WARSHIP
VOLUME VI

Edited by John Roberts

Conway Maritime Press

Naval Institute Press

WARSHIP Volume VI

Managing Editor Robert Gardiner
Editor John Roberts
Art Editor Mark Stevens

Frontispiece: Two views of the unsuccessful
British cruiser submarine *X1*, which is
described by D K Brown in this volume.
CPL

Published in the UK by
Conway Maritime Press Limited
24 Bride Lane
Fleet Street
London EC4Y 8DR

**Published and distributed in the
United States of American and Canada by**
the Naval Institute Press
Annapolis Maryland 21402

Library of Congress Catalog Card No 78-55455
UK ISBN 0 85177 265 X
USA ISBN 0-87021-981-2

Manufactured in the United Kingdom

Contents

Editorial

John Roberts

The US attack carrier *Dwight D Eisenhower* (CVN-69)
USN

This issue of *Warship*, the first of the journal's sixth year, brings a change of style with the introduction of a two column text. This will give an advantage in space (and we hope readability) for both additional text and/or illustration area. As with warships themselves, it is a matter of 'balance', and although the three column system had advantages in magazine layout it is hoped that the increased content of the new arrangement will outweigh any loss in artistic merit. We also introduce two new long running features with this issue, *Warship Wings* and *Warship Details*.

Warship Wings is aimed at warship enthusiasts rather than aircraft enthusiasts, and is intended to give a detailed appraisal of individual aircraft, with particular reference to their importance or otherwise to naval aircraft development and to show the interaction between ship and aircraft requirements. Usually, for example, naval aircraft designs are arranged to fit existing ships so aircraft carrier hanger space and lift dimensions restrict aircraft dimensions, while flight deck arrangements place certain limitations on take-off and landing characteristics. These restrictions have to be balanced with purely aircraft features which, like those of ships, represents a compromise of conflicting requirements. At the same time, however, the increasing limitations of old ships eventually leads to excessive restrictions of aircraft development so new generations of, invariably larger, ships

are naturally designed with future aircraft development in mind. The real problem is, of course, that, the operational life of a ship is so much longer than that normally expected of an aircraft. At least it has been, for it seems unlikely that any future aircraft carriers will exceed the present size of the US attack carriers.

Warship Details will concentrate on providing drawings of parts of warships and details of various items of their equipment and, although this would normally be regarded as a modelmakers' feature, such information can be of value in understanding certain aspects of both technical history and, in some cases, operational history. I have always taken an interest in the widest possible aspects of warship development, from overall strategic requirements and background political history to the minutiae of ship construction and equipment, and it is surprising how often a degree of knowledge in one helps in the understanding of the other.

In fact I dislike the dismissal of certain subjects as of no importance because some find them of no interest – the lack of interest is reasonable, the dismissal is not. Criticism is often made of detail studies, sometimes accompanied by one phrase I particularly dislike – rivet counter – one of those demoralising catch phrases without basis in truth and without any strength of argument behind it.

John Roberts

German Naval Radar to 1945

Part 1

by Erwin Sieche

The story of detecting and ranging on metallic objects by means of reflected high-frequency radio impulses dates back to 30 April 1904, when the German engineer Christian Hülsmeyer registered German and foreign patents for an apparatus he called the Telemobiloscope. The basis for his invention was not, however, new; as far back as 1886 Heinrich Herz, then working at the University of Karlsruhe, had shown, in indoor demonstrations, that electromagnetic waves are reflected by other electric inductors. Nevertheless, Hülsmeyer was too far ahead of his contemporaries for them to appreciate the potential of his invention; even Telefunken rejected an offer to buy his patents.

During the First World War the son of the newspaper-publisher August Scherl, Richard Scherl, also hit on the idea of using radio echoes for detection, without knowledge of Hülsmeyer's previous work. Together with a well-known contemporary science-fiction writer, Hans Dominik, he designed the Raypointer (Strahlenzieler) and successfully produced an experimental set working on a 10cm wavelength. He sent details of his apparatus to the Imperial German Navy in February 1916, but his suggestions were

rejected as 'not being of importance to the war effort'. Again, the inventor was ahead of his time; technology would in fact need decades to provide the necessary operational reliability to match the far-sighted ideas of Hülsmeyer and Scherl.

In the summer of 1926, the Americans Breit and Tuve became the first to use the principles of radar to measure the returning echo of the earth's ionosphere. Also in the 1920s an international army of enthusiastic radio amateurs discovered, and brought to general attention, the field of high-frequency electromagnetic waves, and thus opened the way for a realisation of the potential of radar, the idea being taken up almost simultaneously in France, Great Britain, the USA and Germany.

INITIAL DEVELOPMENT

In Germany it was the *Reichsmarine* which showed interest in the development of this new ranging device, which could 'see behind the clouds', although they entered the field of electromagnetic echo-ranging from a totally different direction. As early as 1929 the *Nachrichten-Versuchsabteilung*

From left to right, the German destroyers *Z39, Z34* and *Z6 (Theodor Riedel)*, the torpedo-boat *T23* (or *T28*), and the destroyers *Z25* and *Z20*, at Kiel on 22 May 1945. The antenna frames above their bridges are for FuMO 21 in *Z39*, and the torpedo-boat; for FuMO 24/25 in *Z34, Z36* and *Z25;* and for FuMO 25 in *Z20. Z25* also has a FuMB 6 *Palau* antenna above the main antenna; the very small dumbbell-shaped antennas on the upper yards of *Z39, Z34* (starboard side) and *Z20* (port side) are for the FuMB 3 *Bali*.

IWM

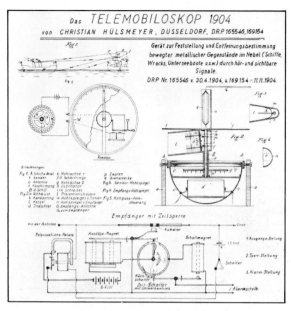

One of the drawings for the patent of Hulsmeyer's Telemobiloscope of 1904. He worked on this invention for two years but the German shipowners of the time could see no advantage in it, the non-expert of that time being unable to distinguish between radio transmissions and radio reflections. During a naval congress at Rotterdam in 1904, Hulsmeyer demonstrated his equipment to the world's press but, although the comments were enthusiastic, nothing further happened – a great pity when one considers the advantages that might have been possible, particularly in such circumstances as those which caused the loss of the liner *Titanic*.

(NVA: Communications trials department) at Kiel were working on a horizontal sound-plummet capable of detecting submerged targets by measuring returning sound-echoes; this was the German forerunner of sonar. NVA's scientific director, Dr Rudolf Kühnhold, decided to use the same basic principles above water by employing electromagnetic waves, and in 1933 NVA managed to pick up echoes from 13.5cm short-wave transmissions via a parabolic dish aerial. However, due to the rather primitive technical possibilities of the time (a transmitting power of only 100 milliwatts), no return echoes were obtained from metallic objects. At the same time, however, one of the leading firms in this field, Philips Eindhoven, produced a 50W magnetron for general sales and the German scientists purchased a few to boost their transmitters to 80W. Unfortunately the transmitting system proved unstable.

Dr Kühnhold now contacted Telefunken to ask if they could take over the development in their highly skilled experimental laboratories. As they rejected this approach, he initiated the foundation of the *Gesellschaft für Elektroakustische und Mechanische Apparate* (GEMA) in 1934 specifically for this promising field of research. GEMA took over the trials sets, which worked on a wavelength of 48cm (630MHz), and found, in trials in the old battleship *Hessen*, that the transmitting impulse had to be pulsed to 'clear' the receiver to allow range as well as bearing information to be obtained.

NVA's original civilian contractor, Pintsch (at Berlin), was in the meantime stimulated by the appearance of this new competitor. After feverish work, they succeeded in trebling the emitting power of the 13.5cm valve to 300mW. With the transmitter and receiver spaced 10m (30.4ft) apart, the echo of the trials vessel *Welle* (ex-*Grille*) could be picked up at up to 2km range but beyond this it faded away due to the limited transmitting energy. Parallel trials with one-way communication (UHF-radio telephone) produced results at over 43km range – from Heligoland to Wangerooge!

These results led to heavy competition between the two contractors, with each trying to overtake the achievements of the other. GEMA now succeeded in producing results at 300m (914ft) range with their improved 48cm set, and later, in October 1934, they managed to obtain a clear echo from *Welle* at over 12km (6.48nm). GEMA trials at the beginning of 1935 showed that longer waves resulted in clearer echoes with no fading effects, and it was realised

that the quality of the echo depended substantially on the silhouette of the target ship (broadside versus end-on). It was therefore decided to build a radar set working on a 2m wavelength (150MHz) and push forward the development of the 13.5cm Pintsch set, although the technical development of the necessary high-energy valves for the latter was proceeding only slowly. Work also continued on the 48cm set, and on 26 September 1935 the improved version was demonstrated in the presence of the German C in C Admiral Raeder; his Commander of the Fleet, Admiral Carls; the head of the *Marinewaffenamt* (Naval Ordnance Department), Admiral Witzell; and other high-ranking naval engineers. The large gunnery training ship *Bremse* was obtained to serve as a radar target and good results were produced. As a result of the ensuing discussion, a number of important development decisions were made, together with a decision to replace the existing term for the system, electric bearing, by the less obvious codename *Dezimeter Telegraphie* (DeTe: decimetric telegraphy). Therefore, all naval radar sets were initially known to the German sailors as *DeTe-Gerät* which, as they did not know its true meaning, they sometimes misinterpreted as *Deutsches Technisches Gerät* (German technical device)! Hence we find this term used for German naval radar sets in the German literature of the first half of the war. The whole matter was so secret that only a handful of specialists actually knew the purpose of the 'grey switchboards' and the curious mattress antenna which began to appear in their ships.

TABLE 1: GERMAN RADAR CODING SYSTEM, c1943

Classification	Translation
Dezimeter-Telegraphie (DeTe)	Decimeter Radio – the first German codeword for radar, sometimes misinterpreted as *Deutsches Technisches Geraet.*
Funkmess (FuM)	Radar set, still used today in the German Democratic Republic to avoid 'Anglo-American' terms.
Funkmess-Ortung (FuMO)	Radar – direction finder, active ranging.
Funkmess-Erkennung (FuMB)	Radar – detector, passive detection (of enemy radar transmissions).
Funkmess-Erkennung (FuME)	Radar – detector, active Identification Friend/Foe (IFF).
Funkmess-Storsender (FuMS)	Radar – interference sender, active jamming.
Funkmess-Tauschung (FuMT)	Radar – deceptor, active deception (by means of transmitting interference signals).
Funkmess-Zusatz (FuMZ)	Radar – with very specialised improvements for various purposes (eg, high-precision bearing).

Before being returned to GEMA, the 48cm set was placed on board *Welle* and she thus became the first German naval unit to carry a radar set. To improve its efficiency and bearing accuracy, this set was modified to a wavelength of 82cm (368–370MHz), and thus became the ancestor of the German *Seetakt* set.

During February 1936 GEMA finished the above-mentioned 2m set, on a final wavelength of 1.8m (165MHz), and with a peak power output of 8kW. By chance this set obtained a clear return from an aircraft at 28km (15.1nm) range and it was, therefore, decided to develop it as an air-warning radar, ultimately leading to the generation of sets known as the *Freyas*.

Although it had no direct connection with naval radar, it should be mentioned that Telefunken also entered the field of radar development in 1935. Their 50cm set, characterised by its parabolic dish and spinning lobe, was the ancestor of the air warning *Würzburg* radar. This was a land service set but at a later date a few were adapted for naval use – of which more will be said later.

Various small German firms became involved in the development of radar as radio and valve technology expanded rapidly, but, due to the need for secrecy and to the limited finance with which to follow up the many proposals made, development was concentrated mainly with the firms GEMA, Telefunken, Siemens, Lorenz and AEG. In the years immediately before the Second World War German scientists tended towards the employment of three fixed frequencies, one for each of the three services, in order to facilitate IFF-definition: 125MHz for aircraft reconnaissance, 368MHz for the Navy and 560MHz for AA-ranging.

RADAR DESIGNATION

With the outbreak of the Second World War, radar development became very complex and, from the historian's point of view, it is difficult to provide a complete record of events. On the one hand the needs of the three services resulted in separate development to meet their individual requirements, and in each case a different system of code designation was adopted. For reasons of secrecy, and due to a degree of jealousy, inter-service communication was poor, and subsequent development depended significantly on personal contacts between the services and the contractors' scientists. On the other hand the contractors themselves were working for all three services and, naturally, used ideas developed for the equipment of one service in that of the others. It was only in the second half of the war that attempts were made to introduce a uniform system of designation for radar sets. Up to this point, there existed no fewer than six different classifications. For example, in the third system introduced, in the surveillance radar FuSE 80 *Freya*, 'Fu' means *Funkmess* (radar), 'S' means Siemens (the manufacturer), 'E' refers to the set's function (in this case *Erkennung*, or reconnaissance), '80' is the running number and *Freya* the set's code word. Sometimes a code was added for the type of installation, *eg* FuSE 62A *Würzburg,* in which 'A' means stationary ground installation with mechanically rotated aerial; to confuse matters the AA gunners of the time referred to this set as FuMG (Flak) 40T/A.

The early sets were simply called DeTe I (or sometimes set A1), DeTe II and so on. When the family of German radar sets began to grow this was found to be insufficient, and arabic numbers were introduced, 100 to 199 being reserved for naval tactical sets working on a wavelength of 80cm. In 1938 a more specific designation system was introduced, giving fuller details of the set; for example the first set installed aboard the armoured ship *Admiral Graf Spee* was FMG 39G (gO). The 'FMG' means *Funkmess-Gerät* (radar device), '39' is the year of introduction (1939), 'G' is the manufacturer (GEMA), 'g' the frequency code (335–430MHz) and 'O' the type of aerial installation (radar tower on top of a rangefinder tower). The full list was a follows:

Manufacturers
G = GEMA
T = Telefunken
L = Lorenz
S = Siemens
A = AEG

Antenna installation
L = trainable antenna on top of bridge
M = trainable antenna on a yardarm
O = battleships; radar tower, or hut, on top of a rangefinder tower
P = battleships; radar room integral with enlarged rangefinder tower
S = fixed antenna on torpedo-boats
U = submarine version

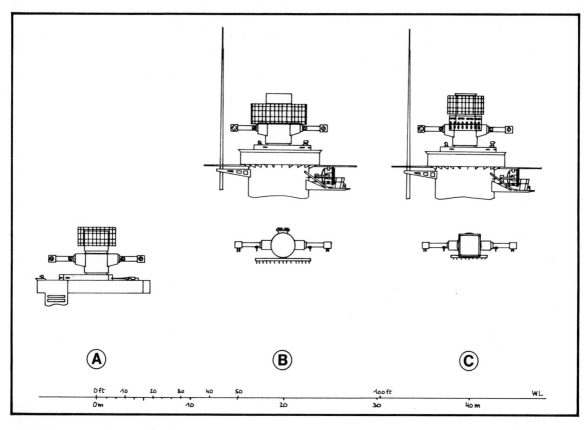

A ⓐ **B** ⓑ **C** ⓒ

0ft 10 20 30 40 50 100ft WL
0m 10 20 30 40 m

SCHARNHORST AND GNEISENAU

Note: The scale line of this and the following drawings also represents the position of the waterline in relation to the profile drawings.

A The after rangefinder tower with its vertically polarised FuMO 27 antenna (2m × 4m), fitted in the summer of 1941.

B The FuMO 22 antenna (2m × 6m) fitted on a new tower above the foretop rangefinder tower in November 1939. The structure is crowned by an open battle-observer's post, *Scharnhorst* and *Gneisenau* being the only German capital ships to have this 'open' type. Also shown (in the plan view) are the butterfly-shaped *Sumatra* antennas probably fitted for the 'Channel dash' in 1942.

C The foretop as modified in February 1942 with a square radar tower and observer's post. The upper antenna is probably for FuMO 26 or 27 (2m × 6m) and the lower antenna the *Timor* frame for the FuMB 4 *Samos*.

Frequency bands

c = 182 to 215MHz
f = 120 to 150MHz
g = 335 to 430MHz
kl = 95MHz

and so on.

In about 1943 these designations were replaced by a standardised system, giving code letters for the type of set and a running number, details of which are given in Table 1 (which also includes the old DeTe code for clarification). Existing sets were recoded under this system, the FMG 39G (gO) for example becoming FuMO 22, the FMG 39G (gP) becoming FuMO 23, the FMG 39G (gL) becoming FuMO 21, and so on. However, the codewords for the sets were retained through all the systems so a *Freya* set, for

example, was always called a *Freya* by its operators. It should be pointed out that the above refers only to the genealogy of the naval coding systems; the *Wehrmacht* and the *Luftwaffe* employed different designations, although some of the basic naval sets were the same as the land-based *Würzburg*. (For reasons of simplicity the following descriptions of the radar installations aboard German ships employ only the last designation system, so only FuMO-, and FuMB-, etc, sets are referred to.)

The various type designations were in fact even more complex than the above indicates, for every small alteration in the type of installation, the function, frequency and other modifications, resulted in the provision of a new code. In addition, each installation consisted of two basic parts – the set itself and the antenna – and as it was possible to inter-change these, using the antenna of one set with the primary equipment of another, yet another level of type designa-tions was possible. Thus a precise listing of all German naval radar sets is almost impossible, and no such list exists in any German literature. Even a simplified listing of radar type designations, with their technical particulars, would require intensive research in German and foreign archives, and the interviewing of surviving witnesses by a researcher expert in both radio technology and naval history. Thus it is not possible to guarantee complete accuracy in describing the radar installations in German warships but it is hoped that this article will provide stimulation for further detailed study in this complex and poorly recorded area.

There is one hope of full clarification: the Allied missions to Germany at the end of the Second World War produced many detailed studies of German developments. Among them was, presumably, a report on radar (possible including drawings and photographs of the sets in surviving German naval units), copies of which are probably buried somewhere in the US and British archives. Hopefully they will eventually be released, allowing somebody to discover and publish them.

For the above reasons the following descriptions of German naval radar concentrates mainly on the visible differences in antennas. As contemporary literature on Second World War German warships includes a great number of excellent pictorials (see Bibliography), this article does not use photographs to illustrate all the variations in radar equipment in *Kriegsmarine* vessels but concentrates on giving general coverage by means of drawings so that the reader may try to identify the different systems in his own personal library by using these as a guide. However, some caution is required because in the majority of such photographs I have noted that the antennas have been carefully turned end-on so one can see that there is a mattress antenna, but cannot see sufficient detail to identify it. Moreover, in the second half of the war the antennas in the centrimetric field became so small that they are often mistaken for blocks or anemometers. The reverse is also true: for example, one of the distinctive items on German naval units in the later period of the war was a trumpet-shaped object which might be mistaken for radar but is in fact an acoustic fog-horn. There only exist about five really good postwar photographs of German warships showing their full complement of active and passive radar antennas, from the 2m × 6m mattress of the FuMO 24/25 to the small cone of the FuME 2 *Wespe* g.

DEUTSCHLAND CLASS

Both *Admiral Graf Spee* and *Deutschland* have been claimed to be the first German naval vessel to be fitted with radar. Trenckle says that *Admiral Graf Spee* had an experimental FuMO 22, and Prager that *Deutschland* had a *Seetakt* set in the autumn of 1937 (which proved very useful for night navigation in Spanish waters). Photographic analysis shows that the frame of this first experimental set was slightly smaller (0.8m × 1.8m) than the final FuMO 22 frame, but it is not known if there were fewer dipoles or alternatively if the dipoles were placed closer together.

R V Jones, in his memoirs (*Most Secret War*, Hamish Hamilton, 1978) describes how the British Admiralty sent L H Bainbridge-Bell to the River Plate to examine the radar installation aboard the wreck of the *Graf Spee*. According to Price (*Instruments of Darkness*, Kimber, 1967) the resultant report took one and a half years to pass through official channels, a statement I find hard to believe considering that Bainbridge-Bell had been sent half way around the world to obtain the information. It adds yet another intriguing possibility of further information, as this report, possibly including photographs of *Graf Spee*'s installation, may yet come to light.

The *Deutschland* (renamed *Lützow* in 1940) had a 2m × 6m mattress antenna for a FuMO 22 throughout her wartime career. From January 1942 until March 1944 she also had a *Timor* frame at the rear of her radar tower, as in the *Scharnhorst*. To follow standard German practice there should also have been fixed *Sumatra* antennas but they cannot be traced in photographs. It is noteworthy that the foretop radar of the armoured ships (later reclassified as heavy cruisers) were provided with the best positioning of

The *Graf Spee* was one of the first German capital ships to be fitted with the prototype FMG 39G (gO) radar set, the experimental forerunner of the FuMO 22. In this view of her bridge structure the antenna on the foretop is covered with canvas.

Author's Collection

TABLE 2: PARTICULARS OF THE PRINCIPAL GERMAN RADAR SETS

Type	Frequency (MHz)	Wavelength (cm)	Power Output (kW)	Frequency Band (KHz)	Range (km)	Bearing (m)	Accuracy (degrees plus & minus)	Employment
FuMO 21	368	81.5	8	500	14-18	70	3	Destroyers
FuMO 22	368	81.5	8	500	–	–	–	Capital ship
FuMO 23	368	81.5	8	500	–	–	–	Capital ships
FuMO 24/25	368	81.5	8	500	15–20	70	0.3	Capital ships, destroyers
FuMO 26	368	81.5	8	500	20–25	70	0.25	Capital ships
FuMO 30	368	81.5	8	500	6–8	100	5	Submarines
FuMO 61 Hohentwiel-U	556	–	30	750	8–10	150	3	Submarines
FuMO 63, Hohentwiel-K	556 to 567	–	30	750 to 1200	12–20	150	2	Cruisers, destroyers
FuMO 81, Berlin-S	3300	–	15	600	20–30	100	5	Surv set, *Prinz Eugen*, destroyers, E-boats
FuMO 213, Würzburg-D	560	53.6	8	500	40-60	35	1.15	AA gunnery

Source: F Trenckle: *Die Deutschen Funkmessverfahren, bis 1945* (see Bibliography).

any of the German heavy units. It was situated at the highest point in the ship, and the foremast was removed, and replaced by a short pole mast, to provide completely unobstructed all-round coverage. Note in the drawings the enclosed battle-observers' post on top of the tower, above which is a lattice construction for the anemometers and the toplights. *Admiral Scheer* was similarly equipped before the removal of her top-heavy pyramidal armoured mast. After that she had a 2m × 4m FuMO 27 mattress antenna and a *Timor* frame, bearing in opposite directions, on the forward rangefinder tower. Three of the four fixed *Sumatra* antennas, spaced 90° apart, were fitted on small horizontal lattice constructions. *Scheer* also had a FuMO 27 antenna on the aft rangefinder tower.

SCHARNHORST AND GNEISENAU

In November 1939 both these vessels were equipped with an 81.5cm (368MHz) FuMO 22 situated in an additional tower above the forward rangefinder tower. The 2m × 6m mattress antenna on the front of the tower rotated with the 10.5m rangefinder so the results from the two instruments could be compared. During their stay at Brest in the summer of 1941 they were fitted with a FuMO 27 on the after rangefinder tower and for their 'Channel dash' in 1942 both were probably equipped with a passive *Palau* antenna on a small frame at the back of their rangefinder tower, which thus operated in the reciprocal direction to the rangefinder and the active FuMO set. During a refit in Germany *Scharnhorst* received a new FuMO 26 or 27 set,

1 *Lutzow* in the summer of 1944 after the removal of her *Timor* antenna, leaving the FuMO 22 on her foretop as her only radar set.

Drüppel

2 The wreck of the *Graf Spee* in the estuary of the River Plate after her scuttling of 17 December 1939.

Drüppel

ADMIRAL GRAF SPEE, LÜTZOW (ex-Deutschland) and ADMIRAL SCHEER

A The foretop of *Spee* with the rangefinder tower topped by a radar hut for the prototype set FMG 39 (gO) – later designated FuMO 22 – and its 1.8m × 0.8m mattress antenna; fitted in 1939.
B The foretop of *Lützow* with the radar hut and 2m × 6m antenna of FuMO 22 added above the rangefinder tower in 1939. The lower drawing shows the *Samos* antenna for FuMB 4, added to the back of the tower in January 1942, and carried until March 1944. Note the battle-observer's post above the radar hut and that her foretop rangefinder is 2m higher, above the waterline, than those of her sisters. *Lützow* was never fitted with radar on her after rangefinder tower.
C The after rangefinder of *Scheer* with the 2m × 4m antenna of the FuMO 27 set added in 1941.
D The forward conning tower of *Scheer* as modified in the summer of 1940. The 10m-rangefinder tower carries the radar hut and antenna for the FuMO 27 which replaced the FuMO 22 (as shown in B) fitted on the original, *Spee*-type, bridge. Note the absence of a battle-observer's post. She also carries four *Sumatra* antennas (forward aft, and at the sides of the tower), three being on lattice extensions. The passive *Timor* antenna was fitted on the back of the radar hut/rangefinder tower in 1942.

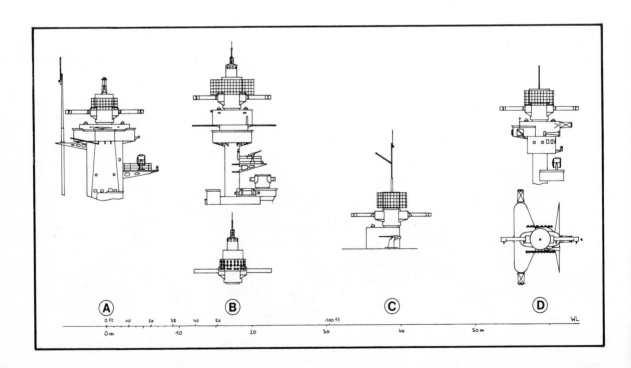

1

2

1

1 *Lützow* at Kiel in April or May 1941. She carried her FuMO 22 radar set throughout her wartime career.

Author's Collection

2 The bridge of *Admiral Scheer*, seen from forward, in about 1945. The rangefinder tower, which is trained to port, has an FuMB 7 *Timor* antenna on its back and the FuMO 27 antenna on its face. Also visible are the short lattice projections, to port, starboard and forward of the screens below the rangefinder, carrying the FuMB 4 *Sumatra* antennas.

Drüppel

with a 2m × 4m mattress antenna, under which was a smaller frame for the two rows of vertical and horizontal *Timor* dipoles serving the passive FuMB 4 *Samos* set.

To follow standard German practice there should also have been passive *Sumatra* antennas somewhere on the screen around the foretop rangefinder platform; however, they cannot be traced in any photography. It can also be assumed that they carried the small omni-directional round-dipole FuMB 3 *Bali*, but the antenna for this set is too small to be clearly identified. It would have been fitted on top of the foremast or on a yardarm.

To be continued.

Readers interested in warship electronics may like to learn that the first real study of the subject was published in November 1981. Entitled *Warship Radar*, by Norman Friedman it is available from Conway Maritime Press (or in North America from The Naval Institute Press).

2

A^s&A^s

BRITISH RADAR from T H Maskell, Bath, Avon

Concerning the radar outfits mentioned in *Warship* 18, I make the following remarks after inspection of various documents at my disposal. Type 288, while listed as for use in AMCs and OBVs, as you remark, was recommended to be phased out as early as January 1941, and a little later was shown in fitting lists as used only for A/S and A/A shore stations and batteries, and then only in very small numbers. It would appear to have been little used. Type 289 was used only by *Isaac Sweers* (two sets) as a close range set. Type 287 is described as the only shore-mounted set of Naval design and as being an observation minefield set (one of the stations shown as using this set was the Coal House, Llanelly!). The very brief details given state it was a 50cm set of 580–620Mc/s, to be used to give precision ranging against surface vessels attempting to pass over the minefields, and to be installed at eight ports in the UK. Type 277 is shown to have had a reliable range of 80,000yds on aircraft. While there is a great deal of information available in various areas on naval radar, regrettably it is inclined to be fragmentary in the 1940–41 periods. Indeed this could be said to apply to the appearance of ships in general, especially regarding camouflage and colour.

BRITISH TORPEDOES from Antony Preston, London

Since my article on torpedoes appeared in *Warship* 19, Martin Douglas has provided me with some additional material on the Mk 20 and Mk 30 torpedoes. There were, it appears, three variants of the Mk 20:
1. Mk 20(E), which was withdrawn very shortly after coming into service, except in the New Zealand frigates *Taranaki* and *Otago*, which had it in service for longer.
2. Mk 20(S), originally Staff Requirements TASW 118 dating from June 1950, which ran at 20kts for 12,000yds. It was eventually accepted into service as Mk 20(S) Mod 1.

3. Mk 20(C), originally Staff Requirement USW 357 dating from February 1961, which ran at 23kts for 7000yds. This was intended to be the submarine version of the torpedo.

The main criticism of the Mk 30 was that it was too heavy and too big – 630lb, 8ft long – whereas the US-pattern Mk 32, on the same length, weighed only 260lb. The Mk 43 Mod 1 of which 75 were purchased ran at only 15kts for 4000yds and could go down to 500ft. Later 500 of the Mod 3 versions were purchased, running at 20kts for 4000yds and capable of going down to 1000ft. The urgent need at this time was for a light torpedo capable of being carried by the MATCH helicopter (Westland Wasp), which was not possible with the Mk 30.

HMS WARRIOR from Captain J G Wells, Research Director, High Firs House, Liss, Hampshire

Although the wrought iron hull of the ironclad *Warrior*, at present under restoration in Hartlepool, is amazingly sound and the majority of her compartments intact, there remains much research to be done in order to bring the ship once more alive, particularly as regards fittings, furniture and equipment, both above and below decks. While official records and original ship's drawings provide valuable information there is lacking the personal recollection and records about life in the Victorian Navy. For this reason I would be grateful to hear from anyone able to assist restoration with the loan of photographs or drawings depicting scenes on board *Warrior* or another ironclad of her period. It would also be useful to learn about the possession of uniforms, accoutrements, etc, likely to be found in the ship, as well as letters, news cuttings or documents relating to those who served in *Warrior*, including the time when she was serving as *Vernon III* (1904–1923).

Correspondence should be addressed to the Research Director, HMS *Warrior* (1860), at the above address. Contributions will be gratefully acknowledged and returned.

The War Service of the Soviet M Class Submarines by Pierre Hervieux

The Soviet 'M' class were small, single-hull coastal submarines, with excellent submerged manoeuvrability and good rapid diving characteristics, which proved of great value in operations in the shallow and restricted waters of the Baltic and northern Black Sea. They were designed for construction in sections, the ultimate aim being mass production, but wartime demands on available material prevented this being put into practice. To suit the widely spread coastal waters of the Soviet Union they were also designed so that they could be dismantled and transported from one operational area to another by rail.

The design was inspired by the Soviet 'Holland' type boats of the 'AG' class built in 1916–24. The prototype,

M1, was laid down by the Ural Machine Works at Sverdlovsk on 29 August 1932, and after running her trials in the Baltic in 1933 she was dismantled and transported to the Pacific by rail in December 1933. She was followed by a further 29 boats, collectively known as the Series VI, all of which were launched in 1933–34. A further four subgroups were subsequently produced – Series VIbis (launched 1934–35), Series XII (launched 1936–37), Series XIIbis (launched 1937–41) and Series XV (launched 1940, 1946 and 1947). Each group incorporated important improvements which included increases in armament and speed. Naturally the dimensions also increased, initially to improve on the inadequate sea-

M32 of Series XIIbis, which were improved versions of Series XII with streamlined conning towers and increased endurance.

keeping of the first series. The boats of the first two series were constructed in four sections, the Series XII and XIIbis boats in six sections, and the Series XV boats in seven sections. The sections were mainly built in yards along the inland rivers and assembled at either Leningrad, Nikolayev or Vladivostok. The first use of welding in Russian submarines was made in the 'M' class; limited initially to the superstructure and bow and stern casings, it was later extended to the pressure hull.

THE 'M' CLASS

Series VI: *M1–M28, M51, M52* (commissioned 1934–35).
Series VIbis: *M29* (ex-*M57*), *M41* (ex-*M82*), *M44* (ex-*M85*), *M54, M55, M56, M58* (ex-*M84*), *M59* (ex-*M86*), *M71–M81, M83* (commissioned 1935–36).
Series XII: *M90, M171* (ex-*M87*), *M172* (ex-*M88*), *M173* (ex-*M89*) (commissioned 1937–38).
Series XIIbis: *M30–M36, M42* (ex-*M61*), *M43* (ex-*M63*), *M45* (ex-*M100*), *M46* (ex-*M101*), *M60, M62, M94–M99, M102–M108, M111–M122, M174–M176, M401* (commissioned 1939–44).
Series XV: *M200–M203* (commissioned 1943–44).

By the end of 1944, 100 'M' Series boats had been commissioned, while *M204–M206*, laid down in 1940–41, were commissioned after the war. In addition, *M207–M213* and *M254–M283* were built postwar. The Series XII boat *M92*, laid down in 1936, was used for experiments in the running of diesel engines under water and was not officially commissioned until after ther war.

OPERATIONAL HISTORY

The following is in chronological order. The abbreviations after the date refer to the area of operation, A being Arctic, B Baltic and BS Black Sea.
June 1941 (B): *M72* possibly badly damaged by a mine in the Gulf of Finland and subsequently scrapped.
23 June 1941 (B): *M78* torpedoed and sunk by *U144* (Capt Von Mittelstädt) west of Windau.

M172 in the Arctic.
J Meister

24 June 1941 (B): *M71* and *M80* scuttled at Libau to prevent capture.

25 June 1941 (B): *M83* scuttled off Libau while returning to port, possibly in a damaged condition.

26 June 1941 (B): *M76* (probably – she did not survive the war) torpedoed and sunk by *U149* (Capt Höltring) off the Gulf of Finland (59°20′/21°12′E).

1 July 1941 (B): *M81* sunk by mine near Laine Bank.

5 July 1941 (B): *M99* sunk by mine north-west of Worms.

21 July 1941 (B): *M94* torpedoed and sunk by *U140* (Capt Hellriegel) off Dago Island (58°51′N/22°00′E).

21 August 1941 (A): *M172* (Capt Fisanovich) made unsuccessful attacks on a steamer in Petsamofjord, at Lumahamaari, and on the hospital ship *Alexander Von Humbolt* (686 tons) off Petsamofjord.

End August 1941 (B): *M103* probably sunk by a mine in the Gulf of Finland.

13 September 1941 (A): *M172* torpedoed and sank the Norwegian coaster *Renoy* (287 tons) in Varangerfjord.

14 September 1941 (A): *M172* made unsuccessful attack on the steamer *Ornulf* in Petsamo harbour.

15 September 1941 (BS): *M34* made unsuccessful attack on the Italian steamer *Tampico* (5000 tons) off Verna.

23 September 1941 (B): *M74* sunk by German aircraft at Kronstadt. She was later refloated and scrapped.

26 September 1941 (A): *M174* (Capt Egorov) made unsuccessful attack on a steamer in Petsamofjord.

2 October 1941 (A): *M171* (Capt Starvkov) depth-charged by patrol vessel *NT05* (*Togo*, ex-Norwegian minesweeper *Otra*), after unsuccessful attack on a steamer in Petsamofjord, but survived.

3 and 8 October 1941 (A): *M176* and *M175* made unsuccessful attacks on ships in Varangerfjord.

27 October 1941 (BS): *M35* (Capt Greshilov) made unsuccessful attack on subchaser *Schiff 19 (Lola)* off Sulma.

November 1941 (B): *M98* probably sunk by mine in western section of Gulf of Finland.

17 November 1941 (A): *M171* made unsuccessful attack on a tanker in Varangerfjord.

December 1941 (BS): *M34* was depth-charged and sunk by Rumanian destroyer *Regele Ferdinand* off the Rumanian coast. (Note: this is sometimes reported as *M54*, which survived the war, the confusion arising from German interrogation of prisoners who were mistaken as to the submarine's identity).

21 December 1941 (A): *M174* torpedoed the German steamer *Emshorn* (4301 tons) off Vando at 13.06, the drifting wreck being sunk by German artillery.

10 January 1942 (A): *M175* torpedoed and sunk by *U584* (Capt Deecke) at 07.22 in position 70°09′N/32°50′E north-west of Fisherman's Peninsula.

End January 1942 (A): *M171* made unsuccessful attack on convoy off the Norwegian polar coast.

19 February 1942 (A): *M171* made unsuccessful attacks on German cargo ships *Oldendorf* (1953 tons) and *J Johanne* (1202 tons) in Persfjord, and was subsequently depth-charged by sub-chasers *Uj1205* and *Uj1214*.

March 1942 (A): *M171* and *M173* made unsuccessful attacks on shipping in Varangerfjord.

13 March 1942 (BS): *M58* sunk by German aircraft off the Crimea.

The submarine *M107*.

J Meister

Early April 1942 (A): *M171* made unsuccessful attack on shipping in Varangerfjord.

15 April 1942 (A): *M172* made unsuccessful attacks on the cargo ships *Oleam* (475 tons), *Nogat* (1339 tons) and *Lowas* (1891 tons). The three escorts dropped 22 depth charges but *M172* was not damaged.

20 April 1942 (A): *M172* made unsuccessful attack on minesweeper *M251*, which counter-attacked with 14 depth charges, south of Vardio.

22 April 1942 (A): at 08.15, *M173* (Capt Terekhin) torpedoed and sank the German cargo ship *Blankenese* (ex-French *Ange Schiaffino*, 3236 tons) off the Varanger Peninsula in position 70°32′N/30°47′E. The German escorts counter-attacked unsuccessfully with 35 depth charges.

29 April 1942 (A): At 18.30, *M171* (Capt Starikov) torpedoed and sank the German cargo ship *Curityba* (4969 tons) off the Varanger Peninsular in position 70°07N/30°33′E,

Mid April–end May 1942 (A): *M176* (Capt Bondarevich) made five unsuccessful attacks on shipping off the Varanger Peninsula.

M72 laid up at Leningrad in 1946.

J Meister

15 May 1942 (A): *M172* made unsuccessful attacks on the hospital ship *Birka* (1000 tons) and the tanker *Gerdmoor* (751 tons). There were five escorts including *Uj1104* and *Uj1108*, and during an eight-hour pursuit 136 depth charges were dropped and 38 shells fired by the German ships. However, they had to turn back when they came under fire from the Soviet shore batteries on Fisherman's Peninsula and *M172* escaped.

19 May 1942 (A): *M176* unsuccessfully attacked the hospital ship *Birka*, escorted by four German sub-chasers which dropped 13 depth charges, off Makkaur.

23 May 1942 (A): *M171* unsuccessfully attacked the Norwegian cargo ship *Vardo* (860 tons) off Varanger. The three escort vessels counter-attacked with 166 depth charges.

15 June 1942 (B): *M95* sunk by mine east of Suursaari Island.

3 July 1942 (A): *M176* was stationed off Varangerfjord to cover the passage of convoy PQ17. No further report was heard from her and she was presumed lost in a German minefield.

12 July 1942 (BS): *M59* sunk by German aircraft off Sochii.

14 August 1942 (B): *M97* sunk by mine off Lavansaari Island.

5–23 August 1942 (BS): *M36* (Capt Kamarov), *M62* (Capt Malyshev), *M111* (Capt Josseliani) and *M118* (Capt Savin) carried out several attacks on convoys in the Bay of Odessa, off the Rumanian coast, but the only success was the sinking of the German tug *Ankara* (112 tons) by *M36*.

24 August 1942 (BS): *M33* sunk by mine off Odessa

24 August 1942 (A): *M173* attacked a convoy off Kyberg consisting of the steamers *Irmstraud* (2843 tons), *Ortelsburg* (1309 tons) and *Lysaker* (909 tons) escorted by seven vessels including *V6105*, *Uj1101*, *Uj1108* and *Uj1112*. In counter-attacks 179 depth charges were dropped and *M179* was sunk by *Uj1112* off Baasfjord.

Mid August 1942–end September 1942 (B): *M96* (Capt Marinesko) operated in the area of Parkkala making only one attack, which was unsuccessful.

September 1942 (BS): *M35* and *M111* made unsuccessful attacks.

October 1942 (B): *M102* made unsuccessful attacks in western section of the Gulf of Finland.

27 September 1942 (BS): *M60* sunk by mine off Odessa.

1 October 1942 (BS): *M118* (Capt Savin) attacked a Ruma-

Commander I Fisanovich aboard his submarine *M172* (ex-*M88*). The gun is a 45mm/46 on an AA mounting which was the standard gun armament in all the 'M' class submarines.

IWM

nian convoy, sinking the German cargo ship *Salzburg* (1742 tons), but she was herself sunk by the Rumanian gunboat *Ghigulescu* off Budaki. On board the *Salzburg* were 2300 Russian prisoners of war, only 200 of whom were rescued.

14 October 1942 (BS): At 13.44 *M32* (Capt Kaltypin) unsuccessfully attacked the Rumanian torpedo-boat *Sborul*, between Odessa and Sulina, which depth-charged and seriously damaged the submarine.

21 October 1942 (BS): At 13.05 *M35* (Capt Greshilov) torpedoed and sank the Panamanian tanker *Le Progres* (511 tons) off Salina. The escorts dropped 32 depth charges but the submarine was only slightly damaged.

October 1942 (BS): The Rumanian tug *Oituz* was probably torpedoed and sunk by *M111* (Capt Josseliani)

November 1942 (B): *M96* was the last boat of the year to sail on patrol in the Gulf of Finland before it began to ice up.

November 1942 (A): *M121* sunk by a mine off the Norwegian coast.

14 December 1942 (A): *M171* unsuccessfully attacked a convoy of four steamers, *Dessau* (5933 tons), *Welheim* (5455 tons), *Poseidon* (3910 tons) and *Utviker* (3502 tons), with three escorts, off Ekkeray.

22 January 1943 (A): at 19.45 *M172* (Capt Fisanovich)

attacked a convoy consisting of two cargo vessels escorted by a destroyer and a patrol vessel, west of Nord Kyn. She missed the destroyer with a torpedo.

29 January 1943 (A): *M171* (Capt Starikov) torpedoed and damaged the transport *Ilona Siemers* (3243 tons), escorted by the patrol boat *V5906*, off Kangafjord.

1 February 1943 (A): At 8.10, *M172* (Capt Fisanovich) torpedoed and sank the patrol boat *V5909* off Kyberg.

February 1943 (A): *M119, M122, M171* and *M172* made several unsuccessful attacks on vessels in the area of Varangerfjord. On several occasions they appeared on the surface so close to the shore that they were fired on by the coastal batteries at Kiberg and Petsamo.

March 1943 (BS): A Soviet submarine was sunk in error by a Soviet surface vessel, off the Caucasus coast. It has been stated that this was *M120*, but this boat was sent to the Caspian Sea in 1942, so the vessel sunk was probably *M36*.

11 March 1943 (A): At 09.10 *M174* (Captain Egorov) hit a mine in one of the defensive fields off Kirkenesfjord but succeeded in returning to her base.

16 March 1943 (A): *M104* (Capt Lykyanov) torpedoed and damaged the steamer *Johannisberger* (4533 tons), which was beached in Narangerfjord.

22 March 1943 (BS): *M117* attacked a German supply convoy between Feodosia and Anapa but the torpedoes fired passed under their targets which were flat-bottomed MFPs.

April 1943 (BS): *M35* and *M112* carried out open sea patrols.

Early–mid April 1943 (A): *M177* operated off Varangerfjord.

22 April 1943 (BS): *M111* operated without success against MFP convoys between Feodosia and Anapa.

April–May 1943 (A): *M104, M105, M106, M122, M171, M172* and *M174* operated in Varangerfjord and off Vardo but although they carried out many attacks achieved no success.

14 May 1943 (A): *M122* sunk by aircraft off the Rybachi peninsula while returning from patrol.

June–July 1943 (BS): *M111, M112* and *M117*, operating between Feodosia and Anapa, made several unsuccessful attacks on German shallow-draught ferry barges supplying the Kuban bridgehead.

June–July 1943 (A): *M105* (Capt Khrulev) made two unsuccessful attacks on convoys off the Polar coast.

5 July 1943 (A): *M106* sunk by depth charges and ramming near Vardo, by escort vessels *Uj1206* and *Uj1217*.

17 July 1943 (BS): *M111* (Capt Tosseliani) attacked a convoy running from Feodosia to Tainan. She hit the small

A series XIIbis boat in the Arctic.

A Series XV submarine in service with the Polish Navy in 1957. Six of this type, M100–M105, were transferred from the Soviet Navy in 1956–57.

BfZ

German motor tanker *Adelheid* (506 tons) but the torpedo did not detonate.

18 July 1943 (BS): *M111* torpedoed and sank the Rumanian lighter *Dunarea I* (505 tons) off Feodosia.

End July–early August 1943 (BS): *M117* and *M35* deployed against expected arrival of German tanker *Firuz* (7327 tons) but this vessel was torpedoed and damaged by another submarine.

Summer 1943 (BS): *M31* mined and sunk off Poti while running speed trials (this is a recent Soviet claim).

28 August 1943 (BS): *M111* torpedoed and sank the German lighter *Hainburg* off Cape Lukall.

1 September 1943 (A): *M104* torpedoed and damaged the steamer *Rudesheimer* (2036 tons) off the Norwegian polar coast.

11 September 1943 (A): *M107* (Capt Kofanov) torpedoed and sank the escort vessel *Uj1217* off Syltefjord.

28 September 1943 (BS): *M113* hit a mine west of the Crimea but reached her base in a badly damaged condition.

13 October 1943 (A): *M172* made an unsuccessful attack on a convoy off Verdo.

25–26 October 1943 (A): *M173* reported in for the last time – it seems that *M174* and *M172* were probably lost on the mine barrages laid by the German minelayers *Brummer II, Ostmark, Kaiser* and *Roland* in the summer and autumn. Captain Fisanovich was not aboard his former command, *M172,* when she was lost. He went to Britain in April 1944 to take over command of the *B1* (ex-HMS *Sunfish*) in which he lost his life on 27 July 1944 when his submarine was sunk with all hands by a Liberator aircraft of Coastal Command. At the time *B1* was proceeding on the surface well outside the area temporarily allotted as an attack-free zone. She should have stayed on the surface during her passage to Russia but when the aircraft approached she dived so the aircraft assumed she was German – an assumption reinforced by the fact the *B1* fired no recognition signal.

25 October 1934 (BS): *M112* (Capt Khakhanov) torpedoed and sank the lighter *Tyra 5* off Ak Mechet.

2 November 1943 (BS): *M35* (Capt Prokofev) torpedoed and sank lighter *No 1293* off Ak Mechet.

12 November 1943 (BS): *M111* (Capt Josseliani) torpedoed and sank the steamer *Theoderich* (3409 tons) off Burpas.

15 November 1943 (BS): *M117* (Capt Kesaev) sank the naval ferry barge *F592* (200 tons)

November–December 1943 (A): *M119* and *M200* patrolled off the Varanger Peninsula.

December 1943 (BS): *M117* made unsuccessful attacks on convoys. The following ships were sunk by unknown submarines in the Black Sea ('M' boats may have been responsible for some or all of them): the Turkish steamers *Tayyari* on 22 July 1943, *Yilmaz* on 25 August 1943, *Verviske* on 26 August 1943 and *Kalkavan* on 16 December 1943; and the German naval ferry barge *F474* (200 tons).

End December 1943–early January 1944 (A): *M105* and *M201* patrolled in Varangerfjord.

19 January 1944 (A): *M104, M105* (Capt Khralev), *M119* (Capt Kolosov) and *M201* (Capt Balin) deployed against enemy convoy traffic off the Polar coast without success.

April 1944 (BS): *M62* and *M117* operated without success

against German ships evacuating troops and supplies from Odessa.

14 April 1944 (BS): *M52* (Capt Matveyev) sighted convoy of five naval ferry barges, escorted by three sub-chasers off the San Georghe canal entrance. She attacked but missed *Uj306* and was counter-attacked with 61 depth charges, also without result.

17 April 1944 (BS): *M111* (Capt Khomiakov) attacked a convoy of two cargo ships, with six escorts, off Sevastopol. She missed the merchantman *Helga* and was counter-attacked, unsuccessfully, with 72 depth charges.

18 April 1944 (BS): *M112* attempted to attack the steamer *Alba Julia* (5700 tons), previously set on fire during an air attack, but was driven off by the escort.

21 April 1944 (BS): *M62* (Capt Malyshev) and *M111* made unsuccessful attacks on the Rumanian cargo vessel *Ardeal* (5695 tons) off Sevastopol.

22 April 1944 (BS): *M35* (Capt Prokofev) torpedoed and sank the German tanker *Ossag* (2793 tons), previously damaged by aircraft, off Sevastopol.

April 1944 (A): *M108* failed to return from patrol off the Norwegian coast – she was probably sunk by a mine.

3–4 May 1944 (BS): *M62* and *M111* made unsuccessful attacks on two convoys between Sevastopol and Constanza.

11 May 1944 (BS): *M62* attacked a convoy (one cargo vessel, one naval ferry barge and five escort vessels) off Sevastopol but was unsuccessful due to the heavy sea.

May 1944 (BS): *M35* sank a barge off Sevastopol.

26 May 1944 (A): *M201* (Capt Balin) unsuccessfully deployed against a convoy off Makkaur.

June 1944 (A): *M200* and *M201* deployed unsuccessfully against convoy traffic off the Polar coast.

17 June 1944 (A): *M200* (Capt Gladkov) approached a convoy east of North Cape (reported earlier as being in Svaerholthavet by a reconnaissance aircraft) but was driven off by the escort vessels *M35, Uj1120* and *Uj1209*.

20 June 1944 (A): *M201* made an unsuccessful attack on a convoy south of Vardo and was seen by an He 115 flying boat as she fired her torpedoes. Forced to dive and depth charged by the escorts *Uj1209, Uj1219, Uj1120* and *Uj1222,* she eventually escaped.

15 July 1944 (A): *M200* made an unsuccessful attack on a convoy near Cape Harbaken (she launched four torpedoes and reported sinking a 5000-ton steamer but none was in fact sunk).

July 1944 (BS): *M111* operated without success off Cautanza.

End July 1944 (BS): *M111* relieved by *M113* and *M117*.

28 July 1944 (BS): *M113* (Capt Volkov) attempted to attack a convoy inside the mine barrages off Cautanza.

18 August 1944 (A): *M201* (Capt Balin) attacked a convoy off Persfjord and torpedoed and sank the patrol coast *V6112.*

End August 1944 (BS): *M62, M111* and *M113* deployed off the Rumanian/Bulgarian coast without success.

10 September 1944 (B): *M96* sunk by mine off Narva.

October 1944 (A): A small Norwegian cutter was sunk by a mine laid off the Norwegian Polar coast by *M171* against the expected sea evacuation of German mountain troops from the Murmansk front.

Warship Details No.1

by John Roberts

These two drawings show the bridge structure of HMS *Hood* as it was after her 1929-31 refit. It illustrates the final development of the tier arrangement in British ships and helps to show why these were abandoned in favour of the block structure introduced in the Royal Navy's next capital ships, *Nelson* and *Rodney*. Despite its size, it had comparatively little enclosed space and the large open platforms were subject to the assault of wind and weather – which involved loss of efficiency among those operating open fire control instruments and signal gear. The entire structure was built around the tripod foremast but, with the ever increasing weights of fire control equipment, it was an arrangement in which rigidity was difficult to achieve and *Hood*'s foretop, like those in other capital ships, suffered from a degree of vibration which did not mix well with fire control gear. In fact, the entire system was the result of a gradual development during the initial dreadnought period, in which expanding technology made increasing demands on bridge space. The block bridge, which followed, resulted largely from a complete reappraisal of control position requirements and although it did not completely solve the conflicting requirements of bridge structures it was a substantial improvement.

Drawings selected from the 320 published in *The Battlecruiser Hood* by John Roberts, the first of the new 'Anatomy of the Ship' series from Conway Maritime Press (January, 1982, £8.50). Available in North America from the Naval Institute Press.

LOWER SECTION OF BRIDGE STRUCTURE

1 24in signalling searchlight (shutter on face portable); **2** Scupper; **3** Voice pipe (signal deck to upper bridges); **4** Upper tactical plotting position; **5** Conning tower platform; **6** Admiral's signal platform; **7** Cleats on guardrail for signal halyards; **8** Sounding machine; **9** Bowlight; **10** Flag locker; **11** Plumber's workshop; **12** Lift for sounding boom; **13** Davit socket; **14** Signal lamp; **15** Flag locker; **16** Boiler room vent; **17** Submarine lookout; **18** Guard to second bowlight; **19** 5.5in director control tower; **20** Voice pipe (director to 5.5in spotting top); **21** Electric cables; **22** Admiral's bridge; **23** Admiral's charthouse; **24** False roof; **25** Admiral's signal house; **26** Foremast; **27** Pillars supporting fore bridge; **28** Mast strut; **29** Cable casing on strut.

FORE BRIDGE AND CONTROL TOP

1 Main W/T aerials; **2** Navigation lights; **3** 15ft rangefinder in aloft director control tower; **4** Anemometer; **5** Wind vane; **6** 15in spotting top; **7** Jackstay; **8** Hammock girdlines; **9** Forward concentrating position; **10** Searchlight manipulating platform; **11** Signal yard braces; **12** Searchlight platform: **13** Chart table; **14** Torpedo control position; **15** Compass platform (roof omitted); **16** Door to compass platform; **17** Teak platform; **18** Fore bridge; **19** Door to remote control office; **20** Voice pipe cabinet; **21** Upper tactical plotting position, on Admiral's bridge; **22** Sliding door to navigating officer's sea cabin; **23** Lagged steam pipes to syrens; **24** Signal yard lift; **25** Manoeuvring lights; **26** Pom-pom director position (director fitted in starboard position only); **27** 5.5in gun, 12ft rangefinder tower, port and starboard; **28** 5.5in spotting top, port and starboard; **29** Siren, port and starboard.

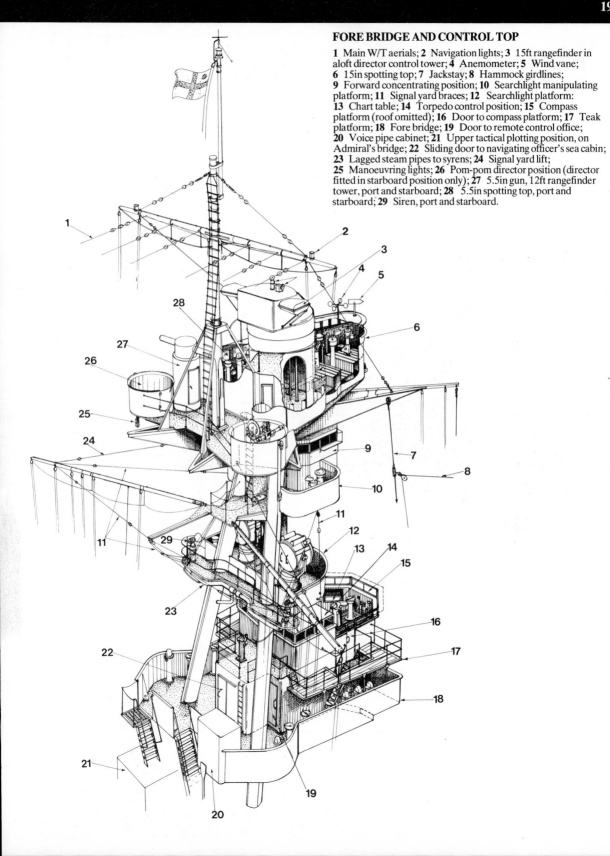

Colonial Cruiser

by Ross Gillett

The naval history of Australia is generally assumed to have begun on 25 March 1859, when Commodore Loring, Commanding Officer of HMS *Iris*, raised his pendant as Senior Officer of Her Majesty's Ships on the Australian Station. Throughout the years up to 10 July 1911, when the Royal Australian Navy formally came into existence, the Royal Navy provided the majority of seaward defence, supported by the odd collection of gunboats and torpedo-boats operated by five of the Australian colonies.

The navy of the colony of Victoria was, by the late 1880s, the largest local naval force; it comprised the monitor *Cerberus*, gunboats *Albert* and *Victoria* and torpedo-boats *Childers, Lonsdale, Nepean* and *Gordon*, as well as a dozen auxiliaries, including the training ship, ex-armoured cruiser, HMVS *Nelson*. It was realised at this time that there was need for a new, improved gunboat-type vessel to augment the unsuccessful *Albert* and *Victoria*, and during 1887 the Victorian Colonial Government began investigations into the feasability of constructing a cruiser for their Colonial Naval Forces. Sir G Armstrong & Co, of Newcastle-upon-Tyne, were invited to prepare suitable designs for the vessel, and on 26 October 1888 the Commander of the Victorian forces commented on the resultant tender.

The letter, addressed to the Honorable Minister of Defence, suggested that the designs offered would undoubtedly be a valuable addition to the defences as they possessed a powerful armament, considerable speed and light draught. He added that any new type of ship should be able to cope with all-comers. Of the two designs, A and B, he considered the former to be the better, the armament being heavier, although a suggestion was made that the Gatling guns be replaced with Nordenfelts. He criticised the position of the pivot guns, as they allowed little depression, and he found it difficult to imagine how those forward could be fired right ahead without damage to the fore part of the ship, although undoubtedly slight alterations could rectify them. The square sails and yards were, except for the passage out to Australia, to be abolished and only the poles and masts required for signalling purposes would be retained. Concern was expressed about the amount of ammunition carried per gun; as each type was quick-firing, plenty of magazine and shell space was required. The cruiser's boats, the same type as those supplied to the earlier gunboats *Albert* and *Victoria,* were to be replaced by improved types. His final comment praised the arrange-

PARTICULARS OF PROTECTED CRUISER DESIGN

	Design A	Design B
Displacement (tons)	1040	1020
Length pp (ft)	195	190
Beam (ft)	33	33
Draught (ft-in)	11-6	11-6
Machinery	Two sets triple expansion	Two sets triple expansion
Indicated horsepower	2600	2600
Speed (kts)	16	16
Coal capacity (tons)	180	180
Armament	3–6in BL	3–6in BL
	4–40pdr	4–6pdr
	8–3pdr	6–3pdr
	4 Gatling guns	6 Gatling guns
	2 torpedo tubes	2 torpedo tubes
Cost: Hull & engines	£55,000	£53,000
Armament	£24,100	£21,700
Torpedoes & Gear	£7550	£7550
Electric lighting	£2520	£2520
Total	£89,170	£84,770

Armstrong's Design 'A'
Photo by L Forsythe

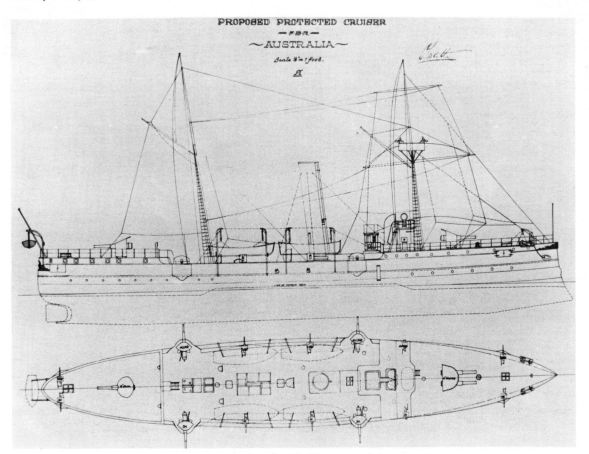

The 3rd class cruiser *Barossa*, a typical small cruiser of the late nineteenth century, shows how the Australian colonial cruiser would have appeared if completed. Although *Barossa* was larger the basic layout is the same, the only major variation being in the funnel which was proportionally taller in the Australian designs (*Barossa* also has two funnels, side by side).
CPL

ments of the steering gear, the compartmentation and the protection of engines and boilers. The complement required for Design A would be at least 150 officers and men.

ARMAMENT

Design A: One twin 6in BL mounting was fitted on a platform on the forecastle and a single 6in mounting on a platform on the poop. Broadside fire was provided by four 40pdr QF guns, mounted on sponsons, and four 3pdr QF guns. Four additional 3pdr were mounted, two in the bow and two at the stern, and four Gatling guns, two in the foremast top and two abreast the bridge. Two torpedo tubes were also provided, on the centreline fore and aft, stowage being provided for six torpedoes with separate magazine stowage for their warheads.

Design B: Carried the same main and torpedo armament as Design A, but four 6pdr QF were fitted on the broadside and six 3pdr QF were carried, two each at bow, stern and amidships. Six gatling guns, two in the military top and four around the topsides, were also provided.

APPEARANCE

Both designs incorporated a protective deck above which the coal bunkers were arranged to assist in the protection. A high forecastle and poop were provided for improved seaworthiness, as well as to allow the bow and stern chase guns to be fitted at a greater height above the waterline, this adding to the fighting efficiency of the cruiser in a seaway. Officers and crew were to have improved living quarters with internal light and ventilation. Ship's boats numbered four large and one small.

Seven watertight bulkheads, two engine rooms and numerous minor compartments provided sufficient watertight sub-division. Two searchlights were to be fitted to the ship, one on each wing of the ship's bridge. The cruiser was to be propelled by two sets of triple expansion engines of the horizontal direct acting type, placed in separate engine rooms, each giving motion to one of the twin screws.

Both hand and steam steering gear were provided, with the main steam steering wheel placed forward in the conning tower. Provision for a sailing rig was also made for the journey to Australia but 'need not, however, be fitted if considered undesirable'.

It was further stated in Armstrong's estimate that the price mentioned included the supply of hull and fittings complete, anchors, cables, boats, masts, rigging, sails, engines, boilers and spare gear, cooking apparatus and tanks for the water and oil. The vessel would be ready except for provisions, consumable stores, nautical instruments, charts, bedding, cutlery, crockery and personal effects of the officers and crew. In fact the cruiser could be completed for sea in from eleven to twelve months of the date of the order.

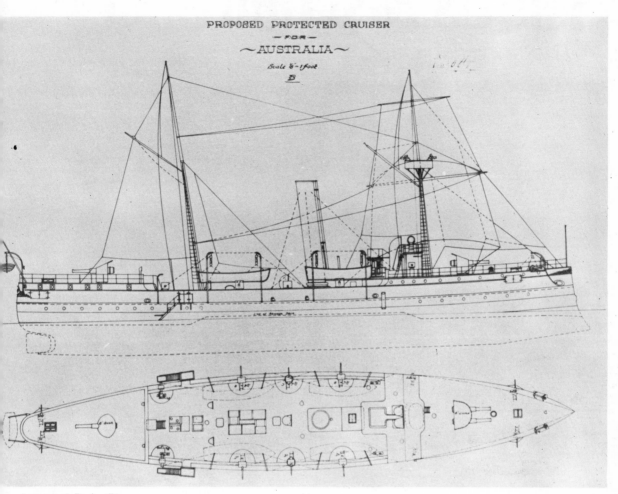

PROPOSED PROTECTED CRUISER
— FOR —
~ AUSTRALIA ~
Scale ⅛=1 foot
B

Armstrong's Design 'B'
Photo by L Forsythe

The *Nelson* from astern.
MoD, by courtesy of R A Burt

CONCLUSIONS

In the event neither design was proceeded with and in 1889 the project seems to have lapsed before the cruiser was laid down. It would have been interesting to see the situation if plans had been approved and the cruiser commissioned into the Victorian fleet. She would have been completed in 1890 and most probably retained in service until the First World War, as were the other colonial vessels *Protector*, *Gayundah*, *Cerberus* and the torpedo-boats. Only one other warship was ordered for a colonial navy after 1889, this being the torpedo-boat HMVS *Countess of Hopetoun* in 1890–91. She may have been the navy's alternate choice following the cancellation of the unnamed protected cruiser. Not long after the arrival of *Countess of Hopetoun* both the older gunboats *Albert* and *Victoria* were reduced to reserve in 1895 and sold out of service one year later. The Victorian Colonial Navy then comprised only *Cerberus*, the torpedo-boat flotilla and the remaining auxiliaries.

The US Fast Gun Boat

by Norman Friedman

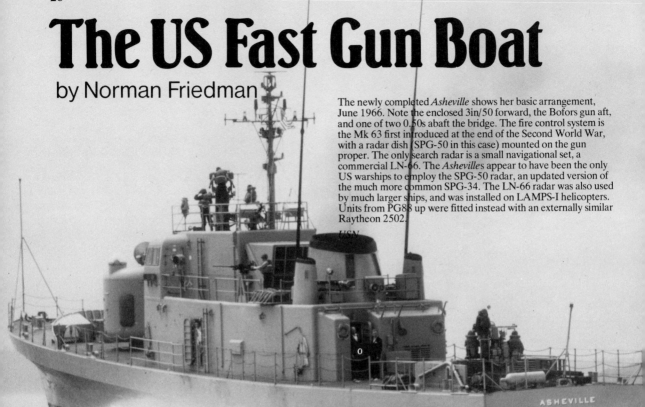

The newly completed *Asheville* shows her basic arrangement, June 1966. Note the enclosed 3in/50 forward, the Bofors gun aft, and one of two 0.50s abaft the bridge. The fire control system is the Mk 63 first introduced at the end of the Second World War, with a radar dish (SPG-50 in this case) mounted on the gun proper. The only search radar is a small navigational set, a commercial LN-66. The *Asheville*s appear to have been the only US warships to employ the SPG-50 radar, an updated version of the much more common SPG-34. The LN-66 radar was also used by much larger ships, and was installed on LAMPS-I helicopters. Units from PG88 up were fitted instead with an externally similar Raytheon 2502.

USN

Fast small craft have only intermittently been popular in the modern US Navy, a force far more concerned with operations in blue than in brown water. Thus their design and construction has generally been associated with particular events and particular requirements, rather than with the staple naval missions. In the case of the *Asheville*s, special conditions coincided with a technological opportunity, so that, in a sense, the well-advertised capability to achieve 40kts was their rationale. All but two are now gone, but in their brief careers they performed both of their principal missions, coastal/riverine warfare and sea surveillance, the latter as 'tattletales' in the Mediterranean. Whether they were the most efficient means of meeting the requirements of coastal warfare in Vietnam is, at best, a matter of controversy. In the 'tattletale' role they appear to have inspired the current, rather controversial missile hydrofoils of the *Pegasus* class.

EXPORT PROJECTS

From 1945 onwards, the US Navy largely abandoned the development of coastal craft. The large fleet of PT-boats

which had survived the war was disposed of, although four new PT-boat prototypes, *PT809–812*, were built. A remnant of the large wartime fleet of amphibious gunboats, including converted small ASW craft, was retained, but most postwar interest in small craft was directed towards replacing the existing 110ft, 173ft and 180ft ASW patrol craft and small escorts, largely for harbour defence. However, several of the smaller Allied navies *did* require small gunboats, and their requirements were the basis for the postwar motor gunboat development which ultimately resulted in the *Asheville*s. In 1955–56 six modified versions of the Second Word War 110ft motor gunboat (PGM) were built for the Philippine Navy under the Military Assistance Program (MAP). Two Coast Guard type 95ft patrol boats were delivered to Iran soon afterwards, and in September 1958 the Chairman of the Ship Characteristics Board asked the Bureau of Ships for studies of a shallow-draught 'river' patrol and gun boat, with a range of possible characteristics giving speeds from 20kts to 45kts and endurances of 800nm to 2000nm at about 10kts. It appears that the Fleet, presumably particularly the naval missions to

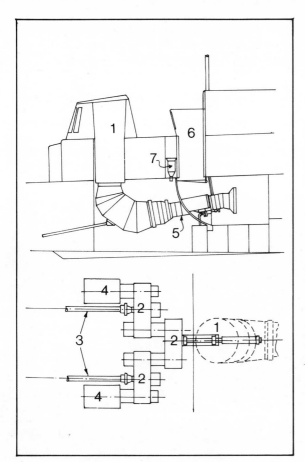

THE MACHINERY LAYOUT OF THE ASHEVILLE CLASS.
1 Turbine exhaust; **2** Reduction Gears; **3** Propeller shafts; **4** Diesel engines; **5** Gas turbines; **6** Air intake; **7** Ventilation fan.

the countries interested in such craft, had its own suggestions, but they have not been preserved.

What is important is that this was a design for export, much as the F-5 'Freedom Fighter' was designed for export to relatively underdeveloped air forces. Simplicity and ease of maintenance therefore took precedence over high performance. BuShips considered three basic types; (a) for moderate speeds, a round-bilge displacement design similar to the successful Coast Guard 95ft patrol boat; (b) for the 30kt to 40kt range, a hard-chine craft similar to a PT-boat; and (c) for speeds above 40kts, a hydrofoil. The minimum suitable craft would be a 65ft reinforced plastic boat capable of 20kts, which could carry one 40mm and one twin 20mm guns. It would cost, in series production, about $475,000 – less than half the cost of any alternative design. It would also be the simplest to operate and maintain. Alternatively, the existing Coast Guard design could be uprated to 25kts at a cost of about $1.2 million, with an additional 40mm gun. It would also carry a 5-ton cargo load, which might be useful in an underdeveloped country where the Navy would have important civil functions.

Other alternatives were 95ft aluminum planing hulls with either three diesels (29kts) or one cruising diesel and two 3000hp gas turbines (38kts) and an 85ft hydrofoil with one 3000hp gas turbine and a cruising diesel (43kts). In each case conventional gun armament was to be supplemented by a flame-thrower and a 106mm recoilless rifle.

The BuShips memo concluded that 'in reviewing the need for the shallow draft patrol craft, it appears that two different threats must be countered. One is the large number of Chinese junks available to potential enemies and the other is the high speed Russian type PT boats which have been made available to them. Since countering the first threat requires great numbers of boats and countering the second requires high performance, it would seem appropriate to consider two different designs for the program.' In fact, the 95ft Coast Guard design, without any significant increase in power, was selected, and substantial numbers were delivered to Brazil, Burma, Ecuador, Ethiopia, Indonesia, Iran, Peru, the Philippines (which received the first of them), Thailand and Vietnam. They were serviceable and they could, if need be, accommodate a substantial armament. For example, the PGM53 class of the Ethiopian Navy normally mounted one single 20mm gun, two depth-charge racks and a Mousetrap ASW rocket launcher. However, it could accommodate one single 40mm gun, two 81mm mortars, four 40mm grenade launchers, four 0.5in machine guns and twelve Redeye surface-to-air missiles. Maximum speed was 20kts, on a 2200hp diesel. Again, that could be remedied; an uprated diesel (3200hp) would propel the same hull at 22kts.

NEW US REQUIREMENT

In 1960 the US Navy held officially that, with the advent of substantial Soviet strategic nuclear forces, central war with the Soviet Union was unlikely; that the Soviets would, instead, foment revolution around the Eurasian periphery. This doctrine, which the incoming Administration would accept (and which would shape early US perceptions of the war in Vietnam), made coastal craft and coastal warfare much more of a naval concern than they had been in the more distant past. The new President, moreover, was a veteran of precisely that unconventional branch of the Navy which had fought a coastal war almost two decades earlier, the PT arm – and with the appearance of Soviet fast coastal craft in Cuba, the US Navy began to see a requirement for fast coastal craft on its own.

Thus in May 1961 the Ships Characteristics Board asked for a new round of studies of a motor gun boat as 'recent developments in the Caribbean and in Southeast Asia have indicated the potential usefulness of a small fast coastal gun boat. Such a boat should be well armed and capable of reasonably sustained and independent operations. Its primary use would be for surveillance, blockade, operations against other small craft in coastal waters, and limited support of troops ashore. The Fast Patrol Boat . . . is considered too limited in endurance and possibly too complex in hull and engineering design to meet all the requirements for a Motor Gun Boat . . .' The new craft would be suitable both for US and indigenous naval operation; it would be able 'to support guerillas or other small groups operating within enemy occupied territory' as well as the more conventional roles of interdiction of coastal shipping, blockade and surveillance, and close support of amphibious operations. Thus shallow draught (a maximum of 8ft) and high speed (30kts) were to be combined with non-petrol engines (to reduce vulnerability) and relatively long endurance (1500nm at 17kts). Major afloat support would come from a base or ship, but the boat would be able to operate on its own for 10 to 14 days; it was to have maximum sea-keeping ability. As for armament, that was to be the maximum possible, 'interchangeable and should include weapons of the sort listed in BuWeps "Weapons shopping list for miscellaneous small craft", such as 40mm or 3in/50 manual controlled guns; recoilless rifles; rocket launchers; grenades or mortars; RED EYE, or other missiles.' Overall

USS *Gallup*, the second of the class, at high speed off Vietnam during Operation 'Market Time', June 1967. It was claimed that these craft could accelerate from 0 to 40kts in less than 60 seconds; in service, however, most were limited in speed due to cavitation-induced propeller damage.

USN

length was to be 95ft to 125ft, the lower figure a tacit admission that the existing 95ft PGM might well have to be adapted.

The project was considered urgent, as the prototype was to be ordered under the FY63 programme. In June, BuShips reported studies of modified 95ft PGMs, noting that an increased armament would be relatively easy to accommodate, but that speed could not be increased materially unless foreign lightweight diesels were installed. Costs would be relatively modest, in line with the SCB demand for low cost: a PGM39 (Philippine type) with increased armament would cost about $580,000. BuShips also suggested as an alternative a somewhat enlarged craft, 115ft long, capable of 27kts, with an endurance of 1300nm at 17kts, and carrying one 3in/50, one twin and two single 0.5in machine guns and two 81mm mortars. It was preferred to two schemes for 95ft hulls with increased power for, respectively, 30kts and 28kts with endurances far short of requirements: 1150nm and 600nm at 12kts. They would be armed with, respectively, one 40mm and one 3in/50 and, in each case, four 0.5in machine guns; the 30kt version would also have two 81mm mortars. The mortars were considered valuable at this time for their high-angle fire (in support of troops) and their illuminating capability.

INITIAL SCHEMES

In October 1961, the Bureau suggested an alternative approach using a gas turbine, for the required 27kt to 30kt maximum speed, and a diesel for the long cruising range. An all-diesel plant of the same power would require considerable reductions in fuel load, lowering the endurance at cruising speed. In the design finally adopted, each of two shafts could be driven either by a single diesel or by the combined power of diesel and gas turbine, the latter exhausting through the transom. A combination of stability requirements, sea-keeping and powering dictated a much longer hull, and a 161ft, 225-ton steel hull was finally adopted as Scheme 5, with a maximum speed at half fuel load of 30kts (28.5kts at full load) and a maximum cruising speed on diesels of at least 16kts (endurance 1700nm at 16kts, 3200nm at 13kts). An armament and ammunition weight of about 20 tons would buy a rapid-fire 3in/50 gun with a Mk 63 fire control system, one twin and two single 0.5in machine guns, two 81mm mortars, twelve Redeyes for anti-aircraft self-defence, and four 40mm grenade launchers. Cost would rise to about $2 million for series units in the FY63 programme. An alternative, Scheme 4, which was discarded, was somewhat simpler, with three rather than two shafts: two powered by gas turbines, one by a diesel, at a cost of $1.8 million. However, the forward location of the machinery spaces dictated mounting the 3in/50 aft of the superstructure, which was not considered acceptable, and the need to windmill the centre or outboard propellers was not liked.

The Bureau was not entirely happy with this result, as 'the design as dictated by performance considerations does not fulfill the requirement for simplicity, low cost, ease of maintenance, and operation by indigenous personnel of Southeast Asian countries. The cost and complexity of Scheme 5 are justified only if the stated performance satisfies a firm requirement of the US Navy.' In fact, the ship

actually built was to be even more complex; but it was to be built (at first) *only* for the US Navy.

Scheme 4 was soon developed into a detailed design, capable (in theory) of 30.5kts at most. However, efforts within BuShips to find a machinery plant suitable for higher speed continued, presumably because it was known that some in the Office of the Chief of Naval Operations would support it – as was in fact the case. Scheme 4b, as reflected in the original Characteristics, employed a British Proteus 3100shp gas turbine and a Curtiss-Wright 3-D 900bhp diesel on each shaft. The Preliminary Design group at BuShips, Code 420, began to look for some alternative, but found only one, Scheme 7b, which promised 36.5kts: it had three shafts, with diesels on the wing shafts (as in the discredited Scheme 4 of the original series of studies) and an 18,000shp Pratt and Whitney FT-4A on the centre shaft. It would cost about $1 million more than the earlier version in FY63, and $0.3 million more in follow-on ships; within a few days it had to be dropped. However, time was very short, and a review even of the original Scheme 4b showed that it was too complex: in mid-June Code 420 still had no acceptable machinery arrangement.

On 20 June four Schemes were compared: 4b (Proteus and 3-D on each of two shafts); 7b (three shafts, FT-4A on centerline, 3-Ds outboard); 9 (three shafts, 3000bhp diesel on centreline, Proteus outboard); and 10a/b (FT-4A on centreline, 300 and 900bhp diesels on Z-drives outboard, which could be lifted from the water at high speed). Scheme 7b might benefit from reduced costs if surplus engines were bought from the Air Force as spares rather than out of FY63 funds. Scheme 7b was chosen, subject to a limit of $4.1 million in the FY63 budget; Scheme 9 was held as an alternative solution 'since it was recognized as the simplest, cheapest means by which the approved characteristics could be met.' In fact the Preliminary Design reflected Scheme 7b, with expected performance, on gas turbines, of 36.5kts (maximum sustained) and 38.8kts maximum. These figures included margins; 'neat' figures were, respectively, 38.5kts and 41.0kts.

DESIGN FINALISATION

However, by August there was still confusion: two alternatives still existed for conversion to Contract Plans. One was a 'low power' PGM, Scheme 4b updated; the other was a new two shaft high-powered design. Gibbs & Cox, the Design Agent, had torpedoed Scheme 7b on grounds of impracticality, as 'it has been understood that this design is intended to be a prototype and is not to be considered experimental.' The centre shaft propeller would have to be super-cavitating because of the high power it would have to absorb within a small diameter; it would also have to adapt to a wide speed range. No existing propeller met these requirements. Controllable, reversible pitch propellers would be required for the outboard shafts; again, no suitable propeller had been tested; alternatively, lightweight clutches and reversing gear would be needed on the outboard shafts. Again, although such a unit could be designed, it did not yet exist and thus could not be provided in time for installation on an urgently needed craft. The Curtiss-Wright diesels were not considered reliable at the high power required for cruising, and the proposed power

The motor gunboat *Antelope* shows her Dutch-designed Mk 87 fire control system, which also provided surface search/navigational radar; note the absence of both the separate radar at masthead and the SPG-50 on the gun shield. The small stacks were diesel exhausts. She ultimately received box launchers aft for two Standard missiles.

USN

turbine had never been operated at sea or under suitable conditions. 'The Design Agent feels that all the above features require development and involve many more uncertainties than are usually associated with a prototype design. None of these problems appear to be insurmountable although any of them could prove to be unexpectedly difficult and could result in troublesome delays in putting a prototype ship into service.'

A 9 August briefing within BuShips noted that the lower power design met or exceeded the approved characteristics and was within the cost limits; but it was deficient in that it used foreign engines (with the attendant foreign exchange problems) and 'because the larger, faster, more seaworthy gunboat is more responsive to needs. High power exceeds the characteristics in speed (and endurance) and is technically an outstanding design of a potential new class. There are no foreign engines, but there are competitive new US engines. This high performance gunboat was not foreseen in the original end-costing; it exceeds the $4.1M by only X . . . Low power meets characteristics and cost but is yesterday's design in cost and engines. High power is an exceptionally good design with US engines but today's cost. We recommend Low Power design be scrapped and end cost augmented to meet High Power costs . . .'

At this time Preliminary Design was much taken with the virtues of the gas turbine, particularly as demonstrated by the new British 'Tribal' class frigates. In Project 'Seahawk' it was beginning to develop a gas turbine destroyer. It seems likely that there was a strong desire to show that the US Navy was indeed capable of matching the latest foreign warship machinery, that BuShips had not given up its interest in new forms of propulsion. Flip charts for presentation outside of the Bureau included the argument that the High Power design would be 'a prestige gunboat' although it would exceed the PT-boat budget level originally worked out, which had called for two boats for $4.1 million in FY63. It would employ a single GE MS240 or Pratt and Whitney FT-3C gas turbine geared to two shafts, each of which would also be powered by a Curtiss-Wright diesel; the lead ship would cost $3.8 million including spares ($2 million for follow-ons) or, without spares (as planned) two could be bought for $4.9 million in FY63. The hull would be of aluminium, and endurance would be 1900nm at over 16kts (1700nm for Low Power design of 375nm at 39kts; 400nm at 31kts). Although projected High Power costs escalated very rapidly (to $5.9 million for two without spares in a 17 August presentation for the CNO, Admiral G W Anderson), it was approved by the CNO – who emphasised that the Bureau should make every effort to keep the ship simple, and that FY63 funds might limit initial procurement to only one ship. Cost was particularly important because a total of 22 ships were scheduled for the FY64-66 programmes, in addition to the two pro-

Benicia was the test-ship for the standard ARM installation (1971); she is shown here in her original form, in April 1970. PGM92 class ships differed in detail from the first series, with increased fuel capacity. The system was removed before her transfer to South Korea.

USN

totypes of FY63. In fact, however, only seventeen were built.

ARMAMENT

Armament was a matter of some controversy, as the slow-firing 3in/50 originally specified was considered rather dated. CinC Pacific Fleet was particularly critical – reflecting the needs of the emerging conflict in South-East Asia – but the Chairman of the Ship Characteristics Board reminded him that only existing systems were to be used, given the urgency of the programme. However, the follow-on units might be given something more suitable. As early as August 1962 the new Dutch M20 series fire control systems (ultimately adopted as the US Mk 87 and Mk 92) were being assessed, and both foreign and domestic weapons were being surveyed to find (a) a lightweight surface gun with an effective range of 6000yds, a high rate of fire and low manning requirements; (b) a simple light-weight anti-aircraft missile for self-defence, at ranges of 3000yds or more, against aircraft and anti-ship cruise missiles; and (c) a lightweight anti-ship homing torpedo. Possibilities included a 3in version of the 5in Mk 45 lightweight gun then under development; a lightweight version of the Army Mauler anti-aircraft missile (then being developed as a Navy point-defence weapon); the British Seacat; the French SS-12; and a Bofors surface-only 3in gun, then being planned for Norwegian and Swedish gunboats. By October, an internal BuShips study had reported that effectiveness of the existing Mk 63 fire control system and of the exposed personnel on a conventional 3in/50 mount would be doubtful at best at 40kts. The Bureau of Naval Weapons was in the process of procuring eight Dutch M22 fire control systems, capable of air and surface fire control. A proposed US lightweight 3in gun was being compared to the Bofors 3in/50; it elevated to 65° (compared to 30) and it appeared that the production cost of $175,000 would match that of licence production of the Swedish gun; however, a development investment of $2 million would be required. None of the proposed missiles was particularly attractive; Mauler had not yet been 'marinised' (and, indeed, would be dead within three years), and both the French SS series and the British Seacat were optically controlled, and hence useless at night.

Alternative weapon suits were considered for the three major functions proposed for the PGM; interdiction, paramilitary operations and perimeter defence of a beach-head against light craft. In each case an enclosed 3in gun, a pair of 20mm machine guns and an M22 fire control system could be justified. Seacat seemed indicated for interdiction, whereas perimeter defence required a more capable system such as Mauler. The paramilitary mission did not require a missile, but it did demand the 81mm mortar and a pair of 0.5in machine guns; a requirement for a 40mm gun was added later. It also gradually became clear that no one would endorse the proposal to develop a new lightweight 3in/50 gun.

In April 1963, the CNO authorised the substitution of a single rapid-fire 3in/50 gun for the open slow-firing weapon previously specified; it would be enclosed to improve its efficiency. As weight compensation, the two 81mm mortars previously specified (and considered rather valuable in

amphibious and riverine operations) would be deleted. At the same time some decrease in specified maximum speed and some considerable increase in allowable draught were accepted; the amphibious readiness branch of the Office of the CNO was unhappy, although the increased draught could not be avoided, given the necessary details of hull lines and propeller size. The only alternative was to accept a considerable reduction in cruising radius so as to combine shallow draught and high speed. That too, was unacceptable, given the sea surveillance mission.

THE ASHEVILLE CLASS

The result of all of this evolution was unique, at least from a US standpoint, so much so that the Contract Design branch, Code 440, of BuShips, proposed in January 1963 that a distinctive hull number series be assigned: 'The size of the new Project 229 even makes it doubtful that they are in the same class as PT or PTF. Their speed and special features are surely going to attract comment . . . Representative Flood has called this [project] *the most exciting in '63.*'

As usual, the reality was somewhat less exciting, although the *Asheville*s did live up to their advertising as regards their maximum speed. The original 24 unit programme fell to 17, and although it had been hoped that the Dutch fire control system would be installed from FY65 onwards, in fact only two (PG86 and 87) had it. All had the rapid-fire 3in/50 Mk 34, plus two twin 0.5in machine guns and a single 40mm gun aft. The self-defence missile issue was never really resolved, although in 1967–68 a navalised Sidewinder was proposed as an anti-'Styx' measure. It was rejected in favour of an offensive surface-to-surface missile which would, in theory, destroy the 'Styx' on its launcher: the ISSM, Standard ARM. *Benicia* was the test platform, and two missiles replaced the after 40mm gun in *Antelope, Ready, Grand Rapids,* and *Douglas* at a cost of 3 or 4kts speed. Such weapons would be particularly effective against an enemy missile boat at some distance from a coast. One reload per launcher was carried, for a total of four missiles.

Operationally, the new gunboats appeared just as the United States became deeply involved in Vietnam; they joined the Market Time coastal interdiction patrol and also fought in the river war. In the former role, they were better seaboats than smaller craft such as Coast Guard picket boats; they could also remain on station longer and had greater firepower. At the same time, they were less expensive than destroyers or the former radar-picket destroyer-escorts. However, they were uncomfortable, and generally operated continuously for only one to two weeks. Similarly, their light draft and heavy battery suited them for the river war – but their light hulls were vulnerable, *Antelope* in particular suffering heavy damage. High speed was certainly no great advantage here, and in 1972 it was reported that two diesel-powered versions were under construction for the South Vietnamese Navy. On the other hand, the *Asheville*s were probably the most powerful units which could operate for extended periods on Vietnamese rivers, and as such they were worked very hard; one unit was underway for 56 days, of which 29 were fire support or patrol, the longest stop being for six hours.

They had both advantages and disadvantages in the open sea. They could make their design speed, although cavitation and the consequent pitting of propellers generally limited them considerably. On the other hand, they were extremely uncomfortable in any considerable sea – although they could certainly ride out severe storms. A US Navy generally unused to craft of their size could comment that they had the worst ride in its experience. On the other hand, their small radar cross-section made them difficult to detect in coastal or near-coastal operations against larger ships. Presumably that was a major reason for Admiral Zumwalt's decision to use *Asheville*s in the Mediterranean to trail major Soviet units, so that it would become impossible for the latter to attack the Sixth Fleet by surprise. In his view the missile hydrofoil (*Pegasus* class) would combine the great virtues of the *Asheville*, its high speed and its considerable firepower (particularly when missile-armed), with satisfactory sea-keeping. Others have been rather more cynical, seeing in the lightly armed tattletale a very ineffective means of countering Soviet surface strike groups. The principal trailers in the Mediterranean were *Defiance* and *Surprise;* both transferred to Turkey in 1973. Their replacements in the Mediterranean, *Antelope* and *Ready*, were stricken in 1977; the other two missile units, which also served in the Mediterranean, were stricken at the same time (*Grand Rapids* was disarmed as a research craft).

Of the remaining ships, PG91 was never completed, as she was destroyed by fire at the Tacoma Boat Yard. PG95, *Benicia*, the missile test ship, stripped of her single missile launcher and transferred to South Korea in 1971, was the first to go. *Beacon* and *Green Bay* were scheduled for transfer to Greece in 1977, but were laid up instead when Congress objected. In 1981 they remain in existence. *Chebalis* became a research craft, and in 1981 only *Tacoma* and *Welch* are left in service, operating at Norfolk to help train Saudi personnel waiting to take over the patrol craft, roughly *Asheville*-size in some cases, being built for Saudi Arabia. The others were all stricken in 1977. Even before that, it was clear that their days were numbered. In 1973, for example, of fourteen units remaining in US hands, seven were patrolling the Marianas Trust Territory out of Guam, three were serving with the Amphibious development unit at Little Creek, Virginia, three were in the Mediterranean and one was refitting as a missile boat. Most of those tasks hardly required the sophistication of an *Asheville*.

All were begun as PGMs, but were reclassified in 1967 as Patrol Gunboats (PG) and as patrol combatants (PG) in 1975. It appears that the entire series of PG84 to PG106 (plus PG108) was reserved for them, although only the numbers to PG101 were used. The *Asheville* design, moreover, lives on in a modified version built for Korea by Tacoma Boatbuilding and the Korea-Tacoma company, the PSMM-5 class, with an all gas-turbine powerplant. Twelve of a modified version have been built or ordered for Taiwan, with surface-to-surface missiles somewhat similar to the Israeli Gabriel, as the *Lung Chiang* class. Four more are being built in Korea for Indonesia. The Korean craft have twin screws with six gas-turbines, the others triple screws with CODOG plants.

HMS APOLLO

by John Roberts

The *Apollo* was a 2nd class cruiser constructed, with twenty sister-ships, under the Naval Defence Act of 1889. She was laid down at Chatham Dockyard in April 1889 and completed in 1892. As built, she carried an armament of two 6in guns, one on the forecastle and one on the poop; six single 4.7in in the waist; eight single 6pdr QF, four in the waist, two forward and two aft; four 0.45in Nordenfelt five-barrelled machine guns, two on the forecastle and two on the poop; one 3pdr QF for the boats (with ship mountings on each side at the after end of the waist); and four 14in torpedo tubes, two fixed in the stem and stern, and two broadside training tubes on the upper deck aft. In 1909 this entire armament was removed when she was converted into a minelayer at Chatham Dockyard, and the accompanying drawing shows her appearance on completion of this refit. The fitting of the mine rails on the upper deck involved some minor alterations to the deck fittings etc, and the removal of the cabins under the poop. Other alterations included extending the after deckhouse, and the conversion of the magazines into store rooms (several, including almost all those aft, were left empty). Six of her sister-ships, *Andromache, Intrepid, Iphigenia, Latona, Naiad* and *Thetis* were similarly converted, except that *Intrepid* and *Naiad* retained six of their 6pdr guns. On the outbreak of war *Apollo* was fitted with four 4.7in, and in 1914–15 she and her sisters formed a minelaying squadron operating from the Nore and Dover. In 1915 she was again disarmed, spending the remainder of the war paid off or serving in subsidiary roles. She was sold for breaking up in 1920.

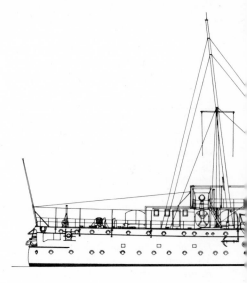

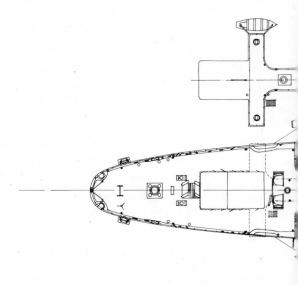

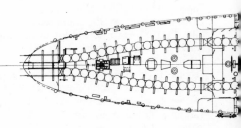

PARTICULARS OF APOLLO

Displacement:	3400 tons (designed)
Length:	300ft (pp), 314ft (oa)
Beam:	43ft
Draught:	17ft 6in
Machinery:	2-shaft steam reciprocating engines, 7000ihp = 18.5kts (natural draught), 9000ihp = 20kts (forced draught); 5 boilers, 535 tons coal.
Protection:	2in–1¼in decks, 3in CT, 5in engine hatch.
Mines:	100
Boats:	One 32ft cutter, one 30ft steam cutter, one 28ft cutter, one 30ft gig, two 27ft whalers, one 16ft dinghy, one balsa raft.
Complement:	273 (as built)

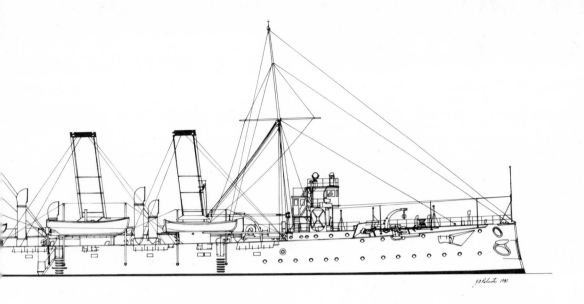
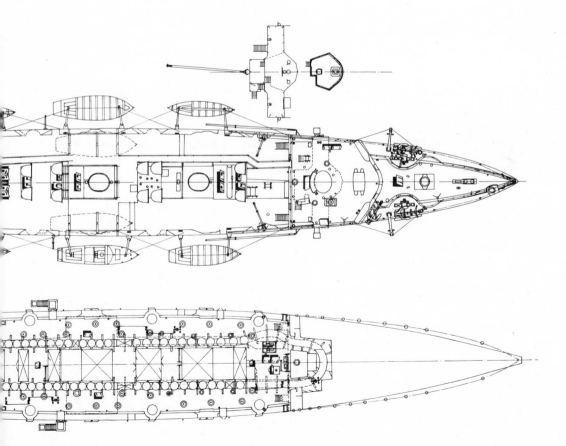

The Last Austro-Hungarian Destroyer Projects

by René Greger

The Austro-Hungarian navy entered the First World War in 1914 with a large number of torpedo vessels (a total of 80), but only a small number were sufficiently large and modern as Table 1 shows. In addition, the fleet list included seven completely obsolete torpedo gun-boats and sixteen obsolete coastal torpedo-boats (80 – 110 tons), which were only suitable for mine sweeping.

TABLE 1: AUSTRO-HUNGARIAN TORPEDO VESSELS, 1914

	Completed	Under construction	Authorised
Large destroyers (870 tons)	6	–	6
Small destroyers (400 tons)	12	1	–
New torpedo-boats (250 tons)	3	24	–
Old torpedo-boats (200 tons)	24	–	–
New coastal torpedo-boats	12	–	–

SHIPBUILDING POLICY

Concentration of effort on the building of battleships caused the construction of large torpedo vessels, and also cruisers to be neglected. Super dreadnoughts were required for operations in the open sea, but the several series of 250 ton torpedo-boats then being built were in no way capable of being employed outside the Adriatic because of their size and the paucity of their artillery armament. Even in the Adriatic the most likely enemy, the Italian Fleet, possessed a large number of new torpedo-boats, all of which carried superior artillery; the large *Indomito* class torpedo-boats carried five 102mm guns, and even the small PN class coastal torpedo-boats generally carried more powerful guns for their displacement (two 76mm) than their Austro-Hungarian counterparts.

The only Austro-Hungarian vessels sufficiently large and modern were the six *Tatra* class destroyers, but the new Fleet construction programme of 1914, which provided for the building of four Super dreadnoughts and three cruisers only allowed for the destroyer flotilla to be increased by six more vessels. If this programme had been carried through, the Austro-Hungarian navy would have had eight modern dreadnoughts at its disposal, but only 12 modern destroyers! It was indeed the *Tatra* class, together with the *Novara* class scout-cruisers, which proved to be the most useful ships of the fleet during the course of the Adriatic War.

WAR PROBLEMS

In 1914, after the outbreak of War, a decision was made to cancel the six destroyers recently authorised which proved to be one of the Fleet Command's greatest mistakes in the shipbuilding policy of the initial stage of the War. It had a substantial influence on the subsequent course of events, the consequences of the error being felt particularly deeply in the Winter of 1915/16. Until Italy entered the war on 23 May 1915 only five new torpedo-boats were commissioned, while the construction of further units made very slow progress, the last boat, *No 97F*, not being delivered to the Fleet until 22 December 1916.

In the meantime, on 29 December 1915 the Austro-Hungarian navy suffered a severe loss when the destroyers *Lika* and *Triglav* were sunk off Durazzo after striking mines. In the period, when the large warships were required to attack transports evacuating the defeated Serbian army retreating from North Albania, the fleet had only four destroyers in service!

It was obvious to the Fleet command that this situation could not be allowed to continue and it was decided to build four new destroyers as quickly as possible, albeit of the same type. These destroyers were built by Ganz-Danubius in Porto Ré (now Kraljevica), and carried the same armament as the first *Tatra* class units (two 100mm/L50 and six 66mm/L45 guns, and four 450mm torpedo tubes) while being of very slightly greater displacement (up to 910 tons normal). Of these ships the *Triglav II* entered service on 27 July 1917, *Lika II* on 6 September 1917, *Dukla* on 7 November 1917 and *Uzsok* not until 25 January 1918.

In the third year of the War the situation became critical; all the small *Huszar* class destroyers and most of the torpedo-boats were in action on convoy duty for the Albanian Front or were on Coastal guard duty, but were also increasingly needed to escort their own submarines, and those of the Germans, as they arrived at, or left their main base of Cattaro. In addition, they were in poor condition, with one third of them always under repair.

NEW DESIGNS

Consequently the Navy called for funds from the Austro-Hungarian government to build new vessels. The Navy's technical committee (MTK) working out the Navy's proposals and producing preliminary designs. In July 1917, the MTK sent a memorandum to the War Ministry, enclosing drawings of a 500 ton torpedo-boat, a 1000 ton torpedo-boat and a 1900 ton torpedo vessel. All the ships were to be exclusively oil-fired, which was an innovation for the Austro-Hungarian Navy.

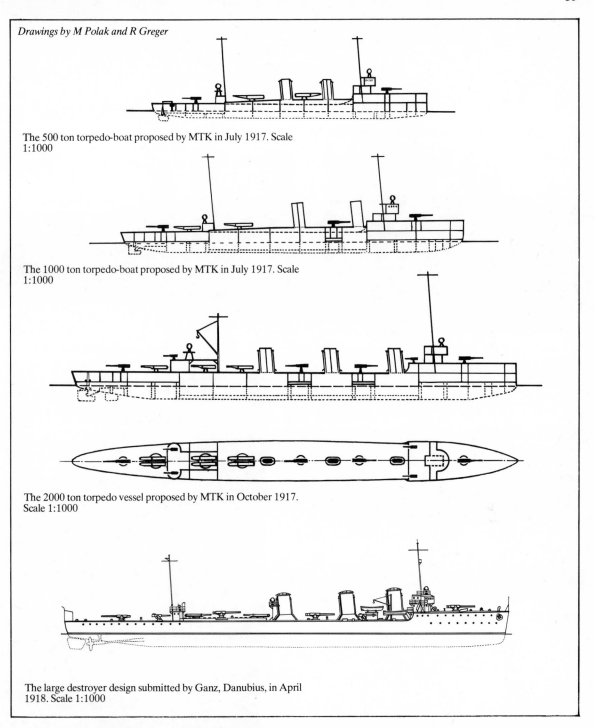

Drawings by M Polak and R Greger

The 500 ton torpedo-boat proposed by MTK in July 1917. Scale 1:1000

The 1000 ton torpedo-boat proposed by MTK in July 1917. Scale 1:1000

The 2000 ton torpedo vessel proposed by MTK in October 1917. Scale 1:1000

The large destroyer design submitted by Ganz, Danubius, in April 1918. Scale 1:1000

Although the MTK document listed the deficiencies of the new 250 ton torpedo-boats, (above all their weak gun armament and limited endurance) it is apparent that the Naval Command did not want to relinquish this type entirely. The proposed 500 ton torpedo-boat was to have a top speed of 32kts and a range of 1000 nautical miles. This would have made it 4kts faster than the 250 ton torpedo-boat, but the endurance would have been the same. The

armament too, consisting of two 90mm/L45 guns, was too weak in comparison with the Italian *Indomito* and *Pilo* class boats, which were of the same size. On the other hand, her torpedo armament (four 533mm torpedo tubes) was too great for her size and, in the final year of the War, the Fleet Command did not approve the construction of this type.

The small 1000 ton destroyer – designated as a torpedo-boat in the document – did carry a powerful armament for

1

2

1 The *Uzsok*, as the Italian *Monfalcone*, carrying Italian 102mm guns in place of the original Skoda built 100mm guns.

Author's collection

2 *Like II* in 1918

Author's collection

3 The vessels of the second *Tatra* class building, under primitive conditions, at Kraljevica (then Porto Re) in October 1916.

Author's collection

its size; three 120mm/L45 guns of a new type made by Skoda. In addition her torpedo armament was the same as in the 500 ton torpedo-boat, while her 32kt top speed and range of 1500 nautical miles would have made this small destroyer an ideal type for the sea war in the Adriatic.

The 1900 ton ship, designated a torpedo vessel, was in reality a large destroyer, which had no equal in the enemy fleets of the time. With her four 150mm/L50 guns she would have been more powerful in artillery terms than the current *Novara* class cruisers, and also much faster. Her top speed was in fact 35kts, and her range 3000 nautical miles. The torpedo armament occupied considerable space, as the 533mm torpedoes were to be carried in three twin tubes. In contrast, the anti-aircraft defences in this first variant of the ship amounted to just two machine guns.

A ship of such qualities was bound to impress the senior officers of the Fleet Command as well as the members of the ministerial council, so it is hardly surprising that this was the type which was chosen. In September 1917, the collective ministerial council, consisting of Austrian and Hungarian ministers, had to consider the Navy's demand for the new large submarines and torpedo vessels which were urgently needed, and for which a special credit of 380 million Kronen was required. The funds were authorised

on the condition that no capital ships were to be built; only ships which could be built within the economic limitations of the monarchy.

FINAL DESIGNS

The Navy finalised its requirements as 12 large submarines of 1000 tons and 20 torpedo-vessels (8 of the smaller type, and 12 large type). Curiously, in December 1917 the 1000 ton small destroyers of the MTK project were replaced by an order for a 'more powerful *Tatra* type'. The extra fire-power being gained by changing the calibre of the two main guns from 100mm to the new 120mm/L45 and replacing the 66mm guns by two 90mm/L45 AA guns. The *Tatra* class destroyers were good ships, subsequently serving in the Italian and French navies until the mid 1930s, so the newly authorised units should also have been capable of providing good service. Due to lack of materials and workers at Ganz-Danubius, only four units were ordered and by the end of the War no keels had been laid, although about 200 tons of materials had arrived at the yard. In contrast, the manufacture of the engine units in Budapest made better progress, and the artillery was also under way at Skoda in Pilsen. All reports that there were destroyers named *Honved* and *Lovcen* at Porto Ré at the end of the

3

Destroyers from both groups of the *Tatra* class at Cattaro in 1917.
From the foreground, *Orjen, Tatra, Lika II* and three of the
Huszar class.

Author's collection

War are incorrect – no names were given officially. The
large submarines were also cut back, only half of them
being ordered in December; and the large destroyers were
never ordered at all.

In November 1917, the Navy sent a new specification for
the revised project to the two most important yards in the
Monarchy. The displacement was now 2000 tons, with four
90mm AA guns, but it was several months before the
yards' tenders, with their own plans, were delivered. Ganz
& Co, Danubius, the firm which had traditionally built
destroyers, sent the most interesting design in April 1918.
Their design, dated 18 April 1918, proposed a large destroyer with the specifications shown in Table 2. In July
1918, three months later, the second yard, Austria of
Trieste (earlier known as the Stabililimento Tecnico Tries-
tino), delivered its two designs. The 'A' variant proposed a
2440 ton large destroyer with only three 150mm guns and
the same top speed of 34kts. The 'B' variant carried four
150mm guns on a displacement of 2650 tons. Only the 'B'
variant was accepted by the MTK, although her anti-

aircraft armament was considered inadequated. However,
neither Ganz nor Austria received orders for these ships so
the last destroyer of the Austro-Hungarian Navy, although
authorised, never progressed beyond the paper stage.

TABLE 2: GANZ DESTROYER DESIGN, 1918

Displacement:	2273 tons normal, 2498 tons maximum (with 747 tons fuel).
Length:	112.4m overall.
Beam:	10.2m
Draught:	3.5m normal.
Shp:	43,000/48,000 max
Speed:	34kts
Armament:	4 – 150mm/L50, 4 – 105mm/L45 AA, 4 – 533mm torpedo tubes (6 torpedoes)

British Naval Guns 1880~1945   No.5
by NJM Campbell

10in Mks I, II, III and IV Of these 32 calibre, trunnioned guns, Mk I was an Elswick design of 1884, not used afloat and limited to coast defence batteries at Aden and Hong Kong. The trunnions were 8.1in further from the breech than in the Mk II, a Woolwich design of 1885, and the guns were thus not interchangeable. However, Mks III and IV, which were Woolwich designs of 1888 and 1890/91, were interchangeable with Mk II. Their use in the navy was limited to the following mountings and battleships: VCP I, 14° elevation, one gun each in *Victoria* and *Sans Pareil*; Turret Mk I, Elswick, 12° elevation, four guns in the rearmed *Thunderer*; Turret Mk II, Whitworth, 13° elevation, four guns in the rearmed *Devastation*; Barbette Mk III, Whitworth, 15° elevation, four guns each in *Barfleur*, *Centurion* and *Renown*.

The last-named mounting was partly steam and partly electric or hand worked, and 35° elevation could be obtained if a section of the shield was removed, but only half charges could be fired at this elevation, converting the

The after 10in guns of the battleship *Renown*. Note the depression rail fitted around the top of the barbette and the sighting port in the top of the open-backed gun shield.
IWM, by courtesy of R A Burt

gun into a kind of howitzer. As originally mounted the gun in *Victoria* and the two in *Thunderer* were Mk II, the four in *Renown* Mk IV and the rest Mk III.

More guns were mounted ashored in coast defence batteries on a variety of disappearing or barbette mountings. Including Mk I, the totals were in Britain: 4 Sheerness, 3 Harwich, 2 Coalhouse (Thames), 2 Plymouth, 1 Milford Haven; and overseas: 8 Bombay, 5 Aden, 5 Hong Kong, 3 Malta, 3 Karachi, 2 Singapore, 1 Halifax. The 2 guns at Port Phillip, Melbourne, were earlier 30 calibre designs, Elswick Patterns 'F' and 'G', and never acquired a Mark number.

Altogether, ten Mk I, 5 Mk II, 52 Mk III and 9 Mk IV were made. All were of built up construction as follows:

1

2

PARTICULARS OF 10in GUNS

	10in Mk I–IV	10in Mk V	10in Mk VI	10in Mk VII	10in Mk VIII
Weight (tons)	29.53	40	39.4	30.69	70.75
Length oa (in)	342.4	517.6	467.6	462.8	432.6
Length bore (cal)	32	50	45	45	40.52
Chamber (cu in)	8370	10,000	9720	9720	8370
Chamber length (in)	54	67.55	65.07	64.54	54
Projectile (lb)	500	500	500	500	500
Charge (lb–type)	252–Pr Br, 76–Cord 30	?172–MD 45	146.8–MD 45	146.8–MD 45	–
Muzzle Velocity (fs)	2040–2046	2930	2656	2656	–
Range (yds)	–	–	14,800/13½°	14,800/13½°	–

Notes: 10in Mk I weighed 32.32 tons. 10in Mk VI* weighed 37 tons. The range tables for the 10in MkI–IV do not extend beyond 10,100yds at 12° 05′. According to calculations in the 1902 Gunnery Manual, with ½ charge and 35° elevation, muzzle velocity was 1393fs and range 11.552yds.

Mk I Complete liner/'A' tube/breech piece, 3 'B' tubes to muzzle/'C' hoop, trunnion piece, jacket

Mk II Liner and alpha tube/'A' tube/breech piece, 2 'B' tubes not to muzzle/'C' hoop, trunnion piece, jacket/'D' hoop.

Mk III 'A' tube/breech piece, 2 'B' tubes to muzzle/'C' hoop and tube/2 hoops and trunnion piece/hoop and screwed ring.

Mk IV 'A' tube/breech piece, 'B' hoop and tube to muzzle/3 'C' hoops/'D' hoop, trunnion piece, screwed ring, jacket.

The breech block was of interrupted screw, cylindrical type with a hand worked 3-motion mechanism, though continuous motion mechanism was reported in *Renown* in 1897. In Mks I, II, III it screwed into the breech piece, but in Mk IV it screwed into a breech bush, itself screwed into the end 'C' hoop.

There were few variants. Mk IIA was for guns with separate bore and chamber liners, and Mk IIIA covered two guns differing from the other Mk IIIs in having one of the 'B' tubes replaced by two hoops and in having shoulders on the 'A' tube over the chamber for greater longitudinal strength. An 'A' in front of the Mark indicated continuous motion breech mechanism, for a later specially ordered coast defence barbette mounting, and Mks I* to IV* indicated loading tray stops and locks for the same mounting.

10in Mk V There was some discussion on introducing an improved 40 calibre gun on the lines of the Elswick Patterns 'P', 'Q' and 'R' used in various foreign navies, and

further consideration in 1901, prompted by the knowledge that the USA were to mount 10in guns in their future armoured cruisers, led to the 50 calibre Mk V which was never made, though the drawings were sealed. The coast artillery had also shown some interest as the 9.2in Mk X was unsatisfactory in its earlier years. The Mk V would have been of normal wire wound type with inner 'A', 'A' and 'B' tubes, and a jacket.

10in Mk VI This 45 calibre gun, Elswick Pattern 'S', was introduced in the battleship *Swiftsure*, originally ordered by Chile. It was fitted in BIV mountings allowing 13½° elevation but limited to 9¾° unless a hatch door in the gunhouse floor was opened. Altogether, five guns were made, of which the first four were wire-wound for part of their length and had two piece 'A' tubes but were otherwise of usual construction except for the addition of a ring piece connecting the hydraulic recoil buffer. The fifth gun, known as Mk VI*, differed in having a single piece 'A' tube and no ring piece. The breech block was of interrupted screw, cylindrical type and the breech bush was located in the 'A' tube. Hydraulic or hand Elswick mechanism was fitted.

When *Swiftsure* was disarmed, in the latter part of the First World War, it was intended that the five guns be re-lined to 9.2in calibre for railway mountings, but this conversion was never completed.

10in Mk VII Another 45 calibre gun, Vickers Mk 'A', introduced in *Triumph*, sister-ship to *Swiftsure*. It was fitted in BV mountings allowing 13½° elevation. A total of five guns were made of normal wire-wound type except that the wire extended for 51.5 per cent of the gun's length. Welin breech blocks and Vickers hydraulic or hand mechanism were fitted. All but one of the guns were lost with *Triumph* and the fifth was to have been relined to 9.2in Mk X for naval (and presumably experimental) purposes, but it is very doubtful if this was done.

10in Mk VIII This Mark covered four 13.5in Mk III or IIIF in the battleship *Revenge,* relined to 10in calibre for training purposes. The front of the chase was reduced in diameter to counterbalance muzzle preponderance.

1 The battleship *Devastation* at the Fleet Review for Queen Victoria's Diamond Jubilee on 28 June 1897. She and her sister *Thunderer* were fitted with 10in guns, in place of the original main armament of 12in muzzle-loaders, during their modernisations of 1890–92.
NMM

2 The battleship *Triumph* as completed. She carried four 10in Mk VII guns in twin BV mountings.

Warship Pictorial

Breaking-Up HM Ships Part 2 by IL Buxton

Following the selection of some of the larger British Second World War ships breaking up which appeared in *Warship 17,* this Pictorial features smaller vessels, mostly at Scottish shipbreakers.

1 This joined view shows two concepts of anti-submarine frigate: 19 kts *Loch Veyatie* of the 1940s and *Teazer*, converted from a war-built Emergency destroyer in 1953–55 at Cardiff, of the 1950s. The latter's 32kts was useful in countering the high underwater speed conventional submarine. Although her two Squids were similar to those in the 'Lochs', they were coupled with the more modern asdic (sonar) outfit of Type 164B search, Type 147F depth predictor, Type 162 bottom target classifier and Type 174 mortar control, compared with the 'Lochs' Type 144 outfit. *Loch Veyatie* was the only ship to mount the improved 4in Mk XXI on the Mk XXIV mounting. The ships are seen here in August 1965 at Arnott Young's Dalmuir yard, now no longer breaking up ships.

2 Although most war-built vessels had been scrapped by 1970, a few survived into the 1980s. *Ulster* was converted from a destroyer to a Type 15 A/S frigate at Chatham in 1954–57, but was used latterly as a harbour training ship at Devonport. She is seen at Ward's yard at Inverkeithing in February 1981 – one of the few British shipbreaking yards left after the closures of 1977–80. The staggered layout of her Mk 10 mortars and handing rooms is clearly visible.

3 The bows of the frigate *Loch Tralaig*, nestling inboard of the Orkney ferry *Earl Thorfinn* at MacLellan's Bo'ness yard in October 1963. The rails for reloading the Squid A/S mortars can be seen leading from the handing room ahead of the bridge. The First World War designed 4in QF Mk V has been removed from its Mk III HA mounting.

1

2

3

1

2

4

1 West of Scotland Shipbreaking's yard at Troon on the Clyde coast
has broken up over 130 naval vessels since the Second World
War. A January morning in 1963 sees, alongside the netlayer
Guardian, the destroyer *Comet* and the frigate *Pheasant*, the latter
having broken her tow on her way from Devonport.

2 The 'River' class frigate *Waveney* showing off her graceful hull at
Troon in May 1958. She had been converted to a landing ship
headquarters vessel, carrying an armament consisting only of
close-range weapons, including a 20mm twin Mk V mounting in
'B' position and single Mk II mountings in 'A'.

3 Another busy scene at Troon in June 1958, with the frigate *Stork*
in the background, then corvette *Tintagel Castle* and the
quarterdeck of *Portchester Castle,* the latter shorn of depth charge
equipment as a training ship. Lightened hulks were towed to the
other side of the pier for beaching – as were bigger vessels from
the associated Arnott Young yard at Dalmuir.

4 A view from *Broadsword*'s masthead after shock trials showing,
left, the remains of the Type 15 frigate *Roebuck* and, right, the
boom defence vessel *Barbican*. The yard is Ward's at
Inverkeithing in October 1968.

3

1

2

3

1 A contrast in bow shapes: two frigates awaiting demolition at Shipbreaking Industries' yard at Charlestown, west of Rosyth, in June 1958. Inboard is the 'Hunt' class destroyer *Ledbury*, outboard the last 'Black Swan' class frigate to be completed, *Sparrow*.

2 Charlestown's principal berth, showing the *Algerine* class minesweeper *Marvel* well cut down by June 1958, revealing the steering gear compartment. The yard closed in 1963, when the harbour area was given over to yacht moorings and executive type houses.

4

5

3 An unusual view of the 'Black Swan' frigate *Opossum* showing
(a) the hull shape at a section through 'A' 4in mounting;
(b) the transverse framing and watertight bulkhead; and
(c) the housing for the retractable transducer of the Type 144
asdic. She was being broken up by Demmelweek and Redding in
Sutton Harbour, Plymouth, in July 1960.

4 The last of some 300 vessels to be broken up at Charlestown over
a period of 40 years: the submarine *Scorcher* lies outboard of her
sister *Saphir* (ex-*Satyr*) under the 30-ton derrick crane in
September 1962.

5 The after half of the Thornycroft-designed 'Hunt' class ship
Brissenden at Dalmuir in May 1965. She still has her Second
World War armament: twin 4in Mk XIX mounting, triple 21in
torpedo tubes, quadruple 2pdr Mk VII, twin 20mm Mk V and
depth charges. Alongside can be seen the minelayer *Ariadne*'s
main deck, cut down to reveal the port mine stowage rails.

1

2

1 The demolition of the submarine *Tapir* is well underway by March 1967 at Shipbreaking Industries' now-closed Faslane yard. The upper section of the all-welded, ¾in thick pressure hull has been removed for easy access to the interior. The shape and structure of the ballast tanks is visible in this view taken from the forward torpedo stowage compartment. *Tapir* had been deliberately sunk in Loch Striven in a submarine salvage exercise in May 1966.

2 The trawler *Skye* beached at Bo'ness in June 1958. Her funnel shows that latterly she belonged to the 50th Minesweeping Squadron, based at Port Edgar a few miles east.

3 The after part of *Sparrow* at Charlestown in June 1958. Although her 40mm guns have been removed, one of the directors (left foreground) remains.

4 Another war-built vessel to survive to 1980 was the cable ship *Bullfinch,* seen under demolition at Blyth in April of that year. With the availability of redundant repair docks, a few small breakers leased drydocks for shipbreaking. *Bullfinch* was broken up by H Kitson Vickers in No 4 Dock, used formerly by Blyth Dry Docks and Shipbuilding Co. In the background the hopper barge *Sir Fon* steams up harbour to take on another load of ash for dumping from Blyth power station.

3

4

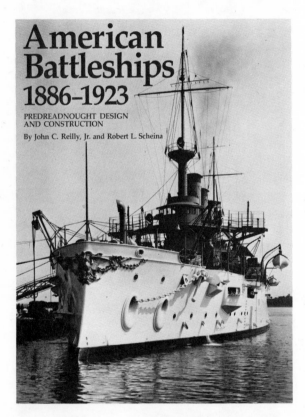

American Battleships 1886-1923
PREDREADNOUGHT DESIGN
AND CONSTRUCTION
By John C. Reilly, Jr. and Robert L. Scheina

Book Reviews

American Battleships 1886-1923 *by John C Reilly, Jr and Robert L Scheina.*
Published by Arms and Armour Press. Price £14.95

Despite the importance of the United States Navy in the development of the modern warship there have been comparatively few books detailing the technical history of their various types of warships, which makes this 259-page volume all the more welcome. It covers the development of the US pre-dreadnought, from the *Texas* and *Maine* of 1886 to the *Mississippi* class of 1903; the dates in the title refer to their period of service – a disappointment to those awaiting a study of the first generations of American dreadnoughts.

There are, for each class, short descriptions of the design origin, detailed descriptions of the completed ships (armour, machinery, armament, etc) and subsequent mod-

ifications and lists of the technical particulars. In fact, the book is almost entirely concerned with the final design and there is little on design development and political/strategic background, which would have added greatly to its value. It may seem unfair to criticise what is, certainly, an excellent publication for what it does not contain, but it is an important consideration given that the book covers a period in which the United States took its initial steps towards becoming a first-class naval power – a situation reflected closely in the development of its pre-dreadnoughts, from low-freeboard, low-endurance vessels to first-class seagoing ships comparable to their European counterparts.

Illustration is provided by 86 photographs and 81 line drawings, five of which are fold-outs. The former are well reproduced and of good size, and include a few very interesting close-up and on-board views. The drawings, despite being reproductions of the original, official drawings, are also clear and well reproduced, although on several it is impossible to read the annotations due to amount of reduction involved. Profiles, deck plans, armour diagrams, sections and the other details are included but are not consistent for each class, presumably due to the availability of suitably clear originals. The *Maine*, for example, has a profile of *Riachuelo*, a profile of *Maine* (with a plan of the forebridge) as built, a fold-out plan of her superstructure deck, a bow end view, a superb perspective cut-away of one of her twin turrets (the only such drawing in the book), a profile of one of her torpedo-boats and a diagram illustrating the damage to the ship when she blew up and sank in Havana harbour.

American Battleships has added greatly to the available material on US warships and is well worth its price to anybody with an interest in the pre-dreadnought period.

John Roberts

The *Oregon*, in San Francisco Bay, is one of the subjects of *American Battleships 1886-1923*, a book which provides a critical view of US pre-dreadnoughts, revealing both their qualities and faults.

by courtesy R A Burt

USS San Francisco *by Chuck Hansen. Available from the author at 1783B Springer Road, Mountain View, Ca 94040, USA. Price $10.95 + $1.25 postage.*

This is yet another technical history, in this case concerning only a single ship – the USS *San Francisco* (CA38), a heavy cruiser completed in 1934 that had a long and distinguished war record. The book is obviously the result of considerable research, and Chuck Hansen has provided both a detailed text and excellent illustrations – an achievement enhanced by the fact that the author has published the work himself. Apart from the depth of detail on the standard features (armament, protection, machinery, etc) the book contains information on items not usually covered, including hull construction, ammunition, aircraft equipment, paravanes, searchlights, etc. There are also details of modifications, camouflage, operational history and other ships named *San Francisco*. There are over 100 photographs, reasonably well produced, the majority of which cover either half or full pages and include many close-up, on-board and unusual views. Particularly interesting are a set of views taken of the ship under construction and another group showing damage received in action with Japanese vessels off Guadalcanal in November 1942 (this section also contains a detailed description of the damage and a profile drawing showing the position of hits). The illustrations are rounded off by some superb drawings of *San Francisco* including a fold-out profile and plan, from the pen of A D Baker III.

Although the price may seem high for a 100-page soft back, it is of large format (11in × 8½in) and is literally crammed with information, which, to this reviewer, makes it excellent value.

John Roberts

Les Cuirassés Francais de 23,500 Tonnes *by Robert Dumas and Jean Guiglini.*
Published by Editions des 4 Seigneurs. Price 240 francs.

This book is similar to *American Battleships* in being largely concerned with the particulars of ships and not with the larger issues which brought them into existence and controlled their subsequent history. It describes in great detail the first two classes of French dreadnoughts – the *Courbet* class (*Courbet, Jean Bart, Paris* and *France*) and the *Bretagne* class, (*Bretagne, Provence* and *Lorraine*). Each class is provided with three chapters giving, in semi-listed form, descriptions of the ship's features as built, details of subsequent alterations and modernisations, and unit histories. In addition, the last 100 pages of this 250-page book consists mainly of eight appendices containing lists of the ships' captains and flag officers; detailed descriptions of the weapons, fire control system and aircraft carried (including basic 3-view drawings); and extracts from documents related to their operational histories.

There are over 160 photographs which, in the majority of cases, are reasonably well produced, but considering only seven ships are covered there are rather too many portrait shots. They are also, with some exceptions, reproduced fairly small, and the publishers would have served the authors better by reducing the number of photographs and printing the remainder at a larger size.

Some drawings are included with the text but the majority are in a separate folder, designed to the same dimensions and style as the book to give the appearance of a two volume set. It contains reproductions, at reduced scale, of official drawings of the *Courbet* and *Bretagne* – an internal profile, plans of the upper- and main-decks, sections and a body plan being provided for each ship. In addition there are 16 sheets (approx 10in × 16in) of drawings by Robert Dumas providing external general arrangement and detail drawings for all ships and details of modifications throughout their lives. These are invaluable for recognition and dating purposes; they are not highly detailed but would be sufficient for a small-scale model. Finally, there are four charts showing the dispositions of the ships at various periods, the divisions they belonged to, etc.

This is very much a book of information, so if you are a collector this is definitely for you; even if you do not speak French it is not difficult to extract particulars from the text, with or without a French-English dictionary.

John Roberts

Luxury Fleet – The Imperial German Navy 1888–1918 *by Holger Herwig, George Allen and Unwin (London 1980). Price £9.95*

Here, at last, is a revisionist at work on the German High Seas Fleet and the period of the great naval arms race. The fact that Professor Herwig is German should add nothing to his scholarship, but somehow his words will have more impact because he is demolishing myths which have been sustained by German, as well as English and American, commentators.

Mythology about the German Navy of the Wilhelmine period takes many forms. English and American authorities, in their zeal to point out the deficiencies of the British, normally assume that up to 1914 everything was going superbly on the other side of the North Sea and that only the strategic ineptitude of the Kaiser, and his Army-minded advisors, prevented the High Seas Fleet from wiping the floor with the Royal Navy. Another myth (first put about by the old fox himself in 1919) was that the High Seas Fleet was only a political tool for Tirpitz to gain an alliance, and that it was not intended for use against England.

Sadly, the premises on which Tirpitz based his First Navy Law were unsound. The State Secretary told the Kaiser that a fleet of sixty battleships would unite the political parties against the rising tide of Social Democracy, rally the workers around the Empire by work and high wages, provide a focus for patriotic sentiment, raise the prestige of the Crown at home and abroad, reduce political interference in the direction of military policy, make Germany an attractive ally, and wring colonial concessions out of Great Britain. Instead, the whole gimcrack structure was wobbling on its foundations. By 1912 the Social Democrats were the largest party in the *Reichstag* and the other parties were hopelessly divided by the ruinous cost of defence, the Kaiser's prestige was somewhat threadbare, the *Reichstag* still controlled taxation and Germany was isolated, unless one counts the dubious value of Austria-Hungary as an ally and a promise of support from Italy.

What was much worse was the strategic outcome of all the manoeuvring, blustering and plotting. The British had refused to play to the Tirpitz Rules and had written a new set for themselves. The Fisher reforms, and above all a vigorous shipbuilding policy, had enabled the Royal Navy to keep pace without the financial ruin predicted by Tirpitz. Instead, it was Germany which was facing ruin. In 1914 the programme was 8 battleships and 13 cruisers in arrears, but 90.1 per cent of the State revenue was devoted to defence and the National Debt had reached 5000 million marks. From 1912, the Army began to fight back against the ever-spiralling Navy share of the budget, cutting it from 49.4 per cent to 32.7 per cent the following year. What did not appear obvious from the outside was that the Imperial German armed forces had to be financed out of customs and excise duties, as taxes on citizens could only be levied by the individual states. It was possible to cover deficits in the Federal budget by voting special grants; of course, an inheritance tax or Federal income tax would have made things much easier, but that would have hit the Junkers in their purses and was unacceptable. Each year, therefore, the man in the street had to pay more for his necessities and luxuries, while the Junkers continued to believe that they could postpone social and fiscal reform indefinitely.

There is much to interest the student of late nineteenth and twentieth century naval history in this book. Once the dazzling sun of Fisher is turned off, much of what was going on in Germany becomes easier to understand, and I would go so far as to say that this is essential reading for students of the Anglo-German arms race. It is not a book for ship-lovers, for technical details of warships and their armaments are by no means accurate in detail, but it explains so much of the bitterness and apparent paranoia which infected the Imperial German Navy. It is also the first detailed analysis of the factors which made Germany's defeat inevitable.

One could hardly fail to notice the parallel with the Soviet Navy of Admiral Gorshkov. Here is another force built up from modest beginnings by a man blessed with superb arrogance and faith in his mission, happening to have the confidence of his political masters. Like Tirpitz, Gorshkov has created a great force but he has achieved it at the expense of the other armed forces, particularly the Air Force and Strategic Rocket Forces. It is also costing an enormous amount of money, and when the bill comes in for replacing the ships after 1985 some awkward questions might be asked by the Politburo. Let us hope that the outcome is not another August 1914, for it is hardly likely to prove any more successful for Gorshkov's High Seas Fleet.

Antony Preston

Attack and Defence Part 2 by DK Brown RCNC

The first gunnery training ship to be named *Excellent* was the former 2nd Rate *Boyne* launched in 1810. The second, illustrated here, was the 1st rate *Queen Charlotte* which took over the role of her predecessor in 1859.

In the first article of this series (*Warship* 18) it was shown how the initial faith and enthusiasm of the Haddington Board in iron ships was weakened by the trials at Woolwich and by the action on the Parana river. During July 1846 doubts continued to grow within the Board, probably because the Government was losing its grip in Parliament and found the results of the Woolwich tests to be inadequate answers to the attacks of Napier and his political allies. On 27 July the Surveyor, Symonds, was asked for his views on the fouling of iron ships. Since he was well known to be hostile to the iron ship programme and had not previously been consulted, it may well be that an adverse report was both expected and desired.

TRIALS AGAINST RUBY

On the 30th of that same month the tender *Ruby* was ordered to be prepared for firing trials at the gunnery school, HMS *Excellent*, by Captain Berkeley.[1] *Ruby* had been built at Bristol in 1842 and, though intended for service on the Niger, had been used as a tender, first at Chatham and then at Portsmouth. From the day of her completion, the correspondence files are full of complaints:

she was too small to tow anything bigger than a lighter; the accommodation was inadequate even for a yard craft; and her machinery was unreliable. She was mainly used to take shipwrights out from Portsmouth to work on ships at anchor in Spithead, but after only four years of life she was worn out: her plates, only $1/8$in thick when new, were seriously corroded, and those between deck beams were said to deflect so much that they were 'hardly safe to carry a man's weight'.[2]

According to the official survey, 'Her state was very bad; the iron of which she was constructed was originally very thin – not thicker than a half crown, the seams of the rivets were many of them almost quite gone, the ribs were very far apart – I should consider it likely that they were about four feet apart instead of being perhaps ten inches or a foot, the heads of her rivets were quite gone, especially internally, the deck was also partially removed for the purpose of lifting the machinery out previous to the experiment; and this made the vessel still weaker.'

This, then, was the river launch which was to face the heavy guns of the gunnery training ship *Excellent*, and as a result has become the focus of controversy ever since. She

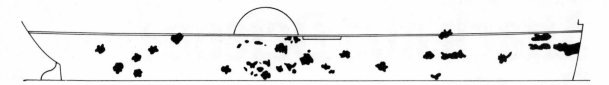

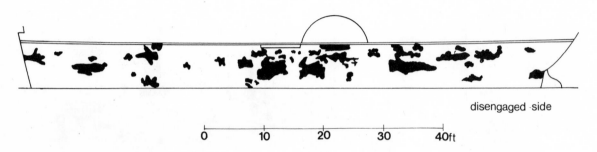

disengaged side

| 0 | 10 | 20 | 30 | 40ft |

HMS *Ruby*: hull damage received 6–7 August 1846 from 40 shots fired by HMS *Excellent*.

was placed broadside on to the guns at a range of 450yds and solid shot, from 8in and 32pdr guns, was fired at her. 'All the shot passed through both sides; the holes made on the first side being of the size of the shot and generally smooth even when striking a rib, but the damage done to the opposite side of the ship was very different, as in the case when the shot struck on a rib, the effect was very great, the iron sheets being torn off and injured to a considerable extent; and even when the shot passed clean through between the ribs, the holes made were of a difficult nature to stop, from their edges being turned outwards. The splinters from the first side were few, but very severe'.[1] See Fig. 1.[3]

'The *Ruby* was afterwards placed end on to the guns, but the shot fired at her so tore the ribs and plates that it was evident that a similar vessel so situated would be in danger of being instantly sunk by one well aimed shot.' A 10in shot, with a 12lb powder charge, passed through the bottom plate on one side and made a hole 4ft long and 3ft wide. Captain Chad, of *Excellent*, reached the obvious and quite unexceptionable conclusion that 'The above experiment clearly proved vessels of the *Ruby* class unfit for war purposes'.[1] No other conclusion seems to have been reached by anyone in authority, and even those who were, at that time, hostile to the iron ship rarely quoted this trial to support their case; only more recent writers have attached undue importance to the *Ruby* trial.

The reason for carrying out the trial remains obscure; it did not need a trial to show that a 90ft launch, either of wood or of iron, was unfit to face a battleship at close range. Those planning any sort of trial must always think beforehand what the possible outcomes may be and what could be learnt from them. It is most likely that someone

decided to save money by expending an unwanted ship rather than by building an expensive target; it is even possible that it was thought less embarrassing to get rid of *Ruby* in this way than to admit that she was a failure. There is no evidence at all to suggest that the trial was rigged to condemn the iron ship. The end came for *Ruby* on 7 August 1846 when the mutilated remains were sold for £20.[2]

FUNNEL TESTS

This was not the only trial carried out by *Excellent* in the 1840s. There were several trials of the effect of shot and shell on coal bunkers, and some very elaborate trials on the likelihood of the destruction of a steamship's funnel,[1] and on the consequences which this would have. In 1846 an old 3ft diameter funnel was fired on at 600yds range by a 32pdr; after eight hits it was still standing, though the report points out that it would probably have fallen in a seaway. A broadside of 14 guns was then fired, of which four shot hit (an interesting measure of accuracy!) but the funnel still stood. Later, two or three shells hit the funnel, and 'afterwards, the braces on the weather side being shot away and there being a strong breeze, the funnel fell.' Further trials were carried out with a 4ft diameter funnel which was hit by 15 bar shot and four round shot and remained upright. Various schemes were then tried for stopping the shot holes, the best being due to Mr Thomas Brown, Engineer of the *Bee*, attached to the Naval College. Two spring catches were fixed to an iron plate, and the springs were pushed in through the shot hole, fixing the plate to the funnel. The security of this patch was proved when two shot were fired through it without it being dislodged.

The security of the funnel was seen as very important since the draught of air which kept the boiler furnace going depended on the height of the flue. For the next part of the trials, five holes were cut in the funnel of the steam tug *Echo* and closed with Brown's patches. The holes were uncovered while the ship was at full power without any noticeable effect on the draught of air, power or fuel consumption. A similar trial was carried out in *Bee*, in which the funnel was removed entirely from just above the deck. This trial illustrates the care and impartiality with which trials were carried out in the mid nineteenth century.

THE IRON FRIGATES
While the fate of the iron frigates is strictly another story, to be told later, it is so linked with the trials of protection in this era that an outline account must be given.[4] The Board of Admiralty received the officer's report of the *Ruby* trials on 8 August 1846 and made their next move on the 27th. A circular letter was sent to the builders of the four iron frigates then under construction, asking them to prepare a target, representing a section of their own ship, for further trials *at their own expense*! This idea was rejected by the builders, or countered with an equally ridiculous quotation for extra costs. The final report of the Woolwich tests was received on 7 September, and by 1 December the Board had asked the Surveyor to find out what would be the cost of cancelling the iron frigates. By March 1847, it was decided to complete them as troopships, with lower power engines to increase their endurance. *Birkenhead*, an iron paddle frigate, already complete, was also converted to a troopship, eventually to meet her tragic fate. It is clear that it was the Woolwich tests and rumours of Parana, and not the *Ruby* trial, which settled this fate.

TRIALS AT PORTSMOUTH
Arguments over the merits of iron ships did not cease. The advantages of iron for merchant ship construction were clear and many of the big liner companies were building iron ships. Many of these received mail subsidies on the condition that they were designed and fitted for conversion to armed merchant cruisers in time of war, but opponents of the iron warship would not accept that an iron ship had any military role, even as a troopship, and demanded that subsidies be withdrawn from such vessels. The directors of these companies, Anderson of P & O in particular, fought back, and in 1849 the Select Committee on Estimates re-examined the arguments for and against the iron ship.[5] They found that the evidence, either way, was negligible and concluded 'that no vessel of that material intended for war had yet been subjected by experiment to any proof of shot whatsoever'. This point had already been accepted by the Admiralty and Captain Chads had been directed to commence a new series of trials. It seems likely that those responsible were unaware of the Woolwich trials.

These trials were carried out by *Excellent* at Portsmouth between 1849 and 1851 in order to determine the effect of shot on iron ships.[1] The first series of tests, on 6 November

1849, was planned to compare the resistance of iron plates and timber to musket balls, canister and grape shot. The first trial used a marine's musket, charged with $4\frac{1}{2}$oz of powder at a range of 40yds against targets of $\frac{1}{8}$in, $\frac{1}{4}$in and $\frac{3}{8}$in thick iron, and of 1in, 2in and 3in thick oak; the $\frac{3}{8}$in iron and 3in oak were proof against musket shot. In the next trial case shots were fired from a 32pdr/56cwt gun with 6lb charges at $\frac{3}{8}$in and $\frac{1}{2}$in iron, and 3in and 4in wood planks, arranged 100yds from the gun. The thicker iron and timber stopped all shot, though the iron was cracked at the back. The next trial was of grape shot fired from the same gun with a 6lb charge at targets of $\frac{1}{2}$in, $\frac{5}{8}$in and $\frac{3}{4}$in, and 4in, 5in and 6in wood planks placed 200yds from the gun. All shots passed through, leaving jagged holes in the iron and the oak planks much splintered.

Captain Chads' conclusions on this series of trials were that:
(a) Resistance to shot by iron and oak is in the ratio of their specific gravity, *ie* 8:1.
(b) The holes in the iron were open and sometimes jagged, whereas those in the oak were always partially closed.
(c) As far as this experiment went, it is perhaps doubtful whether iron or oak of the thickness used was the best as the splinters from the iron, though fewer in number, were more severe than from the oak.

CONTEMPORARY VIEW
Captain Chads' summary of the series was that 'it has been proved, that the disastrous effects of shot upon iron are so great, that it is not a proper material of which to build ships of war and it has also been proved, that these effects are not to be prevented.' Douglas spells out the same conclusion in more detail: 'If the iron sides are of the thickness required to give adequate strength to the ship ($\frac{5}{8}$in or at least $\frac{1}{2}$in) the shot will be broken by the impact; if the iron plate be then enough to let the shot pass into the ship without breaking, the vessel will be deficient in strength; the shot will do its own work, particularly in oblique or raking fire, more effectively than its splinters, and in passing out, make apertures which were more difficult to plug or stop than in passing in . . . the expedient of combining wood and iron makes matters worse. It is generally believed that iron vessels, however convenient or advantageous in other respects, are utterly unfit for purposes of war.'[7]

This verdict was generally accepted by even the most progressive among contemporary builders of iron ships. Fairbairn said to the Institute of Naval Architects, many years later, 'the iron ship was even more dangerous under fire than one built entirely of wood.' John Grantham, another pioneer, wrote: 'In the material points iron warships are deficient. The injury they would receive from shot is probably much greater than in timber built ships; and as there is no effective remedy against fouling their employment on a foreign station, where there are no means of cleaning them every six months, is undesirable . . . I must state my conviction, that the results of careful experiments, and especially of those conducted by Captain Chads were anything but encouraging to the hopes entertained that iron ships would supersede wooden ships in the Navy.' Edward

Reed, so critical of most aspects of Admiralty, accepted the verdict, as did his successor, Nathaniel Barnaby, who much later favoured composite construction for unarmoured ships for this reason.[8,9]

The only naval architect to criticise the Admiralty viewpoint was Scott Russell, who referred to 'seven years of tests on how to make iron plates not resist shot.'[10] Since he did not say how it could be done, this argument can be dismissed as rhetoric. Captain Halsted, in a lecture to the RUSI in 1861, raised a number of objections to the trials.[2] He pointed out that not one of the targets actually represented, fully, both sides of *Simoon*, and that in the trials against the second target, which represented correctly one side of *Simoon*, no measurement was made of the number and spread of splinters. Though these objections are sound, it is most unlikely that they had any bearing on the verdict. He also raised another, more interesting point, when he indicated that even a ½in plate would break up all shells, and that even if they detonated it would be a low order explosion. He did not follow up this line of thought, but since such a plate weighs only 20lb per sq ft it would have

been possible to put such a skin over a substantial area of a line-of-battle ship's side, with a small reduction in number of guns as weight compensation. Such an iron-skinned ship would have been almost invulnerable to the shells of the era, and the timber behind would have prevented splinters from broken shot entering the gun decks.

THE SIMOOM TARGETS

The next series of trials was much more significant. Two sections of a ship's side, each 10ft square, were built at Portsmouth Dockyard to the same designs as the ironwork of the frigate *Simoon*. There was, however, no filling timber between the iron frames or planking fitted inside the frames as there was in the actual frigate. The plates were of ⅝in iron and the ribs 4½in wide, 12in apart. The two sections of the ship's side were then placed 35ft apart between piles, firmly driven, at 450yds from the guns used, one behind the other and reversed, so as to represent the two sides of an iron frigate.

Firing took place over several days in June 1850, and of the shots fired, only a few will be described in detail[6] and

The 42 ton tug *Bee*, launched at Chatham Dockyard in 1842, was employed in various experiments while attached to the gunnery training ship *Excellent*

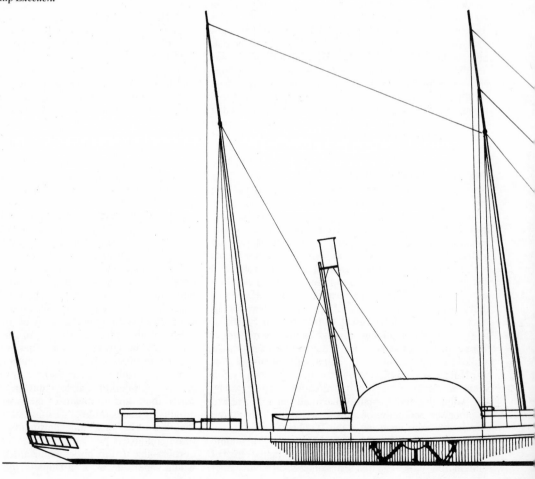

the rest summarised. The first shot was of 32lb fired with a 10lb charge from a 56cwt gun. It hit directly between two ribs, making a 6½in diameter open hole. The shot broke up and the splinters from it, together with those from the plug torn from the plate, were very numerous. The rear section of side was much struck and injured, two of the splinters having penetrated through, one of which made a hole 10in × 9in in the plate. Douglas quotes a letter from Captain Chads in which he says that seventeen 32pdr shot were fired with charges varying from 2½ to 10lb and, of these, 16 split and formed large and numerous splinters.[7] Hits on the ribs made much larger holes. Some rounds were fired from an 8in/65cwt gun and the solid, 68lb shot produced results similar to, but more severe than, the 32pdr. A 56lb hollow shot broke up in a very numerous cloud of splinters which flew some 100–300yds. Similar results came from a 10in/85cwt gun firing 85lb hollow shot.

Nine shells, with Moorsom's fuzes, were fired from a 32pdr, some passing through intact plate and some through holes already made. Most of the shells broke in penetrating the plate but in all cases there was an explosion, sometimes low order, generally not more than 4ft inside the target. Six shells with 3in fuze, but with the caps left on, were also fired. Four of the six hit undamaged structure and broke up without the charge exploding.

Five rounds of grape (45 3lb shot in all) were fired from a 32pdr. Only 5 balls hit (at 450yds) but they all penetrated.

TABLE 1: PARTICULARS OF HMS RUBY

Builders:	Acreman, Bristol
Launched:	1842
Builders measurement tonnage:	73 tons
Length:	90ft
Beam:	12ft 9½in
Depth:	7ft 1in
Nominal horse power	20

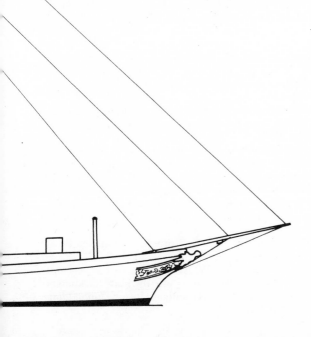

Four hollow shot were fired from a 24pdr howitzer in a boat, with 2½lb charges at a range of 50yds. Two hit ribs and split while the others made clean holes. Captain Chads gives the following conclusions:

'**(a)** All shot hitting ribs, and most in between, split.
(b) Shot hitting between ribs generally made a clean, open hole, slightly larger than the shot. Those striking the ribs made a much larger, jagged hole.
(c) Hollow shot broke into many more splinters than either a solid shot or those produced by a bursting shell.
(d) Moorsom's fuzes ignite the powder of shells passing through ⅝in iron even if the shell is broken, but the breaking of the shell will not ignite the powder in it'.

Finally, it appears that the large, jagged holes would be difficult to stop and hence dangerous if near the waterline. Also, the numerous splinters would cause a few well-directed shot to clear away whole guns' crews and these two facts, more especially the last, must certainly condemn such ships as unfit for war purposes.'

Apart from a few reservations, which will appear later, one cannot dispute Captain Chads' conclusions from the evidence of this trial on the target as tested. However, the lack of the wood filling between frames and the planking behind was a serious deficiency, particularly since the earlier trials at Woolwich had shown their value.

This deficiency was remedied in the next series of trials when a new target was made representing the side of *Simoon* from just below the main deck to just above the upper deck. The iron structure was identical to that used in the previous series but the space between the ribs was filled in solid with 5½in oak timbers. Inside this, oak planking 4½in thick was arranged up to the port sill with 3in fir planking above. The timbers and planks were all bolted through the iron skin, making the target a genuine replica of one side of *Simoon*. As before, the target was secured 450 yds from the gun but this time there was no second structure to represent the disengaged side of the ship.

Firing was carried out on 11 July 1850 when the following projectiles were fired: 32lb solid shot with 10, 6 and 4lb charges; 68lb solid shot with 10lb charges; 8in 56lb hollow shot with 10 and 5lb charges; and 10in 85lb hollow shot with 12lb charges. The holes made by the shot were not so irregular in shape as in the previous series but were just as open. Very few of the splinters from the plate or from broken shot were retained in the wood. With the smaller charges the splinters were not so numerous but with the larger charges there were quite as many as in the first series. The general conclusions were the same as for the first series.

On 13 August another series of shots was fired against another target with ironwork similar to that of *Simoon* but with fir planking 2in, 3in and 4in thick, worked outside (nearest the gun) over different areas of the plating. Once again the conclusions were the same. Some solid shot were also fired against an all-timber butt representing a wooden line-of-battle ship and these gave rise to 'few, very few (splinters) in comparison'.[7] Another iron target was fired against on 10 October 1850. This time the inside was lined with Kamptulicon (see *Warship* 18). It did not prevent the shot breaking up, nor did the holes seal themselves. In yet another series, on 5 July 1851, the target was built up with oak and fir frames, one half being covered with ⅜in iron and the other with 1in iron. Shot, both solid and hollow, hitting the ³/₈in went through without splitting but most broke on the ½in plate. The target was then turned to represent the disengaged side and fired at with reduced charges. On 11 and 12 August a target was tried made up of frames 4½in deep and ⁵/₈in thick, spaced 11½in apart, with 5in teak (10½in wide) outside and 2in teak (9²/₃in wide) inside. A similar butt, reversed, was also tried. A large number of splinters, of both wood and iron, were produced, the iron ones flying some 200–400yds, while the shot flew on for some 1300–1400yds.

CONCLUSION

When considering these trials, some 140 years later, the overriding impression is of the care and impartiality with which they were conducted. The Woolwich trials seem to have been somewhat more scientific and it looks as if those who planned the *Simoon* trials were not aware of them. One complaint against iron hulls was the jagged nature of the holes which shots made when they hit at low velocity, and the difficulty of plugging such holes. The parasol plug was the contemporary answer, which was not really very practical for holes below the water-line. A better solution was the fitting of watertight bulk-heads to limit flooding, but the value of transverse bulk-heads had yet to be fully appreciated.

The major problem was that of splinters, which came partly from the broken shot and partly from the piece of plate which was punched out. Since a piece of ½in plate 6in in diameter weighs only 4lb, it is clear that most of the splinters came from the shot. The effect on the plate is described by Fairbairn who says that wrought iron is very different when broken by bending or by shot.[11] 'In the former case the fibre is elongated by bending and becomes developed in the shape of threads as fine as silk, whilst in the latter the fibres are broken short, and exhibit a decidedly crystalline fracture.' Dr Corlett dis-cusses a related topic: 'The weakness of wrought iron plate was, of course, at right angles to the surface of the plate itself.[12] The slag lamination much affected the strength, and even sound material could be laminated and fractured by quite minor repeated blows on its sur-face.' These two quotations make it clear why the plate would splinter on impact, and since cast iron is even more brittle it is clear that that would splinter too.

The mystery is why *Nemesis*, *Guadeloupe* and *Lizard* did not suffer more from splinters. There seems to be a general law that weapons used in action are much less effective than even in the most realistic trials. The offi-cial verdict was made clear by the decision on the mail subsidy. The Secretary of the Admiralty wrote to Samuel Cunard on 24 June 1850 as follows: 'The Lords Commissioners of the Admiralty direct me to inform you that no vessel commenced after the date of this letter will be approved of, under the terms of the contract, if built of iron.' Similar instructions were given to P & O later. It does not seem that these instructions were ever rescinded, but they were widely ignored and were inef-fective by the end of the Crimean War.

Seen from 1982, these trials appear perfectly fair and the verdict correct in terms of the technology of the 1840s. The answer to the problems raised was to be the armoured, iron hull, to be discussed in the next article of the series. However, the weight of the armour could only be offset by advanced hull and machinery designs – which were beyond the technology of the mid 1840s.

References

1 *Experiments at HMS* Excellent *on Iron Built Ships*, Captain Chad.
2 *Iron Cased Ships,* Captain E. P. Halsted, RUSI 1861.
3 From 'The Introduction of Iron Warships into the RN', D. K. Brown, *The Naval Architect*, March 1977. (Reproduced by kind permission).
4 See also 'The Introduction of Iron Warships into the RN'.
5 *Select Committee on the Steam Navy.* Parliamentary Papers 1844.
6 Wording from Ref 1, slightly amplified for clarity.
7 *Treatise on Naval Gunnery.* Sir Howard Douglas, 1860 edition.
8 *Naval Developments of the Century.* N. Barnaby.
9 *On the fighting power of merchant ships in Naval Warfare.* N. Barnaby; Trans INA 1877.
10 *Fleet of the Future.* Scott Russell, 1862.
11 *On the properties of iron and its resistance to projec-tiles at high velocities.* W. Fairbairn. Royal Institution 1862.
12 *The Iron Ship.* Dr. E. Corbett. Moonraker Press 1974.

See also Fairbairn, W: 'On the law of resistance of armour plates, composed of one or more thicknesses (Trans INA, 1869); and Grantham, J: *Iron Shipbuilding* (Liverpool, 1858).

An early production Albacore, showing to good effect the sturdy undercarriage and the ample all-round visibility afforded to the crew. One of the two torpedo crutches can be seen under the fuselage, with bomb racks under the wings; either station could be filled, but not both simultaneously.

Fleet Air Arm Museum, via author

Warship Wings No.1 Fairey Albacore

by Roger Chesneau

Broadly speaking, there are two avenues by which a military aircraft may be adopted for service use in the British armed forces. In the uncertain pre-First World War days of aviation, when the potential of the aeroplane as an offensive or defensive weapon was not easily appreciated by the authorities, aircraft manufacturers, often small enthusiast concerns, would perceive the need (or what they felt was the need) for a machine with a particular set of characteristics, develop and produce it, and then attempt to persuade the services (in the form of the Admiralty or the War Office) of the advantages of employing it. During 1917, however, the emphasis shifted, and the increasing appreciation of the values of greater co-ordination of equipment led to the formation of the Air Ministry, which began to notify manufacturers of the requirements concerning military aircraft. Specifications (since about 1950 called Operational Requirements) were therefore issued, and companies would tender designs.

The Private Venture (PV) by no means died as a result – indeed, some very successful aircraft have since seen service from these beginnings – but of course the increasing costs of building complex and sophisticated prototypes have made the postwar PV military aircraft something of a rare bird. Since there is now only one British company building fixed-wing military aeroplanes, speculation as to the future is rather academic in any case.

A STILLBORN REQUIREMENT

Specification M7/36 (September 1936) set out the guidelines for a new torpedo-spotter-reconnaissance aircraft for the Fleet Air Arm. Although it was not specifically stated that this was to supplant the Swordfish, which had entered service two months earlier, it was implicit in that the aircraft was to share with that type a number of characteristics: alternative float or wheeled undercarriage (naval aircraft featuring the latter were, somewhat incongruously,

The carrier *Formidable* in 1943, with an Albacore flying off.
Fleet Air Arm Museum, via author

An Albacore of 831 Squadron, with wings folded, aboard *Indomitable*.

CPL

always referred to as *land*planes!); carriage of the 18in Mk XII torpedo; attachment points for ships' cranes; and dimensions (max 18ft folded span, max 37ft carrier-based or 44ft floatplane overall length, height 14ft 9in) to enable it to operate from existing ships or to utilise existing carrier lifts and be accommodated in carrier hangers, as the case may be. Improvements were concerned mainly with crew comfort (enclosed cockpit space, in-flight heating, etc), increased power (183kts cruising speed, with two engines if required provided loaded weight did not exceed 10,000lb) and the installation of a power-operated twin gun turret for the rear crew compartment. Various requirements were laid down regarding performance and carrier suitability, although fundamental issues such as minimum radius of action (range) were apparently not mentioned; neither was the configuration (biplane or monoplane) specifically referred to, which is perhaps indicative of the uncertainties of the time.

M7/36 was subsequently dropped, but the Fairey Aviation Co, who had responded to the Specification, proceeded with their design, which, when S41/36 was issued five months later, was converted into hardware. S41/36 (11

The Albacores of 817 Squadron being positioned on the after end of *Indomitable*'s flight deck preparatory to launch.
CPL

Previously recovered aircraft of 817 Squadron parked forward, while another Albacore lands-on. This, and the other *CPL* photographs accompanying this article, were taken when *Indomitable* was working up in the Clyde in March 1943.

February 1937) requested a TSR design with a dive-bombing capability, and Fairey offered the Albacore (as it was now to be known), the principal visual difference between M7/36 and the aeroplane that actually emerged being the abandonment of the rear turret in favour of a more conventional gunner's cockpit.

SERVICE USE

The Albacore first flew in December 1938 and, as well as incorporating a number of innovatory techniques (despite its somewhat antiquated appearance) in its construction, displayed the whole range of experience accumulated by Fairey over two decades of shipboard aircraft development, particularly the various devices employed for achieving maximum lift during take-off and landing approach: slats on the upperwing leading edges and hydraulic flaps on the lower mainplanes. In the event, ironically, the slats were dispensed with as being unsatisfactory and the flaps were employed principally as air brakes. Carrier characteristics showed themselves in the form of a massive, fixed under-carriage (the added weight of a sufficiently sturdy retract-able unit was still too marginal to contemplate at this stage), good forward vision for the pilot (the tapered engine cowl on production aircraft would improve this even further) and the usual wing-folding, catapult and arrester facilities.

The adoption of the type for Fleet Air Arm service was a protracted affair, owing mainly to problems encountered with the Bristol Taurus XII powerplant, and it was not on strength until March 1940. Carrier embarkation was delayed until November of that year (826 and 829 Squad-rons, *Formidable*), and the Albacore first went into action against the *Vittorio Veneto* (one torpedo hit) and other Italian vessels off Crete (Matapan).

This proved to be the high spot of the aircraft's career, unfortunately, since squadrons operating it off Norway during 1941 (including attacks on *Tirpitz*) encountered little success and unacceptable losses. Although some positive results were achieved with aircraft flying from land bases along the English Channel coast and in North Africa through until 1943, the Albacore was quite swiftly with-drawn from shipboard service, the last carrier-based sorties taking place from *Formidable* during the allied invasion of Southern Italy, August-September 1943.

APPRAISAL

The special characteristics required of a naval torpedo-bomber are effective range, good directional stability, steadiness as a weapons platform (especially at low level), a high degree of manoeuvrability and an ability to absorb punishment, plus of course all the usual requirements of carrier-borne aircraft; a dive-bombing capability requires in addition fast acceleration, an ability to dive steeply and safely, positive control response and unusual structural strength. Speed in itself, it may be noted, is of less impor-

An Albacore about to take-off from *Indomitable*. Note the ASV radar aerials – two receiving dipoles on each outer forward wing strut and transmitting dipoles on the side of the fuselage behind the engine cowling.

CPL

tance, given the scenario in which the Royal Navy found itself in the late 1930s.

The Albacore met all these conditions except one: it displayed a marked lack of agility in the air and did not have the speed which might have gone some way to compensate for this. In short, it was superior to the Swordfish in only one important respect – its increased endurance, which was roughly 50 per cent greater – whilst at the same time it was more complex and thus that much more difficult to maintain; in the event, it was outlived by its legendary predecessor. The design, whilst poking at novelty with its semi-monocoque all-metal fuselage construction, enclosed cockpits and the rest, was essentially anachronistic, and the refinements it did incorporate in no measure contradicted the fact that by the time it entered service the biplane torpedo-bomber had already reached its zenith.

Albacores readying for take-off, *Indomitable*, 1943. The censor has deleted the antennae of ASV Mk IIN from the outer wing struts; the yagis for this, the standard FAA radar equipment during the Second World War, were frequently fuselage-mounted on Albacores, just behind the engine cooling gills and angled outwards at 45°.

Editorial

The English Tourist Board has designated 1982 'Maritime England Year', and we have decided to mark this event with a special extended issue of *Warship*. There will be a large number of general tourist guidebooks available and we have no desire to compete with these; instead we have aimed to give the typical *Warship* reader an insight into the naval aspect of the British maritime tradition, as reflected in the national collection of preserved ships, aircraft and equipment. As usual in *Warship* we have concentrated on the technical aspects of design and development, rather than re-hashing the details of a ship's career, however exciting it may have been. In doing so we have been able to offer information of value about these ships, although the vessels themselves may be familiar to most with an interest in warships.

Britain is singularly fortunate in the range of her surviving ships. When Henry VIII's *Mary Rose* is raised from the bottom of the Solent later this year, the starting point will be 1509 (when the ship was first built) and what is possibly the world's first true line-of-battle ship. The great age of the sailing navy is represented by Nelson's immortal *Victory* (of 1765) and the frigate *Foudroyant*, with *Unicorn* demonstrating the technical innovations of the end of the wooden shipbuilding era. Both ends of the Victorian spectrum, from ironclad to gunboat, can be seen in the *Warrior* and the sloop *Gannet* respectively, with the mid-twentieth century represented by *Cavalier, Belfast* and the submarine *Alliance*. The warship history of the early part of this century is not so well preserved, but the cruiser *Caroline* and the sloops *Chrysanthemum* and *Saxifrage* (of World War I vintage) all survive as drill ships for the RNR, while it is planned to raise the wreck of Britain's first submarine, *Holland I*, during 1982. There are also a number of less well-known survivors such as the ships' boats collection at Gosport and the CMBs and midget submarines at Duxford.

There are, of course, many ship types which warship enthusiasts would like to have seen preserved, but this collection gives many indications of Britain's remarkable contribution to warship design. Some, like *Victory* or *Warrior*, were outstanding designs, whereas others like the sloops or *Cavalier* represent a whole generation of ships and a uniquely British approach to classic problems in warship design. Those ships open to the public are generally 'sold' to tourists on the excitement of sea warfare and the glamour of their careers, but the articles in this issue of *Warship* deliberately avoid this aspect and concentrate on the technical merits of design. No attempt has been made to cover every preserved ship, a selection of the most interesting being combined with other naval subjects, such as RN engineering and the Fleet Air Arm, which can be viewed through the medium of Britain's many museums. This section is concluded with a speculative look, by one of Britain's warship designers, at the types of ship which may be in service about the year 2010.

Bearing in mind that many of *Warship*'s overseas readers may well visit Britain during the year, a short list of places to visit and events to attend has been included. Many others were omitted because details were not yet finalised, and readers are advised to keep an eye on local newspapers, or consult tourist offices, for further information.

Acknowledgements: In compiling this issue the editors have received enormous assistance from individuals and institutions across Britain. We are pleased to acknowledge this help and to extend our thanks to all those concerned. We are particularly grateful to Captain J G Wells, the Research Director of the *Warrior* project, and Commander R Compton-Hall of the Royal Navy Submarine Museum for information and photographs.

Robert Gardiner
John Roberts

MARITIME ENGLAND

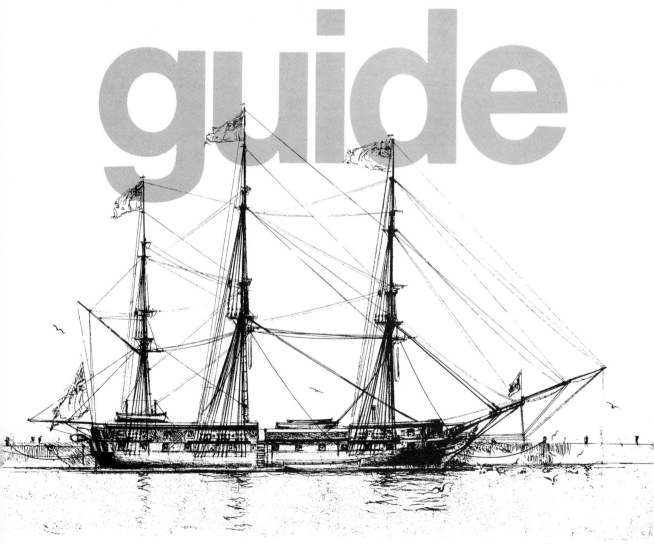

Harold Wyllie's impression of how the frigate *Unicorn* will look when fully restored   *By courtesy of Roderick Stewart*

The cruiser *Caroline*, seen here in 1918, is still afloat at Belfast.

By courtesy of Ray Burt

PLACES TO VISIT

Listed below are some museums and stately homes of particular interest to warship enthusiasts.

BELFAST
HMS Caroline
This light cruiser, launched in 1914, is still in use as an RNR drill ship, but is not open to the public.

BROADLANDS
Broadlands, Romsey, Hampshire. Telephone: 0794- 516878
Home of Earl Mountbatten of Burma. Exhibition includes the 'Kelly Corridor', which contains 50ft:1in models of the ships that Lord Mountbatten served in or commanded, such as *Lion* and *Renown*. The ensign of HMS *Kelly* is also on display.
Opening times: 1 April – 30 September 1982 10.00 – 17.00 (closed on Mondays April to July, excluding Bank Holidays)
Admission charge

CHICHELEY HALL
Nr Newport Pagnell, Buckinghamshire. Telephone: 023-065-252
Home of Admiral Beatty. Contains a small naval museum, devoted to Admiral Beatty's life.
Opening times: Sundays and Bank Holidays 14.30 – 17.00
Admission charge: Adults £1.30

DUNDEE
HMS Unicorn, *Victoria Dock, Dundee, Scotland*
The oldest British-built ship afloat, launched at Chatham in 1824 as a 46-gun Frigate and now being refurbished by the Unicorn Preservation Society.
Opening times: 1 April – 31 October 1982 Monday, Wednesday-Saturday 11.00 – 13.00 & 14.00 – 17.00, Sunday 14.00 – 17.00
Admission charge

DUXFORD
Imperial War Museum Reserve Collections, Duxford, Cambridge CB2 4QZ. Telephone: 0223-833-963
Former Battle of Britain station, now an outpost of the IWM housing over 50 aircraft including a De Havilland Sea Vixen. Naval interest includes preserved CMBs and X-craft.
Opening times: Open all year, Monday – Sunday 11.00 – 16.30
Admission charge

GLASGOW
Museum of Transport, Albert Drive, Glasgow G41 2PE. Telephone: 041-423-8000
Exhibition includes the Clyde Room, a display of models of battleships, battlecruisers and destroyers of both world wars, including the builder's model of HMS *Hood*.
Opening times: Open all year, Monday – Saturday 10.00 – 17.00, Sunday 14.00 – 17.00
Admission free

GOSPORT
HMS Foudroyant, *c/o GPO 136 High Street, Gosport, Hampshire. Telephone: 070-17-82696*
Bombay-built teak frigate (1817) of a design similar to *Unicorn*. Now a training vessel, but some open days are planned for 1982.
Opening times: Monday – Tuesday 10.00 – 12.00, Thursday 14.00 – 16.00; a boat leaves Gosport ferry pontoon at 10.00, 11.00, 14.00 and 15.00 on the appropriate days. A guide will be attached to each party
Admission charges: Adults: 50p. Children 14 years and under: 25p

HMS Gannet, *Fareham Creek, Gosport, Hampshire*
Naval auxiliary steam sloop (1878), at present being refurbished by the Maritime Trust.
Not yet open to the public, but may be viewed from the shore.

Royal Navy Submarine Museum, HMS Dolphin, *Gosport, Hampshire. Telephone: 0705-22351 ext 41250*

Focal point of the museum is the 'A' class submarine *Alliance* built in 1946, but many other exhibits relating to the submarine service.
Opening times: Open all year, Monday – Sunday 9.30 – 16.30
Admission charges: Adults: £1.20, Children:60p

HARTLAND QUAY

Hartland Quay Museum, Hartland Quay, Bideford, Devon. Telephone: 02374-594

Small maritime museum, featuring displays on HMS *Saltburn* and RFA *Green Ranger*, wrecked nearby in 1946 and 1962 respectively.
Opening times: Whitsun – 30 September 1982, Monday – Sunday 11.00 – 17.30
Admission charges: Adults: 25p, Children: 15p

HARTLEPOOL

HMS *Warrior (1860), The Coal Dock, Hartlepool, Cleveland. Telephone: 0429-33051*

The first British ocean-going ironclad battleship, currently being restored by the Maritime Trust.
Opening times: weekends between Easter and August 1982, 14.00 – 17.00
Admission charges: Adults: 60p, Children & OAPS: 15p

LONDON

Artillery Museum, The Rotunda, Repository Road, Woolwich, London SE18 4BJ. Telephone: 01-856-5533 ext 385

The museum of the history of artillery, containing some interesting examples of early guns, including naval types.
Opening times: Summer, Monday – Friday 12.00 – 16.00, Saturday – Sunday 13.00 – 16.00; Winter, Monday – Friday 12.00 – 17.00, Saturday – Sunday 13.00 – 17.00
Admission free

HMS *Belfast, Symons Wharf, Vine Lane, Tooley Street, London SE1 2JH. Telephone: 01-407-6434*

The last survivor of the Royal Navy's big ships, *Belfast* played a key role in the Battle of North Cape in December 1943. Many exhibits on board.
Opening times: Summer, daily 11.00 – 17.50; Winter, daily 11.00 – 16.30
Admission charges: Adults: £1.80, Children and OAPs: 90p

Chrysanthemum, President *and* Wellington, *Victoria Embankment, London WC2.*

The first two are World War I 'Flower' class sloops (the second was originally named *Saxifrage*) used as RNR drill ships, and the last is an inter-war sloop, now the headquarters of the Hon Company of Master Mariners. None is open to the public but can be clearly viewed from the Embankment.

Imperial War Museum, Lambeth Road, London SE1 6HM. Telephone: 01-735-8922

Gallery devoted to Naval Warfare, including German *Biber* submarine and Italian Human Torpedo, a number of gun mountings and many models.
Opening times: Monday – Saturday, 10.00 – 18.00, Sunday 14.00 – 18.00; Reference Department: Monday – Friday 10.00 – 17.00
Admission free

National Maritime Museum, Romney Road, Greenwich, London SE10 9NF. Telephone: 01-858-4422

One of the world's great maritime museums, covering all aspects of British maritime history from the prehistoric period onwards.
Opening times: 1 November – 8 April 1982 Tuesday – Friday 10.00 – 17.00, Saturday 10.00 – 18.00, Sunday 14.30 – 18.00; 10

April – 31 October 1982 Tuesday – Saturday 10.00 – 18.00, Sunday 14.30 – 18.00
Admission free

Royal Naval College, Greenwich, London SE10 9NN. Telephone: 01-858-2154

The eighteenth century Chapel and Painted Hall are open to the public
Opening times: Daily 14.30 – 17.00 (except Thursdays)
Admission free

Science Museum, Exhibition Road, London SW7 2DD. Telephone: 01-587-3456

Exhibition includes ship models and sections of ship's machinery.
Opening times: Open all year, Monday – Saturday 10.00 – 18.00, Sunday 14.30 – 18.00
Admission free

LOWESTOFT

Royal Naval Patrol Service Museum, Sparrows Nest, Lowestoft, Suffolk NR32 1XG. Telephone: 0502-86250
Opening times: 1 April – 31 October 1982, daily
Admission free

PORTSMOUTH

HMS *Victory, HM Naval Base, Portsmouth, Hampshire. Telephone: 0705-22351 ext 22571*

Lord Nelson's Flagship at Trafalgar now in a permanent dry dock.
Opening times: Monday – Saturday 10.30 – 17.00, Sunday 13.00 – 17.00
Admission free

Royal Marines Museum, Eastney, Southsea. Telephone: 0705-22351 ext 6132/6135

An extensive display of Royal Marines history from 1664 to present day
Opening times: Monday – Friday 10.00 – 16.30, Saturday – Sunday 10.00 – 12.30
Admission free

Royal Naval Museum, HM Naval Base, Portsmouth, Hampshire. Telephone: 0705-22351 ext 23868

The museum houses relics of Nelson, ship's models and figureheads.
Opening times: Monday – Saturday, 10.30 – 17.00, Sunday 13.00 – 17.00
Admission charge

Southsea Castle & Museum, Clarence Esplanade, Portsmouth. Telephone: 0705-24584

Displays illustrating Portsmouth's naval history, including finds from the *Mary Rose* (see events)
Opening times: daily 10.30 – 17.30
Admission charge

SOUTHAMPTON

HMS *Cavalier, Berth 45, Southampton Docks, Southampton, Hampshire*

The last destroyer in service with the Royal Navy.
Opening times: from 7 April 1982
Admission charge

YEOVILTON

Fleet Air Arm Museum, RNAS Yeovilton, Somerset. Telephone: 0935-840551 ext 521

The largest collection of historic military aircraft under one roof in Europe, the vast majority being naval types.
Opening times: Monday – Saturday 10.00 – 17.30, Sunday 12.30 – 17.30
Admission free

EVENTS

Listed below are a selection of events of interest to warship enthusiasts.

BRISTOL
World Ship Society Naval Meeting. Includes slide talk on Victorian battleships, quiz and symposium entitled 'Merchant Ships as Naval Auxiliaries during World War II'. Attendance fee £1.25. *Hawthorns Hotel, Woodlands Road. 24 April 1982*

CHATHAM
'Navy Days' at the Dockyard. *30 — 31 May 1982*

LONDON
'Shipwrecks of the Goodwin Sands'. Finds from the excavations of the *Stirling Castle* (1679) and other Goodwin Sands wrecks. *Stock Exchange Gallery, City of London. 5 July to September 1982*

'Toll for the Brave'. Exhibition on the loss of the *Royal George* (1782). *National Maritime Museum, Greenwich. starting late June 1982*

'The Art of the Van de Veldes'. Exhibition of paintings and drawings by the Van de Veldes. *Queen's House, National Maritime Museum. Starting late June 1982*

PLYMOUTH
'Navy Days' at the Devonport Dockyard. *29, 30, 31 August 1982*

PORTLAND
'Navy Days' at the Dockyard. *17 — 18 July 1982*

PORTSMOUTH
The maritime event of 1982 must be the raising of the *Mary Rose*, projected for late August/early September 1982 (See national press for further details)

'Navy Days' at the Dockyard. *28, 29, 30 August 1982*

'Victorian Heyday', the History of the Royal Navy 1861 – 1906. A new permanent gallery devoted to this theme opens in early December 1982. *Royal Naval Museum*

ROSYTH
'Navy Days' at the Dockyard. *3 — 4 July 1982*

YEOVILTON
Exhibition showing the development of the Aircraft Carrier. *Fleet Air Arm Museum. From 6 April 1982*

A gallery of the Submarine Museum at HMS *Dolphin*

The general appearance of the *Gannet* when fully restored will be much like this view of her sister *Espiegle*, except that the latter had a straight stem in place of *Gannet*'s traditional curved 'beak'.

CPL

HMS *Belfast* in 1945. The ship is now a floating naval museum in the Pool of London.

MoD

The Architect of Victory

by Robert Gardiner

MARITIME
ENGLAND
English Tourist Board
Special Promotion

Ask the average Englishman what is the most famous ship in British naval history, and he would probably cite the *Victory*, giving as his reasons the ship's association with Nelson and Trafalgar – and since this was the single most instrumental factor in the preservation of the ship, nobody would argue otherwise.

However, even without Britain's most famous naval hero, or the most successful battle in the era of sail, *Victory* would have been a celebrity. When Nelson hoisted his flag aboard the ship in 1803, *Victory* was nearly 40 years old and had already flown the flags of several famous admirals, including Keppel, Kempenfelt, Lord Howe, Lord Hood and Sir John Jervis. In the American War, *Victory* had fought at Ushant in 1778, was flagship of the Grand Fleet which opposed the Franco-Spanish 'Armada' in 1779, played a leading part in Kempenfelt's massacre of de Guichen's convoy in 1781, and led Howe's fleet in its relief of Gibraltar in October 1782 and the succeeding battle off Cape Spartel. In the French Revolutionary War, *Victory* was Hood's flagship during the occupation of Toulon and the operations against Corsica (1793-94), flew Rear Admiral Mann's flag at the battle of Hyères in 1795, and was present at the battle of St Vincent in 1797 as the fleet flagship of Sir John Jervis.

By the 1790s, she was by no means the largest or most powerful ship in the fleet so her popularity with flag officers cannot be explained simply in terms of her size. Indeed, it is said that Nelson specifically asked for *Victory* as his flagship when she was laid up after St Vincent. The ensuing 'Great Repair' (the equivalent of a present-day 'Mid-Life Modernisation') took from 1800 to 1803, so it was obviously felt that the ship was worth the vast amounts of time, labour and expense at a period when larger First Rates were under construction.

DESIGN AND DESIGNER

What, then, was special about the *Victory*? The answer is simple: her outstanding performance under sail. She had all the attributes of a good line-of-battle ship, being not only a stable gun-platform, but also stiff (ie stable) enough to allow her leeward lower deck guns to be fired in most sea conditions (this was very important in a fleet used to seizing the 'weather gauge' to force action upon the enemy). Furthermore, *Victory* was both weatherly and a fast sailer – indeed she was so fast that she once chased and captured a French frigate (the *Embuscade* which was an ex-British ship and known to be capable of at least 12kts). Every warship design is a compromise in which the military factors of gun-power and steadiness compete with the ship' qualities of structural strength, stability, manoeuvrability and speed. In *Victory* this balance was just

The *Victory* in Portsmouth Harbour in 1886.

CPL

about perfect, which gives the ship a strong claim to being the most successful First Rate of her day – if not of all time.

In the past historians have been inclined to dismiss this pre-eminence as luck, rather than judgement, since naval commentators seem incapable of believing that sailing warships were consciously 'designed'. However, the man who drew up the plans for the *Victory*, Sir Thomas Slade, produced enough similarly outstanding ships to destroy once and for all the notion that only luck guaranteed a good design. Not a lot is known about Slade's life so, perhaps fittingly, it is by his works that we know him. Born in 1703, he spent his whole life in the shipbuilding industry, eventually rising to become Master Shipwright at Deptford in 1753. However, two years later he and William Bately were appointed joint 'Surveyors of the Navy',

The *Victory* with reduced rig, prior to restoration. She has served as the flagship of the C-in-C Portsmouth since the nineteenth century. *CPL*

the contemporary title for the men who designed the Navy's ships. This was obviously Slade's most important promotion, but in many ways it was also the most important appointment to the Surveyorship of the eighteenth century. The naval administration of the 1750s was in a state of transition and the new Surveyors faced novel difficulties, but in turn were offered unprecedented design opportunities. Slade's achievements prove that he was the right man for the job, and not merely a man in the right place at the right time.

In this period the running of the Navy was divided between the Navy Board, which was a permanent bureaucracy responsible for ships and dockyards, and the Admiralty which decided overall policy, and strategy in times of war. Although the Admiralty contained some sea officers, it was politically appointed and changed with the Government, so was at a disadvantage in dealing with the nominally subordinate Navy Board. In the previous decade, the two Boards had been at loggerheads over the state of British ship design, the Admiralty wanting radical improvements but being frustrated by the Navy Board, primariliy in the person of the ultra-conservative Surveyor, Sir Jacob Acworth, who had served in that capacity since 1715. The war of 1739-48 had shown up the deficiencies of the ships built under the various 'Establishments' (standardised dimensions laid down in 1706, 1719, 1733 and 1741) which had hampered the growth of British warships compared with their European rivals. However, the Admiralty had to settle for another Establishment in 1745 which was only a slight improvement, and little could be done until after Acworth's death in 1749.

SHIP REQUIREMENTS

There were two outstanding requirements: the first was for a standard line-of-battle ship that could stand up to European 74-gun ships; and the second was for a fast, and seaworthy cruiser to replace the thoroughly inadequate two-decked 24- and 44-gun ships. Under the energetic influence of Anson, the Admiralty began gradually to usurp the Navy Board's perogative of fixing the details of ship design. As early as 1747 they had ordered two ships built to the lines of a French privateer, so producing the first true frigates in the Royal Navy, and suggesting a long-term solution to the cruiser problem. The line-of-battle ship was more difficult, since the current 70-gun ship was too small, and the three-decker 80, although supported by the Navy Board, was one of the worst designs of the century. The Admiralty began experimenting with 'cutting down' larger ships, or modifying existing designs to try to achieve a satisfactory 74, but without any real success. Allin, Acworth's successor, was a bitter disappointment, and when in 1755 he became 'disordered in his senses', the Admiralty seized the opportunity to bring in new men.

When Bately and Slade took office, the problems were urgent since war with France was imminent. Bately proved a competent surveyor but Slade was little short of brilliant. Three weeks after his appointment, Slade had produced the draughts for the first purpose-designed English 74-gun ships (the *Dublin* class) and early the following year he designed the first English 32-gun frigates (the *Southampton*s). He did not achieve perfection instantly, however, the 74s being subject to a number of detail improvements in succeeding classes, while the *Southampton*s (and the similar 36-gun *Brilliant* class) were followed by the *Niger* class – without doubt the finest all-round 32-guns ships of the eighteenth century. Although the

The *Victory* undergoing restoration at Portsmouth dockyard in the 1920s – at the same time she was reconstructed to her 1805 appearance, including the full rig, and enclosed in a permanent dry dock.

CPL

Royal Navy's usual preoccupation has always been with large numbers of cost-effective 'standard' designs, Slade was willing (and allowed) to experiment. In 1757 he built the frigate *Tweed* to French design principles, and in 1769 produced the plans for the largest British-designed 74 before the 1790s (the *Culloden*). He also designed a number of ships inspired by the lines of the captured French-Canadian-built frigate *L'Abenakise*, so he was open to new ideas from whatever quarter. Considering his success with other ship types, it is not surprising that his only First Rate should have been outstanding – *Victory*, designed in about six months in 1758-59, was certainly one of his greatest achievements, but only one among many.

SLADE'S LEGACY

Perhaps the greatest tribute to his abilities is his posthumous influence over his successors. He died in 1771, but he is the only Surveyor of the era of sail whose designs were built in significant numbers after he died. For example, two ships built to the lines of the *Victory* were launched as late as 1810 and 1811 (the *Boyne* and *Union*). Indeed, even where new designs were attempted, they often followed Slade's basic dimensions and proportions (and usually produced inferior ships). The result was that by the 1790s British warships had failed to keep up with the growth in size of enemy ships, giving rise once again to the complaint that foreign warships were superior. Naval historians have accepted this without proper investigation and have carelessly applied the judgement to the whole period of sail, whereas Slade gave the Navy of the 1760s ships which were more than a match for any in Europe and their outstanding success in the Seven Years War is

more than symbolic. That his very brilliance should have had a stultifying effect is doubly ironic, since historical generalisations based on the later period have obscured the reputation he deserves.

Certainly *Victory* was saved because of her association with Nelson, and public interest could be maintained in no other way, but for those with a more technical interest in naval history she should have a secondary significance. Unlike *Wasa* or even the *Mary Rose* which failed as warships, the *Victory* is one of the very finest examples of an eighteenth century First Rate, and the masterpiece of the sailing navy's greatest designer. In practical terms, Sir Thomas Slade was far more successful than better-known contemporaries like the Swedish Chapman, and his work stands comparison with the great French naval architect Sané. Sir John Henslowe, himself a surveyor during the 1790s summed up Slade in a letter to Earl St Vincent: 'My late very much esteemed friend and patron, Sir Thomas Slade, he was truly a great man in the line he took, such a one I believe never went before him, and if I am not too partial, I may venture to say will hardly follow him'.

History has proved him right.

Seppings Survivor
by W Roderick Stewart

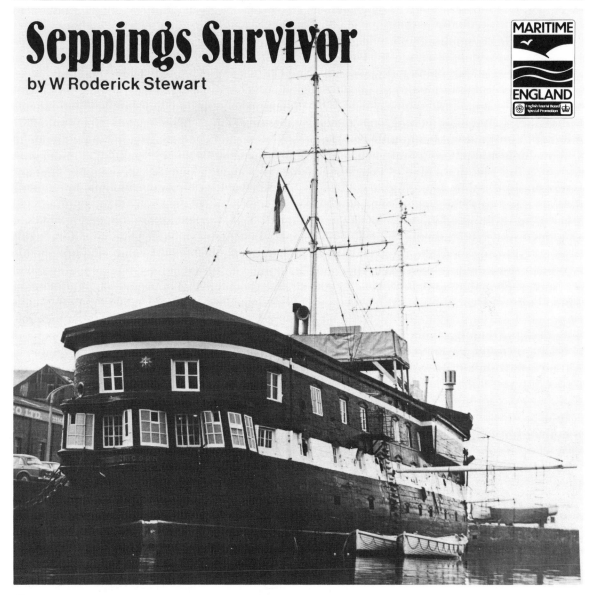

Unicorn as she appeared in 1968 when taken over by the Unicorn Preservation Trust. Note the Seppings' round stern and the roof.

The oldest English-built ship still afloat is alive and well – though in Scottish waters. She is the frigate *Unicorn*, a 5th Rate of 46 guns, launched at Chatham in 1824 for the Royal Navy, and is amazingly almost as sound in hull today as when she was built. However neither *Unicorn* nor her designer, the great Sir Robert Seppings, are anywhere near as famous as their importance warrants, though this is rapidly changing as *Unicorn* takes her place as one of a very select band of preserved ships. Although no longer in the Navy, she continues to serve her country as a place where people may catch a glimpse of the astonishingly hard life which made possible Britain's great and glorious sea power, in the days of sail.

Unicorn spent her early days in reserve, or 'Ordinary', at Chatham and Sheerness, and came to Dundee in 1873 where she acted as the RNR and RNVR Drill Ship, but essentially her story is one of survival rather than great battles. Indeed so ordinary was her history, and so unimportant did she seem that at one stage, when her days as a Drill Ship were over she was almost scrapped. Fortunately the Ministry of Defence was persuaded instead to hand her over to the newly formed *Unicorn Preservation Society*, and *Unicorn*'s future now seems safe.

The Society's aim is to fully rig and restore the ship, and this is well under way. Much work has been done, much money spent, and *Unicorn* is now open to the public as one of the world's most important ships: she represents, along with HMS *Victory*, the Royal Navy in the golden age of sail;

82

she is an example of the sailing frigate, one of the most successful ship types ever built, and one of only four left in the world; she demonstrates a unique form of construction among surviving ships, representing the link between traditional wood – and the fast-developing use of iron in ship building.

THE LEDA CLASS

One of the Royal Navy's most unlikely victories was won in 1782 when the French *Hébé* was captured by the old 44-gun ship *Rainbow* which had been experimentally armed with carronades. The French captain was greatly impressed by the weight of shot these guns fired at his ship but did not appreciate their extremely limited range, and so surrendered.

The *Hébé* was one of the finest frigates of the age, and became a valuable model for future British frigates (including *Unicorn*) for the next fifty years. Indeed so well-balanced was the design that the class must have been one of the most successful ever built, and perhaps the only one which was used by both sides in a major war, since the French also continued to build ships to the original design by their great naval architect Sané. The British ships were known as the *Leda* class and they included such famous ships as the *Shannon* (which defeated the American frigate *Chesapeake*), and the *Trincomalee*, built of teak in Bombay and launched in 1819. Now called the *Foudroyant* this latter is the only ship afloat in Britain older than *Unicorn*. It is thus particularly appropriate that *Unicorn* the only sailing frigate open to the public in Europe should be a member of this illustrious class.

SIR ROBERT SEPPINGS – A NEW SYSTEM OF SHIP-BUILDING

It is often said that the sailor of Drake's day would have been equally at home in one of Nelson's ships. Although this statement does a great injustice to the many brilliant ship designers who laboured during the intervening centuries to perfect the sailing warship, it is certainly true that many basic weaknesses of ship construction in Armada times were still a great problem at Trafalgar. However, the following twenty years saw a great change as the stage was set for the introduction of steam power and iron shipbuilding, and one man in particular was responsible for this change: Sir Robert Seppings, the Surveyor of the Navy (the nineteenth century equivalent of the Director of Naval Construction) from 1813 to 1832.

All his major innovations were incorporated in *Unicorn*'s design, along with several lesser ones, and she now occupies a place of unique importance amongst surviving ships. Externally she appears a traditional ship, similar in many ways to HMS *Victory*, yet structurally she clearly shows the first signs of the coming transformation in shipbuilding. No other ship in the world survives to bridge this gap so effectively.

While the details of many of Seppings' inventions were only applicable to the wooden ship, and passed away with its demise, it is certainly true that, by instituting the first major structural innovations for almost two centuries, he paved the way to even greater developments. It is therefore fitting that there should be preserved, in the *Unicorn*, such a complete illustration of his genius.

Unicorn's immense iron riders. *Spanphoto, Dundee*

The beautifully fitted iron knees and a heavy shelf piece support *Unicorn*'s gun deck.

The gundeck, showing how convincing the fibreglass 18pdr gun barrels look. The carriages are of wood.

Spanphoto, Dundee

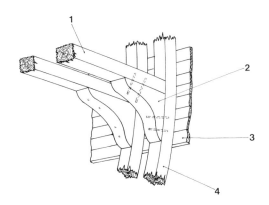

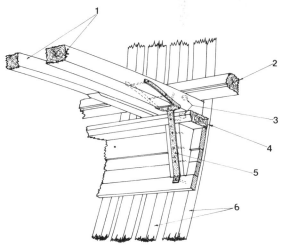

Comparison of old structure (left) with knees, and new structure (right) with shelf piece. Key (old system: **1** Deck beam; **2** Wooden knee; **3** Relatively weak skin planking; **4** Frames. Key (new system): **1** Deck beams; **2** Heavy waterway; **3** Beam coaked at top and bottom into longitudinals; **4** Heavy shelf piece; **5** Iron knee; **6** Frames.

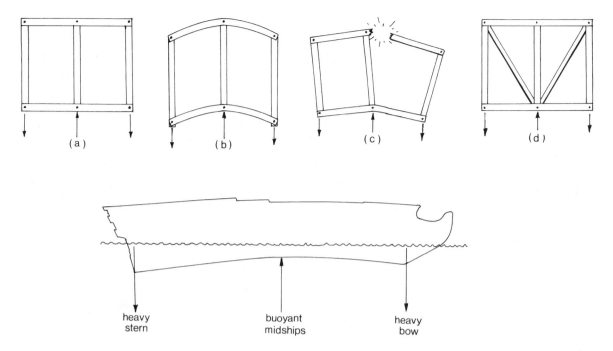

Fig 1: Gate structures and diagramatic illustration of hogging

DIAGONAL RIDERS

When a wooden ship ship has been at sea for any length of time its whole structure would distort and work loose under the action of the waves, and this in turn would lead to small leaks, soon to be followed by the dreaded rot. Even in a static situation great forces would be at work tending to bend the hull as the buoyant midships section was forced up while the heavy bow and stern tried to drop. With all these effects at work a wooden ship would soon start to 'hog' or arch in the middle, and it was not uncommon for a rise in the keel of 18ins or more to occur.

If the plank-and-frame construction of a ship is represented by the structure in Figure 1(a) above, and this structure is submitted to hogging forces, then there are two ways in which it is likely to break: by distortion of the rectangular structure (b) or by failure of a joint in tension (c). It had been seen comparatively early that the simple addition of a diagonal brace (d) to the structure would prevent distortion, but it fell to Robert Seppings, who was then Master Shipwright at Chatham, to produce a comprehensive and workable system for dealing with the whole problem.

The backbone of Seppings' system was the introduction of huge diagonal 'riders' inside the hold. These were first tried on the repair of HMS *Kent* in 1805 and developed further in the *Tremendous*. They proved immediately successful, and the *Howe* of 120 guns, launched in 1815, was the first ship laid down and built on the diagonal principle. An initial disadvantage of the scheme was the extra timber it consumed, and very soon the timber riders were modified to huge straps of iron, over 1in thick and 6ins wide. These great riders can be seen in *Unicorn* where they have done their work so effectively that when the ship was docked in

1972 she was only found to have hogged about an inch, after 148 years in the water! The iron diagonals added enormously to the strength of wooden ships, and were the development which ultimately allowed them to carry the extra weight of boilers and engines.

SHELF PIECES AND WATERWAYS

The second part of Seppings' system was designed to reduce the hogging caused by the loosening of fastenings in the upper part of the hull. This he achieved by the marvellously elegant method of fitting a continuous ring of timber, called the shelf piece, round the interior of the ship at the level of each deck, fastened to the frames and onto which the deck beams were secured. The final touch was to fasten another great ring, the waterway, on top of the beams making the whole structure immovable. The previous method had each beam jointed to its frame by a wooden knee, but only the ship's planking linked each frame to its neighbours. The one real disadvantage with Seppings' system was one which had led to problems in *Unicorn*, is that it is impossible to repair a small section without dismantling a major part of the ship!

FILLING THE BOTTOM, AND DIAGONAL DECKS

At the same time as Seppings tried out his diagonal riders, he packed tight the spaces between the frames in the bottom of the ship with wood and sealed the resulting structure with various compositions of oil and tar, the idea being to increase the rigidity of the bottom of the hull and to reduce the crevices where water could lodge and cause rot. It also produced an extremely solid ship's bottom, well able to withstand considerable damage from grounding etc.

Diagonal deck planking also formed part of the system and was first tried in 1811, but it does not seem ever to have

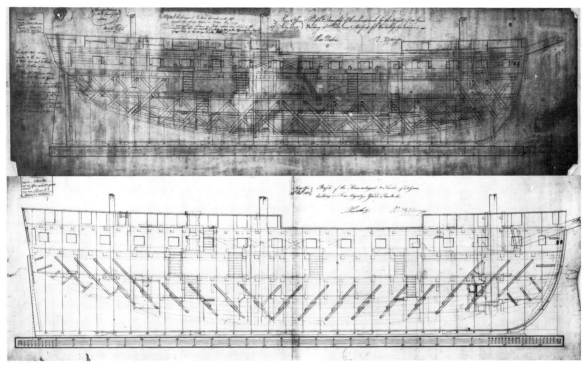

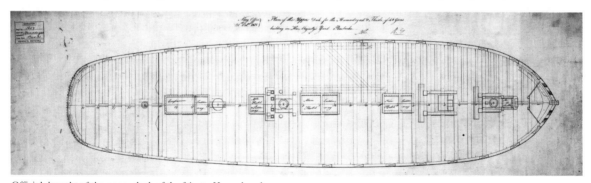

Profiles of two frigates showing (top) the earlier wooden
diagonals and (bottom) the iron diagonals which were both
stronger and cheaper, and took up less space. Official drawings of
HM ships *Arethusa* and *Hamadryad* respectively.

Official draught of the upper deck of the frigate *Hamadryad*,
showing the lay of the diagonal decking.

NMM

become common. Aside from its more obvious advantages,
this form of decking allowed the use of shorter deck planks.

IRON KNEES

Traditionally a ship's deck beams were joined to the side by
great curved pieces of wood called knees, each carved from
a piece of oak which had been grown to just the right shape.
However, by the Napoleonic Wars, timber of all sorts – but
particularly the curved 'compass timber' – had become
scarce, whereas the Industrial Revolution was well under
way and iron was becoming cheap and reliable. The first
attempts at change were made in the late eighteenth century, when a wooden knee with iron reinforcements was
developed, but the all-iron knee, such as can be seen in
Unicorn, was perfected in 1810 by Sir Robert Seppings.

This represents the earliest use of iron as a major structural
material in shipbuilding, and is a very important stage in the
ancestry of the modern ship.

Quite aside from the technical advance of this development, the sheer craftsmanship of these knees is extraordi-
nary, as each one is formed to a slightly different angle from
its neighbours, yet each enormous piece of iron fits with an
amazing accuracy.

THE ROUND BOW AND STERN

Two weak points in the construction of the old men-of-war
were the square bow and stern. The stern consisted of
elaborate, but lightly built, windows for the officers'
accommodation, and because its full weight fell on only one
beam (the transom beam), it could not be significantly
strengthened. The bow was strong up to middle deck level,
but above that there was only a flimsy bulkhead. Both these
points could be easily penetrated by heavy weather or

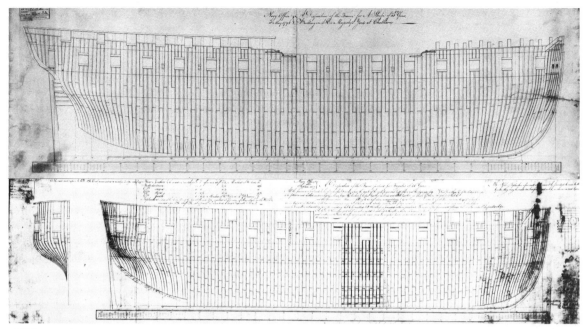

Official draughts showing the framing of the 38 gun frigates *Leda*, (top) and *Diana* (bottom), with the old and complex transom stern and elegantly simple round stern, respectively.

NMM

enemy shot, and it became a standard manoeuvre for a ship to attempt to 'rake' her opponent by firing a full broadside in through the enemy's bow or stern. Each shot would then travel the full length of the ship, leaving a terrible wake of destruction, and no effective retaliation was possible, since the bow and stern were not strongly enough built even to withstand the recoil of heavy bow or stern chasers. Consequently when Seppings had the job of 'cutting down' the *Namur* from a three- to a two-decker, in 1805, he decided to leave the bows fully planked. By 1817 he further developed this idea, when building the *Asia*, into his famous round stern, which was fully framed and planked, and had only small windows. This not only kept out enemy shot

more effectively and was strong enough to withstand the recoil of heavy stern chasers, but also allowed a wider arc of fire. In a sense it was the first move towards the modern gun-turret.

THE ROOF IS ORIGINAL!

Surprisingly, *Unicorn*'s curious 'Noah's Ark' roof is every bit as old as the ship herself. *Unicorn* was built as part of a great programme of replacement of worn-out ships after the Napoleonic Wars, but it took place at the start of a long period of peace, so many of these ships, including *Unicorn*, were put straight into reserve, or 'Ordinary'. It was at this stage that *Unicorn*'s strangely modern-looking roof was fitted to protect her hull. As it took two years or more to build a ship's hull, yet as little as two weeks to fit the rigging,

The redrawn lines of *Diana* and *Latona*. *Unicorn* was built to the same drawings.

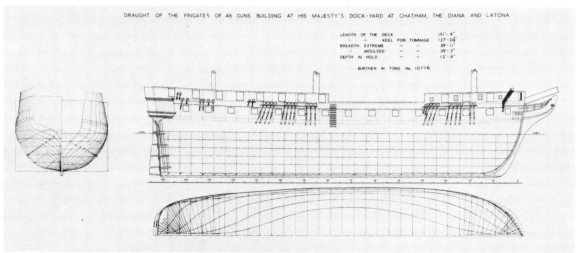

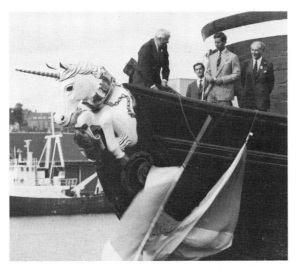

The figurehead unveiled by HRH the Prince of Wales in June 1979.

Spanphoto, Dundee

A bow view of *Unicorn* in drydock, 1972.

it made good sense to stockpile ships in this way against an emergency.

The ships launched just after the Napoleonic Wars were possibly the finest wooden warships every built, as the shipbuilding art was at its zenith, and their construction was not rushed as it would have been in wartime. In addition to this fine start, *Unicorn*'s hull has been safely protected by its roof for 158 years, with the result that it is almost certainly the best preserved, and least repaired, old wooden hull in the world.

RESTORATION AND THE FUTURE

Over the years a great warren of partitioning and miscellaneous structures had been added to the ship (including radar!) and one of the first tasks was to clear this away, allowing the full size and beautiful construction of the hull to be appreciated. The two small signal masts were also removed, as was a small section of roof, so that the long term effects of the weather could be estimated. This uncovered the ship's beakhead, which was carefully restored, even to the four 'seats of easement' which were the entire toilet facilities for 250 sailors!

The first six guns of the ship's main battery, which were copied in fibreglass from an original 18pdr in Edinburgh Castle, have been installed, together with two of the upper deck carronades. The latter were presented by the same Carron company who invented this weapon over 200 years ago, and yet was still able to cast the guns for *Unicorn* from the original pattern. The officers' cabins and part of the ship's company mess deck were refitted, and this left the interior work in a fairly complete state for visitors to see.

MASTING BEGINS

Attention could now be focussed on masting and rigging the ship, and a symbolic start to this exterior work was made in 1979 when HRH Prince Charles unveiled a splendid new figurehead, of a demi-unicorn, wearing the naval crown and supporting the Royal Arms. 1980 saw the completion of the constructional drawings for the bowsprit, and in early 1981 this immense spar was carefully eased into its position. It measures $54\frac{1}{2}$ft × $28\frac{1}{2}$in diameter, and cost over £10,000 with its fittings.

With the bowsprit safely installed, the next stage will be to raise £75,000 needed for the fore lower mast and its rigging. Though this seems a vast sum of money, it will buy a very large mast, $84\frac{1}{2}$ft high. Even the fore top will be $17\frac{1}{2}$ft by $10\frac{1}{2}$ft, which is as large as a good sized room!

HOW YOU CAN HELP . . .

The association of Friends of the Frigate *Unicorn* is open to all, and Ordinary membership costs only £5.00 per year. Its aim is to enable those who have an interest in old ships to help financially, to identify with *Unicorn* in a tangible manner, and to follow, via a newsletter, the progress of work on board. Full details are available from: The Project Manager, The Frigate Unicorn, Victoria Dock, Dundee, Scotland. Even if becoming a Friend is too much, reading an article is no substitute for visiting the real thing. *Unicorn* is open to the public from April to October each year (not Tuesdays) and is easily found right in the heart of Dundee's docks.

Warship Pictorial

HMS Warrior

The photo feature in this issue is devoted to the most ambitious warship restoration project currently under way in Britain. HMS *Warrior* was the first seagoing iron-built battleship, and it is singularly appropriate that this epoch-making vessel should have survived to represent the ironclad period and fill a gap in Britain's otherwise impressive range of preserved ships. By a quirk of fate, *Warrior* is also Britain's last surviving battleship, and a tribute to her designers and builders. Originally completed in August 1861, she was used as a depot ship from 1902, hulked in 1923 and used as an oil pipeline pontoon at Milford Haven until 1979, when she was towed to Hartlepool for restoration work to begin. This is proceeding steadily, but more help is required. There is a 'Friends of the Warrior' organisation, and anyone interested should contact Colin Doram (College of Further Education, Stockton Street, Hartlepool) for a leaflet.

This bow view taken in 1870 emphasizes *Warrior*'s fine lines, which, combined with great length, were necessary to achieve her high speed – she once logged 17kts under sail and steam.

By courtesy of Captain Wells

Warrior at Plymouth in 1863 – the earliest known photograph of the ship.
IWM

A rare early view of the ship taken a few years after commissioning.   *CPL*

Warrior and her sister *Black Prince* were the last first-rate British warships to be built with the traditional stem knee and full figurehead. Both ships had superb examples of the latter, *Warrior*'s being shown here in about 1867.   *CPL*

The original *Warrior* figurehead, removed from the ship late in her career. The buildings in the background give some idea of the giant scale of the carving.   *CPL*

Warrior's stem as it was when restoration began. The end of the stem knee was broken off when a tanker collided with the ship at Milford Haven during Warrior's time as a pipeline jetty. A new stem was fitted in June 1981, and a new figurehead is being carved.

By courtesy of Captain John Wells

A general view of the Warrior alongside the Coal Dock in Hartlepool (June 1981). Initial work has concentrated on clearing the ship of nearly a century of minor additions, including an inch-thick layer of fire-resistant compound on the gundeck and 4 inches of concrete on the weather deck. Plating and timber on the upper deck are being replaced, but probably the most spectacular addition will be the new figurehead, currently being carved at Henry Spencer's yard on the Isle of Wight.

By courtesy of Captain Wells

When the ship was drydocked at Devonport in 1958 (seen here) the hull was found to be remarkably sound, a tribute both to the materials with which she was constructed, and the men who built her. It is this basic soundness which makes the whole restoration programme possible.

By courtesy of Captain Wells

This lithograph by Dutton, published in 1861, gives some idea of the appearance the restoration programme is working towards. Research is aimed at an exact reconstruction of the ship as in 1862, during her first commission. It is the most ambitious venture ever undertaken by the Maritime Trust and probably the biggest restoration project of its type so far attempted anywhere in the world.

By courtesy of Captain Wells

The after section of the ship seen about 1964 when *Warrior* was serving as a pontoon at Milford Haven. As well as a figurehead *Warrior* also had a traditional frigate stern with a full set of 'lights' (windows) and quarter galleries, although the latter were removed long before this photo was taken.

By courtesy of Captain Wells

The Warrior has meant the revival of old skills in Hartlepool, an area badly affected by unemployment in traditional manufacturing industries. Here work is proceeding on the new stem, necessary to carry the figurehead.

By courtesy of Captain Wells

The Steam Engine & the Royal Navy
by John M Maber

Henry Bell's *Comet* made her debut on the Clyde in August 1812 but it was not until 1821 that the Royal Navy acquired its first steam vessel, the 212-ton *Monkey*, a wooden paddler fitted with simple machinery of 80nhp. The 238-ton *Comet*, the first built expressly for the naval service, followed a year later and in 1824 the 298-ton *Lightning* achieved fame as the first to be engaged on active war service by her presence, albeit in a limited role, at the blockade of Algiers. However, these small vessels were intended primarily for duty as tugs and had no claim to be warships in the accepted sense. Their machinery was of the simple side-lever type, an adaptation of the overhead beam engine where the beam was placed abreast the cylinder in order to keep the centre of gravity low. Usually two 'engines', opposite handed, were installed side-by-side to drive the paddle shaft, the two halves of which could be disconnected.

EARLY DEVELOPMENT

Side-lever engines, working at pressures only a little above atmospheric, were fitted in a number of early steam warships, but for the first paddle frigates, *Gorgon* (launched in 1837) and *Cyclops* (1839), Messrs Seaward & Capel of Millwall built vertical direct-acting engines with their two

Model of the engines for the paddle frigate *Gorgon* (1837). This was the first vertical direct-acting engine with fixed cylinders and represented a considerable saving in space and weight compared with the almost universal side-lever engine of the day.

Science Museum

Model of a side-lever engine, circa 1845. In this design the two cylinders are arranged fore-and-aft instead of athwartship as was usually the case.

Science Museum

cylinders mounted beneath the cranks each of which was coupled via a short connecting-rod. The small end of the connecting-rod was guided by a complex parallel motion which also drove the air pump used to maintain a partial vacuum in the condenser and to clear the accumulated condensate through to the hotwell. Machinery of this direct-acting design occupied much less space and was considerably lighter than the side-lever type, although the short connecting-rods were probably responsible for the excessive wear and uneven running of these engines in service.

In the meantime, the Admiralty had been watching with interest the development by Francis Pettit Smith and others of the screw propeller and in April 1840 representatives witnessed the trials at Dover of the screw steamship *Archimedes,* built in 1839 to demonstrate Smith's two bladed screw. In the light of a favourable report[1] the Admiralty reacted with surprising alacrity and in December 1840 placed an order for the construction of a wooden screw sloop to be named *Rattler*. This contract was followed in 1844 by orders for the wood screw frigates *Arrogant, Dauntless* and *Termagant* of which the first named entered the water at Portsmouth on the 5 April 1848[2]. Classed as an auxiliary screw frigate, the *Arrogant* (2615 tons) was engined by John Penn & Sons with twin cylinder, simple expansion, horizontal trunk machinery

The screw steamship *Archimedes* (1839) built to demonstrate Francis Pettit Smith's screw propeller.

Science Museum

sited below the waterline and thus well protected from shot and shell. In this engine, in order to save athwartships space, the connecting-rod was coupled directly to the piston within an annular trunk passing through the cylinder covers and taking the place of the piston rod.

TRUNK TO TRIPLE EXPANSION
Trunk machinery driving a single screw was also fitted in HMS *Warrior* (9210 tons) the first iron hulled armoured warship which entered service in 1861. Box through-tube boilers supplied steam at 20psi and on trials at 54rpm the *Warrior* achieved a mean speed of 14.35kts under steam alone. However, the trunk engine was not without its problems, due largely to the excessive heat loss from the trunks and the restricted access for maintenance, so that its use, confined in fact to warship installations, was abandoned by the late 1860s in favour of the horizontal direct-acting engine. Like the direct-acting paddle engine, however, this form of screw engine suffered from the shortness of the connecting-rod. Compound expansion development of this type was built for the twin screw despatch vessels *Iris* and *Mercury* of 1878 but thereafter warships, like contemporary merchant ships, were fitted with compound or, from 1884, triple-expansion vertical inverted machinery taking steam at pressures up to 200psi. In general, warship engines were of shorter stroke and faster running than the mercantile type resulting in a lower profile and an improved power/weight ratio, albeit at the cost of increased maintenance.

The triple-expansion inverted (early vertical engines were arranged with the cylinders beneath the crankshaft) engine, in which the steam is expanded in three stages, represented the peak of reciprocating machinery design. Refinements were introduced, such as forced lubrication in the twin screw armoured cruisers of the 14,600-ton *Shannon* class of 1908-09, but in general the triple-expansion engine fitted in large numbers of frigates, corvettes and ocean minesweepers during the Second World War differed little from its predecessor of a half century earlier.

THE STEAM TURBINE
Meanwhile, back in 1884 the Hon Charles Parsons had taken out a patent for a parallel-flow reaction turbine designed to drive an electric generator. Steam was expanded through alternate rows of fixed and moving blades placed at an angle of 45° to the axis of the rotor but the high speed, at 18,000rpm, precluded any immediate development of the turbine as a propulsion unit. Ten years later Parsons realised this latter objective and secured a patent '. . . for propelling a vessel by means of a steam turbine . . .' In that same year, 1894, following tests with models to determine the power required, a propulsion set was built for installation in the 44.5-ton yacht *Turbinia*. This machinery comprised a radial-flow reaction turbine taking steam at 155psi from a double-ended water-tube boiler and driving the single shaft at 2400rpm. At this high propeller speed, however, cavitation (the formation of voids on the blade surface) resulted in such loss of power that *Turbinia* could only manage a disappointing 19.75kts.

The problem was that the turbine could only operate efficiently if the moving blade speed was high, whereas the screw propeller is most efficient at relatively low speeds. Gearing of sufficient accuracy to transmit the power involved was not then available so turbine and propeller had, necessarily, to be directly coupled. Thus the direct-drive turbine required a large diameter rotor, to give a reasonably high peripheral blade speed with the lowest possible shaft speed. Space in the *Turbinia* was limited but she was successfully rebuilt with a 3-shaft arrangement driven by a 3-stage parallel-flow turbine set wherein the steam was expanded progressively through a high-pressure turbine on the starboard shaft, an intermediate-pressure turbine to port and a low-pressure turbine on the centre shaft which, since the turbine is non-reversing, was provided also with a separate astern turbine. Each shaft carried three propellers thereby increasing the blade area as much as possible and despite the fact that propeller speed remained very high, the *Turbinia* managed an impressive 34.5kts with the machinery developing 2400shp.

TURBINE DESTROYERS

The rebuilt *Turbinia* was demonstrated to the public on the occasion of Queen Victoria's Diamond Jubilee Review at Spithead in June 1897, when she astonished all present by her performance. In the wake of this demonstration, the Admiralty ordered from the Parsons Marine Steam Turbine Co in 1898 the 344-ton turbine-engined destroyer

Transverse section of HMS *Warrior* (1861), showing details of the horizontal double-trunk engine with the condenser, bilge pump and suctions.

Science Museum

Viper, a vessel similar in all other respects to the contemporary destroyers of the 30-knot type. At about the same time Armstrong's on the Tyne built, as a private venture, the 375-ton destroyer *Cobra* which was purchased by the Admiralty on completion of her trials. Both were engined with compound turbine sets on four shafts, high-pressure on the outer shafts and low-pressure, plus astern turbines, on the inner shafts. The *Viper* had two screws and the *Cobra* three on each shaft, and both achieved over 34kts on trials, albeit in a light condition without armament. They were accepted for service in 1901 but before the year's end both had come to grief, the *Viper* on the Casquets, off Alderney, where she broke her back and the *Cobra* off the Yorkshire coast, when she broke in two during heavy weather.

Trials had demonstrated the poor efficiency of the direct-drive turbine at low speeds, but in 1904 Hawthorn Leslie & Co completed the 420-ton destroyer *Velox*, engined on four shafts with compound-expansion turbines but fitted additionally with triple-expansion reciprocating engines, in line with the low-pressure turbines and driving the inner shafts only. These engines exhausted into the high-pressure turbines on the outer shafts and were declutched at speeds in excess of 13kts. She was followed by the 540-ton 'River' class destroyer *Eden* which, in place

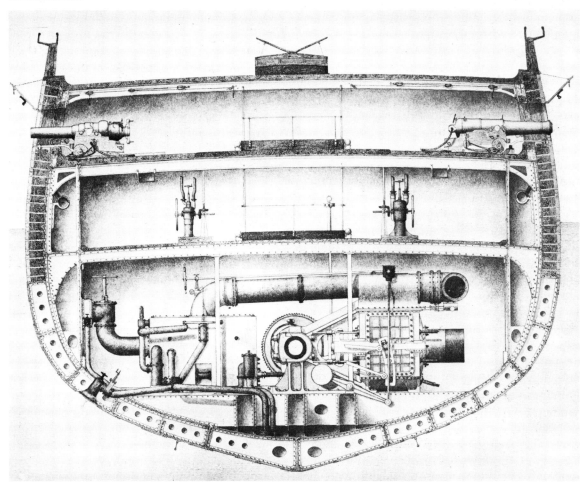

of the reciprocating engines of *Velox*, was fitted with cruising turbines, while in March 1905 Armstrong's delivered the 3000-ton turbine-engined cruiser *Amethyst* fitted likewise with cruising turbines and capable of 22.5kts at 12,000shp, against the 21.75kts with 9800ihp of her triple-expansion engined sisters. Also in 1905 the Admiralty Committee on Designs under the chairmanship of the First Sea Lord, Admiral Sir John Fisher, decided, in the light of accumulating experience, that all future destroyers and larger warships should be fitted with steam turbine machinery.

The few British turbine engined warships to this time had been fitted exclusively with machinery of the Parsons' reaction type, although of course, Parsons himself had been by no means the only engineer active in this field. De Laval (Sweden) had patented his single stage impulse turbine in 1889, and in 1896 both Rateau (France) and Curtis (USA) had taken out patents for velocity-compounded impulse turbines.

The decision to fit steam turbines to all major warships was marked on the 10 February 1906 by the launch at Portsmouth of the 17,900-ton all big gun battleship *Dreadnought*, engined on four shafts with Parsons direct-drive machinery designed for a maximum output of 23,000shp at 21kts. Like her predecessors she was coal-fired, although Admiral Fisher was himself a persistent advocate of the advantages of oil fuel. Largely as a result of Fisher's advocacy the turbine-engined destroyers of the contemporary 'Tribal' class were in fact oil fired, although there was a reversion to coal in the case of the succeeding *Beagle* class completed in 1910.

In the second decade of the century Brown-Curtis impulse type turbines achieved considerable popularity, being fitted first in the 4800-ton cruiser *Bristol* in 1911 and thereafter in many of the destroyers and larger vessels built for the Royal Navy. The main advantage was the economy obtainable at low powers and the Brown-Curtis turbine was accepted as a satisfactory alternative to the Parsons type until it lost favour following a series of damaging blade failures in the 1920s.

GEARED TURBINES

Meanwhile, in 1909 the Parsons company had re-engined the 22 year old cargo steamship *Vespasian* with a compound single-reduction geared turbine set resulting in a saving of some 15 per cent in fuel consumption against that required for the original triple-expansion reciprocating machinery. This saving apart, however, the turbine and the propeller were thus enabled to run at their optimum speeds, the turbine rotor itself being at the same time much reduced in diameter. The Admiralty took considerable interest in this development and in 1910 orders were placed for two destroyers of the *Acheron* class (*Badger* and *Beaver*) to be fitted with semi-geared machinery, the high-pressure and cruising turbines being geared to forward extensions of the direct drive low-pressure turbine rotor spindles. All – geared turbines, in this case of a Parsons impulse-reaction type, first appeared in the destroyers *Leonidas* and *Lucifer* in 1914.

By 1918 practically all new construction destroyers and larger craft were being fitted with single-reduction geared

Model of the horizontal direct-acting screw engines for HMS *Prince Albert* (1864), coastal defence armoured turret ship. This machinery, built by Humphrys & Tennant, indicated 2121 horse power at 61 rpm.

Science Museum

Model of the simple horizontal trunk machinery for HMS *Northumberland* (1868). These engines had two cylinders of 112ins diameter by 52ins stroke and trunks 41ins diameter, which at full power drove the single screw at 58 rpm.

Science Museum

Model of the four cylinder triple-expansion machinery (port set) for the twin screw battleship *Duncan* (1901).

Science Museum

The turbine steam yacht *Turbinia* alongside the quadruple screw turbine engined Cunard express liner *Mauretania* at Wallsend (1907).

Science Museum

The turbine engined destroyer *Viper* (1901) which achieved a speed on trial of 37.118kts.

Science Museum

turbines but in that year the Federal Steam Navigation Co of London took delivery of the turbine steamship *Somerset* fitted with double-reduction gearing. This permitted a further increase in turbine speed and an accompanying improvement in the overall economy of the installation. The *Somerset* proved successful but double-reduction gearing proved troublesome elsewhere and came to be regarded by British designers as unreliable[3]. Thereafter, apart from an experimental high pressure (500psi) installation in the Thornycroft-built destroyer *Acheron* of 1930, developments for the Royal Navy through the remaining years before war erupted in 1939 centred upon the single-reduction geared turbine of the Parsons reaction type with an impulse first stage in the high-pressure turbine and an

The original Parsons radial flow turbine built for the experimental steam yacht *Turbinia* (1894). Trials with this machinery proved disappointing and she managed only 19.75 knots.

Science Museum

One of the two sets of single-reduction geared turbines of the destroyer *Verity* (1920). The gear case is on the left, the high-pressure turbine in the centre and the low-pressure turbine beyond.

J Brown

all-impulse astern turbine. As it turned out, the practical certainty of war inhibited any major change in turbine or transmission design after 1936 and the well proven plant of the 1930s remained virtually unchanged in design until the early 1950s.

POSTWAR DEVELOPMENT

The Pacific war showed up the poor steaming efficiency of British turbine-engined warships against US Navy vessels with their double-reduction gearing and advanced steam conditions. Thus in 1943 the Admiralty invited industry to match American practice for the proposed *Daring* class fleet destroyers and in response there was formed an organisation known as the Parsons and Marine Engineers Turbine Research and Development Association (PAMET-RADA) to build a research and test establishment. In the event, the war ended and completion of the eight *Daring* class was delayed until the early 1950s, by which time the Royal Navy was able to make full use of PAMETRADA developments coupled with the experience of the English Electric Co and the British Thompson Houston Co in the electricity supply industry.

In the meantime, the need had been generated for a lightweight integrated machinery installation to power a new class of fast anti-submarine frigates the first of which, HMS *Torquay*, entered service in July 1956. Double-reduction gearing and careful turbine design, without recourse to extreme steam conditions, resulted in high efficiency at cruising speeds. Apart from detail improvements, machinery of this Y-100 type was employed for all the earlier Type 12 derived frigates, for the RN and other navies, and led to the development of the Y-160 installation for the later 'wide beam' *Leander* class vessels, the ultimate all-steam design for the Royal Navy and probably

Single reduction geared turbine set for the destroyer HMS *Fury* (1934) assembled prior to installation.

Cowes Branch Library and Maritime Museum

the best of its day for any navy. The final unit of this class, HMS *Ariadne*, commissioned for service in February 1973, by which time the Royal Navy had opted for a policy based on the employment of gas-turbine propulsion for all warships of frigate size and larger.

Only in the nuclear submarine is there now any foreseen future for steam and the geared turbine. However, diminishing supplies of oil fuels may yet enforce a change in policy and hence dictate a revived interest in steam plant for surface ships. For the present, on the other hand, there are many, with memories of long hours spent in making good defects under tropical conditions, who will not regret the end of an era.

1 *Reports Relative to Smith's Patent Screw Propeller as used On Board the Archimedes* by Captain Edward Chappell, RN (London 1840).
2 That is prior to the much publicised 'tug of war' between the screw sloop *Rattler* and the paddle sloop *Alecto* which took place on the 3 April 1845.
3 It is interesting to note that double-reduction gearing had been introduced in the US Navy in 1915 and that the problems encountered had been solved by 1918.

Model of a 3-shaft Parsons direct drive turbine set (1904).

Science Museum

Dolphins & Brass Funnels
by Peter Hollins

MARITIME ENGLAND
English Tourist Board Special Promotion

HMS *Malaya*'s second picket boat, probably heading for the Squadron steps during Cowes Week, 1934. Notice the exceptionally tall brass dolphins aft and the Stoker POs head at the engine-room hatch.

Beken of Cowes

Mention 'steamboats' and it will almost always bring to mind brass funnels with bell tops. Since most civilian steam launches had buff painted funnels with plain tops – polished brass at sea was much too labour intensive – the reference is to the steam picket boats, barges and cutters of HM Service, where the men needed to fight a Victorian man-o-war could be spared at other times for polishing substantial areas of brass.

Naval steam boats are perhaps the image leaders, and rightly so, for the steam pinnace – either as 'vedette', picket boat or liberty boat – was a highly successful concept from its introduction in 1867 to its general demise between the two world wars. This article traces the background, as far as we known it to date, of the last Royal Navy picket boat to survive in its original form, and two other examples of less well-known types, now in care of the Steam Launch Restoration Group at the Maritime Trust Boatyard, Ferrol Road, Gosport, Hampshire.

STEAM PINNACE NO 198 A

When Robert Whitehead introduced the 'locomotive torpedo' in the late 1860s, he sparked off various trains of development in counter-measures. Its predecessor, the spar torpedo, which required a boat to creep undetected to within 20ft of its enemy, had little real offensive potential but the new, relatively long-range device seemed a promising small boat weapon for night attacks on enemy ships at anchor. One of the resulting defensive requirements was for a reasonably fast steam launch, sufficiently small and sturdy to be carried by a capital ship yet large enough to be equipped with effective weapons to deal with any fast and lightly built torpedo craft which might penetrate a fleet anchorage.

Thornycroft's at Chiswick were quick to develop the offensive torpedo-boat, the first in service with the Royal Navy being the 18kt *Lightning* in 1876; but J Samuel White's, then of Cowes but originally of Gosport, were pre-eminent from 1867 in developing what became their ultimate counter-measure, the highly manoeuvrable 56ft 'turn-about' boat of the 1890s. These were lean twin-funnelled vessels capable of 15kts and equipped with a second rudder in place of the usual deadwood, giving them the reputation of being able to 'turn-about' on a sixpence. Battleships carried two each of these boats, not the least of their minor roles being to provide training in command for midshipmen.

Ordnance manufacturers were quick to supply suitable weapons: in 1885 the Nordenfelt multi-barrelled machine gun, a reasonably compact weapon for ship and boat use, provided the first practical answer for naval defence

The final development of combined picket boat and admiral's barge – HMS *Royal Sovereign*'s second picket boat, slightly down by the head under the weight of her 3pdr Hotchkiss gun, steaming out of Weymouth Harbour in June 1938:

P A Vicary

against fast moving targets, although the famous Gatling gun had been tried a few years previously. At about the same time Benjamin Hotchkiss, an American arms designer, went into business with William Armstrong of Jarrow to produce the ubiquitous 3pdr quick firing (QF) gun with a vertically sliding, wedge-shaped breech block, a revolutionary system at a time when muzzle-loaders were still widely used. Quickly trained by one man and with a range of nearly two miles, it was capable of the astonishing rate of fire of 12 to 15 rounds per minute. Moreover, its weight at 4¼cwt, would not seriously affect the stability and performance of a 56ft 'vedette' boat. Such a boat, weighing some 20 tons, was very near but not beyond the practical limit for hoisting in and out with a capital ship's main derrick. The size of boat was, therefore, a compromise which, nevertheless, largely satisfied all requirements

and it was even found possible to carry two side-slung 14in torpedoes when offensive action was demanded.

By the turn of the century the tactic of infiltrating enemy anchorages with small torpedo-boats had been defeated by the combined defensive measures of new artificial harbours, such as those at Portland and Cherbourg, by torpedo nets carried aboard ship and by the development of heavy machine guns and QF guns mounted in the fighting tops and in the picket boats of capital ships. By 1908, the threat had so diminished that steam pinnaces had become much more useful as liberty boats and for general duties than as defensive picket boats. In that year, Lord Fisher, the arch-rationalist, is said to have been responsible for standardising the design of all naval boats then in use.

His prime alteration in the case of the picket boat was a decrease in length to 50ft, with a corresponding reduction in speed to 11.5kts and 'all-up' weight to 16.8 tons. The stern cabin was enlarged and the top swept up to provide headroom and the shelter of a porch. In about one boat in twenty, the gun mounting forward was omitted in case a conversion to Admiral's Barge became necessary. However, policy over the need for the gun mounting vacillated

until, in 1914, the necessity for harbour patrols resolved the problem and in those boats without mountings, timber bases were constructed to carry the standard conical frustrum and gunmetal clamping rings.

Picket boat *No 198A*, under restoration by the Maritime Trust's Steam Launch Restoration Group (SLRG) at White's original yard in Gosport, is now the premier boat in a collection being established by the Royal Naval Museum, Portsmouth. She was built in 1911 to Lord Fisher's new standard 50ft design, although curiously she retained the very small stern cabin of the earlier 'vedette' boat. There is, however, no trace of the forward gun mounting ever being permanently fitted. She was therefore a boat intended for conversion to an admiral's barge if needed and in 1916, due to wartime expansion of the fleet, this work was put in hand with the addition of a counter stern. This never faired sweetly into the run aft however and has recently been removed. The brass funnel survived her later service as the Netley Hospital duty boat and was almost undented when, in March 1949, the boat was purchased by the late David Tyzack from Admiralty Small Craft Disposals through Fred Watts, a boatbuilder at Gosport, Hampshire.

A similar steam cutter to *No 463* under construction. Alternate planks of the diagonal inner skin have yet to be shaped and fitted. They will be followed by an oiled calico membrane and an outer skin laid fore and aft.

Probably the most ambitious voyage of her career occurred in July 1950 when four enthusiasts stoked and steamed the boat around the coast to the upper reaches of the Thames. But interest in her waned and her nadir occured in January 1959 when a Mr Cheeseman bought her for £10, restored the vessel and subsequently cruised in her with a petrol engine until 1967. After two further owners, one of whom, Mr Tamieska-Elliot, had very extensive hull renovations carried out at Tough's Yard, Twickenham, she was bought in July 1979 by the Royal Naval Museum and returned by road to Portsmouth where the SLRG took charge.

STEAM PINNACE 198A – TECHNICAL DATA	
Length:	50ft (pp)
Breadth outside planking:	9ft 9in
Depth, top of hog to top of gunwale:	4ft 10½in
Keel, hog, frames:	Canadian elm
Planking and deck:	2 skins ½in and ⅜in teak
Displacement fully loaded:	16.8 tons
Draught (mean):	3ft 7in
Weight of hull:	6.59 tons
Weight of machinery (inc water in boiler):	6.42 tons
Engine:	enclosed compound surface condensing
cylinders	6½in and 13in dia × 8½in stroke
rpm	about 624
ihp	162
Boiler:	White-Forster water tube
heating surface	320sq ft
grate surface	8.5sq ft
working pressure	185lbs/sq in
Propeller	3 bladed gunmetal; 3ft 4in dia × 2ft 5in pitch; surface area 600sq in
Speed:	11.65kts trial

Probably taken about 1905, the steam cutter from the Royal Yacht *Victoria and Albert* heads into Cowes.

Beken of Cowes

Re-assembling the steam plant has been a vast jig-saw puzzle but with help from all quarters, is proceeding steadily. HMS *Sultan*, the Navy's Engineering School, has donated a Mumford compound engine, similar to the original, and a Forster-White boiler from an 1898 56ft 'vedette' boat. On of the original auxiliaries has been located in Twickenham and her two steam pumps near Namur in Belgium. Much plumbing remains to be done at the time of writing but the target is to have the vessel in steam by Easter of Maritime Heritage Year, when she will be active in the Solent area and will take part in various public events.

HSL 376 carrying visitors to the Camber Basin, Priddys Hard, Gosport for a special occasion in September 1975.

T McShee, Esq

STEAM CUTTER NO 463

The earliest naval boats to be successfully equipped with steam machinery were six heavily built launches in 1864. They were fitted with removable twin screw machinery in which the single cylinder engines were probably bolted to the after end of the boiler. The drill was to hoist out boat and machinery separately and, even as late as 1878, drawings of sloops such as HMS *Gannet* show the chocks on the upper deck where the boiler was stowed. They were reported as most useful boats and encouraged the building in the late 1860s and early 1870s of a range of purpose-built steam cutters, based on the medium weight and rather finer-lined pulling and sailing cutters. Their development continued until the First World War and they formed the principal powered boat for vessels of the size of light cruisers, having an offensive capability consisting of a Nordenfelt and later a Maxim gun. Early experiments with spar torpedoes were made with these cutters in Portsmouth Harbour but they were generally too small and slow to use the later Whitehead torpedoes.

Steam Cutter *No 463* was a standard mahogany boat of 32ft, built in 1899/1900 and allocated to the Royal Yacht *Victoria and Albert III*, then under construction. Although her stern board is proudly carved *V & A: No 1 Steam Cutter 463*, she relinquished pride of place when the specially designed 30ft 'life cutter' *Osborne*, built of teak for Queen Victoria in 1897, was transferred to the yacht. *No 463* survived the twilight period of the parent vessel during and after the last war, being used on Portsmouth Dockyard business in wartime when petrol was scarce and being sold through Belsize Boatyard shortly after to Mr Hayes, a Guernsey market gardener. Mr Hayes restored and ran the boat in the Channel Islands most successfully but in 1974 she was bought by the Maritime Trust and loaned to the Royal Naval Museum, Portsmouth. Partly rebuilt in the dockyard, the hull was completed by a group of young men under a Job Creation Scheme in 1977/78 and now awaits internal refitting and a new boiler.

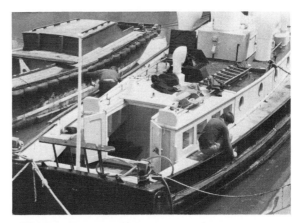

HSL 376 receiving attention from her volunteer crew.

Steam Launch Restoration Group

STEAM CUTTER 463 – TECHNICAL DATA

Length:	32ft pp
Breadth outside planking:	7ft
Draught:	2ft 5in
Planking and deck:	2 skins ⅜in mahogany (outer skin now teak)
Engine:	Open compound surface condensing by J S White
cylinders	4¾in and 9in × 5in stroke
rpm	485
ihp	32
Boiler:	White horizontal direct tube gunboat type
heating surface	85sq ft
working pressure	130sq in (forced draught fan driven from main engine)
Propeller:	3 bladed gunmetal, 2ft 4in pitch
Speed:	8.33kts on trials.

HARBOUR SERVICE LAUNCH (STEAM) 376

From early in the nineteenth century, steam power had been used in small craft built for towage and general harbour duties but, with the advent of steam cutters and pinnaces, a tendency developed of using the fleet's cast-offs for this purpose. This was particularly so during the lean years at the end of the Victorian period. However, a general duty harbour service launch *was* developed during the first half of the twentieth century and an example, surviving from 1919, suggests that the design was based on the 50ft steam pinnace but with some 3ft extra beam and a much reduced speed of 7 – 8kts.

It was to this 1919 design that the Admiralty turned when, in 1939 – 40, the need for a small harbour service launch (HSL) became urgent. Wartime petrol being scarce and coal indigenous, the choice of coal-fired steam machinery was logical, particularly since spare manufacturing capacity was available at the LNER locomotive workshops while diesel production was at full stretch. So were born 65 HSLs of the last war. The first batch, built in 1940 – 41, were 52ft 6in long, with a 13ft beam and a 5ft 3in draught; they had coal-fired, heavy Scotch boilers and compound condensing engines with 8in and 16in cylinders and an 8in stroke. They had a raked stem with considerable sheer down to a low freeboard amidships. An open shelter served

the coxswain but the flue from the coal fired galley stove passed through the shelter to provide some warmth and the crew of four could sleep on board in relative comfort. Their slow turning propellers, 46in in diameter, gave them excellent towing qualities for their size.

HSL(S) 376 is the last of the sixty-five to have remained in service, having been sold in September 1973 from Portland Naval Base to the Maritime Trust. She is of the amended 54ft design used for the second batch built in 1944 and was, until recently, oil-fired. Most of her service career was spend towing targets and performing similar duties in Weymouth Bay, but under her new ownership, the launch has taken divers on reconnaissance against the incursions of Japanese Seaweed around the Isle of Wight and has regularly appeared in steam during Portsmouth Navy Days.

During 1981, the launch was given a very thorough overhaul and converted to coal firing at the Maritime Trust Boatyard, Gosport, by the SLRG. She will, it is hoped, be seen frequently in steam again for Maritime Heritage Year.

HSL 376 – TECHNICAL DATA

Length:	54ft (oa)
Beam over rubbers:	13ft 7in
Draught:	5ft 6in
Planking	2 skins ⅝in and ½in larch, double diagonal
Frames:	sawn oak
Stringers:	columbian pine
Engine:	open compound surface condensing by Lissons
cylinders	8in and 16in × 8in stroke
rpm	250
ihp	75
Boiler:	wet back return tube Scotch by Ruston & Hornsby Ltd
heating surface	264sq ft, steam atomising burner for furnace fuel oil
working pressure	120lbs/sq in
Propeller:	3 bladed gunmetal, 46in dia × 59in pitch
Speed:	7kts

OTHER NAVAL SMALL CRAFT

Other boats in this representative collection include an admiral's barge thought to have been built in 1888 when steam barges were first introduced into the Service. At the moment she is no more than a bare hull but when restored, will have all the grace and yacht-like qualities of the boat in the accompanying photograph.

The collection is not confined to steam – included is a fast and sleek 30ft sailing gig in 1935, traditionally rigged with two dipping lugs and fully restored. A 'pusser's dinghy' is being returned to her original appearance and it is hoped to obtain one of the earlier, more graceful Montague whalers shortly.

Another item recently acquired of particular interest to embryo naval architects is a 55ft Thornycroft high-speed Coastal Motor Boat of World War I design. This was the direct successor of the steam torpedo-boats of the 1880s by the same firm but built thirty years later and being over twice as fast.

WHERE TO SEE
Work in Progress:
Maritime Trust Boatyard, Ferrol Road, Gosport (adjoining St Vincent School in Forton Road) Boats, Steam machinery, Models, Steam Shop. Admission: 30p per head
Completed Boats in Use:
52′ steam picket boat No *198A*
30′ sailing gig
Cowes Week; Portsmouth Navy Days (29/31 August 1982); Southampton Boat Show

Static Boats, Photo Display:
RNAD Priddys Hard, Camber Basin, as an adjunct to the Armaments Museum – apply to the Curator, RNAD Priddys Hard, Gosport, Hampshire, by letter giving one week's notice. Admission: Free
All Enquiries to:
Peter Hollins, 30 Ranvilles Lane, Fareham, Hampshire PO14 3DX. Telephone: Titchfield (0329) 43359

The Vice-Admiral's Barge, Portsmouth, approaching Whale Island steps in April 1934.

Wright and Logan

A close-up of the elegant after cabin of an Admiral's barge.

Wright and Logan

The Fleet Air Arm

by Roger Chesneau

In one well-known guide to the warships of the Second World War the following information appears for the aircraft carrier *Ark Royal*:

'*Armament*: 16–4.5in AA (8×2), 48–2pdr AA (6×8), 32–.5in MG (8×4) guns; 72 aircraft.'

It is typical of the type of entries one comes across in popular reference books. The accuracy of the information is not being questioned. What is surprising, however, is the emphasis: the ship's primary armament, indeed her *raison d'être*, is shunted to the back of the list as though an afterthought. It seems often to be forgotten that the aeroplane is the most important of the carrier's weapons: it is the main armament of that type of vessel, or more accurately the primary means by which its main weapons (both offen-

sive and defensive) are delivered, and represents the best method of achieving very long range for its warheads whilst retaining optimum flexibility. Many naval writers see the aircraft carrier only in terms of its design and development as a ship type, but from another point of view it is merely a mobile base: at once a runway, a hangar, a maintenance shop, an ordnance depot, a refuelling facility. But what 110pdrs are to HMS *Warrior* or 6in guns are to HMS *Belfast*, so Skuas, Swordfish and Fulmars are to our *Ark Royal*. It might be added, by way of redress, that aviation experts frequently view naval aircraft using solely the criteria that they apply to their more numerous land-based counterparts!

These apparently barely relevant points are in fact important; they are central to any discussion of shipboard aircraft and go a long way to explain the somewhat chequered history of the Fleet Air Arm: shunned on the one hand by 'ship men', especially in the early days of naval aviation when they were regarded as little more than an

A Sopwith 2F1 Camel on a 'fixed' flying-off ramp built over the forward 6in gun of the cruiser *Calliope*, 1918. Revolving platforms were also developed and these became a standard fitting in British cruisers during the 1920s. *IWM*

adjunct to naval gunnery, and viewed askance by many air force protagonists, who held that aerial warfard was hardly the province of the Royal Navy. Legacies of these attitudes can still, regrettably, be traced to this day.

It is perhaps paradoxical, then, that the Fleet Air Arm is the best preserved aspect of Royal Navy history, and one that stretches back over 70 years. Those years have seen an astonishing increase in the size, speed and versatility of the rather special shipboard weapon referred to as an aircraft, and it is no exaggeration to say that naval thinking has, as a result, undergone no greater revolution since the day somebody decided to mount a gun on board ship. In the paragraphs which follow, we can only touch upon some of the high points in the development of the naval aircraft, and make particular reference to some of the most outstanding machines to have lined a British carrier flight deck, examples of many of which can still be seen today.

Perhaps the most famous of all British carrier aircraft, and certainly one of the most effective, was the Fairey Swordfish. Its exceptionally low stalling speed made it an ideal weapon for operation from the short escort carrier flight decks.

Fleet Air Arm Museum

THE FORMATIVE YEARS

The First World War saw the introduction and baptism of the seaborne aeroplane as a practicable means of projecting naval power. The Naval Wing of the Royal Flying Corps was formally redesignated the Royal Navy Air Service on 1 July 1914, and for most of the first three years of the conflict operations were centred around the seaplane and flying boat bases on the coast and landplane air stations further inland; for the first eighteen months, too, RNAS machines were entrusted with the home defence of Great Britain. Shipboard operations were confined to sorties by seaplane-carrying ex-merchantmen such as *Engadine* and *Ben-My-Chree*, and a particularly celebrated occasion was when a Short 184, flying from *Engadine*, observed the presence of units of the *Hochseeflotte* during the Battle of Jutland. This very aircraft, 8359, or rather part of it, is now one of the treasures preserved at the Fleet Air Arm Museum at RNAS Yeovilton.

With longer ranges and the unreliability of navigational aids, it was not at all certain that a pilot would be able to bring his machine safely back to a parent carrier on his own, and FAA doctrine insisted on a second seat for a navigator. Even in 1940 this still held, as these Fairey Fulmars demonstrate.

Fleet Air Arm Museum

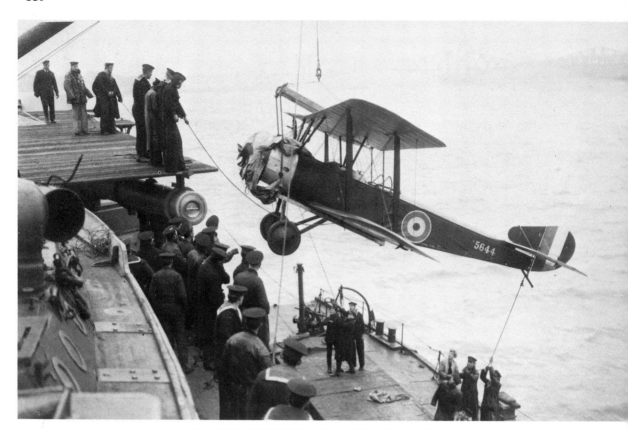

The battlecruiser *Australia*, Firth of Forth, 1918, a Sopwith 1½ Strutter being hoisted from a lighter onto the flying-off ramp fitted on the roof of 'Q' turret.

IWM

Other representatives of these first tentative excursions into shipboard aviation are also to be seen at Yeovilton, including a Short S27 replica, symbolising the aircraft flown by early naval trainee pilots and the types used in prewar take-off experiments on board ship. Of considerably less grandiose dimensions than the Short 184 but, like it, equipped with slab-sided pontoon floats fore and aft and employed with success in the same environment, was the Sopwith Baby, and an example of this compact scout/bomber biplane has been the subject of a rebuild and is one of the Museum's most prized exhibits.

Sopwith aircraft figured prominently in the early annals of naval aviation: the Tabloid scout/bomber, the Schneider and Baby seaplanes, the 1½-Strutter maid-of-all-work and, right at the end of the First World War the Cuckoo torpedo-bomber. But two Sopwith creations rank amongst the most outstanding designs ever produced – and both played a significant part in the development of the aircraft carrier as a viable vehicle for the launching and recovery of wheeled aeroplanes. To the Sopwith Pup, a machine of similar proportions to the earlier Baby, goes the distinction of two notable 'firsts': the first take-off from a gun turret platform (*Yarmouth*, June 1917), and the first ever carrier landing (*Furious*, August 1917) – events consolidated into

practice by both the Pup and the slightly bulkier Sopwith Camel, the 2F1 variant of which was designed specifically for use aboard ship. Fortunately, examples of both these epoch-making aircraft are preserved in Great Britain: Lt Culley's 2F1 Camel, in which he took off from a towed lighter and shot down a Zeppelin, is to be seen in the Imperial War Museum at Lambeth, an F1 Camel (virtually indistinguishable from the later variant) is preserved at the Royal Airforce Museum at Hendon, London, and two replica Camels are maintained in flying conditions at Thorpe Park Leisure Centre, Surrey; a rebuilt Pup (converted from a two-seater Sopwith Dove) is on display at the Shuttleworth Collection, Old Warden, Bedfordshire and one other Pup is privately owned. A Sopwith 1½-Strutter, the first two-seater aircraft to fly off a turret platform, is owned by the RAF Museum.

BETWEEN THE WARS

It is no anomaly that the 1½-Strutter, essentially a *naval* aircraft, should be preserved by the RAF, since the Royal Naval Air Service ceased to exist on 1 April 1918: it merged with the RFC to form the new Royal Air Force, which was to be responsible for all British military aviation, including shipboard aviation. In 1924 the naval branch of

A Fairey IIIF seaplane on the quarterdeck catapult of the battleship *Valiant* in July 1931.

NMM

A Fairey Flycatcher, the standard fleet fighter from the late 1920s to the early 1930s, endeared itself to its pilots by its superb handling characteristics. This example is overflying HMS *Eagle*, about 1927.

Fleet Air Arm Museum

the RAF was officially designated the Fleet Air Arm, and by this time much valuable work had been done in full-blown carrier operating techniques. HMS *Argus* was commissioned just after the end of the First World War; *Furious* was in dockyard hands undergoing full conversion to a flush-decked carrier; and the new carriers *Eagle* and *Hermes* had just commissioned and were working up. Within six years the two large carriers *Courageous* and *Glorious* had also joined the fleet, and the turret-mounted platforms on board the larger ships had begun to give way to catapults. Despite the advances in launching, retrieval and general operating capabilities, little radical change was evident in the aircraft themselves over this period, and although several types gave splendid service in the Fleet Air Arm very little hardware survives today. Yeovilton does have a replica of a Fairey Flycatcher, the standard fleet fighter from the time the FAA was established in 1924 until the early 1930s (on display during the winter months only), and in storage are remnants of an equally renowned Fairey product, the IIIF spotter/reconnaissance biplane, which served aboard all six of the Royal Navy's carriers as well as three capital ships and a number of cruisers.

The word 'legendary' is an overworked adjective with respect to aircraft types, but among the handful deserving of such a description must surely be counted the Fairey Swordfish. Entering fleet service in mid-1936 when it was already technically obsolescent, and serving in the torpedo-bomber/spotter-reconnaissance roles both on board carriers and with catapult flights, the viceless 'Stringbag' was on strength until the last months of the Second World War, gained fame in such exploits as the Taranto raid and the sinking of the *Bismarck*, and was one of the main naval weapons in the prosecution of the anti-submarine war. Two Swordfish are kept at RNAS Yeovil-

To the Blackburn Skua, the Fleet Air Arm's first operational monoplane, belongs the distinction of the first FAA 'kill' of the Second World War: a Dornier Do 18 flying boat off Norway. These are 803 Squadron machines operating from *Ark Royal*.

Fleet Air Arm Museum

An early production Grumman Martlet I, seen here at Prestwick on its arrival in the UK, August 1940. This particular machine was one of the initial batch of aircraft that would have equipped the *Aeronavale* had France not fallen two months earlier.

Conway Picture Library

Landlubber in sea boots: the first Seafire, a Mk IB, converted from a Spitfire Mk VB whose serial number it still (temporarily) retains. From this angle the aircraft is physically indistinguishable from its land-based prototype.

Fleet Air Arm Museum

ton, one of which is maintained in flying condition and performs regularly at air shows throughout the country; the Imperial War Museum also preserves an example.

Another apparent anachronism during the Second World War was the Supermarine Walrus amphibian, primarily a spotter-reconnaissance biplane but serving also in other roles. The only preserved example is to be found at the Fleet Air Arm Museum, although a Seagull V, the original (Australian) version of the type, is on display in the Battle of Britain Museum, RAF Hendon.

Two other representatives of the prewar era that should be mentioned are the Hawker Osprey fighter-reconnaissance seaplane/carrier aircraft and the Gloster Sea Gladiator, a biplane fleet fighter which replaced the Hawker Nimrod, a close relative of the Osprey. Examples of these aircraft are not preserved, but the landplanes from which they were derived (and differed very little), the Hart and the Gladiator respectively, are on view at Hendon, whilst Yeovilton has an example the latter. Visitors to old Warden, too, will see an airworthy Gladiator, whilst recently restored to flying condition at the same aerodrome is an ex-Afghan Hind, another Hart derivative and similar in general configuration to the Osprey.

A Grumman Avenger leaves the deck of an unknown British lend-lease escort carrier, probably in 1943, Although nominally a torpedo-bomber, the Avenger in FAA service was more usually employed as an all-purpose strike aircraft.

Conway Picture Library

THE SECOND WORLD WAR

The Admiralty had regained full control of naval aviation by 1937, but the sleek monoplanes that were about to equip the RAF took somewhat longer to reach the Fleet. It was not until late 1938 that the first, the Blackburn Skua dive-bomber, entered service aboard the new *Ark Royal*, and not until mid-1940 did the first monoplane fleet fighter, the eight-gun, two-seat Fairey Fulmar, arrive. The first prototype Fulmar survives at Yeovilton, where a Skua, dredged up from a Norwegian lake late in 1974 and displayed in the condition in which it was found, is also on view.

The shortcomings of the Fleet Air Arm's inventory during much of the Second World War were symbolised by the adoption of, first, extemporised landplanes and, second, four US combat aircraft. With the arrival in squadron service during 1941 of the Hawker Sea Hurricane, the Fleet Air Arm for the first time possessed a fighter that was capable of sustained speeds of over 300mph. The Sea Hurricane, also used extensively as a 'Hurricat' aboard catapult-armed merchant ships (CAMs), was very little different from its RAF progenitor – indeed many were straight conversions from ex-RAF machines, simply with catapult attachment points and arrester hooks added. The Seafire, initially a 'hooked Spitfire', was taken aboard carriers a year later and, despite the inherent problems associated with navalising this immortal aircraft (particularly those caused by the narrow-track undercarriage and the effect of high landing speeds), the type was progressively developed and remained in service for over a decade. The four US aircraft, in chronological order of service entry, were the

Grumman Martlet (Wildcat), the Grumman Hellcat, the Grumman Avenger and the Vought Corsair. All were designed exclusively for carrier operation and all except the Avenger were primarily fleet fighters and hence fulfilled the role of carrier long-range air defence; the last-named was arguably the finest naval fighter of the Second World War. Examples of all the US machines are preserved at Yeovilton, and the Museum also houses a Seafire XVII, a postwar Griffon-engined variant; no Sea Hurricane or Merlin Seafire is preserved, although of course specimens of their land-based equivalents are numerous.

Torpedo-bomber development continued from the Swordfish through the Fairey Albacore, one of the comparatively few biplane aircraft to feature an enclosed cockpit, and the ungainly, high-wing Fairey Barracuda, to the Avenger already mentioned. In the event, the Albacore was outlasted in service by its illustrious predecessor, whilst the Barracuda pursued a wide variety of pastimes, including, in particular, dive-bombing. An Albacore and a Barracuda II are held in storage at the Fleet Air Arm Museum, although regrettably they are not on public display as yet.

THE JET AGE

In the early postwar years it was all too obvious that the day of the piston-engined naval combat aircraft was almost over, and new carrier-based operating techniques, heavier and faster machines and a rapid evolution in the roles assigned in shipboard aviation all combined to bring about a drmamatic change in the composition of the Fleet Air Arm. The closing years of the piston-engined aeroplane were typified by the Fairey Firefly (developed from a wartime two-seat fighter-reconnaissance type through to a strike and anti-submarine aircraft); the ill-starred Blackburn Firebrand strike/torpedo fighter; the final variants of the Seafire; and the superlative Hawker Sea Fury and De Havilland Sea Hornet.

Experiments in jet landings aboard ship had taken place in 1945-46, and in 1951 the first Royal Navy jet type, the tail-sitting Supermarine Attacker, entered a squadron serivce. A further six jet aircraft were to equip the Navy's fleet carriers: the twin-boom De Havilland Sea Venom all-weather fighter, distant derivative of the Vampire, the type used in the world's first jet carrier landing; the superbly elegant Hawker Sea Hawk fighter; the Sea Hawk's successor, the Supermarine Scimitar; the Sea Venom's suc-

cessor, the twin-boom Hawker Siddeley Sea Vixen; the Blackburn (Hawker Siddeley) Buccaneer strike bomber; and the US-built McDonnell Phantom, the one and only FAA machine capable of supersonic speed in level flight. The last two formed the bulk of *Ark Royal's* complement up to her final paying-off, and all were transferred to the RAF, with which service they continue to operate. There are at Yeovilton examples of all these postwar types, with the exception of the Firebrand, the Sea Hornet and the Phantom, whilst the station maintains two Sea Furies and a Firefly AS5, and RNAS Culdrose a Sea Hawk, in flying condition. The RAF Museum displays a Sea Fury in the Camm Memorial Hall, whilst another is preserved at Southend Museum. Sea Venoms and Sea Vixens are also held by a number of other organisations.

Two other elements within the postwar Fleet Air Arm must not be forgotten. One is the development of AEW aircraft, first the piston-engined Douglas Skyraider and then the turbo-prop Fairey Gannet, the latter redesigned from the pure anti-submarine aircraft that bore the same name. Examples of all these are on display at Yeovilton, together with an Eagle- (piston-) engined Westland Wyvern, the later turboprop-driven version of which

served aboard *Albion* and *Eagle* and distinguished itself at Suez in 1956.

The other element is of course the development of the helicopter within the Royal Navy for communications, search and rescue, ASW strike, and assault, from the 1950 Dragonfly, through the Whirlwind, Wessex and Wasp, to the current Sea King and Lynx. Specimens of the first three may be seen at Yeovilton, whilst a Saunders-Roe P531, the prototype Westland Wasp, is also on view.

With the commissioning of *Invincible*, the Fleet Air Arm, after a gap of three years, has once again a fixed-wing capability, in the form of the British aerospace Sea Harrier FRS1. Sea Harriers, too, may be seen at Yeovilton, since the air station serves as 'home' for disembarked aircraft and for training and operational conversion. A public enclosure/picnic area has been provided by the Station authorities, so that on many days through the year one may watch the present while comparing the past: the entire legacy of the British naval air arm, from the downward-sloping platform take-off aboard HMS *Africa* in 1912 to the upward-sloping 'ski-jump' launches of today, is here for the seeing.

5

6

1 The Fairey Firefly served the Fleet Air Arm in various guises for over fifteen years. This is a Mk 5, over its parent carrier *Ocean*. The fuel tank under the port wing provided balance for the similarly contoured radome beneath the starboard wing.

   Fleet Air Arm Museum

2 A May 1951 photograph of Hawker Sea Furies on board HMS *Theseus*, with Fireflies right aft. The Sea Fury, the FAA's last operational piston-engined fighter, was widely used in Korea, where it fought with considerable success.

   Conway Picture Library

3 Engine start-up for six Sea Hawks, fired by special explosive cartridges. Sea Hawks served in the Royal Navy from 1953 to 1960 and were one of the most aerodynamically clean designs ever built.

   Conway Picture Library

4 The Hawker Siddeley Sea Vixen FAW2 differed from the earlier FAW1 version in its ability to carry the Red Top missile (seen here on the inboard wing pylons) and in its longer range, bestowed by the massive overwing boom extensions. The aircraft depicted is the first FAW2, converted from an FAW1, in 1962.

   Conway Picture Library

5 An 807 Squadron Supermarine Scimitar about to be catapulted from *Centaur*, June 1961. Primarily a fighter, the Scimitar could, however, carry a small nuclear weapon and was the first Fleet Air Arm aircraft to have such a capability. Scimitars served from 1958 until 1967.

6 The Hawker Siddeley Buccaneer provides one of the few examples of an aircraft designed for shipboard operation which has found its way into land-based air forces. This is an S2, shown here landing aboard *Ark Royal*; the Fleet Air Arm Museum preserves an S1 (distinguishable principally by its smaller intakes) and also the third (Blackburn NA39) prototype aircraft.

   Royal Navy

The Last Fleet Destroyer

by Antony Preston

The keel of the destroyer *Cavalier* was laid in February 1943; eleven months later, on 7 April 1944, she was launched and only seven months after that she commissioned. With her sister ships of the 6th Destroyer Flotilla, she was initially employed escorting Home Fleet aircraft carriers in three operations against German shipping in Norwegian waters in February 1945, and for her work in escorting convoys to Murmansk she was later awarded a Battle Honour. After a short refit she sailed to the Far East in August 1945, just too late for the final campaign against Japan. However she took part in 'mopping up' operations in the East Indies and shared the unhappy task of putting down unrest in the Royal Indian Navy. In June 1946 she returned to Portsmouth, with her sister *Cavendish*, and went straight into the Reserve Fleet, after a service life of less than two years.

Most warships which are paid-off into the 'mothball fleet' go from there straight to the breakers' yard but in 1955 *Cavalier* was taken in hand for a two-year modernisation at the Woolston yard of John I Thornycroft. When she recommissioned in July 1957 she had been completely transformed, with a new fire-control director above the bridge, a new anti-aircraft armament of four 40mm Bofors guns and the after bank of torpedo tubes replaced by a deckhouse carrying twin depth-charge mortars. The threat to the Fleet required anti-aircraft and anti-submarine firepower, and *Cavalier* could now be said to be more of a general-purpose fleet escort than a traditional fleet destroyer.

With a considerable number of Royal Navy warships still based 'East of Suez' the late 1950s and the 1960s were a busy time. The ship took part in numerous exercises and visited many ports in the Far East between 1957 and 1968. During this period she suffered severe damage in a collision with a Liberian tanker, and while under repair received the final modifications which resulted in her appearance as she is today. The torpedo tubes were removed along with the twin 40mm Bofors AA gun, but in their place she was given a new deck-house carrying a quadruple Seacat guided missile launcher and its fire-control.

The *Cavalier* now entered the last and in many ways the most exciting part of her long career. After a spell with the Beira Patrol screening the carrier *Eagle*, she returned to Home waters to join the Western Fleet. As a result of a challenge issued during an exercise in September 1970 she and the frigate *Rapid* ran a two-hour race in the Firth of Forth, for the honour of 'Fastest in the Fleet'. With the support of a national newspaper the event attracted considerable publicity, and to everyone's surprise the 26 year old *Cavalier* averaged no less than 31.8kts over a distance of 64 miles, beating HMS *Rapid* by a mere 30yds. It seemed that the *Cavalier* could not help attracting publicity, for just after the challenge had been issued she had received a distress call from a coaster on fire near Lundy Island. The blazing ship was boarded and brought safely into harbour, with the happy result that nearly two years later the officers and ratings were awarded £11,000 as their share of the salvage money.

Many would have liked the 'Laughing *Cavalier*' to remain in service for longer but the lack of spares for her elderly equipment made this impossible. However, by the time she paid off in 1972, a Trust had been formed to preserve her as a destroyer-memorial. Raising the large sums of money needed first to buy her and then to refurbish her as a museum-ship has taken nearly ten years, but thanks largely to the enthusiastic support of the late Admiral of the Fleet Earl Mountbatten of Burma she is now ready to be opened to the public. From Easter 1982 she will lie at Berth No 45 in Southampton Docks, 100yds or so inside Gate No 4 to the west of the old Ocean Terminal. The berth is a temporary one, leased by the Southampton Harbour Authorities to the *Cavalier* Trust for two years, and at the end of that period it is hoped to move her to a permanent dredged berth of Mayflower Park, facing Southampton Water.

Embodying as she does the classic features of British destroyers: the open bridge, four single guns and a single funnel, she is a fitting memorial to the hundreds of destroyers which served in two World Wars. It is intended to open more of the ship to the public as time goes by, and it will eventually be possible to see a complete steam turbine partially stripped and one of the boilers cut away to show its interior. The *Cavalier* will also serve as a centre for destroyer momentoes such as photographs, models and relics.

HMS *Cavalier* during her race with the frigate *Rapid*; the latter ship was converted from a destroyer of the same basic design as *Cavalier* but retained her original engine plant so the two vessels were well matched.

Ambrose Greenway

Into the 21st Century

by DK Brown RCNC

History is an interesting subject which can often be enjoyable but the past is also the only guide available to the trends which govern the future. The designers of a new warship must look far ahead; the first studies for the *Whitby* class frigates, for example, were begun in 1944 and their direct descendants, the *Leanders*, are likely to be in service 50 years later. The Constructors of the *Whitby* and *Leander* classes (N G Holt and M P C Purvis) produced one of the finest groups of warships of all time, but even an average design will have a life of some 30-40 years from its first conception.

To look ahead some 30 years is difficult, in fact well nigh impossible, but the designer who fails to make the attempt to do so is abdicating his responsibility. While one cannot say what *will* happen, there are quite a number of clear trends as to what *will not* happen and a number of indication on what *could* happen. Some of these trends will be explored in the context of the United Kingdom and the Royal Navy.

MONEY

The enthusiast is prone to forget that warships are very expensive and are getting more expensive. A few examples of cost are shown in Table 1, both as recorded on completion and with the effects of inflation taken out by converting to the value of the £ in 1950. Some of this increase in cost is due to growth in size; *Broadsword*, for example, is $1\frac{3}{4}$ times the displacement of *Whitby*, but even so the real cost per tonne is now about twice what it was in 1950 (Ref 1a). Similar high costs occur elsewhere in the Naval programme – the 1980 Statement on Defence Estimates quotes the price of a nuclear powered fleet submarine as £140 million and the Sting Ray torpedo project as £920 million. Such increases cannot go on; there is no sign of rapid exconomic growth in the United Kingdom and hence the chance of significantly more money becoming available for defence in general or the Navy in particular is remote. There will either be fewer ships or cheaper ships and yet each one must be capable of playing an effective part in resisting an increasing threat.

TASKS

The true tasks of the Royal Navy have changed little since the end of the Second World War. Every day about 120 ocean-going ships arrive in the ports of Western Europe, bringing about one million tons of cargo of which around a half is destined for the United Kingdom. In times of tension, there would be a requirement for the rapid reinforcement of the NATO forces in Central Europe and on the flanks – Norway and Italy. The Royal Navy, together with

The US Navy's SES-100B launching an SM3 missile in the Gulf of Mexico in April 1976.

USN

Table 1: COMPARATIVE COSTS OF BRITISH FRIGATES

Date	Ship	Cost on Completion (£ million)	Cost Reduced to 1950 Value of £
1950	*Whitby*	3½	3½
1961	*Ashanti*	5¼	3½
1965	*Leander*	4½	3
1978	*Broadsword*	80	12
1981	Type 22, Batch II	120	13

its NATO allies, must help to protect this flow of ships, for if the normal trade is interrupted for any length of time, Western Europe will collapse without the need for a tank battle in Germany. The potential threat to NATO shipping is increasing rapidly, from submarines and aircraft, from large surface warships such as *Kirov* and *Kiev* and from the fast growing Soviet force of hovercraft and hydrofoils.

VULNERABILITY

The surface warship faces an ever growing threat from long-range missiles launched from aircraft, submarines and surface craft of all kinds. It is difficult to put a figure to

the percentage of hits which such missiles will achieve; the last Arab-Israeli war and the Indo-Pakistan war suggest that the number of hits will be fairly low. Many missiles will be jammed, seduced electronically or by decoys, and some may even be destroyed by point defence missiles.

However, there will be hits and, as the accompanying photograph of *Undaunted* shows, a modern missile will cause such damage to a frigate that it will be out of action for many months at best. An interesting example has been quoted by Rear Admiral J S Lake USN (Ref 1b). While operating off the Gulf of Tonkin in 1972 the USS *Worden* was accidentally attacked by a Shrike anti-radar missile. The missile worked perfectly, homing on the ship's radar and exploding some 80-100ft above the *Worden*. The ship was sprayed with fragments of missile body and of the warhead, which contained a mere 50lbs of explosive. The destroyer was completely out of action with no power, light or communications for 30 minutes. When the *Worden* was under way again, it had lost 60 per cent of its combat effectiveness and needed a lengthy spell in a shipyard for repairs. The problem of vulnerability further suggests the need for numerous small and fairly cheap ships, though they must not be so simple that they lack all defence, passive or active, against missiles.

SUBMARINES

The main threat to transatlantic shipping is from the very large and powerful Soviet submarine force and it is important to understand how submarine technology may change in the next few decades. The main aspects of

USS *Worden* (DLG 18), seen here on 8 December 1970 off Bath, Maine, was put completely out of action for 30 minutes after a misdirected Shrike anti-radar missile detonated above the ship in the Gulf of Tonkin in 1972.

USN

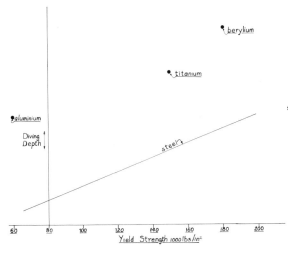

FIG 1

Graph of submarine diving capabilities with various pressure hull materials.[11]

FIG 2

Speed/wave height comparison.

performance are speed, diving depth and noise, all of which are highly classified subjects. The following passages are illustrative only and are based on published data which may, or may not, be entirely correct.

A current nuclear powered attack submarine is usually described as having a displacement of about 4000 tonnes, with about 20,000shp to drive it at a speed of 30kts. It can be estimated (ref 2) that the bridge fin alone accounts for some 10 per cent of the drag and that if this is removed – as it was on *Scotsman* – the speed will increase by one knot. If all excrescences are removed (casing, hydroplanes, sonar and water inlets) leaving a perfectly stream-

lined body, the speed will increase to 35½kts without increase of power.

If a more powerful reactor is available, say 40,000shp, the original submarine complete with fin, casing etc, but increased in size to 5000 tons to carry the bigger machinery, will reach nearly 36kts. Much of this power is used in overcoming the friction of the water on the hull and it has been shown by Canham and others that this component of drag can be much reduced by injecting polyethylene oxide into the water flow (Ref 3). At present the quantities required, even for a mixture of 30 parts per million, make the cost prohibitive but it is not impossible that this situation will change. With friction halved, the 40,000shp, 5000-ton submarine could reach 41kts!

There are even fewer facts publicly available on diving depth but *Fig 1* indicates some of the possibilities for

The frigate *Undaunted*, serving as a target, after being hit by an Exocet surface-to-surface missile fired from HM guided missile destroyer *Norfolk* in 1974.

MoD

increasing the safe limit. Higher strength steel, titanium, berylium and even plastic, reinforced with glass or carbon fibres, can all give greater diving depths for a given weight of hull. Many of these materials have already been tried on research submersibles but in an optional submarine the main difficulty lies in designing the systems which penetrate the hull to accept increased diving pressure. There is no doubt that much greater diving depths than those at present used can be achieved if the increased cost is accepted.

The main advantage to a submarine of going deep is that the characteristics of the sea make it possible to hear surface ships, and often submarines, at much greater distances. If full benefit is to be obtained, the listening submarine itself must be quiet. The main noise sources, both for submarines and surface ships, are the propeller, the machinery and the water flow round the hull. Once again, much can be done to reduce such noises – at a price. The initial stages of noise reduction cost comparatively little but each futher decibel costs more and more to eliminate, and the techniques used tend to require frequent, skilled and very expensive maintenance if they are to continue to function.

To sum up, the submarine can be developed very considerably beyond today's performance levels as indeed the Soviet *Alfa* class seems to have done. An anti-submarine force designed solely to counter today's submarine potential might be out of date very quickly.

THE SURFACE FLEET

Cost and vulnerability suggest that surface ships will be quite small individually but they will be highly sophisticated in order to meet the growing submarine threat, hence there will still be few such ships. In addition to anti-submarine warfare, the surface fleet will be required to take part in offshore protection, mine countermeasures and a number of minor tasks. It is suggested that shipborne area air-defence and anti-surface strike will be either impossible or too expensive for the RN and will be carried out by shore-based aircraft. In general, the smaller the frigate, the more hulls become available from a fixed sum of money, but if the ships are too small they become ineffective either because of an inadequate weapon-fit or because their operational performance is degraded by motion in bad weather.

The minimum anti-submarine equipment is a good passive sonar, probably towed, and the ability to operate a helicopter of about Sea King size. It is probably uneconomic to base a single such helicopter on a frigate as this would mean that all the expensive maintenance facilities and crew must be provided in each ship. A better solution is to arrange a helicopter 'garage', possibly on a replenishment ship, and to provide only a landing deck, with refuelling and rearming capability, on the frigates. Adding communications and some ECM equipment to the sonar and helicopter deck is already implying a ship of about 2000 tons to provide the force required.

ROUGH SEAS

The effect of bad weather on such a ship is interesting, to say the least! Table 2 shows the percentage of time for which various sea states are experience by weather ship *India* off N W Scotland and their effects on a 3000-ton ship. Below sea state 5 the weather will have little effect on the crew or weapons of a 2–3000-tonne ship but in sea state 5 some of the crew will be sick, particularly during the first few days of a patrol, and the effectiveness of some weapons and sensors will be slightly affected. The effect of sea state 6, met some 21 per cent of the year in Northern latitudes, is much greater. About one-third of the crew will be sick and there will be a significant degradation in weapon performance. For the 9 per cent of the year when sea state 7 and above is met the ship will be almost totally ineffective.

The simplest way to reduce ship motions in bad weather is to increase the length. The value of this approach is clearly seen in accounts of life at sea in the wartime escorts of the 'Flower', 'Castle' and 'River' classes. There are many accounts of life in the 'Flowers' (55m in length) of which *The Cruel Sea* is best known. All such accounts are dominated by the sea and it seems the crews of the 'Flower' class could do little more than survive in rough weather and that their operational effectiveness was negligible for a sizeable part of the year. Accounts of life in the 'Castle' class (69m) are few in number but it seems that fighting the U-boat was a more memorable aspect of life than fighting the weather. Mention of severe weather is rare in narratives of the 'River' class of 92m length (Ref 5). Length is the most important ship parameter governing pitch and heave in bad weather and modern technology has enabled the ship designers to put figures to the effect of length.

THE LONG AND THE SHORT OF IT

A ship of some 90-100m length and of about 2000 tonnes can carry a minimum weapon fit and there are, as always, advantages in a bigger ship is the cost is acceptable. The proportion of weight and space which can be devoted to armament increases rapidly in the bigger ship, so improving its apparent cost-effectiveness. The true measure is the cost-effectiveness of the whole fleet which may show advantage to more, smaller ships. A longer ship will have reduced motions in rought seas so increasing the number of days a year on which it is effective, as shown in Table 4.

In effect, the longer ship will be able to operate at the same level of effectiveness in weather about half a sea

TABLE 2: SEA STATES EXPERIENCED BY 'INDIA'

Sea State	Description	Significant Wave Height (metres)	% of Year	Roll Unstabilised° Stabilised	Pitch°	Heave (metres)
1–4	Calm–Moderate	Up to 2.5	39	$3\frac{1}{2}/2\frac{1}{2}°$	1°	0.5
5	Rough	2.5–4	31	$4\frac{1}{2}/3°$	$1\frac{1}{2}°$	1
6	Very rough	4–6	21	6/4°	2°	1.5
7 or over	High and over	6+	9	Over 14/9°	$2\frac{1}{2}°$	2

The RN's first jetfoil, HMS *Speedy*, built in the US by Boeing, serves to evaluate the type for future employment in British service.

MoD

The US prototype SWATH, *Kaimalino*, in 1976. The type shows great promise for future development.

TABLE 3: SEA PERFORMANCE OF SECOND WORLD WAR ESCORTS

Class	Pitch		Heave (metres)	
Wind force (Beaufort)	5	7	5	7
Flower (55m)	$2\frac{1}{2}°$	4°	$\frac{3}{4}$	$1\frac{1}{2}$
Castle (69m)	2°	$3\frac{1}{2}°$	$\frac{1}{2}$	$1\frac{3}{4}$
River (92m)	$1\frac{1}{2}°$	3°	$\frac{1}{3}$	1

state worse than the shorter ship. Such an increase in effectiveness can be given a cash value. If the total cost of the frigate force, together with a proportion of training and support costs is divided by the number of ships and by the number of days at sea, it will appear that the cost of having one frigate at sea for one day is £100,000 (1981 Defence Statement). The extra value of the longer ship, described above, is therefore about £5 million per year. This is not the only benefit to be gained from the longer ship. Most warships operate in a moderate speed range defined by:

Speed in knots $\sqrt{\text{Length}}$ in feet, giving a ratio of between 1.0 and 1.4

Over this range any practical increase in length will reduce the power required for a given speed and save fuel. For a typical operating pattern, the longer ship (B, Table 4) will require some 15 per cent less fuel, saving about £90,000 a year on its fuel bill at today's prices – and the cost of fuel will double or treble by the end of the century! The longer ship will be more expensive to build and in this example the difference will be of the order of £½ million – a very small sum compared with the benefits of improved sea keeping and reduced fuel consumption over 20–25 years. It is always difficult to balance future benefits against present costs but even the most pessimistic discount rate will show a considerable increase in 'present value' for the longer ship. The long ship will be easier to lay out; in particular the arrangement of sensors and weapons so as to avoid mutual interference will be eased. The spacious

hull will also allow the superstructures to be smaller, reducing the windage which upsets stability and handling at low speeds.

MACHINERY

The obvious fuels for the future fleet are oil, coal, and nuclear. Oil will get much more expensive, at least doubling in real price by the end of the century. However, at that price level there are a number of low grade sources of oil, such as shale, which become viable, and it will also become economic to convert coal into oil. The direct use of coal in warships seems less attractive. Coates (Ref 10) has given a comparison of a coal fired Type 42(C) with HMS *Sheffield*, Table 5. Nuclear power is very expensive and is only sensible for large (10,000-tonne), high speed ships which it is unlikely that the RN can afford.

It seems that the surface navy is likely to use oil fuel well into the 21st century, possibly made from the rich coal deposits under the UK. Modern gas turbines, such as the SM1A (Spey) have a fuel consumption very similar to that of a diesel and are likely to be used for the bigger ships but diesels will increasingly be used for smaller craft.

TABLE 4: COMPARISON OF A CONVENTIONAL FRIGATE WITH A LONGER SHIP

Ship	Length (metres)	Displ M (tonnes)	Pitch		Heave (metres)	
Wind Force			5	7	5	7
Frigate A	107	2700	5.5°	10°	1.7	4.3
Frigate B	125	2835	4.2°	7.7	1.5	3.8

Note: Motions are double amplitude, significant ($\frac{1}{2}$), ie mean of the one third highest out-to-out motion

TABLE 5: COMPARISON OF HMS SHEFFIELD AND A COAL FIRED TYPE 42

	Displacement (tonnes)	Power (MW)	Speed (Knots)	Crew	Cost Ratio
Oil	4000	36	28	220	1
Coal	7500	40	28	330	1.4

SWATH (Small Waterplane Area, Twin Hull)

Prototypes are already in service of more advanced vehicles which can give even more dramatic improvements in seakeeping. The SWATH is a catamaran with two submerged, cylindrical hulls connected to a platform, well above most waves, by slender struts. Many oil exploration rigs operate on this principle but they are usually slow moving craft. The US Navy has operated an experimental SWATH, the *Kaimalino*, for a number of years and experience with this craft, together with model tests and theoretical studies, has shown the potential of the SWATH concept for warships of frigate size.

There are two aspects of the motion of a ship which affect the liability of the crew to sickness or may degrade their performance. These are the magnitude of the vertical acceleration caused by pitch and heave and the frequency at which these motions occur. Nausea (derived from the Greek word for ship) only occurs over a fairly limited range of frequencies – roughly when one complete cycle of motion takes between 3 and 10 seconds. Conventional warships tend to pitch and heave right in the middle of this band, while the slower motions of the SWATH are clear of the worst of it. The pitch and heave periods of a frigate are about 4.7 seconds while those of a SWATH are about 14 seconds. The actual motions of a SWATH are very much less too. In 1978 the US Coast Guard compared *Kaimalino* with two conventional cutters as shown in Table 6. In moderate seas off Hawaii the motions of *Kaimalino* and *Mellon* were very similar while those of *Cape Corwin* were several times greater. Medical tests confirmed that the SWATH was the most comfortable of the three ships. It should be almost impossible to be sick in a large SWATH, and its motion characteristics make it an ideal helicopter operating platform.

There are, of course, problems as well. The technical difficulties relate to strength and to control in following seas. These problems have been solved in *Kaimalino* and can be solved for bigger SWATHs, but the extra work involved does mean that a SWATH will need many more graduate engineers in the design staff than a conventional ship. The cost of these will be insignificant in relation to that of the ship, but such men are scarce and it will require a major decision to commit so many to one job. The other technical problem is that of machinery arrangement and power transmission. To reduce the noise levels which pass into the sea it is desirable to put the machinery in the platform and transmit the power down the struts to a propeller behind each hull. In the small *Kaimalino* this arrangement has been applied using chain drive to the propellers, but the mind boggles at such an arrangement transmitting the power from an Olympus turbine. Almost certainly such engines will be positioned in the submerged hulls, with some complication and loss of efficiency due to the long uptakes and downtakes.

It is generally estimated that a SWATH, built in steel, will displace about 10 per cent more than a conventional ship to carry the same payload and that the hull cost (roughly half the total) will be up to 10 per cent more. Thus a SWATH will be about 15 per cent more expensive than a conventional frigate with the same weapon fit, but it will remain effective in weather conditions in which the conventional frigate cannot operate – but in which sub-

TABLE 6: SWATH SEA PERFORMANCE

Vessel	Length (ft)	Displacement (tons)
Kaimalino	89	200
Cape Corwin	95	100
Mellon	378	3000

marines and aircraft can. A considerable amount of work has been done on the development of SWATH both in the USA and in other NATO nations and, since it involves no really new technology, one may well expect prototype warships of this style in the early 1990s (Ref 6).

THE HYDROFOIL

The power required to drive a ship through the water is mainly dissipated in friction and wave making (*See* 'Where the Power Goes', *Warship 16*). The only solution is to get out of the water, a feat which has been performed for many years by the hovercraft and hydrofoil and gives a big advantage in speed both in calm water and in rough water up to a high limiting sea state.

Hydrofoils are already in service with the world's navies in surprisingly large numbers – about 130 from China and half that number from Russia. With a few significant exceptions these are of the simple surface-piercing foil design which gives a fairly high performance, even in moderate sea states, at low cost.

The US Navy has developed the much more sophisticated, and expensive, fully submerged foil craft in which the incidence of the foils can be controlled by a computer in reference to the anticipated wave profile. A 100-tonne craft of this type can operate at full speed into low sea state 3 (waves some $2\frac{1}{2}$m high). The Royal Navy purchased such a craft, HMS *Speedy*, from Boeing Marine Systems to explore their capabilities. The first and most important lesson learnt from the *Speedy* is that her actual performance is exactly that forecast by her designer (Ref 7). This gives confidence in the accuracy of estimates for 400 tonne and larger craft and there seems little doubt that any small strike craft in service in the 21st century will be hydrofoils or hovercraft, though it is not clear that the role itself is viable in the face of air opposition.

The great virtue of the hydrofoil is very high speed in rough seas and this can be used in anti-submarine warfare; after all the hydrofoil is almost the only surface craft which is faster than a nuclear submarine. There seems little prospect of using sonars at 40–50kts but hydrofoils can either use aircraft techniques – sonar buoys – or can stop to listen and regain position using their high speed. Such craft can either be a fully capable ASW ship or a mobile listening post. An example of the former is the study carried out by Grumman for the USN into a hydrofoil destroyer. This would have a displacement of 2400 tonnes with a calm water speed of 53kts (51.6 in sea state 6). It has a payload – weapons, fuel, crew and stores of 1080 tonnes and in 1978 was estimated to cost $218 million. The design is described in great detail and there is little doubt that it is feasible in terms of today's technology – though the project manager would undoubtedly have a few headaches. The alternative approach recognises that hydrofoils are inevitably expensive and that there is no reason why, for example, a helicopter and maintenance equipment should be carried on board. The helicopter is

An artist's impression of the 3000-ton surface effect ship (SES) proposed for the US Navy by Rohr Marine. The vessel is designed to achieve a speed of over 80kts.

best carried in a support ship (or even a merchant ship in convoy) and called up when required. Such hydrofoils, carrying little more than a towed sonar, come out at around 400 tonnes for Atlantic operation.

The actual need for high speed requires careful justification. The fishery protection operations with *Speedy* have shown the value of her speed, not in pursuit of delinquent trawlers, but in rapid transit from one group of fishing vessels to another. HMS *Speedy* has already proved her value in fishery protection work while at the same time demonstrating commendable reliability. These operations also accustom the operators to the concept of a craft with most of its stores and maintenance ratings on shore; to a craft with a rather low endurance in terms of hours but a high endurance in terms of distance covered.

HOVERCRAFT

There are two basic configurations, side-wall craft (sometimes referred to as surface effect craft) and the fully skirted, amphibious craft. The side-wall craft, pioneered in Britain by Hovermarine, offers performance rather similar to that of a hard-chine patrol boat at low cost. The world-wide sales of Hovermarine show that this concept is commercially viable and patrol boat variants are available. The US Navy has developed this concept and built two research craft of about 100 tonnes with speeds of 80kts. These craft were part of the programme intended to lead to a 3000-tonne, 80kt SES frigate. This programme has progressed very slowly due to lack of funds and it has been said that such a craft would cost as much as a 10,000-tonne cruiser.

The fully skirted craft with air propulsion, has three

most valuable characteristics; it is amphibious, has very low underwater noise levels and is resistant to underwater explosions. There can be little doubt of the value of hovercraft in amphibious operations; repeated operations of the RN Hovercraft Trials Unit in support of Royal Marine exercises from Norway to Borneo have made that clear. This lesson has been well learnt by the USSR with the *Aist* class and the USN with its JEFF development vehicles. One may well doubt the feasibility of opposed landings against air opposition but even support landings in friendly countries, over unprepared beaches, need hovercraft. The problems are that hovercraft are expensive to buy, operate and even more expensive to develop. The cost of development means that almost all British designs are rather elderly – the biggest, the British Hovercraft Corporation SRN4 is 13 years old. Modern designs, such as the BHC AP-188, with more economical engines could be far cheaper to build and run and have much better endurance in naval roles.

The Hovercraft's most obvious role lies in mine warfare (Ref 1a). Conventional craft can, at great expense, be made quiet, non-magnetic and shock-resistant while the hovercraft, held above the sea by its supporting cushion, does not have these problems. Exercises with the BH7 craft and simulated trials with a chartered SRN4 have demonstrated that hovercraft can operate all forms of minesweeping gear up to the limits of the gear. BHC have published proposals for mounting conventional minehunting sonars on a stalk under the hull and developments in towed sonars, such as the US Navy's AQS 14, show great promise in searching for mines at a much higher speed than can be achieved, in safety, by conventional minehunters.

The RN has recently taken a step along the road of hovercraft for mine warfare. The Vosper Thornycroft VT

2 has been purchased to carry stores from the shore based Forward Support Unit to *Hunt* class MCMVs at sea. Her immunity to mine explosions, proven in actual trials with the crew on board, means that short cuts can be taken across suspect minefields and that the store carrier is unlikely to set off mines under the *Hunt* class as might well happen with a conventional ship. There are many subsidiary roles for hovercraft including: towing damaged ships out of minefields (SRN4 can tow a destroyer); mine laying; army support.

MODULAR SHIPS

Much of the versatility of the hovercraft is due to the large and unobstructed deck of craft designed as vehicle ferries onto which can be dropped containers or pallets with a wide range of military equipment. The same approach can be adopted on conventional ships. Several navies have seen the need to install equipments in bigger packages, arranged in standardised spaces, with appropriately sized access and local supply of essential services. The depth and height of modules must be closely related to the height and arm length of the human body and it is no coincidence that the three main systems, British, German and American are multiples, one of the other. This approach should lead to considerable reductions in pipe and wiring work and, even more valuable, it is possible to test and tune large blocks of electronic equipment in the factory.

The UK Ministry of Defence has developed a system known as Cellularity which embraces a number of concepts contributing to: ease in build, and in subsequent refit and modernisation; arrangement to minimise the effects of damage; incorporation of margins to allow for update later in the life of the ship. It is hoped to save about 20 per cent of drawing office time and 25 per cent of the man-hours required for weapon and electrical system installation. The German (MEKO) system is based on larger modules often, but not essentially, based on the standard container dimensions, and the US system uses even bigger modules. In general, the bigger the box, the greater will be the saving on installation cost but the less will be the flexibility.

It does not look likely that it will be possible to supply a bolt-on kit to convert an ASW ship to an AA ship overnight. There are too many other requirements – quiet propulsion, masthead electronics, supplies of electricity at different voltage and frequency, and of chilled water, to name but a few.

CONCLUSIONS

Since the life of a warship after commissioning is about 20–25 years it seems likely that a few of the ships of the 21st century fleet are already in service. Design and building takes the best part of ten years implying that almost half the fleet of AD2001 is in the design stage – not on the drawing board, please, but on the storage discs of the computer.

Most of the remaining half are likely to be quite ordinary looking ships, quite small but long for their size with little visible armament. Such ships will provide a great challenge to the skills of the Naval Constructor since the

An artist's impression of the proposed 2400-tonne hydrofoil destroyer designed by the Grumman Corporation.

design of a cheap ship which is also effective is one of the most difficult tasks which can be presented. Simple ships are not produced by simple minds but are the result of the most sophisticated skills; only the result looks easy.

The fleet may also have one or two SWATH ships of 2000–3000 tonnes and an increasing number of hovercraft in mine warfare. Surface strike in coastal waters should be the preserve of the hydrofoil with a few prototypes of larger ocean-going ASW craft. Submarines will be faster, quieter and deeper diving. While the ships of the Navy may change, the role of protecting the shipping which feeds and supplies the United Kingdom does not.

REFERENCES

1 International Naval Technology Expo. Rotterdam 1980
(a) 'The design of cheap warships', D K Brown RCNC and D J Andrews RCNC
(b) 'Warship Survivability', Rear Admiral J S Lake USN
2 *Fluid Dynamic Drag*, Schoenherr
3 'Boundary Layer Additives to reduce ship resistance', H J S Canham RCNC, J F Catchpole and R F Long (*Trans RINA*, 1971)
4 'Naval Architectural Aspects of Submarine Design', Captain E S Arentzen USN, P Mandel (*Trans SNA*)
5 'Small Warships in the Royal Navy and the Fishery Protection Task', D K Brown RCNC and P D Marshall RCNC (RINA Symposium on small fast warships, 1978)
6 'Seakeeping and the SWATH design', Lt Cdr S R Olsen, US Naval Institute (March 1978)
7 'A Hydrofoil Fisheries Patrol Vessel for the UK', J T S Coates (RINA Symposium, 1978)
8 'Grumman Design M163, a 2400 Metric Tonne air capable Hydrofoil Ship', G Pieroth AIAA/ASNE (Advanced Marine Vehicles Conference, 1978)
9 'Hydrofoils, a review of their History, Capability and Potential', D K Brown RCNC (Inst of Engineers and Shipbuilders of Scotland, 1980)
10 J F Coates RCNC (Contribution to RINA, 1979)
11 Graph adapted from 'Naval Architectural Aspects of Submarine Design'

Acheron & Avernus

by Ross Gillett

Acheron.

Author's collection

The early maritime defence of the colony of New South Wales – and more particularly of Port Jackson – was, for most of its recorded history, provided by the Royal Navy ships based on the Australian station. Britannia's presence had been an integral part of the early colony's make-up since the arrival of the first fleet under Captain Arthur Phillip in January 1788.

When, on 1 March 1859, HMS *Iris* became flagship of the Australian Station, a continuing presence in local waters was guaranteed. For the ensuing 52 years another twelve flagships would lead the Royal Navy squadron, with occasional visits from special task groups, such as the Flying Squadron in 1869 and the Detached Squadron in 1881. Usually the permanent force would comprise the flagship and between six and twelve other warships, of all types from cruiser downwards.

Naturally, local residents, although content with the might of Britannia in Sydney Harbour, desired a visible local effort to protect their homes and families. This desire also manifested itself in the other colonies, due to the Russian threat of the 1870s and 1880s – a threat which failed to materialise.

Frequent reports in the daily press warning of Russian warships off the coast led in 1877 to the Government of the colony of New South Wales ordering the construction of two 'outrigger' torpedo-boats, to be built to a Thornycroft design. Tenders for the two boats closed on 17 January 1878, with £8784 being allotted. The construction of the two craft in Sydney was a remarkable achievement for the colonials, as this revolutionary type of warship had only entered service with the Royal Navy a few years earlier.

The Atlas Works, located in Pyrmont, Sydney Harbour, were the successful tenderers, with completion scheduled in March 1878, a remarkably short period for any shipbuilder. The two torpedo-boats were named *Acheron* and *Avernus*, the former in Greek mythology being one of the rivers of the lower world, the name being taken from a river in southern Epirus which flowed through a deep gorge into the Ionian Sea. *Avernus* bore the name of a small lake near Naples which ancient civilisations believed to be the entrance to the lower world.

Acheron, the first boat to complete, ran trials in Sydney Harbour on 1 March 1878, the trip proving most successful. A speed of 16kts was attained on a number of runs. As well as their defensive function, *Acheron* and *Avernus* were deployed for other military purposes and on occasions served as despatch boats.

ACHERON AND AVERNUS – DATA AS COMPLETED

Type:	Second class 'outrigger' torpedo-boats
Displacement:	22 tons
Length:	82ft 6in
Beam:	10ft 6in
Draught:	4ft
Machinery:	Surface condensing engines, 200ihp, single screw
Boilers:	Multi-tubular type
Speed:	16kts (18 maximum)
Bunkers:	4 tons of coal
Armament:	Two sets of dropping gear for 14in Whitehead torpedoes
Cost:	£8,784 (total)

Acheron, described as 'the first torpedo launch ever constructed in Australia', was divided into ten watertight compartments. The first, enclosed by a collision bulkhead, bore the torpedo spar and was adjacent to the fore cabin. Moving further aft, there was a small stores compartment, then the steering compartment, torpedo compartment, the boiler room, the engine room, the after cabin (for 12 people) and another two separate divisions before the stern.

Each boat could be steered from the stern or from a small sunken position directly forward of the funnel. A bullet-proof steel visor protected the helmsman in the sunken position, who also had the duty of launching the torpedoes. The engines were mounted on steel columns with wrought-iron sole plates to obtain the maximum power

Avernus, with *Acheron* in the background, in Sydney Harbour, about 1890.

Author's collection

with the minimum weight.

The careers of *Acheron* and *Avernus* were confined to harbour waters and both were almost exclusively active at weekends and on public holidays. Fortunately for Sydney Harbour and the boat's crews, the two craft were never called upon to meet an adversary; what the results might have been can only be conjectured. Experiments with the boat's propellers were carried out in 1879 in an effort to increase speeds, but these proved unsuccessful.

By April 1885, *Acheron* and *Avernus* were in a state of disrepair and they had to be drydocked at Cockatoo Island. After another docking in May, both were fitted to use spar torpedoes in addition to launching their torpedoes from the cradles on each beam amidships. Neither boat saw active duty in 1886 and late in that decade they were being described as Sydney's third line of defence, the first being the Naval Artillery and the second, the defensive mines. During May 1896, both boats were again refitted, their boilers lifted and repaired and hulls overhauled.

In 1901 they were integrated into the Commonwealth Naval Force and on 6 November 1902, it was announced that *Acheron* and *Avernus* were to be sold to the Federal Government, the state receiving re-imbursement for their value. The next month *Acheron* was sold for £425, while *Avernus* fetched £502.

Acheron received a new lease of life as Sydney's quarantine boat, before being paid-off in the late 1930s. *Avernus* had a less spectacular ending; she was abandoned on a harbourside beach before finally being sunk for reclamation of land in the 1940s.

Today, nothing but the history remains of New South Wales' first true warships.

Akagi & Kaga Part 1

by Hans Lengerer

Kaga under conversion at Yokosuka Navy Yard.

BfZ

On the opening day of the Washington Conference – 12 November 1921 – the American delegate, Secretary of State Charles Evan Hughes, surprised the delegates with detailed proposals for reducing naval strength. Amongst other things, he suggested a limitation on the total tonnage of aircraft carriers to 80,000 tons for the USA and Britain, and 48,000 tons for Japan. When the problem of the aircraft carrier was discussed on 28 December 1921, the Japanese Navy minister, Vice-Admiral Tomosaburo Kato, came out strongly against the American plan; demanding 81,000 tons as, according to Kato, the defence of Japan required at least three carriers, and these would need to be of the maximum permitted size – 27,000 tons. As Britain was already demanding five carriers, the Japanese delegation's demand was conceded. Article 7 of the Treaty laid down the limits at 81,000 tons (82,296 tonnes) for Japan, and 135,000 tons (137,160 tonnes) each for the USA and Britain.

The treaty defined the aircraft carrier as ship of more than 10,000 tons standard displacement, designed for the particular and exclusive purpose of carrying aircraft, and constructed in such a way that aircraft were able to take off and land on it. In addition, it could not be designed or constructed to carry gun armaments with calibres in excess of 8in (20.3cm), a limit imposed later. Maximum displacement was limited by Article 9 to 27,000 tons standard. However, each nation was allowed two carriers with a maximum standard displacement of 33,000 tons, on condition that the total tonnage limit was not exceeded. Any two ships, which otherwise would have had to be scrapped under the conditions of Article 2, could be used for this purpose, whether already completed or currently under construction. For these ships a maximum gun armament of eight 8in was permitted, while ten 8in were permitted as armament for the carriers below the 27,000-ton limit (Article 10). In each case, AA armaments up to a calibre of 5in (12.7cm) were excluded from restriction.

The principles of Japanese national defence policy had to be altered as a result of the restrictions of the Washington Treaty, American shipbuilding policy and the differences between Japan and America over the extension of military bases in the Pacific (defined in Article 19 of the Washington Treaty). After about three months of negotiations, the defence committee agreed, amongst other things, on a future fleet strength of 9 battleships, 3 aircraft carriers (of

Kaga running trials in 1928, showing clearly the long funnel casing trunked aft to exhaust under the after end of the upper flight deck. The forward 8in turrets and the foremost of the three 8in casemate guns have yet to be fitted.

Courtesy Norman Polmar

27,000 tons standard displacement each), 40 cruisers and 70 submarines; this policy was officially laid down on 28 February 1923. The USA, Russia and China were considered as potential enemies, in that order, and Britain was added to the list later.

AKAGI AND KAGA – SELECTION

In pursuance of Article 9 of the Washington Treaty, the Japanese Navy chose the battlecruisers *Amagi* and *Akagi* for conversion into aircraft carriers of 27,000 tons displacement. Both ships belonged to the 8–8 Fleet Completion Programme *(Hachi hachi kantai kansei keikaku)* of 1920, as battlecruisers No 4 *(Amagi)* and No 5 *(Akagi)*. This programme was aimed at expanding the Navy into an 8–8 Fleet, as laid down in the principles for national defence policy of 29 June 1918, *ie* a fleet consisting of a division of 8 battleships less than 8 years old, and a division of 5 battleships and 4 battlecruisers more than 8 years old.

Amagi had been laid down on 16 December 1920 at Yokosuka Navy Yard, and *Akagi* at Kure Navy Yard on 6 December 1920; both ships were about 40 per cent complete at the time the treaty was signed. On the day before the signing of the Washington Treaty – 5 February 1922 – the Naval authorities ordered construction work on the majority of major warships to be stopped, allowing work to continue on only 18 ships, amongst them the two carriers. The final decision on their construction was not made, however, until after ratification of the Treaty on 17 August 1923.

Initially, both units were included in the new post Washington fleet expansion programme *(Washington Joyaku niyoru kantei seizo shin hoju keikaku)*, together with other ships, the building of which had been proposed as early as July 1922. This programme was accepted in March 1923 during the 46th sitting of the Imperial Assembly (27 December 1922 – 27 March 1923);, and superseded all previous programmes. However, on 1 September 1923, during the great earthquake in the Kanto region, *Amagi* was so severely damaged that she was stricken from the Navy list on 14 April 1924 and assigned for scrap on 12 May 1924. The battleship *Kaga*, designated No 7 in the 8–8

Fleet Programme, was selected as her replacement. *Kaga* had been laid down on 19 July 1920 at the Kobe yard of the Kawasaki Company, and launched on 17 November 1921. On 5 February 1922 the yard received the order to suspend her construction and five months later, on 11 July 1922, the incomplete hull was transferred to the Japanese Navy prior to being moved to the Navy yard at Yokosuka. Orders for the conversion of *Akagi* and *Kaga* were finally given on 19 November 1923 and two days later they were added to the register of aircraft carriers, after *Wakamiya* (1 April 1920), *Shokaku* (3 March 1921) and *Hosho* (13 October 1921).

AKAGI AND KAGA – CONVERSION

Work on *Akagi* was resumed by Kure Navy Yard on 9 November 1923, that is, a few days before the official order. By this time Constructor Captain Kikuo Fujimoto, the leader of the basic planning department in the Navy's design office, had worked out the conversion plans, and Constructor Captain Suzuki was appointed overseer at the shipyard. The carrier was launched on 22 April 1925, and officially commissioned on 25 March 1927, although trials had not been completed; these lasted until November 1927.

Conversion work on *Kaga* began officially on 13 December 1923, but the hull was not, in fact, converted until 1925, as Yokosuka Navy Yard had been damaged, and the conversion plans had not in any case been completed as *Kaga*, being a battleship, was of different dimensions from *Amagi*. The official commissioning, on 31 March 1928, actually marked the commencement of trials, which lasted until the ship joined the Combined Fleet *(Rengo kantai)* on 30 November 1929, during which period she was moved to Sasebo, for some final fitting-out work, on 28 December 1928.

Until this time, Japan's experience in building aircraft carriers was limited to the construction of *Hosho*, which had been commissioned on 27 December 1922. The construction of a carrier three times the size of that ship caused grave difficulties, compounded by the fact that the conversion was from a different class of ship; these problems concerned design as well as construction. For instance, prior to conversion *Akagi* was complete as far as the armour deck. This had to be lowered by one deck, and its thickness reduced from 96mm to 79mm generally and to 57mm over the area between the belt armour and the longitudinal torpedo bulkhead. Therefore, the upper part of the torpedo bulge, and the height of the belt armour and

PARTICULARS OF AKAGI AND KAGA

	Akagi as built	Akagi as modernised	Kaga as built	Kaga as modernised
Builder	Kure NY	Sasebo NY	Kawasaki (Kobe)	Sasebo NY
Laid down	6 December 1920	–	19 July 1920	–
Launched	22 April 1925	–	17 November 1921	–
Conversion begun	19 November 1923	24 October 1935	19 November 1923	25 June 1934
Commissioned	25 March 1927	31 August 1938	31 March 1928	25 June 1935
Standard displacement (tons)	26,900	36,500	26,900	38,200
Trial displacement (tons)	34,364	41,300	33,693	42,541
Length oa (m/ft-in)	261.21/857	260.67/855-3	238.5/782.6	247.65/812-6
Length wl (m/ft-in)	248.95/816-9	250.36/821-5	230/754-7	240.3/788-5
Length pp (m/ft-in)	234.7/770	234.7/770	217.93/715	217.93/715
Beam, max (m/ft-in)	31/101-8	–	31.67/103-11	–
Beam, wl (m/ft-in)	28.96/95	31.32/102-9	29.57/97	32.5/106-7
Draught (m/ft-in)	8.08/26-6	8.71/28.7	7.92/26	9.48/31.1
Hull depth to flight deck (m/ft-in)	29/92.2	28.65/94	29.57/97	29.57/97
Freeboard at trial displacement (m/ft-in)	–	19.46/63-10	–	19.7/64.8
Length of main flight deck (m/ft-in)	190.2/624	249.17/817-6	171.3/562	248.58/815-6
Width of flight deck amidships (m/ft-in)	30.48/100	30.48/100	30.48/100	30.48/100
Width of flight deck forward (m/ft-in)	–	19.00/62.4	–	14.32/47
Width of flight deck aft (m/ft-in)	–	23.77/78	–	30.48/100
Number of hangars	3	3	3	3
Number of lifts	2	3	2	3
Size of forward lift (m/ft-in)	11.8 × 13/ 38-8 × 42-8	11.8 × 16/ 38-8 × 52-6	10.67 × 15.85/ 35 × 52	11.5 × 12/ 37-8 × 39-5
Size of midships lift (m/ft-in)	–	11.8 × 13/ 38-8 × 42-8	–	10.67 × 15.85/ 35 × 52
Size of after lift (m/ft-in)	12.8 × 8.4/ 42 × 27-7	12.8 × 8.4/ 42 × 27-7	12.8 × 9.15/ 42 × 30	12.8 × 9.15/ 42 × 30
Aircraft capacity:				
Fighters	16 Type 3	12 (+4) Type 96	16 Type 3	12 (+3) Type 96
Torpedo bombers	28 Type 13	38 (+16) Type 96	28 Type 13	36 (+9) Type 95
Dive bombers	–	19 (+5) Type 96	–	24 (+6) Type 94
Reconnaisance	16 Type 10	–	16 Type 10	–
Armament:				
20cm Type 3	10 (2×2, 6×1)	6 (6/1)	10 (2×2, 6×1)	10 (10×1)
12cm AA Type 10	12 (6×2)	12 (6×2)	12 (6×2)	–
12.7cm AA Type 89	–	–	–	16 (8×2)
25mm AA Type 96	–	28 (14×2)	–	22 (11×2)
Turbines	Gihon	Gihon	Brown Curtis	Kampon
Boilers	19 Kampon Type B	19 Kampon Type B	12 Kampon Type B	8 Kampon Type B
SHP	131,000	133,000	91,000	127,400
Speeds (kts)	32.5	31.5	27.5	28.34
Fuel (tons)	3900 (oil), 2100 (coal)	5770 (oil)	3600 (oil), 1700 (coal)	7500 (oil)
Endurance (nm/kts)	8000/14	8200/16	8000/14	10,000/15

its supports, had to be altered. The thickness of the side armour plates, which had already been manufactured, was reduced from 254mm to 152mm by re-rolling. Other parts of the ship also had to be remade to a different design.

At this time, aircraft technology had made rapid progress but war experience was scarce – and what was known had not been analysed in full. For these reasons an aircraft carrier of unique form evolved, incorporating original ideas in layout and shape of flight deck, in flight deck equipment, in funnel arrangement and in gun armament. However, this unique design did not prove successful, and a substantial reconstruction became necessary.

AKAGI – FLIGHT DECK ARRANGEMENTS

A new and characteristic feature was *Akagi*'s three-stage flight deck. The top deck, 190.20m long and 30.48m wide, was designed as a take-off and landing deck. Over 40 per cent of its length it sloped down towards the bow, while the after 60 per cent was inclined 1.5° towards the stern relative to the waterline, the intention being to achieve a favourable airflow over the deck for landing aircraft. The middle flight deck, which began immediately forward on the bridge, was only 15m long and hence was so short that the smallest aircraft must have had problems in taking off. The lower flight deck was 55.02m long by 22.86m wide, and was intended as a take-off deck for the larger torpedo aircraft. Although this deck was very short by today's standards, it was adequate for the slow, lightweight aircraft of the time. In fact, it was used later as the take-off deck for fighter aircraft, which normally would have used the middle deck. The arrangement was intended to facilitate simultaneous take-off and landing without obstruction (achieved in modern carriers by the angled flight deck), as well as allowing the rapid launch of aircraft directly from the hangar, without the need to transport the machines via a lift. However, the advantages which the Japanese Navy had hoped to obtain with this design eventually became disadvantages due to the enormous strides in aircraft development made subsequently. With ever heavier machines of higher and higher speed requiring ever longer take-off and landing distances, the three-stage flight deck gradually became less and less practical.

No other Navy can show examples of this arrangement, the only ships in any way comparable being the British carriers *Furious, Courageous* and *Glorious,* (especially *Furious*), although there is no evidence that the two-stage arrangement of these carriers served as model for the Japanese design. Nevertheless, the thinking was very close, and some Japanese writers have interpreted the similarity as evidence of adoption of the British system, with the addition of the middle stage for the take-off of small aircraft to improve the battle strength still further.

Longitudinal arrester gear, of British origin, was adopted for the braking and guidance of landing aircraft. From the middle to the after end of the upper flight deck about 60 steel cables of 12mm diameter, spaced about 15cm apart, were stretched towards the stern over a length of approximately 100m, parallel to the centreline. They could be raised to a height of about 15cm by means of flaps designed to tip forward when lightly struck by aircraft tyres. The landing aircraft's arrester hook, mounted on the undercarriage axle, engaged on these cables, and was guided along them; the friction between the hook and the cables and the resistance of the flaps provided the braking effect. The braking force was very low, and there were many accidents, as it was usually impossible to abort a landing.

The British had fitted the system in *Furious*, and had found it inadequate in practice, despite its theoretical efficiency. The Japanese had already come to the same conclusion with *Hosho*, which possessed the system until her refit of November 1930 to March 1931. At the time *Akagi* was completed, no workable Japanese alternative had been developed, so this ship again featured the longitudinal system, but in 1931 the carrier was fitted with a cross-deck arrester system developed by Shiro Kabaya. The gear consisted of athwartships cables with their ends run around hydraulically controlled brake drums which applied increasing resistance as the arrester hook on the aircraft hauled on the wire. This was later supplanted by the Kure Model 4 type (Kure shiki 4 gata) system, incorporating 12 arrester wires, which was also fitted in *Kaga*. This was in turn replaced by a more advanced arrester gear when the ships were modernised. Hangars were provided on three levels aft and two levels forward, total capacity being 60 aircraft – a remarkably small number considering the size of the vessel. The upper hangar was designated the 'wartime hangar' *(Senji kakunoka)*. The forward aircraft lift, offset to starboard, was 11.8m × 13.0m, and was designed to handle the larger aircraft, while the aft one, 12.8m × 8.4m, was intended for the smaller types.

The ship's command centre was located below the forward end of the upper flight deck, and extended aft as far as the rear wall of the twin 20cm turrets, fitted on each side of the mid-level flight deck.

AKAGI – MACHINERY

One of the greatest design problems of the conversion was how to arrange the funnel uptakes. The swivelling funnels of the *Hosho* had not proved ideal, as the smoke often streamed across the flight deck. The hot gases caused air turbulence, and at times the disturbances were so severe that no aircraft could land. Consequently, a 1/48 scale model of *Akagi* was constructed, with a scale volume of 1:110,600, which underwent extensive testing in the wind tunnel of the Kasumigaura Technical Research Institute *(Gijitsu kenkyo sho)* before the conversion. No suitable solution was found, and as a result the authorities agreed on one large funnel projecting obliquely about 0.4m to starboard, just below the upper flight deck, cranked through an angle of 120° so that its mouth pointed downwards at about this angle, plus one small funnel fitted immediately abaft it, which was routed vertically past the end of the upper flight deck. To accommodate this funnel arrangement, the upper flight deck was offset to port, and consequently the shape of the sponsons for the 12cm AA armament varied.

The upper rear section of the larger funnel's casing (facing to port) was fitted with an opening sealed with a blind cover. This was a safety measure in case damage caused a severe list. If the mouth of the funnel reached the surface of the water, the cover could be raised allowing the exhaust gases to escape directly through the opening. The funnel was also fitted with a cooling system, utilising sea water,

Akagi as completed with flight decks on three levels.

CPL

which was intended to avoid or reduce the turbulence caused by exhaust gases by reducing its temperature. The principle was similar to that used, for example, in the French carrier *Béarn*, in which the exhaust gases were mixed with cold air.

The propulsion system consisted of the original four geared turbine sets planned for the ship as a battlecruiser. Each set consisted of a high-pressure, a low-pressure and a cruising turbine geared to a single shaft. Designed performance was 131,000shp on four shafts producing a speed of 30kts. The turbines weight 311 tons and the gear drive 272 tons, giving a total of 583 tons. The power/weight ratio was 224shp/ton.

Akagi's designed maximum speed as a battlecruiser was 28.5kts but, as her displacement was reduced from 41,200 tons to about 34,000 tons by the conversion, the same machinery naturally produced a higher speed. Hence, on her full power trial (17 June 1927), she reached 32.5kts.

AKAGI – ARMAMENT

Akagi's displacement was officially reported as 26,900 tons but was, in fact, about 29,500 tons. The 2500-ton excess on the Washington limit allowed for the installation of ten 20cm guns, as compared with the eight 20.3cm guns of her US rivals *Saratoga* and *Lexington*. One twin turret was located on each side of the middle flight deck abreast the bridge and three single mountings in casemates along each side aft. It was planned to fit six 12cm guns in the casemates – to be replaced by the 20cm guns in the event of war – but this idea was abandoned before the conversion was completed. The Japanese had aimed at providing a superiority in fire power but the arrangement adopted actually placed them at a disadvantage compared with the US carriers. The Americans had fitted their guns in twin turrets fore and aft of the island structure which allowed all eight guns to fire on the broadside, while the maximum broadside in *Akagi* was five guns.

The installation of 20cm guns in casemates was unique in the Japanese Navy. Until then the secondary armament of battleships and battlecruisers had always consisted of 14cm guns. The gun used was the 20cm/50cal Mod 3 No 1, which had an actual calibre of 20.32cm (8in), and which also formed the main armament of the heavy cruisers of the *Furutaka*, *Aoba* and *Myoko* classes before their conversion. The reasoning behind fitting them in a carrier was that they might be engaged in a gun action with a heavy cruiser. At that time the fitting of heavy surface weapons was considered to be an important component of the ship's combat effectiveness. In fact, such an armament for a carrier is completely illogical because of the vulnerability of the flight installations (hangars, flight deck, aircraft fuel tanks, supply systems) in a gun battle. Nevertheless, virtually all Japanese authors stress that this armament was an impressive feature. In reality it was inappropriate, reflecting the uncertainty prevailing at that time about the use, and design features, of aircraft carriers, further examples being the three-stage flight deck and the funnel arrangement. However, it must be admitted that such armaments had some origin in the political, and even psychological, effects of the Washington Treaty, a fact which is also reflected by the 20.3cm armament of the US carriers.

It was not until the strategic and tactical requirements of the carrier were harmonised, and the technical problems overcome, that a basis for design was developed which took account of the carrier's special features and operational principles. Even then, this could not be exploited immediately for political (Washington and London Treaties) and budgetary reasons. The gap between requirements and technical solutions led to an extensive modernisation some years after completion, during which the external appearance of both ships was completely altered, bringing them into line with the modern carrier configuration.

AKAGI – PROTECTION

The side, horizontal and underwater protection of the original design was adopted virtually unchanged, with the exception of the reduction in belt thickness and the lowering of the armour deck which have already been mentioned. The distribution of the armour can be seen in the accompanying transverse section drawings.

AKAGI AS MODERNISED IN 1938

Drawing by Michael Wünschmann from material supplied by the author

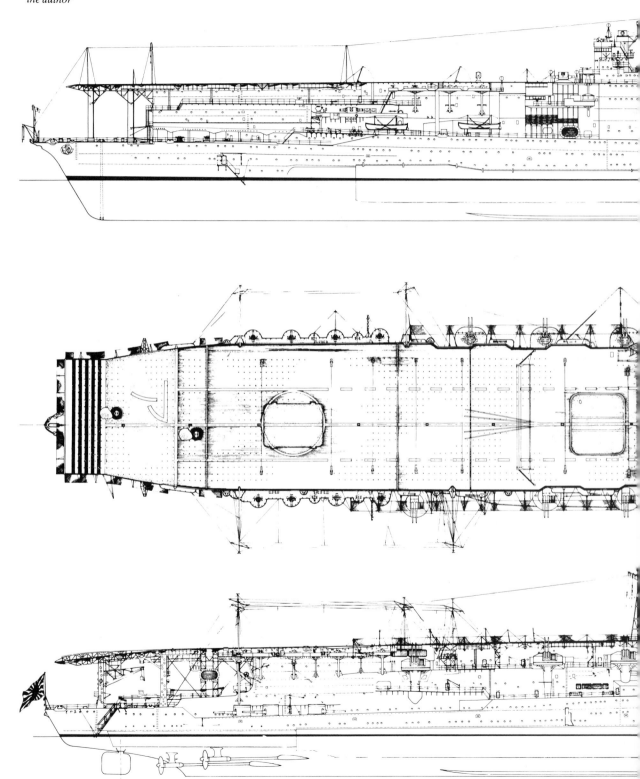

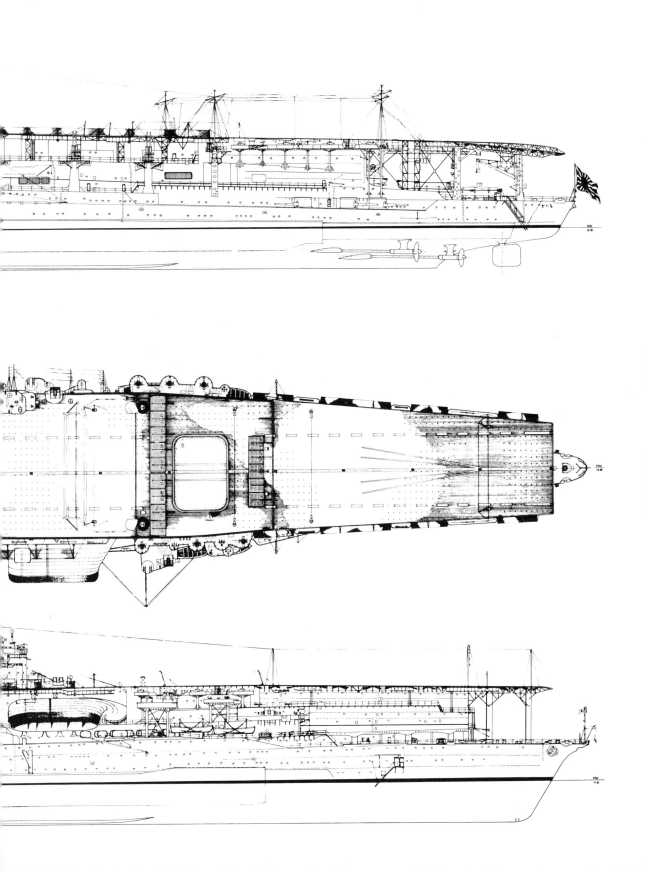

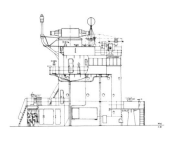
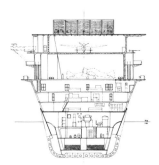
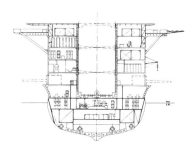

An aerial view of *Kaga* c1930, showing clearly the twin 8in turrets fitted on the middle flight deck, forward.

Courtesy Norman Polmar

KAGA – FLIGHT DECK ARRANGEMENTS

The main features of the conversion were identical to those of *Akagi*, but the *Kaga*, having been designed as a battle-ship, had a shorter but broader hull. The upper flight deck was, therefore, only 171.20m long, despite being extended as far as the stern, and it was level and not sloped towards the stern as in *Akagi*. *Kaga*'s broader hull allowed the lower flight deck to be wider (at 24.38m, compared to 22.86m in *Akagi*), and there were considerable differences in flight deck outline at all levels. The conversion of *Kaga* was begun later than that of *Akagi* and the lifts were enlarged to take account of the trend towards larger aircraft. The arrester system initially fitted was a transverse cable arrangement developed by the French firm of Schneider for the carrier *Béarn*; introduced in 1930 it was known as the Model Fju *(Fju shiki)*.

KAGA – MACHINERY

A major feature differentiating the two carriers was the funnel. On both sides of *Kaga* a broad tube was routed below the upper flight deck almost as far as the stern, where the mouth was directed obliquely downwards and out-wards. This method was chosen by the designers because the wind tunnel experiments had not produced an efficient solution, and hence the ships were to be compared for efficiency of exhaust gas elimination. The arrangement was hotly disputed right from the beginning, and designers such as Yuzuru Hiraga, who had been responsible for the design of Japanese cruisers from the *Yubari* to the *Myoko* class, as

well as many other ships, made very derogatory remarks about it. They were proved absolutely right, as the aim of keeping the hot exhaust gases remote from the flight deck was not achieved and as a result of *Kaga*'s lower speed, the airflow at the stern was disturbed and landing operations obstructed. In addition, the accommodation for the non-commissioned officers and deck officers, which was located beside the funnels along the ship's sides was almost unin-habitable. A further disadvantage, if somewhat less impor-tant, was the greater weight of the *Kaga* arrangement.

The ship was fitted with four sets of Kawasaki Brown-Curtis geared turbines giving 91,000shp on four shafts, for a speed of 26.5kts as a battleship. As a result of the reduc-tion in weight from the original 39,900 tons to 33,693 tons standard, *Kaga* achieved 27.5kts on trials on 15 September 1928.

As in *Akagi*, steam was supplied by type B (Ro) Kampon boilers with a working pressure of $20kg/cm^2$. However, while *Akagi* had 19 boilers (11 large oil-burners and 8 small mixed oil/coal burners), *Kaga* had only 12 boilers (8 oil-burners and 4 mixed oil/coal burners). All boilers operated on saturated steam.

KAGA – ARMAMENT

The armament was the same as that of *Akagi*.

KAGA – PROTECTION

As in the case of *Akagi*, the thickness of the armour deck was reduced, here from 102mm to 38mm, but it was retained at the originally planned level so that the torpedo bulge did not need to be changed. The belt armour was reduced from 280mm to 152mm, and where the bulge met the bottom edge of the belt armour that part of the bulge which projected obliquely outwards was provided with 127mm armour.

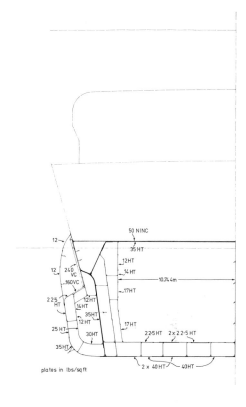

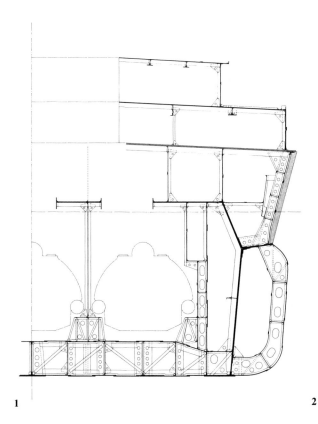

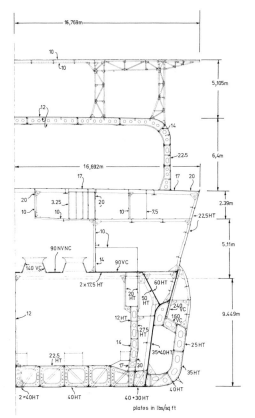

plates in lbs/sq ft

1 Midships section of *Kaga*, showing designed arrangement as a battleship.

All drawings by Jurg Tischhauser from material supplied by the author

2 Midships section of *Akagi*, after modernisation, at frame 198. Plate size given in lbs (40lbs = 1in thickness); HT = high tensile steel, VC = Vickers cemented armour plate.

3 Midships section of *Akagi*, after modernisation, at frame 174.

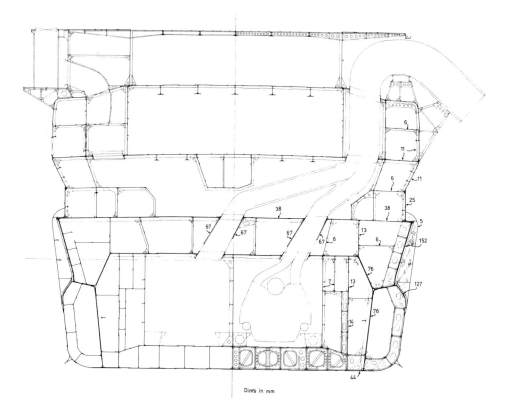

Dim's in mm

Midships section of *Kaga*, after modernisation. Plate thickness in mm.

KAGA – MODERNISATION

Although completed later than *Akagi*, *Kaga* was the first to be modernised, with a view to improving her aircraft handling and stowage arrangements. This was because, with her funnel configuration, low speed and smaller flight deck, she was inferior to *Akagi* and therefore more in need of improvement. Major modernisation had been proposed, and plans drawn up, at an early date but financial restrictions caused several postponements and, although approved in May 1933, work did not begin until 25 June 1934 when she was taken in hand at Sasebo Navy Yard. She completed exactly one year later with the following principal features.

The upper flight deck was extended to 248.58m length to project over both bow and stern and the two lower flight decks removed to allow for extending the two upper hangars forward. A third lift was fitted to serve the new hangars and the lowest hangar, fitted to accommodate reserve aircraft, was also enlarged. The increased hangar area provided for a maximum stowage of 90 aircraft, 72 operational and 18 reserve. The bomb and torpedo lifts were modified so that they could transport their ammunition directly to the flight deck or hangar, whereas previously they had had to be unloaded and reloaded during transit.

During modernisation *Kaga* became the first Japanese carrier to be fitted with the Type 1 arrester system (earlier Types were classified as 'braking' rather than 'arrester' systems – hence the Type 1) developed by the air transport technology office (*Koky gijitsu*). At a later stage this was replaced by the Type 3 system, which has also fitted in *Akagi*.

Kaga as completed
Author's collection

To improve the ship's speed she was fitted with a new propulsion system and new propellers, and the hull was lengthened at the stern by 10.3m to improve the drag coefficient. The new machinery consisted of four sets of Kampon equal-pressure geared turbines (each consisting of one high-pressure, one low-pressure and one cruising turbine geared to a single shaft) and eight Type B (Ro) Kampon oil fired boilers with a working pressure of 22kg/cm² at a steam temperature of 300°C. The boiler rooms were extended forward and subdivided to allow one room per boiler, two groups of four boilers each being provided with one uptake. The two uptakes were led into a single casing and, as in *Akagi*, this was provided with a cooling system and a blind cover. This funnel, referred to as the *Ryujo* type, was similar to that in *Akagi* but of smaller dimensions. The designed speed was 28.5kts with 125,000shp at normal load, and on trials *Kaga* achieved 28.34kts with 127,400shp at a displacement of 42,700 tons. The fuel stowage was modified to 7500 tons oil, providing an increased endurance of 10,000nm at 16kts.

The space on either side of the upper hangar, originally occupied by the funnel ducting, was divided into two decks in order to provide living quarters for the additional air and maintenance crews of the larger aircraft complement.

As the earlier navigating bridge had to make way for the extension of the aircraft hangars, an island superstructure was fitted on the starboard side of the flight deck which provided improved direction for flight operations as well as a better conning position.

The AA armament was improved by replacing the 12cm AA guns with sixteen 12.7cm 40cal Type 89 (1929) AA guns in eight twin mountings (starboard: 2 forward, 2 aft; port: 1 forward, 3 aft), which were fitted in raised sponsons to obtain arcs of fire across the flight deck. For close-range defence 25mm machine guns were fitted in eleven twin mountings which were also located in sponsons. The guns employed were the Type 96 (1936), which had been developed from the Hotchkiss machine gun. There were also six 6.5mm Type 11 (1922) machine guns on board. The complete restructuring of the flight decks necessitated the removal of the twin 20cm turrets and these were replaced by two 20cm in casemates on each side, forward of the casemate guns already fitted.

During the conversion the lessons learned from the capsizing of the torpedo-boat *Tomozuru* on 12 March 1934 were taken into account, and the opportunity was taken to move the centre of gravity as low as possible to increase the level of stability. This was largely achieved by increasing the beam by adding a torpedo bulge above the side armour abreast the upper part of the existing bulge. The conversion was a success and *Kaga* returned to the Fleet as its largest and most powerful carrier.

AKAGI – MODERNISATION
Akagi was also modernised at Sasebo Navy Yard, the conversion lasting from 24 October 1935 until 31 August 1938. Despite the conversion period being virtually three times as long as that for *Kaga*, it was far less extensive, the principal reason for the delay being financial.

As in *Kaga* the three-stage flight deck was replaced by an extended upper flight deck, although in this case the slope towards the stern was retained. Until *Taiho* was commissioned, *Akagi* (which had been sunk in the meantime) possessed the largest flight deck of the Japanese carriers; the conversion of *Shinano* relegated her to third place. The aircraft hangars and aircraft capacity were enlarged, a third lift was installed, and the ammunition transfer and refuelling systems were improved. As modernised she could carry 91 aircraft, 66 operational and 25 in reserve – one more than *Kaga*, although that ship had older aircraft types. To provide sufficient bomb, torpedo and petrol stowage for three full attacks by all aircraft, as well as extended reconnaissance capability, the munition store rooms and aircraft petrol tanks below the armour deck were enlarged.

The original turbines were retained and the only modifications to the machinery were the replacement of the boilers by oil-fired units and the improvement of the ventilation arrangements. However, since the ship's weight had increased, her speed dropped slightly and on the official trial run she achieved only 31.2kts at a displacement of 41,300 tons, with 133,000shp. Her new fuel oil stowage of 5770 tons provided an endurance of 8200nm at 16kts.

The shape of the small funnel, which had previously been angled upwards behind the cranked funnel, was matched to

Kaga c1930. The white rectangle on the upper flight deck is the after lift.

BfZ

that of the large one, and enclosed in the same casing, giving *Akagi* a truly mammoth uptake. A smokescreen system (black smoke) was also fitted.

The equipment for navigation and control of flight operations was assembled in an island bridge but differed from that in *Kaga* in being fitted on the port side and located approximately half way along the ship's length. The Japanese Navy had investigated the ideal arrangement of the island bridge during *Kaga*'s conversion and during the building of *Soryu*, when these ships, both with islands on the starboard side at the forward end of the flight deck, were being planned and built respectively, the Air Armament Office *(Kaigun Koku honbu)* produced a report which claimed that this arrangement had a disadvantageous effect on aircraft taking off. The speed of the aircraft was still comparatively low at this time, and the turbulence which was produced by the island made control more difficult. Consequently it was decided to move the island further aft, to roughly half the ship's length, which automatically necessitated a move to the port side, as the funnel was located to starboard. However, it did have the advantage of balancing the unequal weights of bridge and funnel. A wooden model of the planned bridge was constructed before *Akagi* was converted and fitted in the proposed position for a voyage from Yokosuka to Sasebo. During this run test take-offs and landings were made, and the airflow monitored. From this experiment the air technol-

Akagi as built, note the unique 8in casemate guns.

Author's collection

Kaga prior to modernisation.

Author's collection

ogy office came to the conclusion that the arrangement had advantage, and should be adopted in future. So it was that *Akagi* and *Hiryu* were the only carriers in the world to have their islands placed on the port side of the flight deck.

Naturally the Air Armament Office was not without critics, and pilots who had flown in *Akagi* and *Hiryu* reported severe turbulence and consequent difficulties. By now faster and heavier aircraft were in use, and the take-off distance consequently longer, so the advantages expected by the Air Armament Office were nullified. After heated discussion the pilots eventually prevailed and the Office modified its opinion, deciding that the arrangement of the bridge in *Soryu* was the ideal.

As in *Kaga* the extension of the flight deck necessitated the removal of the 20cm twin turrets, but in this case no additional casemate guns were fitted. Moreover, the original Type 10 (1921) 12cm/45 AA guns, carried in the Type G (G = *Gata*) mountings low down in an ineffective location, were not replaced by the more modern 12.7cm AA weapons. However, 25mm Model 96 machine guns were fitted for close-range AA defence in 14 twin mountings (3 forward and 4 aft on each side.

To be continued

The Bad Weather Flotilla Part 1

by Przemysław Budzbon & Boris Lemachko

Yard No *S 322* during trials. Note the absence of the minesweeping gear, and the open bridge.

All photographs, Boris Lemachko Collection

Work on the first Soviet naval shipbuilding programme began early in 1925, but feasibility studies for submarines and MTBs had already started in 1923. Soviet leaders soon realised that hopes for a large shipbuilding programme, influenced by the 1909 Czarist scheme, had to be abandoned because of both economic and technical restrictions. Soviet war doctrine of that time was based on experiences in the Civil War and regarded the support of land armies as the most important role of the naval forces. Furthermore, the closest possible association between surface and submarine forces as well as cooperation with the naval air force was insisted on.

All these conceptions, together with the material limitations which severely frustrated the Soviet economy at that time, led to the modest five-year programme which was announced by the Revolutionary War Soviet (*Revvoensoviet*). This called for 12 submarines, 18 guard ships, 36 MTBs as well as the completion of 2 cruisers, 4 destroyers and the modernisation of a battleship. This programme was approved by the Soviet of Work and Defence on 26 November 1926 and 64 million roubles were issued for the fiscal year 1926/27 – twice the 1925/26 figure.

DESIGN

The term guard ship (*Storozhevoj Korabl'*) in Russian nomenclature indicates a general purpose patrol and/or escort vessel. After the Civil War about 36 old torpedo-boats were used as guard ships for local patrol work by both the GPU (later known as the NKVD) and the Red Navy. However, owing to the deteriorating conditions of these boats, they were subsequently scrapped or relegated to auxiliary duties and only 11 remained in service by the mid-1920s. Therefore, it was decided to replace them with a new class of craft which could also be used for patrol duties.

The early staff requirements of the new guard ships were issued just as the future naval programme was being discussed by the Soviet naval authorities. The general characteristics of these ships – with the exception of speed – bear a striking resemblance to those of the old torpedo-boats.

TABLE 1: PRELIMINARY CHARACTERISTICS FOR THE GUARD SHIPS

Displacement:	not exceeding 300 tons
Machinery:	2-shaft diesel engines, 6000bhp = 30kts (max)
Armament:	2-4in (2×1), 3-18in TT (1×3), mines

Four 1500bhp high-speed Beardmore diesels were proposed for these ships and it was planned to mass produce 'Chinese copies' of these engines.

The above specifications were passed to the Technical Headquarters of the Naval Forces (Techhead) for preparation of preliminary designs. However, after the production of 10 design variants, the likelihood of obtaining diesel engines from Britain deteriorated as anti-Soviet feeling in that country increased, mainly due to the Soviet financial contribution to British coal miners during the General Strike of 1926. Therefore, the Techhead begun additional studies for a turbine version of the guard ship design. Consultation with the Shipbuilding Trust (*Sudotrest*) was recommended at that time since the design bureau of this organisation, unlike that of the Navy, had recent design experience with the first Soviet mercantile construction. Lack of experienced naval architects was a major problem for Soviet shipbuilding in those years simply because no naval or merchant construction had been ordered in Russia between 1917 and 1924. Only refits and repairs were carried out during this period, so when the question of new construction arose they were in short supply. Numerous naval architects had changed profession, some had emigrated, and others were considered politically suspect and

were not allowed to work. The remainder often lacked experience and were not familiar with current developments.

All the preliminary designs were revised in November 1926 and it was realised that not one of them fulfilled the staff requirements. Two extreme variants (of 650 tons and 300 tons the latter having only 8 tons of load left for the armament) proved that too much was hoped from the 300-ton limit. Therefore, it was decided to prepare one more design for the 350-ton ship powered by 2-shaft 6000shp direct-drive turbines, as the value of gearboxes was only to be learned later. Obviously 30kts would not be possible under these conditions and 28 – 29kts was estimated at best. This variant, despite a lower speed than required previously, was approved and the preliminary design was passed to the *Sudotrest* on 24 November 1926 together with the order for the general ship design and the design of the power plant.

Further design was entrusted to the design bureau of the Shipbuilding Works of A A Zhdanov in Leningrad (Zhdanov Yd) which had been chosen as the lead builder for the type. The yard proposed two design variations – a low (20atm), and a high (35-40atm) steam pressure power-plant – giving deadlines for design completion January and February 1927 respectively. Techhead rejected the high-pressure power-plant, however, and work commenced on the first version only.

When the design progressed, Techhead supplied additional requirements such as the provision of a double bottom, an astern turbine, and a reserve of buoyancy sufficient to float the ship with two compartments flooded.

Shkval in the mid 1930s. Her gun armament still comprised only two 4in, but the bridge was covered with an awning.

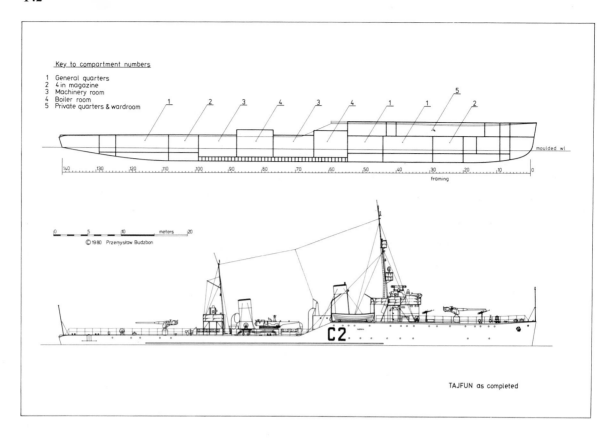

Key to compartment numbers

1 General quarters
2 4 in magazine
3 Machinery room
4 Boiler room
5 Private quarters & wardroom

moulded wl

framing

meters

© 1980 Przemysław Budzbon

TAJFUN as completed

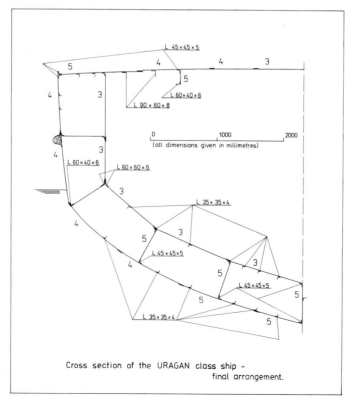

Cross section of the URAGAN class ship -
final arrangement.

L 45×45×5

L 60×40×6

L 90×60×8

0   1000   2000
(all dimensions given in millimetres)

L 60×40×6   L 60×60×6

L 35×35×4

L 45×45×5

L 45×45×5

L 35×35×4

Shkval in the mid 1930s.

Moreover, additional studies were ordered on the following versions of the power-plant:
(i) 3-shaft combined plant with 2-shaft geared turbines plus 1-shaft diesel engine for cruising
(ii) diesel-electric
(iii) diesel

As a result of the above-mentioned and other additions, moulded displacement of the turbine version eventually reached 400 tons. Such radical changes, and the additional design studies, caused considerable delay in the design process. Finally, the turbine version was declared the best it was possible to build in the Soviet Union at that time. Even after this version was presented for approval, the C-in-C of the Naval Forces of the Republic R A Muklevich*, ordered another drastic change to the design, adding a third 4in gun. This requirement was hardly well-timed, as the design process was practically concluded, and it caused unnecessary delay with no significant results whatsoever. Increasing the ordnance by 50 per cent produced stability problems, so it was decided to be satisfied with what had already been achieved. The twelfth version of the general design for the guard ship was finally approved on 23 June 1927 and received the designation *Project No 2*.

PROJECT NO 2

Hull. The single deck steel hull with long forecastle was divided by transverse bulkheads into 14 main watertight compartments which were subdivided into a total of 52 watertight spaces. The power-plant, occupying one-third of the hull, was arranged *en echelon* with alternate boiler and engine rooms, which produced the twin funnelled silhouette. The double bottom of 0.6m depth was carried under the boiler and machinery compartments only.

The riveted hull of typical construction – longitudinal framing between the main gun mounting and transverse framed ends – was built from a steel described by the Russians as 'second category'. The thicknesses of the hull plating were 5mm at the keel and bilges, 4mm at the sides, 5mm for the deck stringer and 3-4mm for the other deck

plating. The main longitudinal framing was of 5mm thickness (keel, floors and deck girders, and the inner bottom plating was 3mm thick. The steel sections used for stiffening and angle connections was of the angle-bar type in the following dimensions (mm): 35 × 35 × 4, 45 × 45 × 5, 60 × 40 × 6, 60 × 60 × 6.

* Ranks abolished after the Revolution were to be restored on 22 September 1935.

TABLE 2: MAIN DIMENSIONS OF THE HULL

Displacement	395m³ (moulded), 450 tons (standard), 530 tons (normal), 619 tons (full load)
Length:	70.0m (pp*), 71.5m (oa)
Beam:	7.1m (moulded), 7.4m (max)
Depth:	3.6m (moulded)
Draught (mean):	1.9m (moulded), 2.6m (max)
Immersion:	3.3m³/cm (moulded)
Coefficients	
Block	0.419
Cylindrical	0.626
Metacentric height:	0.6m

*Equal to the length on designed waterline in British practice.

Machinery. The power-plant consisted of two 3-drum watertube boilers and 2-shaft geared steam turbines. The boilers were placed in 2 separate boiler rooms between frames 54 and 65 and 76½ and 87½. They were to give 20-tons/hour of superheated steam each, at a pressure of 21atm and a temperature of 280°C. Both turbine sets were placed in two separate machinery rooms between frames 65 and 76½ and 87½ and 99. Each turbine set consisted of a high-pressure turbine designed for 8400rpm and a low-pressure turbine designed for 4200rpm. An astern turbine was housed in the casing of the low-pressure turbine, both driving the same shaft. The total power of the turbine sets was designed to be 7500shp; with a propulsive coefficient estimated at $c0.521$ they could achieve up to 29kts maximum at 630rpm. Two 3-bladed bronze propellers were provided, connected to the turbines via two single reduction gearboxes.

The normal oil fuel capacity was 48 tons, which would give an endurance of 700nm at full speed or 1500nm at an economic speded of 14kts. The maximum oil fuel stowage was 160 tons.

The 115v electrical systems was supplied by two 30kW turbo-generators of the type which had been built for the *Novik* class destroyers. One auxiliary 11kW generator was fitted, powered by an Izhora type 20hp kerosene engine. The electric power demand reached 58.4kW under battle conditions.

Armament. Two single 4in/60 old type guns were placed at either end of the superstructure, with the magazine below. Each magazine contained 2000 fixed rounds which were hand supplied to the after mounting while a hoist was installed forward. AA defence was provided by 3 single Vickers 2pdrs and three 0.5in MGs. One triple 18in (referred to usually as 450mm) TT mounting was placed between the funnels. Mine rails for a maximum of 50 mines were provided on the main deck where depth charges could also be stowed. These latter were operated in a very rudimentary fashion – simply by dropping them overboard. Two drop platforms were provided on the counter.

Minesweeping gear was introduced just after the design was finalised and consisted of 2 paravanes of the *K1* type stowed amidships and served by a trawl winch and a jib derrick on the after deck. This equipment was not to be placed aboard before conclusion of the acceptance trials.

Control and Communication. One 2m rangefinder was placed atop the open bridge and a 1m searchlight was sited on the platform abaft the second funnel as well as a small one on the foremast flatform. The wireless equipment occupied the main deckhouse abaft the fore funnel while the antenna were spread between the main and forward masts. The DF equipment was housed in the after part of the bridge.

Crew. The complement, as designed, was c90 officers and men. The general quarters were placed on the upper deck fore and aft while the officers' quarters and wardroom were in the forecastle.

CONSTRUCTION

A total of 18 guard ships was planned but it was decided to build them in series, because of the limitations of Soviet shipbuilding in those years. Series I comprised a group of 6 ships built by the Zhdanov Yd, while Series II was the 2 ships to be built by the Shipbuilding Works of A Marti in Nikolaiev (Marti Yd). The latter yard prepared its own variation of the working design which received the designation *Project No 4*. Laying down of the Series I ships was planned for 13 Aug 1927, for completion of the prototype on 1 August 1929. The Marti Yd planned to lay down its pair on 24 September 1927.

At the beginning of August 1927 the *Sudotrest* was pressed by the Chief of the *Revvoensoviet* K J Voroshilov, to accelerate the above building times. However, an analysis of the possibilities of Soviet industry proved that this demand would be impossible to enforce. In order to deal with orders from the *Sudotrest* other bránces of Soviet industry had to overcome the lack of experienced engineers

and skilled workmen, the deficiency in technology and know-how, and problems caused by the generally low quality of Soviet industrial products.

For the above reasons, large overseas orders were necessary to meet the needs of the warship construction programme. At first it was planned to import tools for the machining of turbine gears and rotor blades as well as stainless steel for their manufacture. Furthermore the need to place orders in Czechoslovakia for castings and forgings for the turbine and other gears soon became evident, and turbine gears for the first pair of guard ships had to be ordered in Germany. As foreign firms were not able to fulfill Soviet orders in the short times required, the incomplete power-plants retarded work on the guard ship programme. Later, when it became apparent that machine tools for toothed parts would not be available until the end of 1929, 8 sets of turbine gears had to be ordered abroad, instead of the 2 originally envisaged.

Construction of the hulls was also late from the very beginning. Just when the prefabrication of the first 3 hulls was begun in the Zhdanov Yd on 13 August 1927, serious omissions and errors were found in the strength analysis of the longitudinal joints of the hull. All work was stopped until the end of November 1927 when the improved version of the hull framing design was issued. Additional angle bars were added in the area of deck stringers, bilges, keel and mid-plating of the inner bottoms, as compared with the original version. Furthermore, all main members of the longitudinal framing were led continuously through all transverse bulkheads. As the *Sudotrest* was unable to solve problems of general vibration with the means available, the Techhead agreed to work out these analyses themselves but left the local vibration problems to the responsibility of the builder. The *Sudotrest* then decided to strengthen the hull joints near all sources of vibration. For examhle, two stringers were added near the shaft brackets as well as plating being thickened in this area.

Besides inaccuracy in the general strength analysis some problems arose in the field of local strength. Controversy between the *Sudotrest* and the Techhead concerning pressure tests on the fuel tanks were not solved until the full scale tests were finished in October 1928.

Work on the above-mentioned hulls was resumed in November 1927 and at that time prefabrication of the remaining 3 hulls of the Series I began.

All these teething problems with the first Soviet naval design slowed down construction considerably, but hull assembly was held up mainly by lack of suitable slipways in the Zhdanov Yd. Construction of 6 slipways was only possible by the end of 1927 and only 3 of them were ready in May 1928 – 9 months after the planned laying down of the prototype ship. It was finally possible to begin the hull assembly of the first 'troika' on 15 May 1928, when keels numbered *S1*, *S2* and *S3* (S for *Stroitelnyj Nomer* ie Building Number) were laid down. These ships were given the names *Uragan*, *Tajfun* and *Smerch* respectively. During May–July 1928 work on the remaining slipways was concluded and the next 3 hulls were laid down on them: *S4* named *Tsiklon*, *S5* named *Vikhr'* and *S6* named *Groza*. The two guard ships laid down in the Marti Yd received the names *Shtorm* and *Shkval*.

Vikhr' c1935.

Purga firing a ceremonial salvo in 1939. Note the 45mm gun forward of her 4in mounting.

Shtorm in a moderate sea in the mid 1930s. Note that almost half her main deck is subject to permanent wetness.

Construction of the hulls proceeded with moderate vigour, with one significant exception – the hull of *Uragan* was erected 'at Stakhanov's tempo' and was thus ready for launching within 10 weeks of keel-laying. Perhaps she was built quickly to gain as much experience as possible. Owing to a lack of experience, excessive safety precautions were provided to guarantee the success of the launching. The thickness of launching grease was doubled and the launching ways were extended for 4m underwater. The slipway was of the broadside type with 4 launching ways of 7° pitch; the launching weight of the ship did not exceed 180 tons.

to be continued

German Naval Radar to 1945 Part 2

by Erwin Sieche

Prinz Eugen at Copenhagen in May 1945 with the tender (ex-*F1*) alongside. She carries the antennas for FuMO 26 on her foretop rangefinder; FuMO 81 *Berlin-S* on her foretopmast head; FuMO 25 on the mainmast; and FuMO 23 on her after rangefinder tower.

IWM

BISMARCK AND TIRPITZ

As the added weight of the radar tower resulted in a critical surplus load on the sensitive bearing engines of the range-finder tower, both these battleships were fitted with enlarged towers, for all three gunnery rangefinders, housing both a FuMO 23 set and the optical equipment. The installation of a fourth mattress antenna on the front of *Bismarck*'s conning tower is the subject of controversy in German literature. The dimensions of the structure appear to indicate that it had two rows of dipoles for active or passive detection, but the clarifying details are obscured in all photographs by a canvas cover.

Tirpitz was re-equipped while she was based in Norway as part of the German standby force. Probably in January 1942 the foretop rangefinder tower was topped with an additional radar tower, carrying a FuMO 27 mattress antenna and a smaller frame, for the *Timor* antennas, above it. The sides and the rear of the radar tower were fitted with *Sumatra* antennas. In about the spring or summer of 1944 *Tirpitz* received an enlarged 3m × 6m mattress antenna, probably for FuMO 26. Careful examination of *Tirpitz* photographs reveals a small frame on a pole on top of the foretop tower, later moved to a bracket on the foremast to avoid interference with the FuMO 26. It is possible that this was either an experimental installation for a FuMO 30 or the later standard frame for the *Palau* dipoles serving a FuMB 6. The addition of a trainable antenna frame to supplement the fixed antennas seems logical, but this would be the only appearance of a FuMO 30 on a German surface unit, it having originally been developed for submarines (see *Warship* 15, p165).

Again in the spring or summer of 1944, the third AA director, fitted just abaft the mainmast (German nickname '*Wackeltopf*') was raised by 2m and equipped with an AA gunnery radar, probably a *Würzburg-C* or *Würzburg-D*. As previously mentioned the *Würzburg* had originally been developed for the *Luftwaffe*, but it was later navalised for

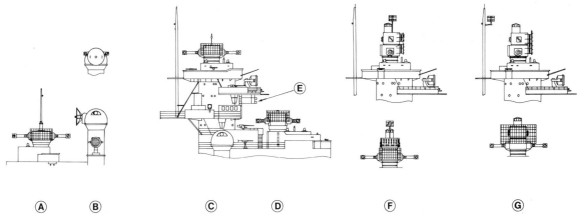

BISMARCK AND TIRPITZ

A The after 10.5m rangefinder tower with FuMO 23 antennas, 1940–12 November 1944 (*Tirpitz*).
B The third 3-D, stabilised AA director with the 3m diameter parabolic dish antenna of FuMO 212 or 213. The base ring of the director was raised 2m in the spring/summer of 1944 (*Tirpitz*).
C Foretop 10.5m rangefinder tower and FuMO 23 antenna, 1940 – January 1942.
D Forward 7m rangefinder tower and FuMO 23 antenna, 1940–12 November 1944 (*Tirpitz*).
E Possible FuMO 21 dipoles in *Bismarck*, no definite proof available for this assumption.
F Foretop rangefinder tower crowned by an additional radar office, with FuMO 27 antenna, and topped by a battle observer's post. On the short pole on the roof of the radar hut is the *Timor* antenna of FuMB 4 *Samos*, January 1942–Spring/Summer 1944.
G Foretop tower and radar hut supporting the large FuMO 26 antenna. FuMO 30 *Hohentwiel* placed on a small bracket on the foremast, Spring/Summer 1944 – 12 November 1944.

All drawings by the author

the German Navy's AA shore batteries under the following designations: FMG 39T/C (later FuSE 62C) *Würzburg-C* became the Navy FuMO 212, and FMG 39T/D (later FuSE 62D) *Würzburg-D* became the Navy FuMO 213. This reveals a fact that has not previously been published: *Tirpitz* had the most sophisticated radar equipment of all the larger German surface units. However, without interviewing the surviving eye-witnesses we cannot know that these sets were not experimental, nor how effective they were under battle conditions. In this connection it would be most interesting to read the British intelligence reports on the ship and to see Torstein Raaby's photographs of her. Torstein Raaby, who became famous after the war as member of Thor Heyerdahl's *Kon Tiki* expedition, was with the Norwegian resistance during the war and for ten months spent much of his time at the top of the church tower in the village of Alta watching the movements of the German capital ships lying in Kaa Fjord. He had a radio set, and a camera with a telephoto lens, and his detailed reports to the British helped to ensure the ultimate destruction of the *Tirpitz*. As far as I know, his photographs have never been published, so where are they now?

Bismarck in September 1940 at Kiel. She carries a rectangular object under the searchlight platform of the bridge tower which has the dimensions of a mattress radar antenna, but it is yet to be established if this is the case.

Author's collection

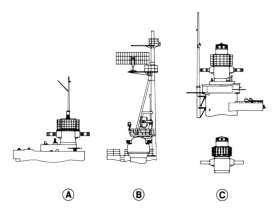

HIPPER AND BLÜCHER

A *Hipper* only: after 7m rangefinder tower with radar office in roof carrying antenna for FuMO 27, end 1941 early 1942 – 3 May 1945.

B *Hipper* only: probably during her last refit (begun February 1945), FuMO 24/25 antennas added on mainmast.

C *Hipper* and *Blücher*: foretop 7m rangefinder with radar office, added in November 1939, for FuMO 22, removed from *Hipper* end 1941/early 1942 and replaced by FuMO 27 on face of radar office and *Timor* frame on rear. Drawing shows latter configuration, with the battle observer's post that was added at the same time. During 1941/42 – May 1945 *Hipper* was probably re-equipped with FuMO 26 and other more modern sets such as FUMO 63 and FuMO 81.

THE HIPPER CLASS

The most modern unit of this class, the short-lived *Blücher*, had her foretop rangefinder tower crowned by an additional radar tower carrying the 2m × 6m mattress of FuMO 22, but no battle-observer's post. *Admiral Hipper* had similar equipment, but probably during her refit of late 1941 to early 1942, she received a battle-observer's post atop the forward radar tower and a *Timor* frame on its rear. The after rangefinder was also topped by a radar tower for a FuMO 27. There are astonishingly few photographs showing this ship after her recommissioning in March 1944, and little information is therefore available on her final radar fit. After February 1945 she docked at the Deutsche Werke, Kiel, where she was scuttled by her crew in May 1945. Two postwar photographs taken during an examination by high ranking British officers immediately after the German capitulation, show that *Admiral Hipper* was to have been equipped with a FuMO 25 similar to *Prinz Eugen* (as detail B), the scaffolding and the central revolving pole being clearly visible. *Prinz Eugen*, which did not commission before August 1940, was, in contrast to *Bismarck*, fitted with enlarged rangefinder towers, one aft and one on the foretop, for FuMO 27 sets with 2m × 4m mattresses. Probably during her refit after the dash, her foretop rangefinder was crowned by an additional radar office, the equipment fitted being in some ways very similar to that of *Tirpitz*: above the 2m × 4m mattress of FuMO 26, below the slightly smaller *Timor* frame, both bearing in the same direction, while passive *Sumatra* antennas, bearing in all four directions, were situated on the screen of the foretop platform. She was, however unique in having a special heightfinder set with an aerial consisting of two rectangular frames which could be switched in elevation. The left one carried the active dipoles, the right the passive 'butterfly' dipoles with vertical polarisation. This may have been an experimental set for air search and/or for AA fire control. It was removed at the same time as *Tirpitz* received her superior *Würzburg*. In her final configuration *Prinz Eugen* carried a huge 3m × 6m mattress for FuMO 26 on the face of her radar tower and an antenna on the foremast for the most sophisticated German set of the war – a FuMO 81 *Berlin-S* panoramic reconnaissance radar working on a wavelength of 6cm. The passive equipment consisted of the standard *Sumatra*, and the cone-shaped FuME 2 *Wespe-G* (2) atop the forward radar tower. It may be assumed that there were also *Bali* dipoles, but these are too small to be

Prinz Eugen in the summer of 1942 at Kiel, with an impressive array of antennas attached to her foretop rangefinder tower. In the centre is the FuMO 26 mattress, below that the *Timor* frame and on each side the 'owl ears' of an experimental height-finding set. Due to the poor quality of the photograph the *Sumatra* dipoles around the foretop screen are not visible.

Author's collection

detected in photographs. From August 1944 the *Prinz Eugen* carried a FuMO 25 (as fitted in destroyers) on her

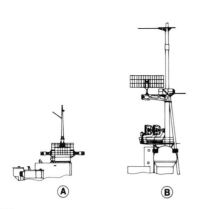

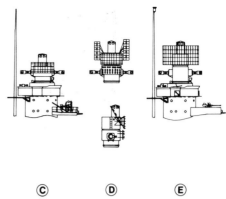

Ⓐ   Ⓑ   Ⓒ   Ⓓ   Ⓔ

PRINZ EUGEN

A After 7m-rangefinder tower with antenna for FuMO 27, August 1940 – May 1945.

B FuMO 25 antenna on mainmast platform (training 35° to 325°). August 1944 – May 1945.

C Foretop 7m-rangefinder tower with antenna for FuMO 27. The hut on the roof is an octagonal battle observer's post, August 1940 – September 1942.

D Foretop tower, enlarged by addition of second level supporting the antenna for the improved FuMO 26 with sided 'owl ears' for height-finding. Lower array is the *Timor* for the FuMB 4 *Samos* set, September 1942 – August 1944.

E Final configuration with FuMO 26 antenna on foretop tower and FuMO 81 *Berlin-S* on foremast head, August 1944 – 1945.

mainmast yardarm. Due to its position, this set could only be used on bearings from 35° to 325°, although it had 360° training.

THE LIGHT CRUISERS

None of the German light cruisers which took part in the assault on Norway had radar. Two of the three 'K' class cruisers were lost in this operation, so the only remaining modern light cruisers were *Köln* and *Nürnberg*, *Leipzig*'s fighting potential having been so reduced by a torpedo hit, that she served as a cadet training ship for the rest of the war as did the obsolete *Emden*. While *Köln* and *Nürnberg* served with the Norwegian stand-by force, they were fitted with a FuMO 21, with 2m × 4m mattress antennas in place

of the forward rangefinder. In the summer of 1944 *Nürnberg* received a large FuMO 25 frame on one of the yardarms of her armoured tower, above that, on a smaller yardarm was a rotating frame carrying two *Palau* dipoles. However, one photograph of *Nürnberg* indicates that earlier she had a FuMO 22 with a 2m × 4m mattress, placed on her prominent forward yardarm. The flanks of the armoured spotting top were surrounded by some five fixed *Sumatra* dipoles which remained in place when the *Palau* frame was installed later, only one *Sumatra*, bearing in the foward direction, being removed. *Leipzig* was similarly equipped after her recommissioning in August 1943, only the form of the large supporting outrigger and the position of the yardarm supporting the *Palau* frame being different. As *Köln* was active until the end of war it may be assumed that she was modified to the same standards, but there are no photographs showing this. As the only remaining active major German surface vessel in the latter stages of the war *Nürnberg* was fitted with a fully trainable FuMO 63 *Hohentwiel-K* on top of her mainmast, which had to be strengthened with tripod legs. In the last phase of the war *Emden* received a FuMO 25 in similar configuration.

The destroyer *Z39* in 1943 during her final fitting-out at the Germaniawerft, Kiel. She shows the typical radar equipment of a Type 1936A-Mob boat up to the end of the war: a FuMO 21 on the bridge and *Sumatra* dipoles around the foremast searchlight platform.

Drüppel

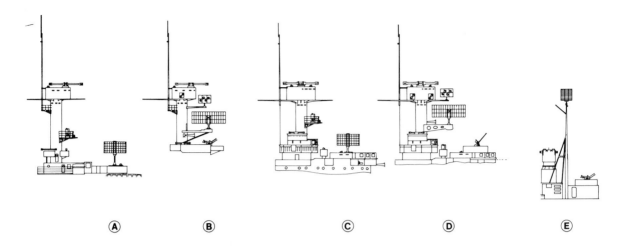

(A) (B) (C) (D) (E)

KÖLN, LEIPZIG AND NÜRNBERG

A *Köln*'s forward rangefinder replaced by FuMO 21 antenna (as fitted in destroyers) in the summer of 1941 or 1942; carried until 30 April 1945? Modification, similar to those in the FuMO 25 of *Leipzig* (B), is possible but uncertain.

B *Leipzig* after recommissioning, 1 August 1943, with the large FuMo 24/25 antenna forward of her bridge tower and a FuMB 6 *Palau* above it. Note the fixed *Sumatra* dipoles on the flanks of the armoured spotting top, summer 1943 – May 1945.

C *Nürnberg* with forward rangefinder replaced by FuMO 21 antenna, summer 1941 – summer 1944.

D *Nürnberg* with a FuMO 24/25 antenna on a *Prinz Eugen*-type bracket, a FuMB 6 *Palau* antenna above and fixed *Sumatra* antennas on the spotting top, summer 1944 – May 1945.

F *Nürnberg*'s mainmast with a FuMO 63 *Hohentwiel-K* at its head and tripod struts added for stiffness, summer 1944 – May 1945.

The French destroyer *Desaix*, ex-German *Paul Jacobi* (Z5), on 23 April 1948. Although the original radar equipment was removed immediately after the war by British examination groups, the distinctive 'goal post' mast, abaft the bridge, remains.
Marius Bar

The torpedo-boat *T20* at Wilhelmshaven probably in January 1946, with another torpedo-boat (possibly *T14*) and the destroyers *Paul Jacobi* (*Z5*) and *Theodor Riedel* (*Z6*) beyond. The torpedo-boats have FuMO 63 *Hohentwiel-K* fore and aft, while *Z5* has the antenna of FuMO 24/25 above her bridge. The original photograph also shows some small passive antennas, not generally visible in contemporary photographs; both torpedo-boats have FuME 3 *Bali* round-dipoles on their topmast heads, FuMB 26 *Tunis* antennas just above the upper yard, and the FuMB 4 *Sumatra* antennas in a cluster about halfway between the bridge and masthead. On the foretopmast head of *Z5* is FuME 2 *Wespe-G* (2).

Marius Bar

OTHER MAJOR UNITS

During extensive refits in the last weeks of the war, the two old pre-dreadnought battleships *Schleswig* and *Schleswig-Holstein* were equipped with radar similar to that in *Nürnberg* and *Leipzig*: a FuMO 25 with a large 2m × 6m mattress on an outrigger, and a smaller training *Palau* frame above.

Most of the larger auxiliaries, such as the tenders of the *Wilhelm Bauer* class, the *Gustav Nachtigal* class and the *Carl Peters* received a standard FuMO 21. The floating AA batteries *Undine*, *Ariadne*, *Niobe* and *Arcona*, built on the hulls of hulked First World War cruisers, were fitted with the AA fire control radars FuMO 212 or 213 *Würzburg-C* or -*D̂*.

DESTROYERS

The radar equipment of German destroyers followed a standard pattern, and only at the end of the war do we find some individual layouts. The first standard equipment was the FuMO 21 (*Zerstörerdrehsaule*) with a 2m × 4m mattress installed above a special radar-office between fore-

mast and bridge. In the earlier types, with their short bridges, the frame could not be trained over its full arc but all German destroyers were in any case limited to this bearing angle by the mast. From the summer of 1943 the improved FuMO 25, with 2m × 6m mattress, was introduced, and was first fitted in the older boats.

To fully train the frame a distinctive 'goal post' mast was developed, the later types having sufficient space around their radar office for this structure. From the summer of 1944 some boats were fitted with a FuMO 63 *Hohentwiel-K* in place of the after searchlight platform, and a FuMB 6 *Palau* on a yardarm of the foremast. The passive equipment consisted of four fixed *Sumatra* dipoles situated either around the forward searchlight sponson, or at the level of the tripod junction. Postwar photographs show the usual variety of small passive antennas – the omni-directional round-dipole of FuMB 3 *Bali*, the conical IFF antenna of FuME 2 *Wespe-G* and the diagonal 9cm dipoles of the FuMB *Tunis* forward of a small cheese-type reflector. The location of these antennas varies, but as they were

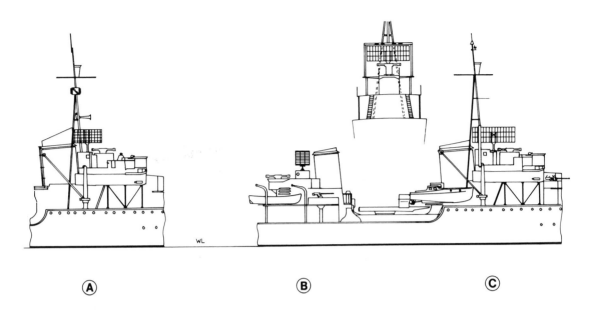

(A)   (B)   (C)

TYPE 1934A DESTROYER, PAUL JACOBI (Z5)

A With FuMO 21 on the bridge (hindered in training by the mast) and four fixed *Sumatra* antennas on the foremast, 1941 – autumn 1943.

B After searchlight platform removed and replaced by radar office and antenna for FuMO 63 *Hohentwiel-K*, mid 1944 – May 1945.

C The distinctive goalpost mast (inset transverse view) for the FuMO 24/25 antenna at the rear of the bridge. At the foremast head is the conical antenna for FuME 2 *Wespe-G* and on the spur below that the round dipole of the *Bali* set, autumn 1943 – May 1945.

small and light they were usually fitted high on the foremast.

A most interesting system was developed for the projected Type 1944 destroyer *Z52*. It consisted of an AA director, similar to US Navy types, fitted with the 1.5 parabolic dish antenna of a FuMO 231 *Euklid*. In the next stage of development, it was planned to switch down the set to 3cm wavelength to become the *Euklid-Z*.

TORPEDO-BOATS

Originally the smaller types of German torpedo-boats had no radar equipment. As the *Zerstörerdrehsaule* FuMO 21 was too heavy for them, some of the 1935 type boats (*T1* – *T12*) and the 1937 type boats (*T13* – *T21*) received a FuMO 28, with fixed mattress; two fixed 2.4m × 3.8m antenna being installed on the tripod foremast. The radar scanned by lobe-switching, but it was obviously an inferior system because, when the FuMO 63 *Hohentwiel-K* became available at the beginning of 1944, the surviving boats were fitted with two of these sets – one on the foremast and one on the mainmast. The same modification was made in the few surviving boats of the old 1923 and 1924 types. The

passive equipment matched the contemporary standard in destroyers.

The larger boats of the 1939 type (*T22* – *T36*) received a FuMO 21, but with limited arcs of training. Two forms of outrigger were employed to support the 2m × 4m mattress antennas of this set. Although this class of ships numbered no less than 15 boats, which served throughout the war, there are surprisingly few photographs of them. One shows that at least one boat had her after searchlight replaced by a FuMO 63 *Hohentwiel-K* as in some of the destroyers.

SMALL UNITS

As Germany was rather late in developing centimetric radar, it was not until the last weeks of the war that a few experimental 'small' sets became available. There is a photograph showing a minesweeper of the 1943 Type (*M801* series) with a FuMO 62 *Hohentwiel-S*.

The German S-boats which mainly operated at night and had to navigate the difficult waters of the Channel, also requested radar sets. As the Luftwaffe replaced their night-fighter FuG 202 *Lichtenstein-B/C* with more modern units, the Navy took over the old sets, as they worked at high frequency, required only small antennas. It was navalised, largely by discarding the high-bearing tube, and redesignated FuMO 71 *Lichtenstein-B/C*. An experimental set was installed aboard an S-Boat and, as the fixed array necessitated training the boat in order to detect a target, a rotating antenna (1.6m × 1.3m) was developed under the designation FuMO 72. However, this increased the silhouette of this particular experimental boat in such a way that it was always sighted first, consequently receiving the nickname 'grenade collector'. Later a *Vorpostenboot*, the *VP1107*, was fitted with an experimental FuMO 72. As with all Luftwaffe sets, but unlike most of the Kriegsmarine sets, the *Lichtenstein* had vertical polarisation. As far as is known, no German S-Boat received an operational radar set.

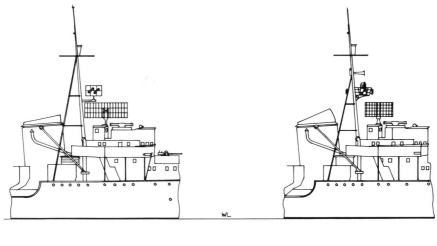

D   E

TYPE 1936A DESTROYER Z25, 1943–45

D FuMO 24/25 radar on bridge with office moved sufficiently to allow full rotation of antenna. The FuMO 24/25 was replaced by a FuMO 21, with a smaller 2m × 4m mattress antenna, in the same position in 1944. The antenna on the foremast spur is the FuMB 6 *Palau* and that on the masthead is the FuMB 3 *Bali*.

1936A Mob TYPE DESTROYER Z38, 1942–45

E Drawing shows the basic FuMO 21 which was carried until the end of the war and the four fixed *Sumatra* antennas fitted around the foremast searchlight platform and on the after edges of the mast struts. Note the differences from the 1936A Type: curved forward funnel cap, height of tripod struts and square forward edge to bridge wing.

SUBMARINES

The whole range of German submarine radar sets, from the first FuMO 29 with fixed dipoles to the FuMO 30 with rotating frame and the FuMO 61 *Hohentwiel-U* have been described in *Warship* 15 (pages 163-165).

CONCLUSION

Although German radar development was very promising in its early stages it was quickly overtaken by allied technology. One major reason for this was that the German Navy, which was the most conservative of the three services, did not realise the full potential of active radar, leaving the Allies in a favourable position to force the pace of the microwave war. The German Navy had decided that radar

A close-up of the bridge of *Z43* in the summer of 1944 showing the mattress antenna of FuMO 24/25 above, her bridge. Also visible are the four fixed *Sumatra* dipoles – around the foremast just above the top of the mast struts.

Wolfgang Harnack

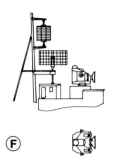

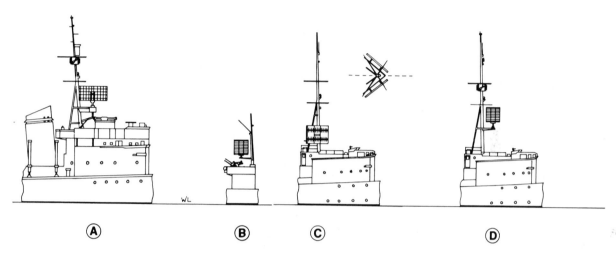

1944 TYPE DESTROYER, Z52

F The uncompleted *Z52* would have had an impressive radar outfit. The gunnery radar FuMO 231 *Euklid* was to be combined with the 3D stabilised bridge director, carrying a 1.5m diameter parabolic dish antenna. The twin 128mm DP gun turrets would have been the first genuine radar controlled armament in a German warship. Other radar equipment is uncertain, the larger antenna having dimensions of 2m × 4m although FuMO 21 was by this time obsolete; the antenna on the foremast was either for a FuMO 63 *Hohentwiel-K* or a FuMB 6 *Palau*.

TORPEDO BOATS

A 1939 Type, *T22-T36*, with FuMO 21 antenna on a foremast spur, four fixed *Sumatra* dipoles under crowsnest and a FuMB 3 *Bali* antenna at the masthead.
B Type 1937, *T13-21*, with a FuMO 31 *Hohentwiel-K* added on the mainmast (from the end of 1944 on). Note the after searchlight replaced by a 2cm quadruple AA mounting.
C Type 1937, *T13-T21*, FuMO 28 with two fixed mattress antennas of 2.4 × 3.8m fitted to foremast (inset plan view of antennas and mast).
D Type 1937, *T13-21*. Some boats of this group received a fully trainable FuMO 63 *Hohentwiel-K* antenna on the foremast during refits from the end of 1944 on; the *Sumatra* and *Bali* antennas remained as in drawing A. The small cheese type antenna, near the top of the mast, could be a FuMO 26.

The large 6m × 2m FuMO 21 antenna of the destroyer *Z39*, taken at Boston Navy Yard on 11 August 1945.

USN, courtesy of Robert F Sumrall

transmissions would provide a source from which an enemy could obtain a 'fix' on a ship's position, in the same way that direction-finders could be used to obtain a 'fix' on the source of a radio transmission. Extensive use of radar was therefore discouraged, a decision reinforced by the German belief in the superiority of their optical equipment. It is significant that young officers were taught absolutely nothing about radar and had to learn from scratch about the complex microwave war while on active service, in conditions where any fault could be fatal. It was not until March 1945 that the German Naval Command issued *Tacitcal order No 10* entitled *Instruction for the use of radar aboard surface units*.

Thus the story of German naval radar in surface units is one of 'too lates'. The other services, especially the Luftwaffe, the Flak (AA) troops and even the coast defence artillery, employed radar skilfully and extensively, while the Navy was tardy in providing information and training in the new technology. Knowledge of high-frequency radio emissions was therefore limited and the quality of the radar aboard German ships depended substantially on the personnel interest of the responsible radio officer. Only a few of these were electronics experts, by virtue of being enthusiastic, and even fewer had good contacts in the electronic industry, thus reducing their chances of improving sets in service. It is not surprising therefore that, under the rough conditions aboard a ship, the sensitive electronic equipment soon deteriorated and became faulty. Many

A view taken on the bridge of *Z43* with the FuMO 24/25 antenna in the background.

Wolfgang Harnack

surface units did not have their radar equipment re-calibrated during the long periods of their careers! Thus sets became so unreliable that the commanders refused to use them – an easy decision, when asked to hold strict radar-silence whenever possible.

To counter the superior Allied radar technology, German surface vessels were fitted with more and more passive sets, the field becoming so extended that a description of the German passive radar-sets, the *Funkmess-Beobachtungsgeraete* or FuMBs has been reserved for a separate article, to appear in a later edition of *Warship*.

SELECTED BIBLIOGRAPHY

Beaver, Paul: *U-Boats in the Atlantic*, Patrick Stephens, Cambridge 1979;
    German Capital Ships, Patrick Stephens, Cambridge 1980;
    E-Boats and Coastal Craft, Patrick Stephens, Cambridge 1981;
    German Destroyers and Escorts, Patrick Stephens, Cambridge 1982.
Bekker, Cajus (pseudonym for Hans Dieter Berenbrok): *Die versunkene Flotte*, Gerhard Stalling, Oldenburg 1969;
    Das große Bildbuch der deutschen Kriegsmarine, Gerhard Stalling, Oldenburg 1972
Breyer, Siegfried/Gerhard Koop: *Von der Emden zur Tirpitz*, 2 volumes, Wehr & Wissen, Bonn 1981
Brown, David: *Tirpitz, the floating Fortress*, Arms & Armour Press, London 1977
Harnack, Wolfgang: *Zerstörer unter deutscher Flagge*, Koehlers, Herford 1978
Herzog, Bodo: *Die deutsche Kriegsmarine im Kampf, eine Dokumentation in Bildern*, Podzun, Dorheim 1969
Herzon, Bodo and Ulrich Elfrath: *Schlachtschiff Bismarck, eine Bericht in Bildern und Dokumenten*, Podzun, Dorheim 1975
Humble, Richard: *Hitler's High Seas Fleet*, Pan/Ballantine, 1971
Jung, Dieter, Arno Abendroth and Norbert Keling: *Anstriche und Tarnanstriche der deutschen Kriegsmarine*, Bernard & Graefe, Munich 1977
Kroschel, Günther and August-Ludwig Evers: *Die deutsche Flotte 1848 — 1945*, Lohse-Eissing, Wilhelmshaven 1974
Mallman-Showell, Jak P: *The German Navy in World War Two*, Arms & Armour Press, London 1979
Prager, Hans Georg: *Panzerschiff Deutschland, schwerer Kreuzer Lützow*, Koehlers, Herford 1981
Thomas, Egbert: *Torpedoboote und Zerstörer*, Gerhard Stalling, Oldenburg 1970
Schmalenbach, Paul: *Kreuzer Prinz Eugen*, Koehlers, Herford 1978
Warship Profiles: *No4 Admiral Graf Spee, No6 Prinz Eugen, No18 Bismarck, No33 Scharnhorst and Gneisenau*

Special books concerning Radar

Bekker, Cajus: *Augen durch Nacht und Nebel, die Radar-Story*, Gerhard Stalling, Oldenburg 1962.
Friedman, Norman: *Naval Radar*, Conway Maritime Press, London, 1981.
Giessler, Helmuth: *Der Marine-Nachrichten und -Ortungsdienst*, Lehmann, München 1971.
Jones, R V: *Most Secret War*, Hamish Hamilton, London 1978.
Niehaus, Werner: *Die Radar-Schlacht*, Motorbuch, Stuttgart 1977.
Price, Alfred: *Instruments of Darkness*, W Kimber & Co, London 1967.

The 4m × 2m antenna of FuMO 21 aboard the torpedo-boat *T35*, taken at Boston Navy Yard in 1945.

USN, courtesy of Robert F Sumrall

The '3-T' Programme Part 1

by Norman Friedman

Although it originated as a supersonic test vehicle for Talos
components, Terrier entered service first. Here, in April 1962
both major components of the fleet air defence system of the time
come together, as the carrier *Constellation* fires a Terrier with
Demon all-weather missile-armed interceptors in the foreground.
The missile is the early wing-controlled configuration.

USN

Although it is often suggested that the United States prefers revolution to evolution in its weapons, the US Navy surface-to-air missile programme must be considered a major exception. A clear line of descent can be traced from the first designs of 1945 through to the Terrier of about a decade later, and the current Standard missile and the coming Aegis/SM-2 system. Indeed, apart from the short-range Sea Sparrow, *all* US Navy anti-aircraft missiles currently in service share a common ancestry; and even the massive Talos, no longer in service, had much in common with the smaller Terrier and Tartar. All of these weapons were initially conceived by the Applied Physics Laboratory (APL) of John Hopkins University, an organisation formed during the Second World War to develop the proximity (VT) fuze under the leadership of Dr Merle A Tuve – whence the 'T' names chosen by APL for Terrier, Talos, Tartar and the abortive Typhon. More than three decades after the beginning of the 'Bumblebee' project for naval surface-to-air weapons, APL continues to have a major influence on US Navy approaches to fleet air defence.

GENESIS
US naval interest in anti-aircraft missiles can be traced back to Bureau of Aeronautic Studies for pilotless drone fighters, but the current series of weapons began with the threat of attack by German stand-off weapons such as the Fritz-1400 guided bomb and the Hs 293 anti-ship bomber-launched missile. By May 1944 the Office of Scientific Research and Development (OSRD) was seeking countermeasures, and the Bureaus of Aeronautics ('Lark') and Ordnance ('Bumblebee') both proposed surface-to-air missile projects in the summer of 1944, well before the beginning of the Japanese Kamikaze threat. Project Bumblebee formally began on 4 December 1944, envisaging a ramjet missile (which ultimately became Talos). By early 1945 the guidance system had been fixed as well: the missile would ride a radar beam directed at the target, and it

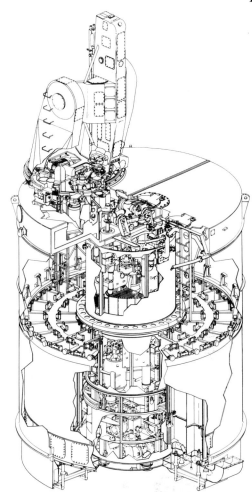

The automatic Mk13 missile launcher

would home semi-actively at the end of its flight. At that time an interim test version and an ultimate combat version were envisaged, only the latter employing terminal homing. Each would carry a 300lb warhead to a range of 10 to 20nm at a speed of Mach 2.

In 1945 the big ramjet missile was a rather ambitious concept, in keeping with a general willingness to accept considerable technological risk in the pursuit of a new era of naval (and other) weapons – a climate which now seems to have departed. In fact, it proved so ambitious that a supersonic rocket-powered test vehicle (STV-3) designed largely to test the control system entered service first as Terrier. On 24 March 1948 an STV made the first successful supersonic beam-riding flight, and in December it was fired successfully from a zero-length launcher. The pre-tactical Talos first flew only in 1950, a true prototype flying in March 1951. By that time the STV/tactical missile programme had been accelerated, and work on a ship to fire what was then called Terrier was already well underway.

MISSILE SHIPS
In retrospect it seems odd that both Talos and its smaller derivative were developed for some considerable time

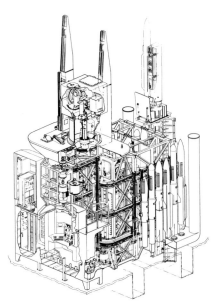

The Mk26 missile launcher

without any definite plans for ships to carry them. There were some tentative studies of missile ships in 1946, amounting to little more than weight and space studies. However, at the same time there was serious consideration of converting the large cruiser *Hawaii* into a missile test ship under the designation SCB 26; she would have carried a combination of ballistic missiles (presumably V-2s), SAMs (the XPM or interim test version of what became Talos) as well as aircraft and air-breathing missiles, the latter to be launched from a catapult set in a short flight deck forward. The *Hawaii* conversion was shelved, but in 1948 there was considerable interest in a cruiser conversion to fire the new small missile.

By that time many in the US Navy considered the bomber-launched stand-off missile the chief future threat to carrier task forces at sea. It had to be conceded that a bomber could approach a fleet in weather too rough for the carrier to launch her own fighters, and that the Soviets, the most probable future enemy, had captured (and would probably improve on) German anti-ship missile technology. In fact, the Soviets by this time had a considerable programme, Komet, and reportedly it was considered so

A tail-controlled Terrier is shown after launch by the missile cruiser *Leahy*, 16 July 1975.

USN

important that Stalin assigned the son of Beria, his security chief, to run it. In bad weather only a very long range anti-aircraft weapon could defend the fleet. Thus the General Board was willing, in 1948, to accept the cost of modifying the cruiser *Wichita*, replacing each of her 8in turrets with a missile launcher, even though the Bureau of Ordnance could not then guarantee a rate of fire of more than one missile every 30 min per launcher. At this time no missile launching system had yet been devised, the Bureau not even being certain as to whether missiles would be stowed vertically or horizontally; no tactical version of the STV test missile yet existed, even on the drawing board. However, it was pursued as a matter of national urgency in parallel with the Army Nike.

The precise reasons for choosing the *Wichita* as a missile platform are not clear at this remove. She was close enough to the later generation of heavy cruisers to embody many of their more useful features, yet not so modern that her withdrawal would deny the Fleet modern gun-cruisers at a time when guns remained important. Several times, larger ships, including the *Hawaii* and some of the battleships, were proposed as alternatives, but they would have been

far more expensive. There was also some fear that the guided missile experiment might fail, and thus a desire to contain its risks. On the other hand, suggestions that a dedicated test ship, such as the *Norton Sound*, be converted instead of a cruiser were rejected: the bomber/missile combination was so potent a threat that the Fleet needed some operational capability as soon as possible, even though that initial capability might be very badly flawed.

CRUISER CONVERSIONS

In fact matters moved far more slowly than had been expected. The *Wichita* was ultimately rejected as too cramped, and a *Baltimore* class hull substituted, several alternative ships being considered before the *Boston* and *Canberra* were chosen. Similarly, early hopes for a double-ended conversion with a total of four of even five launchers were ultimately rejected in favour of a very austere conversion in which the two forward 8in turrets were retained. However, at the same time the efficiency of the missile installation increased very considerably. At first, it appeared that most missiles would be stowed partly or completely disassembled, with only about 12 or 16 in ready-service configuration, out of a total of about 100 weapons per launcher. However, in the *Boston* design all missiles were stowed in ready-service configuration, requiring only the fitting of fins and wings before firing. By leaving this operation until last, the designers could achieve much denser missile stowage, which in turn made possible the elimination of all but ready-service stowage. The Characteristics (staff requirements) for the *Boston* design called for 60 missiles per launcher, but a total of 72 were provided so as to allow for a 20 per cent dud rate. As the cruiser design progressed, Terrier was being credited with a 50 per cent probability of killing a subsonic target (up to 600kts) at a range of up to 20,000yds (10nm) for a salvo of two missiles. Each launcher carried the two-weapon salvo, and it was provided with a single guidance radar (channel) for that salvo, either a redesigned Mk 25 or the new SPQ-5.

Talos was a much larger weapon, requiring more elaborate stowage and handling techniques. On the other hand, by the early 1950s it appeared that it would achieve very great ranges: as of December 1950 it was required to reach targets at up to 50nm and 60,000ft, compared to 10nm and 50,000ft for Terrier. During 1953 and 1954 several sketch designs for new cruisers to carry it were drawn, but there were also studies for *Cleveland* class cruiser conversions. Ultimately the only new cruiser the United States built after 1945 was the nuclear *Long Beach*, as much a demonstration of the reliability of nuclear surface combatants as of the value of Terrier and Talos; all other Talos platforms were conversions. The missile was far too large to be accommodated aboard anything short of a large cruiser, while Terrier could be mounted aboard large destroyers (frigates, DLG, many of which were later designated cruisers) and even a *Gearing* class destroyer, the *Gyatt*. Even conversions of the surviving battleships and large cruisers (CB) were considered. Not only was the missile itself massive, it also required more radar than did the Terrier. Terrier, in its early version, rode a beam, all the way to interception. Talos rode a beam and then switched to semi-active homing at the point of interception. It emp-

loyed an SPG-49 target-tracker and an SPW-2 beam-generator, the target tracker driving the beam through a shipboard computer. This combination permitted the missile to ride the most energy-efficient trajectory towards its target, a feature repeated in the command mid-course guidance system of the SM-2 missile (both Aegis and upgraded Terrier/Tartar versions). In addition, the very long range of the Talos missile requiring target detection at extreme range, eg by means of the immense SPS-2 radar; Terrier could make do with much simpler systems.

MISSILE HANDLING

The Talos missile system actually installed aboard the first three conversions (of *Cleveland* class light cruisers) was reminiscent more of early BuOrd missile studies than of the highly-automated 'Coke machine' system of the *Bostons*. In these early designs, missiles had been stowed and moved horizontally, from components (missile body and booster, stowed separately) through assembly to ready stowage (for 16 weapons per launcher) through finning while hung from

USS *Dewey* was the first US missile frigate; in 1975 she was redesignated a missile destroyer, a measure of the general growth of all ship categories. Her two Terrier launch rails aft were associated with a pair of SPQ-5 beam-rider guidance radars, which were themselves closely related to the SPG-49 tracking radar developed for Talos, indicating how unified the '3-T' programme was. SPQ-5 was later replaced by SPG-55, which was more reliable and which could provide illumination for semi-active homing as well as a guidance beam.

USN

As the cost of new technology began to become evident in the late 1950s, several expedients to provide the fleet with missile air defence at lower cost were examined. One was to save the cost of additional hulls by placing missile launchers on carriers: after all, given the range of the weapon, it did not really matter very much where in the task force it was located. This is the carrier *Constellation*, 17 April 1962; one of her SPG-55 guidance radars is visible, just forward of a missile launcher, on her port after sponson. Terrier was actually installed aboard the *Constellation, Kitty Hawk,* and *America*. It was planned for the nuclear *Enterprise*, but was deleted to save money; more recently it has been replaced by Sea Sparrow, indicating a change in the role of the carrier-launched defensive missile, from contributing to the area defence of the task force to defending the carrier herself against missiles 'leaking' through other defences. To some extent, too, installing Terrier on the carrier limited the carrier's ability to maintain the Combat Air Patrol which is a major part of task force air defence.

USN

overhead rails, to ramming onto the launcher. From a conversion point of view, such systems had the advantage of requiring no structure below the main (weather) deck, although they did consume considerable centerline space. For example, there could be little hope of superimposing Talos launchers, a point emphasised by the number of superimposed guidance radars which would have been required. Nor does it appear that *Cleveland* class hulls could have accommodated a second launching system forward. *Cleveland* class Terrier ships had a similar system, unique among Terrier launcher/loaders in having no ready-service 'rings'.

BuOrd preferred an alternative scheme in which all Talos were stowed assembled (albeit without their fins) and arranged in tiers below deck. An elevator moved them into a finning space above decks from which they could be rammed onto the launch rails. This sytem appears in the Talos design studies of 1953-54 and in early studies of double-ended *Talos* conversions of *Cleveland* class cruisers (SCB 140). It was actually fitted only to the three Talos conversions of heavy cruisers and to the *Long Beach*; it required very considerable rearrangement of a ship's hull.

As for Terrier, only the two earliest conversions had the vertical missile arrangement. It was too expensive for the austere *Cleveland* class conversions and required far too much hull depth for large destroyers. Instead, in the *Gyatt* and later ships, the Terriers (without their fins) were set on large horizontal 'rings' each of which could accommodate 20 (7 in *Gyatt*) missiles. The topmost was in line with an overhead rail which carried to the finning space, after which it could be rammed onto a launch rail. In such a launcher, only the finning was manual, and until later it was not considered a significant limit on firing rate. That is, each guidance radar could handle only one target and, in the beam-riding mode, one missile, so that firing rate was limited by engagement rate rather than by the rate at which the system could place missiles on the launcher. About 1960 BuOrd observed that ASROC missiles could occupy alternate spaces in a Terrier ring launcher, and some versions of the Mk 10 Terrier launching system had three rings, the upper pair of which carried, between them, 20 ASROC. The lower ring fed the upper two as they were exhausted, but it could not accommodate ASROCs. The cruiser *Long Beach* was unique in having four-ring Terrier launchers forward, superimposed.

TARTAR

About 1951 APL began studies for a new missile suited to smaller ships. The next year it began to consider semi-active homing as a replacement for the beam-riding guidance of Terrier, and at the same time adopted tail- rather than wing-control for future versions of that missile. Tail guidance was important because the missile tail was much shorter than the wing, short enough to be folded around a weapon in storage. Terrier still needed finning, since its booster required large fins for stability. However, the combination of tail control, semi-active guidance (which implies a less complex shipboard guidance radar), and a new dual-thrust rocket motor (with initial boost and sustaining thrust in one unit) made possible the development of a single-stage small-ship missile, which became Tartar. Semi-active

guidance was also applied to late models of Terrier, which entered fleet service about 1960; it could not be fully applied to Talos because at the latter's extreme range targets would appear to be so close to the horizon that the missile would not be able to home on them. Single-stage operation with tail control also made possible the design of a highly automated missile launching system, which became Mk 11 (or, in single-arm form, Mk 13). Missiles were stowed vertically around a drum, and relatively little vertical space (compared, say, to the *Boston*'s Mk 4) was needed because they were not finned manually. As a result the firing rate could be greatly increased, from one salvo every 30 seconds to one every 20, to better than one missile per second in the current Mk 13.

By the mid-1950s there was considerable commonality among the '3-T' missiles. For example, the primary Talos guidance radar, the SPG-49, was also the basis for the SPQ-5 Terrier radar, which added a guidance-beam generator to the the basic target-tracking radar. The Terrier airframe was largely duplicated in the Tartar missile, and late semi-active Terriers used the same guidance system as Tartars, although generally they did not use the latter's tracking radar (SPG-51).

IMPROVEMENTS

The new missiles were all improved on a incremental basis, the results being quite spectacular in retrospect. Thus the original wing-controlled Terrier was credited with a range of 10nm. However, within a few years there was a tail-controlled version, Terrier BT-3, using a new end-burning booster which doubled range to about 20nm. The next stage was semi-active homing (Terrier HT series), which reportedly improved kill probability per missile by 30 per cent. Late production Terrier HT-3s had a new sustainer and power supply, which again doubled missile range, to 40nm. They were designated RIM-2F, in a unified Defense Department missile designation series.

Tartar was also subject to considerable evolution. The original missile was effective between 2000 and 15,000yds; however as early as May 1957 there was a requirement for an Improved Tartar effective out to 25,000yds. Two years later the Tartar Reliability Improvement programme (TRIP) projected a range of 25nm, better than that achieved by Terrier HT-3; effective range was usually quoted as 17.5nm. By this time missile range was set more

Talos was the weapon originally envisaged by Project Bumblebee; here two are shown on their launcher aboard the missile cruiser *Little Rock*, November 1960. They lack the four-pronged nose antenna (interferometer) of homing weapons and are therefore probably either unguided training rounds or nuclear (non-homing) rounds. The single nose probe is a static pressure probe. The large lens radars are SPG-49s for target tracking; the small dish below them, SPW-2, projected the guidance beam. Another SPW-2 is hidden by the upper SPG-49. The large diamond-shaped radar is SPS-2, for very long range air-search and monopulse height finding. Missile magazine blast doors are visible behind the launcher.

USN

All three of the '3-T' missiles were to have been replaced by a new Typhon series, the Long Range variant of which (illustrated) was to have had Talos or better performance within Terrier dimensions. It incorporated new ramjet technology. The first prototype is shown at White Sands Missile Range, 23 March 1961, just before firing. Although the missile proved quite successful aerodynamically, the entire Typhon programme failed as a result of over-optimism concerning its massive fire control radar, SPG-59. Aegis is its descendant. *USN*

A Standard Missile, externally identical to a long line of Tartars, is shown being fired from a Mk 26 launcher aboard the test ship *Norton Sound*, 10 October 1973, Note that, in contrast with the launcher configuration to fire ASROC, the forward part of each launch rail is pivoted away from the accelerating missile, for minimum energy loss due to friction. Standard is descended from Tartar through a variety of improvement programmes and also through the abortive Typhon (Medium Range), which used a slightly modified Tartar airframe.

USN

by flight profile than by the potential of the weapon; in the Typhon system a command-guided Tartar airframe was credited with a range as great as 40nm, the guidance system assuring an energy-efficient flight path, with terminal homing near the target. Similar guidance concepts account for much of the very long range of the Aegis system.

Finally, Talos was also greatly improved. It entered service in 1959 with a range of about 50nm, but in 1960 a version with a range of 100nm entered service; this latter range characterised all later Talos variants, the limit presumably being set more by guidance equipment than by the state of missile technology. Talos was already considered a somewhat dated design; in the Typhon programme a radically improved (and Terrier sized) ramjet was credited with a range of 200nm, flying an energy-efficient (command-guided) trajectory.

To be continued

Anatomy of the Ship:

The Aircraft Carrier INTREPID

by John Roberts

Each volume features:
- Full description of the ship, including modifications and appearance changes
- Pictorial section emphasizing close-up and on-board photographs
- Dramatic cover painting with back cover camouflage or colour guide
- Around 300 drawings of virtually every detail of the ship – general arrangements, construction, machinery, superstructure, rig, armament, fittings, boats and aircraft, all with in-depth descriptive keys.

Each volume covers an internationally famous vessel that is also representative of a type – in this case, USS *Intrepid* which was built to one of the most successful aircraft carrier designs of all time, the *Essex* class. The series was launched with *The Battlecruiser Hood* which has already been highly praised for the quality of its drawings.

This exciting new series aims to provide the finest documentation of individual ships ever published. What makes 'Anatomy of the Ship' unique is its complete set of superbly executed line drawings – conventional 3-view plans, perspectives and cut-aways – offering enthusiasts, historians and modelmakers a novel insight into ship design and construction, literally down to the nuts and bolts.

240 × 254mm (9½″ × 10″), landscape, 96 pages, 20 photographs, 300 line drawings. ISBN 0 85177 251 X Published in May 1982. £8.50 (plus £1.50 post and packing when ordering direct).

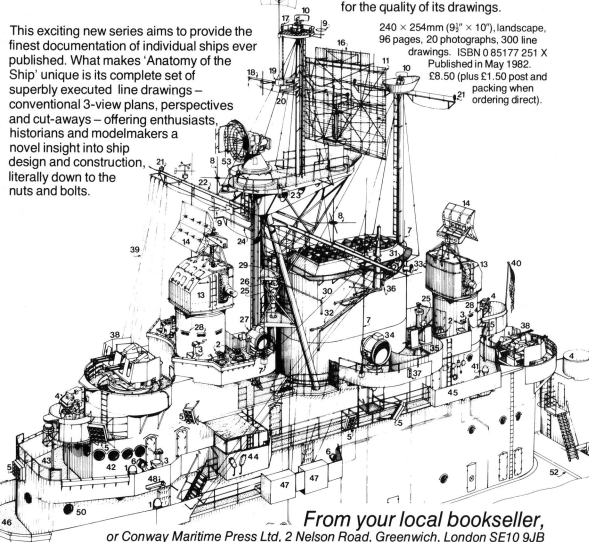

From your local bookseller,
or Conway Maritime Press Ltd, 2 Nelson Road, Greenwich, London SE10 9JB

NAVAL BOOKS

Conway Maritime offer an unrivalled range of authoritative and well-illustrated titles on naval subjects. A free catalogue is available, but some of the leading titles are listed below:

NAVAL RADAR*
by Norman Friedman
The theory, functions and performance of seaborne radar systems explained for the layman. Pictorial catalogue of every major piece of equipment.
11" × 8½", 240 pages, 200 photos, 100 line drawings.
ISBN 0 85177 238 2. £18.00 (plus £2.00 p +p)

THE PACIFIC WAR*
As seen by US Navy Photographers during World War 2
by Larry Sowinski
Nearly 500 of the most spectacular photos of the Pacific campaign, including 16 pages of rare colour shots.
12" × 9¼", 208 pages, 478 photos (38 in full colour).
ISBN 0 85177 217 X. £12.50 (plus £2.00 p +p)

CARRIER AIR POWER
by Norman Friedman
A penetrating analysis of how carrier warfare operates, with extensive data on the ships and their aircraft.
12" × 9", 192 pages, 187 photos, 32 line drawings. ISBN 0 85177 216 1. £12.50 (plus £2.00 p + p)

CAMERA AT SEA 1939–1945*
edited by the staff of *Warship*
"A unique collection of some of the best photographs of World War II at sea" — *Sea Power*
12¼" × 8½", 192 pages, 250 photos, 24 colour plates. ISBN 0 85177 124 6. £12.00 (plus £1.50 p + p)

THE BIG GUN*
Battleship Main Armament 1860-1905
by Peter Hodges
The first fully comprehensive history of capital ship gunmountings, from the first ironclad to the end of the big gun era. Illustrated throughout with the author's detailed plans and drawings.
10" × 8", 144 pages, 74 photos and 86 line drawings.
ISBN 0 85177 144 0.
£9.50 (plus £1.25 p + p)

THE NAVAL AIR WAR 1939-1945
by Nathan Miller
A highly readable account of naval air forces in action, covering the pilots, their aircraft and carriers, and all the major battles.
9" × 6", 236 pages, 170 photos, 3 maps. ISBN 0 85177 201 3. £8.50 (plus £1.25 p + p)

CONWAY'S ALL THE WORLD'S FIGHTING SHIPS 1922-1946
The second in this highly acclaimed series, the 1922-1946 volume covers all significant warships built between the Washington Treaty and the end of the wartime construction programmes. With over 1000 illustrations, it is the ultimate reference book on the navies of World War II.
12¼" × 8½", 464 pages, 506 photos, 530 line drawings. ISBN 0 85177 146 7. £30.00 (plus £2.00 p + p)

CONWAY'S ALL THE WORLD'S FIGHTING SHIPS 1860-1905
The first complete listing of all warships between the first ironclad and the *Dreadnought*. "... must rank with the all-time great naval reference works ..." — *The Navy*. "... all the thoroughness and attention to detail we have come to expect from Conway Maritime ... excellent value". — *Ships Monthly*
12¼" × 8½", 448 pages, 471 photos, 506 line drawings. ISBN 0 85177 133 5. £24.00 (plus £2.00 p + p)

BATTLESHIPS OF THE WORLD 1905-1970
by Siegfried Breyer
A spectacular collection of photographs of all capital ships from the *Dreadnought* onwards. "*Battleships of the World* is a lot of book, and it will certainly enthrall all historians, enthusiasts, modellers and general readers alike." — *Airfix Magazine*
11¾" × 8¼", 400 pages, 557 photos, 32 line drawings. ISBN 0 85177 181 5. £25.00 (plus £2.00 p + p)

DESTROYER WEAPONS OF WORLD WAR 2*
by Peter Hodges and Norman Friedman
A detailed comparison between British and US destroyer weapons, including mountings, directors and electronics. "... one of the greatest possible additions to the ... range of naval books ..." — *The Navy*
9½" × 7¼", 192 pages, 150 photos, 73 line drawings. ISBN 0 85177 137 8. £7.50 (plus £1.25 + p)

BATTLESHIP DESIGN AND DEVELOPMENT 1905-1945
by Norman Friedman
The first layman's guide to the design process and the factors governing the development of capital ships. "... an eye-opening study of an extremely complex business ..." — *Nautical Magazine*
10" × 8", 176 pages, 200 photos, plans and line drawings. ISBN 0 85177 135 1. £8.50 (plus £1.25 p + p)

MODERN WARSHIP DESIGN AND DEVELOPMENT
by Norman Friedman
"... never before have the problems and parameters of modern warship design been set out so comprehensively, informatively and clearly ... the book should be read by everyone with a concern for the modern naval scene, professional or amateur, uniformed or civilian." — *Journal of the Royal United Services Institute*
10" × 8", 192 pages, 167 photos, 65 line drawings. ISBN 0 85177 147 5. £9.50 (plus £1.25 p + p)

AIRCRAFT CARRIERS OF THE US NAVY
by Stefan Terzibaschitsch
"... a definitive history of the US carrier fleet from 1920 until the present day ..." — *Journal of the Institute of Marine Engineers*
11¾" × 8¼", 320 pages, 322 photos, 94 plans and line drawings. ISBN 0 85177 159 9. £15.00 (plus £1.50 p + p)

ESCORT CARRIERS and Aviation Support Ships of the US Navy
by Stefan Terzibaschitsch
The first definitive work on escort carriers and other aviation auxiliaries. Extensive tabular data, career summaries and numerous illustrations.
11¾" × 8¼", 208 pages, 238 photos 38 line drawings. ISBN 0 85177 242 0. £15.00 (plus £1.50 p +p)

*These titles are available in North America from the Naval Institute Press, Annapolis, Md 21402.

Editorial

The warship designs produced by the Admiralty's design organisation – now DG (Ships), formerly the Department of the Director of Naval Construction – have, throughout the history of the Royal Corps of Naval Constructors (RCNC), been subject to criticism. To a certain extent this is to be expected given that any ship design is a balance of requirements which often conflict and which must therefore produce a compromise on which 100 per cent agreement is unlikely. It can, moreover, be helpful in its official application, as part of the designer's function is to take account of the opinions of sea-officers and the heads of the multitude of Admiralty departments both in relation to existing and future designs. However, there has also been much ill-informed criticism, sometimes internal, but more often external from naval commentators (both in contemporary and historical publications) and other sources.

Some of these criticisms are justified but one of the unfortunate results of the analysis of warships is that any imperfections are usually referred to as design errors. This tends to imply a fault by the designer but, in fact, the majority of problems in British warships have been the result of either poor concept (the responsibility of the Board and Staff of the Admiralty), poor equipment (the responsibility of the various technical departments of the Admiralty all of which except ship design, electrical engineering and scientific research were headed by naval officers) and lack of finance (the responsibility of the Government).

Examples are easy to find: the battlecruisers often referred to as bad designs, but in fact the result of poor concept, were exactly what the Admiralty – or more properly Admiral Fisher – asked for. It is after all essential to judge a designer's work on the basis of how well it met its specification not on whether the whole idea was a good one; as described within these pages, the submarine *X1* was a failure largely due to poor concept and inadequate machinery (principally some ex-U-boat diesels!); the 'County' class cruisers were criticised for being too large and inadequately protected (and for having three funnels!) when first generation treaty cruisers of other nations were no better and in many cases worse; the inadequate AA capability of British destroyers in the Second World War – the responsibility of the Department of Naval Ordnance and the result of pre-war Admiralty policy giving priority to surface action, and to limited financial and industrial capacity; the comparatively heavy British machinery and electrical equipment of the Second World War, again the result of limited industrial capacity combined with Admiralty conservatism.

It would not be true to say that the DNC's department had no influence on all these items – the preparation of Staff requirements for example, was carried out in cooperation with the DNC and it was not uncommon for the DNC to press the other technical departments for improvements in equipment – particularly machinery, an area closely integrated with ship design. However, this was largely an advisory role and was usually restricted to areas which directly affected the ship design; with armaments for example the DNC was largely concerned with weight and space requirements, protection and size of magazines, etc and not with the detailed design and performance of guns and mountings.

As the Second World War progressed the DNC's department came under increasing criticism from naval officers, usually as a result of comparisons between British and American ships which appeared to show that the latter achieved much more on a given displacement than the British. However, demands to compare like-with-like, pointing out the advantages gained by the Americans with lightweight machinery and equipment and the fact that many of the features of US ships would not have met the Staff requirements of their British contemporaries seems to have had little effect, largely one suspects because those making the criticism saw these replies as excuses. This attitude seems to have worsened gradually since the war to a point where many naval officers are now openly hostile to the RCNC, a situation reflected in the media where not only ship design but the very existence of the RCNC are being questioned. It would indeed be a black day for the Royal Navy if it lost the RCNC; although it might take a few years to become apparent it would eventually be realised that commercial organisations are no substitute for a specialised professional body.

Oddly enough British warships have improved dramatically since the Second World War, the lessons of that conflict having been applied to produce some superb vessels among which such ships as the *Leander*s (the Dutch variants of whch are discussed in this issue), the *Broadsword*s and *Invincible* stand out. There have of course been vessels of doubtful value, such as the *Blackwood* and *Tribal* class frigates but these result largely from an attempt to produce 'cheap' ships which historically have been vessels of short life and limited capability which cannot by their nature prove anything more than an expedient to produce numbers in place of quality.

The above is no more than a crude generalisation but the future appearance of the first history of the RCNC, written by D K Brown and to be published by Conway Maritime Press in 1983, will with hope go a long way to improve the understanding of the value of the RCNC and the difficulties under which it has operated for the last 100 years, not least the peculiarly British habit of regarding engineers as of a lower order than those in other professions, a situation reflected in their relative status and salary.

John Roberts

Akagi & Kaga Part 2
by Hans Lengerer

Kaga as completed
CPL

AKAGI – PREWAR SERVICE

The *Akagi* was laid down, as battleship No 5 of the 8-8 Fleet Completion Programme of 1920, at Kure Navy yard on 6 December 1920. Construction was interrupted on 5 February 1922 and then resumed on 9 November 1923 after conversion of her design to an aircraft carrier. She was launched on 22 April 1925, and commissioned on 25 March 1927.

On 1 August 1927, the *Akagi* took her place in the Combined Fleet, and shortly after, participated in the main fleet manoeuvres. As early as 1 November 1927 she was classified as a first reserve ship (first class), and exactly one month later Captain Shozaburo Kobayashi assumed command of the carrier. On 1 April 1928 the *Akagi* and *Hosho* formed the First Carrier Division, which was placed under the command of the Combined Fleet. For the fleet manoeuvres one carrier was allotted to the 'blue' (own forces) and one to the 'red' (enemy) fleet, and for the first time in the history of the Imperial Japanese Navy her fleets fought a mock battle using carrier aircraft. After this, the First Carrier Division was disbanded and the *Akagi* returned to her status of first reserve on 10 December 1928, at which time Captain Isoroku Yamamoto (later Commander in Chief of the Combined Fleet) assumed command. On 1 April 1929 the ship again became part of the First Carrier Division, and participated in the Spring manoeuvres – during

which, on 20 April, a storm forced aircraft to make emergency landings in the water off Saishutoshima. The carrier returned to Sasebo on 22 April. Captain Yamamoto was in command of the *Akagi* for not quite twelve months, and on 1 November 1929 the ship received a new commander in Captain Kiyoshi Kitagawa. On the 30th of that month the carrier was again, classified as a first reserve ship, and did not return to her place in the First Carrier Division until 1 December 1930, on which date Captain Hideo Wada assumed control. He was replaced by Captain Jiro Onishi on 28 August 1931, after being struck and injured by a landing aircraft on 18 August. Onishi only remained in command for about two months, Captain Hoshio Shibayama taking over the vessel on 1 November 1931.

Classification as a second reserve ship on 1 December 1931 indicated her preparation for refit, and at Yokosuka Navy Yard, the ventilation equipment and the radio system were overhauled and improved. Exactly one year later the *Akagi* became a first reserve ship again, and from 25 April 1933 resumed her active service by joining the Second Carrier Division and taking part in the Special Fleet Manoeuvres of that year. The vessel joined the First Fleet, First Carrier Division on 20 October 1933; at the same time there was a change in command, Captain Nishizo Tsukahara replacing Captain Shibayama. On 25 November 1934 the carrier joined the Second Fleet, Second Carrier Division and one year later on 15 November 1935 she was reduced to third reserve ship prior to being taken in hand for major modernisation. The work which has already been described (see *Warship* 22) was completed at Sasebo Navy Yard on 31 August 1938. She was reclassified once again as a first reserve ship on 15 November 1938 and one month later rejoined the First Fleet, First Carrier Division at the same time as receiving a new commander, Captain Kimpei Teraoka.

On 30 January 1939 the *Akagi* left Sasebo, and took part in operations off South China until 19 February and after a further change in command on 15 November 1939, when Captain Ryunosuke Kusaka took over the ship, the carrier left Ariake Bay on 26 March 1940 to participate in operations off central China until 2 April. On 5 September 1940 the *Akagi* steamed from Yokosuka to the South Pacific where she supported army operations before returning to Kure on 18 September where she was registered as a special purpose ship (*Tokubetse Ilomokan*) on 15 November 1940. This classification remained in force while the hull and the weapons system were overhauled.

On 25 March 1941 she received her last commander prior to the outbreak of the Second World War, Captain Kiichi Hasegawa. She joined the newly formed First Air Fleet, First Carrier Division as flagship on 10 April 1941. Leaving Saeki on 18 November 1941, she dropped anchor in Tankan (Hitokappu) Bay, the secret assembly point for Vice Admiral Chuichi Nagumo's attack group for Pearl Harbor, on the 22nd.

Kaga before reconstruction. Note the three twin 120mm AA guns on the starboard side.

KAGA – PREWAR SERVICE

Kaga's keel was laid at the Kawasaki AG Yard at Kobe on 19 July 1920, as battleship No 7 of the 8-8 Fleet Completion Programme. Launched on 17 November 1921, the order to cease work on her construction came on 5 February 1922, and her hull was transferred to the Navy on 11 July when she was taken to Yokosuka Navy Yard. Work on her conversion to an aircraft carrier officially began on 13 December 1923 in Yokosuka Navy Yard and was completed on 31 March 1928, at the end of the 1927 budget year, again according to official reports. On the same date the *Kaga* was placed under the command of Captain Giichiro Kawamura at the Navy station of Sasebo, and immediately classified as fourth reserve ship. (Captain Kawamura also received his commission on that data.) In fact, work was by no means complete, and after being reclassified as a third reserve ship on 15 June 1928 and a second reserve ship on 28 December 1928, the *Kaga* was transferred to Sasebo on the latter date where work was resumed, the conditions of the budget being circumvented by including the work under 'repair costs, costs of new equipment and modernisation'. When the ship received her aircraft on 1 November 1929 she was classifed as a first reserve ship, and joined the Combined Fleet, First Carrier Division on 30 November. The carrier left Sasebo on 28 March 1930 and saw service in the Tsingtao district until 3 April. On 1 December 1930 the *Kaga* was once again reclassified as a first reserve ship, and Captain Sekiya Uno assumed command. It was not until exactly one year later that the ship rejoined the Combined Fleet, First Carrier Division, this coinciding with the appointment of a new commander, Captain Jiro Onishi. On 29 January 1932 the *Kaga* left Sasebo and steamed to

Shanghai, on account of the first Shanghai incident, and from 31 January protected the army's landing force. On 5 February her aircraft and the landing troops moved to the Kodai supply base. The fighting ceased on 3 March and on the 22nd the carrier returned to Japan via the Terashima Straits. On 28 November 1932 Captain Goro Hara took over command, but was replaced by Captain Naokuni Nomura on 14 February 1933.

Reclassification as a second reserve ship on 20 October 1933 indicated the commencement of her reconstruction at Sasebo Navy Yard. Although the reconstruction officially lasted from 25 June 1934 to 25 June 1935, the work did in fact begin earlier.

After joining the Second Fleet, Second Carrier Division, the *Kaga* again saw active service from 15 November 1935. After the Lukuch'iao incident of 7 July 1939, at the famous Marco Polo bridge in Peking, the situation in China deteriorated, and on 10 August 1937 the *Kaga* left Japan, under the command of Captain Ayao Inagaki, to escort a convoy to North China via the Straits of Terashima. On 15 August 1937 the carrier arrived at Shanghai, her aircraft flying patrols over the city on the following day. An air attack on Hangchou on 17 August ended with a disaster; the bombers lost contact with their fighter escort, due to the poor weather, and flew on to their target without protection. They were met by Chinese fighters, which shot down 11 of the 12 aircraft involved.

The *Kaga* was ordered back to Japan to embark new type 96 (Claude) fighter aircraft and reached Sasebo on 26 August; after taking the aircraft on board she steamed out the following day. Until 25 September she provided air support for the fighting around Shanghai and, among other things, her aircraft took part in the first aerial attack on Nanking on 18 September, and in the attacks on shipping and army positions along the Yangtse. These operations provided valuable experience in the tactical employment of carrier aircraft.

On 26 September the *Kaga* again steamed into the port of Sasebo for supplies, sailing again on 4 October for South China, via Bako, where she took part in operations until the 24th. She again returned to Sasebo on 27 October, took on supplies and left harbour on 1 November, escorting the landing forces which landed in Hangchow Bay south of Shanghai on 5 November. The carrier returned to Sasebo on 17 November, and left again on 21st for South China where she participated in the offensive around Canton from 24 to 29 November, returning to Sasebo on 2 December. At this point Captain Katsuo Abe assumed command and the carrier left harbour once more on 10 December to take part in air attacks on various targets in South China during 12 December 1937 to 21 January 1938. Four days later the carrier was once more at Sasebo prior to moving to Yokosuka, which she left on 28 February 1938. She headed for South China where, amongst other missions, her aircraft took part in the aerial attacks on Canton and Amoy. From 12 October she was employed in support of the occupation of Canton.

The return to Sasebo on 12 December 1938 was followed on 15 December by reclassification as a second

reserve ship prior to a refit which included new arrester equipment and the modernisation of, and fitting new equipment in the bridge. On 15 November 1939 the carrier was reclassified 'special purpose ship' and the hull and weapons system were overhauled. Exactly one year later the ship returned to active service after joining the Second Fleet, First Carrier Division.

When the First Air Fleet was formed on 10 April 1941 the *Kaga*, together with *Akagi*, joined the First Carrier Division of this unit. From 1 to 14 May 1941 the *Kaga* lay in dock in Sasebo, then steamed to Ariake Bay on 21 June. On 31 June she entered the port of Yokosuka, then moved to Tateyama, leaving on 8 July to return to Ariake Bay, where she arrived on 11 July. On 15 September she received her last Commander in Captain Jisaku Okada.

From 11 to 14 November 1941 the carrier was again in dock at Sasebo Navy yard, prior to moving to Saeki Bay where she took on board 100 torpedoes specially designed for the shallow water of Pearl Harbor, on 17 November. On the 19th she sailed for Tankan Bay, where she arrived on 22 November.

HAWAII OPERATIONS (HAWAI SAKUSEN)

The purpose of the Hawaii operation was to contain the US Pacific Fleet in their supply base at Pearl Harbor, Oahu for about 6 – 12 months. The surprise attack, due to take place about 30 minutes after the declaration of war, was intended to prevent the US Navy interfering with the conquest of south-east Asia and the occupation and fortification of strategic key positions to form a strong defensive ring around the newly won territories.

The attack group sailed from the isolated Tankan Bay under the command of Vice Admiral Chuichi Nagumo on 26 November. The group consisted of 6 aircraft carriers (*Akagi, Kaga, Soryu, Hiryu, Shokaku* and *Zuikaku*) with a total of 441 aircraft (including 54 reserve aircraft), two battleships (*Hiei* and *Kirishima*), two heavy cruisers (*Tone* and *Chikuma*), the light cruiser *Abukuma*, 9 destroyers (*Tanikaze, Urakaze, Hamakaze, Isokaze, Shiranui, Kasumi, Arare, Kagero* and *Akigumo*), 3 submarines (*I19, I21* and *I23*) and 7 tankers and supply vessels (*Kyokuto Maru, Kokuyo Maru, Shinkoku Maru, Toho Maru, Kenyo Maru, Nippon Maru* and *Toei Maru*). The tanker *Akebone Maru*, which was also listed in Vice Admiral Nagumo's command group, and which is usually included by naval historians, did not in fact take part, as alterations to her connections for oil transference were not completed in time.

On the morning of 8 December the ships reached a point on the north route about 230nm to the north of Oahu. Between 01.30 and 01.45 (Tokyo time) 89 B5N2 (Kate), 51 D3A1 (Val) and 43 A6M2 (Zeke, Zero), totalling 183 aircraft, took-off from the carriers, to attack the aircraft and airfields on Oahu and the ships in Pearl Harbor. This first wave reached the target at 03.25.

At 02.45 the second air attack unit began to take-off from a point 200nm from Oahu and, 15 minutes later, there were 54 Kates, 80 Vals and 36 Zeros in the air. Two Vals, from *Soryu* and *Hiryu*, and one Zero, from

Aircraft ranged on the flight deck of *Kaga c*1937.
BfZ

Akagi after reconstruction showing the extended flight deck,
*c*1941.

BfZ

PEARL HARBOR

TABLE 1: NUMBER OF AIRCRAFT CARRIED

Carrier	Zero	Val	Kate	Total	Grand Total
Akagi	18 (3)	18 (3)	27 (3)	63 (9)	135 (18)
Kaga	18 (3)	27 (3)	27 (3)	72 (9)	

Reseve aircraft in Parenthesis

TABLE 2: NUMBER OF AIRCRAFT PARTICIPATING IN ATTACKS

Carrier	Attack Wave	Zero	Val	Kate	Total	Grand Total	Grand Total Per Attack
Akagi	1st	9	–	27	36	63	71 (1st wave)
Akagi	2nd	9	18	–	27		
Kaga	1st	9	–	26	35	70	62 (2nd wave)
Kaga	2nd	9	26	–	35		

TABLE 3: ORGANISATION OF AIR ATTACK UNITS

Attack Wave	Leader	Aircraft	Carrier	Weapons	Target According to Order of Attack
1st	Cdr Mitsuo Fuchida	15 Kates	*Akagi*	1 800kg AP bomb Type 99 No 5	Battleships
1st	Lt Cdr Takashi Hashiguchi	14 Kates	*Kaga*	1 800kg AP bomb Type 99 No 5	Battleships and Carriers
1st	Lt Cdr Shigeharv Murata	12 Kates	*Akagi*	1 Type 91 torpedo	Battleships and Carriers
1st	Lt Kazuyoshi Kitajima	12 Kates	*Kaga*	1 Type 91 torpedo	Battleships and Carriers
1st	Lt Cdr Shigeru Haya	9 Zeros	*Akagi*	2-20mm, 2-7.7mm MG	Hickam Field, Ewa, Wheeler Field
1st	Lt Yoshio Shiga	9 Zeros	*Kaga*	2-20mm, 2-7.7mm MG	Aircraft in the air and on the ground
2nd	Lt Takehiko Chihaya	18 Vals	*Akagi*	1 250kg GP bomb	Hickam Field, Ewa, Kaneohe
2nd	Lt Saburō Makino	26 Vals	*Kaga*	1 250kg GP bomb	Ford Island
2nd	Lt Saburō Shindō	9 Zeros	*Akagi*	2-20mm, 2-7.7mm MG	Hickam Field, Ewa, Wheeler Field, Kaneohe
2nd	Lt Yasushi Nikaido	9 Zeros	*Kaga*	2-20mm, 2-7.7mm MG	Aircraft in the air and on the ground

Note: Fuchida was overall commander

TABLE 4: AIRCRAFT LOSSES

Carrier	Attack Wave	Zero	Val	Kate (bomb)	Kate (torpedo)	Total	Grand Total
Akagi	1st	1	–	–	–	1	5
Akagi	2nd	–	4	–	–	4	
Kaga	1st	2	–	–	5	7	15
Kaga	2nd	2	6	–	–	8	

Note: Total losses were 29 (*Soryu* 5, *Hiryu* 3, *Shokaku* 1)

TABLE 5: NUMBER OF AIRCRAFT DAMAGED IN ATTACKS

Carrier	Attack Wave	Zero	Val	Kate (bomb)	Kate (torpedo)	Total	Grand Total
Akagi	1st	3	–	3	4	10	23
Akagi	2nd	1	12	–	–	13	
Kaga	1st	2	–	2	5	9	28
Kaga	2nd	3	16	–	–	19	

Note: At least 109 aircraft damaged in all carriers (*Soryu* 22, *Shokaku/Zuikaku* 37, *Hiryu* ?)

TABLE 6: US AIRCRAFT LOSSES IN ATTACKS ON AIRFIELDS, OFFICIALLY CREDITED TO AKAGI AND KAGA

Carrier	Attack Wave	Ford Island	Hickam Field	Wheeler Field	Ewa	Kaneohe	Bellows Field	Shot Down	Total
Akagi	1st	–	8	–	11	–	–	3	22
Akagi	2nd	1	2	–	–	–	–	1	4
Kaga	1st	–	7	–	15	–	–	1	23
Kaga	2nd	1	–	1	2	–	–	2	6

A view down *Kaga*'s starboard side on 11 May 1937 with, in the foreground, an AA director, one of her twin 25mm AA mountings and the downward angled funnel. In the background can be seen one of her wireless masts, partly lowered, and one of the twin 127mm gun mountings.

Hiryu, had to turn back because of engine trouble, leaving 167 aircraft in the second wave, which reached the target at 04.32 (Details are given in Tables 1 – 7).

On 24 December 1941 *Akagi* returned undamaged to the western Inland Sea, which she left on 8 January 1942 for Truk, where the carrier dropped anchor on 14th.

TABLE 7: RESULTS OF THE ATTACKS ON SHIPS CREDITED TO AKAGI AND KAGA

Target	Hits
Nevada (BB 36)	1 torpedo (*Kaga*), more than 6 250kg bombs (*Kaga*)
Oklahoma (BB 37)	4 torpedoes (*Kaga*), 6 torpedoes (*Akagi*)
Arizona (BB 39)	2 800kg AP bombs (*Kaga*)
California (BB 44)	2 torpedoes (*Kaga*)
West Virginia (BB 48)	4 torpedoes (*Kaga*), 3 torpedoes (*Akagi*)
Maryland (BB 46)*	2 250kg bombs (*Kaga*), 5 250kg bombs (*Akagi*)
Raleigh (CL 7)	1 250kg bomb (*Akagi*)
Shaw (DD 373)	2 250kg bombs (*Akagi*)

*Only one 250kg bomb hit confirmed by US sources. It is probable that a near miss was judged as a hit.

The *Kaga* anchored at Hashirajima, the Combined Fleet's anchorage in the Inland Sea, on 23 December 1941, shortly afterwards she moved to Kure and then sailed for Truk on 9 January 1942, where she arrived one day later than *Akagi*.

RABAUL AND KAVIENG

Vice Admiral Nagumo's ships were assembled at Truk to take part in the R-operation (operations off the Bismarck Archipelago, in particular the capture of Rabaul and Kavieng) as a distant support group. Rabaul and Kavieng were key positions in the southern section of the defensive ring – against Australia and for blocking a push by General MacArthur's armies in the direction of the Philippines.

The group consisted of the same ships which had taken part in the Hawaii operation, with the exception of the Second Carrier Division (*Hiryu* and *Soryu*) the patrol group (*I19*, *I21* and *I23*) and an altered supply group (*Kyokuto Maru*, *Shinkoku Maru*, *Nichiro Maru*, *No 2 Nyoei Maru* and *Hoko Maru*). The units left Truk at 07.30 on 17 January 1942 and reached the starting point for the first aerial attack at 05.00 on 20 January. The start was postponed until 10.00 hours because of heavy rain, and at that time a total of 109 aircraft (47 Kates, 38 Vals and 24 Zeros) took off from the four aircraft carriers. The aircraft found few targets; the 7 defending

Wirraway fighters (an eighth aircraft crashed on take-off) were either shot down or had to make emergency landings, and only one aircraft escaped undamaged in the clouds. The Vals of the *Shokaku* had the greatest success in finding and sinking the Norwegian freighter *Herstein*. One Kate from the *Kaga* was shot down by AA fire, and one Val from the *Shokaku* had to make an emergency landing on the return flight.

After the attack on Kavieng was called off at 10.30, Vice Admiral Nagumo reassembled his group, and the Fifth Carrier Division (*Shokaku* and *Zuikaku*) separated from the main group. Their aircraft attacked Lae, Salamaue, Madang and Bulolo on the following day.

On 21 January, aircraft from *Akagi* and *Kaga* attacked Kavieng, which ended with similarly disappointing results to the attack on Rabaul; all aircraft returned. Rabaul was attacked again on the following day: the Vals bombarded Praed Point and put the coast battery out of action (two 15.5cm guns), while *Akagi*'s Zeros attacked Vanakanau airfield and *Kaga*'s Zeros attacked Lakunai airfield. Two of *Kaga*'s Vals had to make emergency landings but the crews were rescued. On 23 January 3 Vals and 3 Zeros from each of the four carriers flew aerial support missions over the landing areas but met no opposition, and all aircraft landed undamaged.

TABLE 8: ORGANISATION OF AIR ATTACK UNITS FOR ATTACK ON RABAUL (20 January 1941)

Leader	Aircraft	Carrier	Losses
Cdr Mitsuo Fuchida	20 Kates	*Akagi*	–
Lt Ayao Shirane	9 Zeros	*Akagi*	–
Lt Cdr Takashi Hashiguchi	27 Kates	*Kaga*	1
Lt Yoshio Shiga	9 Zeros	*Kaga*	

Note: Fuchida was overall commander

TABLE 9: ORGANISATION OF AIR ATTACK UNITS FOR ATTACK ON KAVIENG

Leader	Aircraft	Carrier	Losses
Lt Takehiko Chihaya	18 Vals	*Akagi*	–
Lt Masanobu Jbusuki	9 Zeros	*Akagi*	–
Lt Shoichi Ogawa	16 Vals	*Kaga*	–
Lt Yashushi Nikaido	9 Zeros	*Kaga*	–

Note: Chihaya was overall commander

TABLE 10: ORGANISATION OF AIR ATTACK UNITS FOR ATTACK ON RABAUL (22 January 1941)

Leader	Aircraft	Carrier	Losses
Lt Cdr Shigeharu Murata	18 Vals	*Akagi*	–
Lt Ayao Shirane	6 Zeros	*Akagi*	–
Lt Shoichi Ogawa	16 Vals	*Kaga*	2
Lt Yashushi Nikaido	6 Zeros	*Kaga*	–

The *Kaga* dropped anchor at Truk on 25 January, the *Akagi* on the 27th and, two days later, *Shokaku* and *Zuikaku*. The *Shokaku* returned to Japan the same day, while the *Zuikaku* remained with Vice Admiral Nagumo's group. (Details of the air attack units can be found in tables 8 – 10.)

OPERATIONS AGAINST THE US CARRIERS

At Truk Vice Admiral Nagumo's ships prepared to leave for Staring Bay (Celebes), to support operations in the South-West Pacific. However, on 1 February American naval forces bombed and shelled several islands in the Marshall and Gilbert groups, these forces including the aircraft carriers *Enterprise* and *Yorktown*. This being the first definite intelligence of the whereabouts of the US carriers, Vice Admiral Nagumo decided to cancel the departure for the Celebes and attempt a surprise interception of the American group off the Marshall Islands, about 1200nm distant from Truk. Steaming eastward at speed the Nagumo force consisted of the carriers *Akagi*, *Kaga* and *Zuikaku*, the battleships *Hiei* and *Kirishima*, the heavy cruisers *Tone* and *Chikuma*, the light cruiser *Abukuma* and the destroyers *Urakaze*, *Isokaze*, *Tanikaze*, *Hamakaze*, *Kasumi*, *Arare*, *Kagero*, *Shiranui* and *Akigumo*. His carriers had 180 aircraft aboard, which he believed would give him superiority over the US carriers but at 23.20 on 2 February, when his group was in position 8°N, 162°36'E, he received orders from the Combined Fleet to return. At 03.05 on the 3rd he turned 270° and retraced his course at 16kts to the West, arriving at Palau on the 8th. On the following day *Zuikaku* left the group and returned to Yokosuka to protect the motherland.

While engaged in changing her anchorage on 9 February *Kaga* struck an uncharted reef and although facilities at Palau were inadequate and only allowed for temporary repairs, she was patched-up sufficiently to take part in the operation against Port Darwin.

THE AIR RAID ON PORT DARWIN

After the conquest of Kendari on 24 January 1942 air attacks on the southern part of the Dutch East Indies became possible. The naval and air forces of the USA, Britain and Holland had been pushed back to Java, a major target for the Japanese, and Port Darwin, in the North-West of Australia, quickly assumed importance as the rear supply base and reception port for the retreating ABDA groups. From Darwin the invasion of Java could be disrupted by air and naval forces and the Japanese determined to eliminate its port and airfield facilities by a suprise air attack, similar to that on Pearl Harbor. It was also hoped that it would serve to demoralise the Australians. The occupation of Port Darwin was

TABLE 11: ORGANISATION OF AIR ATTACK UNITS FOR ATTACK ON PORT DARWIN

Leader	Aircraft	Carrier	Losses	Total
Cdr Mitsuo Fuchida	18 Kates	*Akagi*	–	
Lt Takehiko Chihaya	18 Vals	*Akagi*	–	45
Lt Cdr Shigeru Itaya	9 Zeros	*Akagi*	–	
Lt Takashi Hashiguchi	27 Kates	*Kaga*	1	
L Shoichi Ogawa	18 Vals	*Kaga*	–	54
Lt Yoisushi Nikaido	9 Zeros	*Kaga*	–	

also considered but had been turned down by Imperial headquarters.

At 24.00 on 7 February Admiral Yamamoto ordered Nagumo to join the southern area fleet and at 14.00 on 15 February the group, consisting of the carriers *Akagi, Kaga, Hiryu* and *Soryu*, the cruisers *Tone* and *Chikuma* and the first destroyer squadron with light cruiser *Abukuma* and the destroyers *Tanikaze, Urakaze, Isok-aze, Hamakaze, Kasumi, Shiranui* and *Ariake* sailed from Davao. They steamed westwards from Halmahere through the Straits of Manipa into the Sunda Sea until, at 06.20 on the 19th, the carriers were about 240nm NNW of Port Darwin. Here a total of 188 aircraft were launched by the carriers (81 Kates, 71 Vals and 36 Zeros) which, after assembly, flew off in the direction of Port Darwin at 07.00, under the command of Commander Mitsuo Fuchida. The aircraft reformed at 07.45 over the island of Melville, the fighter protection taking the lead, and at 08.10 Fuchida gave the order to attack. Between 08.20 and 09.20 the aircraft attacked ships, airfields and other military installations in and around Darwin, taking the town and its defences by surprise. The harbour was full of ships. Eight of them, including the American freighter *Meigs* of 12,596 tons, the British tanker *British Motorist* of 6891 tons and the US destroyer *Peary*, were sunk, 14 more were severely damaged, 23 aircraft, including 10 American Kittyhawk fighters intended for the defence of Timor, were shot down or destroyed on the ground, while 2 more were damaged. The landing strips and hangars of the sur-rounding airfields were destroyed by land-based bombers from Kendari and Ambon, which attacked at the same time. Shelling from the sea set fire to the wooden houses, and the local people, fearing an invasion, left the town for several days. Port Darwin was thus eliminated as a supply base for Java, Timor and Bali.

The Japanese aircraft returned to their carriers and landed between 10.40 and 11.40. The attack cost only one Kate from the *Kaga*, and one Zero from the *Hiryu* which was forced to make an emergency landing on Melville island. The group retreated to the north-west and at 13.06 *Soryu* and *Hiryu* each launched 9 Vals to attack a camouflaged cruiser which had been sighted near Cape Foureroy (Bathurst) by aircraft returning to the *Akagi*. The aircraft saw two ships at 14.56 at 290°, 32nm off Cape Foureroy. They attacked at 15.12 and sank the vessels, which were claimed to be a cruiser and a merchant ship of 1000 tons. In reality they were the American freighters *Don Isidro* and *Florence D*. The Vals landed on their carriers at 17.00, one of them being damaged. The group continued to the north-west and reached Staring Bay at 10.45 on 21 December. (Details of the air attack units are given in Table 11.)

To be continued

The starboard quarter of *Kaga* as built.

Warship Wings No. 2
The Lockheed S-3A Viking

by Roger Chesneau

First flown on 21 January 1972 and entering service on 20 February 1974, the S-3 Viking is the current US Navy fixed-wing anti-submarine aircraft. It is a complete ASW package, equipped with computerised surface and sub-surface search technology and also with the weapons to deal with the threat once identified. Successor to the piston-engined S-2 Tracker, the Viking is turbofan-powered, giving a dash speed capability which its predecessor did not possess, enabling it to close a threat more rapidly and to make better use of its long-range, wide-angle detection equipment.

PROCUREMENT

The acquisition of the S-3 for the US Navy is a saga in itself and contrasts interestingly with the procedures that led to the adoption of the Fairey Albacore for the Fleet Air Arm (see *Warship* 21). The project (VSX Program) was submitted just at the time when taxing questions were streaming out from various hostile sources about the cost-effectiveness of the ASW carrier (CVS); it will be remembered that in 1967, when the VSX Request for Proposals was first issued by the USN, ASW was conducted by these specialised carriers. Three factors ensured that the Navy got its way: vigorous support from Secretary of Defense Melvin Laird; a realisation that ASW prosecution solely by means of land-based Navy aircraft would leave significant 'holes' in the ocean surveillance net; and the arrival of the 'CV Concept', which envisaged the carriage of ASW aircraft on board multi-role vessels (CVs), rubbing shoulders with strike and fleet air defence (FAD) types.

Competition among several leading US manufacturers to gain the VSX contract was intense, though of course, owing to costs, the contests these days are generally for design work only. Lockheed, in collaboration with Ling-Temco-Vought, were pronounced the winners in August 1969, and began work on 8 pre-production machines; 13 production aircraft were authorised in April 1972, and Board of Inspection and Survey (BIS) trials were successfully concluded some two years later. Production of 187 S-3As for the US Navy is now complete (twelve squadrons are equipped), but a Weapons System Improvement Program, including modification of the aircraft to deploy the Harpoon ASM, is now underway.

DESIGN CONSIDERATIONS

The CV Concept[1] is central to the design of the S-3A. Firstly, its turbofan (GE TF-34-400A) powerplants give it fuel commonality with other elements deployed on board fleet carriers, thereby simplifying fuel stowage problems. Turbofans are a comparatively recent innovation, and make for economical consumption whilst still permitting high maximum speeds. Secondly, deck and hangar space utilisation has to be kept to an absolute minimum to lessen the impact on total numbers of aircraft embarked.

Elsewhere, the interplay of the various factors involved in the Viking's design give a fascinating glimpse of the complexities of modern aircraft construction. The main requirements are: long range; high airframe capacity, not only for maximum fuel stowage but also for the many systems required for the collection, storage and processing of ASW data, for an effective complement of weapons and stores, for maximum sonobuoy stowage, for the four crew members called for by the S-3s mission, and for radar and other sensors; and, finally, the traditional carrier requirements such as low stalling speed, airframe and undercarriage strength, high lift capability and the rest.

The S-3 is a compact aeroplane, but it is not a small one. The USN requirement for a 2500-plus nm range dictated that the wings be as thick as possible, and tapered as little as possible, in order to house the necessary fuel, whilst decisions governing the thickness: chord ratio were determined to give maximum lift: drag ratio at the optimum mission (cruise) speed – about 375kts. The large span (68ft 8in) is required mainly because of the need for single-engined operation, as well as for the usual precision low-speed handling characteristics; the use of one powerplant also means a large-area vertical

[1]For further discussion of the CV Concept see Norman Friedman: *Carrier Air Power* (Conway Maritime Press, 1981).

Vikings from VS-29, USS *Enterprise*, showing the folding arrangements of the flying surfaces. Notice how the deck-edge type lift does not necessarily limit aircraft dimensions – at least not to the extent inboard lifts used to. 300 US gallon tanks are fitted to the external stations of this S-3A.

Lockheed-California

An S-3A Viking from VS-22, USS *Saratoga*, with extended
MAD boom. Note 'twist' in wings, helping to minimise wingtip
stalling. The thickness of the wing at the root can easily be
seen.

Lockheed-California

stabiliser for good directional stability, with the consequent need for hingeing – which adds weight. The wings
also need to be capable of folding for stowage (the
mechanism is not symmetrical, owing to the need for one
wing to fold aft of the other, to keep the overall height
down), and the large span, plus the full-width flaps and
slats and their attendant mechanisms for low-speed
operations, *plus* the need to support large quantities of
fuel, podded engines and external hardpoints, all add up
to still more in the way of weight penalties. A far cry
indeed from the wartime ASW Swordfish, armed with
ASV radar, 8-60lb rockets and a good deal of hope!

CAPABILITIES
There is no doubt that the S-3A is, electronically, the
most sophisticated US military aircraft in service. Avionics include both passive and active sensors, the primary
passive variety being a maximum 60 sonobuoys stowed

in chutes in a ventral fuselage bay aft of the main undercarriage. Forward-Looking Infra-Red (FLIR), the modern equivalent of the old searchlight, is housed in a
retractable dome below the cockpit, whilst an
AS/ASQ-81 Magnetic Anomaly Detector (MAD) is
carried in a retractable tail boom. AN/APS-116 search
and navigation radar is fitted in the nose, and
AN/ALR-47 ESM equipment is mounted in wingtip
fairings.

Strike weapons comprise (internal bays) four Mk 46
torpedoes or Mk 53 mines or Mk 54 or 57 depth charges
or Mk 82 bombs; and (wing hardpoints) a variety of
flares, rockets, mines, bombs or Harpoon ASMs. The
S-3A also has a nuclear capability. Fuel tanks instead of
externally carried offensive stores increase range by
something of the order of 40 per cent.

Derivatives of the Viking comprise the US-3A Carrier
Onboard Delivery (COD) vehicle, four of which – converted standard S-3As – are now flying (3750lb cargo
and five passengers can be accommodated); and the
KS-3A tanker, also modified from a standard airframe
but only one example of which is in service. Retrofitting
of S-3As to take on more advanced equipment (and
Harpoon) in the late 1980s is likely to result in an S-3B
designation.

The '3-T' Programme Part 2

by Norman Friedman

MISSILE POLICY

Through the first postwar decade, the Navy surface-to-air missile programme was pressed ahead urgently, at what would now be described as considerable technological risk. Although there was no solid intelligence of Soviet efforts to duplicate the wartime German anti-ship missile technology, at least at first, there was a strong presumption – which proved entirely correct – that the Soviets would press ahead with what the Navy regarded as the most effective challenge to its primary strike asset, the attack aircraft carrier. Thus, although the first two operational units, the heavy cruisers *Boston* and *Canberra*, were not commissioned until 1956, by that time a wide variety of other conversions had been planned. In fact the great bulk of US missile ships were authorised before FY 62; the '3-T' programme was wound down in the late 1950s because a superior missile system, Typhon, was in immediate prospect. Thus official documents of the late 1950s refer to Terrier and even to Tartar as 'obsolete' – with reference to a hypothetical 1960–1970 era threat. The headlong progress of the missile installation programme had unfortunate consequences, primarily in reliability of weapons and of their control radars rather than in problems with the basic missile system designs.

In 1962 an internal Defence Department report proposed suspension of the Typhon programme because the existing systems were clearly incapable of meeting the requirements already laid down, largely in terms of reliability and readiness. It seemed to follow that system improvement would be a better alternative than the development of an entirely new family of missiles and control radars, which was already perceived as extremely expensive. Secretary of Defense McNamara cancelled the Typhon programme in December 1963, shifting most of the funds allocated into a '3-T Get-Well' programme concerned much more with reliability than with improved missile performance. Ultimately it produced the current Standard missile family, as well as improved (more reliable) versions of the SPG-51 and -55 radars. However, attempts to replace the Talos tracking radar (SPG-49) with either a specialised set (SPG-61) or a modified version of the existing SPG-51 (SPG-51E) failed, and these failures appear to have been a factor in the ultimate demise of Talos. As for Typhon, the current Aegis system is its lineal descendant, but it is entering service about 17 years after the planned appearance of Typhon, and a full decade after the initially planned appearance of the Advanced Surface Missile System (ASMS), as Aegis was initially known.

The actual acceptance of a new weapon system depends very much on the appearance of platforms suitable for its employment. Thus the mere existence of the *Boston* and *Canberra* made Terrier an important element of fleet air defence tactics within the fleet. However, no new missile ships were authorised after the FY 52 budget until the Talos cruiser *Galveston*, in FY 56. A third cruiser conversion had been suggested in the FY 53 budget, presumably as a Talos test platform, but it was dropped early in the budget process; Talos was not yet ready. Five more *Cleveland* class missile cruisers followed in the FY 57 budget.

TALOS CRUISER DESIGNS

In 1956 a new policy for missile installations was announced: from FY 58 onwards, wherever possible, ships would be double-enders, since missile installations were essential and there was pressure to increase the number of missile launchers in the fleet. New guided missile cruisers would have Talos at each end, with (if possible) Tartar as a secondary battery, and with one SPG-49 tracker per missile launching arm, ie, with a capability to engage one target per missile of a four-missile salvo. The forward Talos system would, however, have three SPW-2 beam-riding guidance radars, the after system, two. At this time BuOrd projected such progress with Tartar (which had not yet flown) that it would be able to discard the intermediate Terrier entirely; two years later APL would propose a Terrier-size replacement for the much larger Talos, as Typhon (Long Range). Thus, although missile frigates (now redesignated cruisers) were still being designed to fire Terrier, there was declining interest in Terrier for cruisers.

The Bureau of Ships produced a variety of sketch designs for future cruiser conversions. The available classes were *Cleveland, Baltimore, Worcester* and *Des Moines*. It was argued that the *Cleveland*s had very limited internal hull volume, and that most of them had their CICs above the protective deck. The *Worcester* and *Des Moines* class were the most modern, and had both received major electronic improvements – which would be scrapped upon conversion. However, *Baltimore* (and the similar *Oregon City*) class cruisers in the reserve fleet had not been refitted and were considered poor prospects for future activation. Both of the newer classes incorporated what were considered the most effective existing gun mounts, all of which would have to be removed and scrapped in the course of conversion. In the case of the 8in cruisers, that would leave only the slow-firing 8in mounts for future use for gun-

The guided missile cruiser USS *Canberra* (CAG-2) being manoeuvred into position at the Jamestown International Naval Review on 12 June 1957.

USN

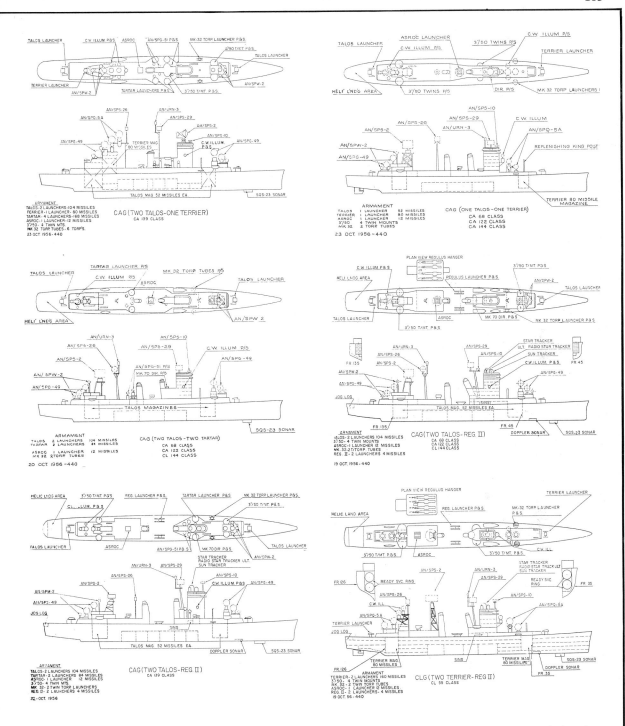

fire support. Finally, it could be argued that among the inactive *Baltimore*s were ships with the least time on their engines, ie with the greatest remaining machinery life (*Oregon City, Chicago,* and *Fall River,* all with less than three years in service). In fact the active cruisers *Albany* and *Columbus* were ultimately selected, apparently to save money, since their inactivation costs could be avoided.

The 1956 sketch designs for double-ended cruisers included a *Des Moines* with two Talos (fore and aft) and Terrier (80 missiles) superimposed aft (with what was described as a 'cascade' of guidance radars); a CAG (*Baltimore* or *Worcester*) with Terrier forward and Talos aft; a CAG with Talos fore and aft; and a CAG with Talos fore and aft and Regulus II strategic missiles (2 launchers and 4 missiles) amidships. In each case there was ASROC and the associated SQS-2 sonar; the Regulus ship had, in addition, special navigational equipment associated with the long-range missile, comprising a doppler sonar (to measure actual speed over the bottom), a 'star-tracker', and a 'jog-log', which was paid out astern to measure ship speed precisely in water too deep for the doppler sonar to be effective. Finally, there was a double-ended *Cleveland* conversion (80 missiles in the deep four-ring mounts at each end) with Regulus II and ASROC.

THE ALBANY CLASS

The double-ended CAG with Talos and Regulus (installation of which was deferred) was chosen for a programme of six conversions, tentatively scheduled for the FY 58 – FY 60 programme. However, two ships of FY 58 were deferred to FY 59, as the Navy's shipbuilding funds were severely stressed by, among other things, the carrier and Polaris programme. One remaining ship of the FY 58 programme, *Albany* became the prototype of this SCB 173 conversion. Three ships planned for FY 60, as CB 13 – 15, were never converted. They would have had a new Talos guidance radar, SPG-56. After FY 60 interest shifted to ships suited to Typhon construction or conversion – and the conversion programme stagnated. Although there were later proposals to fit existing missile systems in the old cruisers, they were generally part of other projects, such as proposals for cruiser conversions to amphibious flagships (LCC).

The three *Albany*s were unique in their mast and funnel design. Early sketches showed conventional masts, but tests of smoke patterns showed considerable interference with the large number of radars planned. Moreover, the heavy pole masts planned were not rigid enough; vibration could lead to considerable errors in the interpretation of radar data, with consequent failure of interception by missiles, or at the least, loss of vital time between initial target detection and handover to missile tracking radars. The solution was the mast-stack or 'Mack', in which radars were mounted atop the extended smokepipe. The smokepipes were far taller than in conventional practice, and it appeared that the new structures could also simplify radio installation by serving as 'sleeve' antennas. BuShips adopted them not only for the *Albany*s, but also for the *Belknap* and *Leahy* class missile frigates (now cruisers) and for destroyer escorts (now styled frigates) from the *Bronstein* class onwards.

DESTROYER INSTALLATIONS

Terrier proved amenable to large destroyer installation, at a time when new construction of cruisers was fiscally impossible. Thus it soon predominated over Talos in the US new construction programme, with the first six (*Dewey* class, half initially planned as all-gun ships) in the FY 56 programme, and four more following in FY 57. The FY 58 frigates were double-ended: the *Leahy* class (3 in FY 58, 6 in FY 59, plus a nuclear version, *Bainbridge*, in FY 59). In addition there was the nuclear cruiser *Long Beach* (FY 57), the design of which began as a large frigate and soon graduated to cruiser

USS *Dale* (DLG-19) launching a Terrier missile off Point Muga, California in April 1964.
USN

The guided missile cruiser *Columbus* fires a Tartar missile from her port launcher amidships, 28 May 1957. Her aft main battery (Talos) launcher, with one arm loaded, can be seen on the quarterdeck.

size, with Talos aft and Terrier forward. The *Gearing* class destroyer *Gyatt* was converted to fire Terrier under the FY 56 programme, proving that such weapons could be accommodated even on very small hulls. However, Tartar was reserved for destroyers and, later, for destroyer escorts. Its installation was considered a very high priority, again considering the magnitude of the expected threat; studies of a missile destroyer based on the *Forrest Sherman* hull began as early as the Fall of 1955. Eight were included in the FY 57 programme, with five more in the FY 58, five in FY 59, three in FY 60, and two in FY 61 (*C F Adams* class).

There was some dissatisfaction within the influential Atlantic Destroyer Force concerning the *Adams* design: Tartar was perceived, in 1955-56, very much as a second-rate missile, and BuShips was forced to produce sketch designs of an alternative installation of Terrier in a *Forrest Sherman* hull. One of the costs of

A Tartar missile in its launcher on the after superstructure of the French guided missile destroyer *Kersaint*.

ECPA

A Talos missile, hung from an overhead transportation rail, being fitted with its fins prior to loading into the launcher – USS *Galveston*, 28 May 1957.

USN

such an installation would have been about half the boiler power of the earlier ship. Similarly, attempts were made to revise the *Adams* design to fulfill the double-ender policy of the FY 58 programme. At the same time the original SQS-23 sonar was to have been replaced by an SQS-26; the result was far too expensive, and the project dropped. In fact there was some feeling that the *Adams* class was far too expensive, and in 1959 attempts were made to develop a more austere missile destroyer. At the same time, however, the new ship was to have had much greater endurance and an SQS-26 sonar. The result, paradoxically, was a much larger ship, roughly of missile frigate (cruiser) size – which became the *Belknap*; Terrier was adopted in view of the other sunk costs represented by the new designs, and there were some design savings achieved by using the hull of the earlier *Leahy*, somewhat modified. Three ships were planned under FY 60, but they were deferred to FY 61 in view of the costs of the new Polaris missile programme. Six more (plus a nuclear version, *Truxtun*) were built under FY 62. They were the last US non-nuclear missile frigates/cruisers. The only other missile installations of the late 1950s and early 1960s were aboard six Tartar-armed missile destroyer escorts (DEG, *Brooke* class) and aboard the carriers *Kitty Hawk*, *Constellation*, and *America*.

Attempts to continue missile ship construction encountered, first, the great promise of the Typhon system, which was so different from that of the '3-Ts' that it could not be back-fitted to an existing missile ship, at least not without enormous expenditure. To some extent it appeared, in 1959-60, that the existing force of postwar all-gun frigates and destroyers were candidates for conversion: *Norfolk* could be fitted with Terriers, the *Mitscher*s with Terrier or with Tartar, and the *Forrest Sherman*s with Tartar. The programme actually began, with conversion plans drawn for Tartar in both *Mitscher*s and destroyers, but it was discontinued by Secretary of Defense McNamara in view of the low effectiveness of Tartar and the high cost per ship: ultimately only two frigates and four destroyers were converted, most of the *Forrest Sherman*s receiving instead an ASW improvement programme. A new DDG planned first for FY 66 and then for FY 67 was never built; instead a DDG programme was embedded in the surface combatant replacement programme which produced the *Spruance* class. In this sense the four ex-Iranian *Kidd* class missile destroyers are the true (and very belated) descendants of the '3-Ts'.

Readers may be interested to know that the author's detailed study US Naval Weapons *will be published in the spring of 1983 by Conway Maritime Press in the UK and the Naval Institute Press in North America.*

THE RN's 1960 CRUISER DESIGNS

by Antony Preston

Hitherto very little information has been published about a series of large cruisers intended to be ordered under the 1960 Naval Estimates. All that was revealed at the time was a cryptic reference in *Jane's Fighting Ships* to the effect that a new 20,000-ton cruiser armed with missiles was under consideration. This project then vanished, apparently a victim of retrenchment, and nothing further was heard of it. Only recently has any new information come to light, and I must express my gratitude to the Ministry of Defence (Navy) for their willingness to declassify the drawings and details. I must

also add a note of caution: this is by no means the full picture as the relevant papers have not yet been made available under the 30-year Rule. Until those documents can be examined we will know very little of the politics behind the design and its subsequent fate. Having said that, what follows is an educated guess, based on what documents I have been able to examine.

A large cruiser project, the *Minotaur*, which had been under development since 1947 finally lapsed in the early

The 'County' class guided missile destroyers were the first and only operational ships to be armed with Seaslug, the launcher for which can be seen on the quarterdeck in this view of *Devonshire*. The 1960 cruiser would have been the second Seaslug type, with double the missile stowage of the 'County' class, but loss of faith in the system and financial limitations led to the abandoning of the project.

C & S Taylor

1950s. However its influence over later designs was strong, for no design team can afford to throw away the results of so many years of labour. As a result, after some 100 design-studies, a new anti-aircraft cruiser evolved in the late 1950s to meet a Staff Requirement for a major fleet escort armed with a powerful anti-aircraft battery.

SEASLUG

The major weapon system available was the Seaslug Guided Weapon System No 1 (GWS 1), a first-generation surface-to-air guided weapon based on the JTV2 ramjet test vehicle and the RTV test vehicle, both of which were descended from the wartime Ministry of Supply's LOP/GAP project. The Staff Requirement was issued as early as 1946 and two years later a development contract was given to industry. The first test vehicle of what was known as Project 502 flew in 1951, and it was then possible to fix the dimensions of the weapon.

The first ships built to fire GWS 1 were the 6000-ton 'County'class DLGs, or large destroyers, but they were armed with only 24 rounds, and it was recognised that a larger fleet escort would be needed if more missiles (preferably double the complement of the 'Counties') were to be embarked.

Most of the problems of the design stemmed from the sheer size of Seaslug. Large boost-motors were not available, and so four smaller boosters were 'wrapped' around the main body of the missile, resulting in a very large diameter and great weight. Had a single booster been used it might have been possible to adopt an end-to-end configuration, and this would in turn have permitted vertical loading through a deck-hatch. But it was not possible, and so the designers were saddled with a requirement for horizontal loading. This meant that a substantial part of the ship's internal volume had to be devoted to a hangar, armoured if possible to protect against splinter-damage.

The guns also posed problems. The 5in/56cal currently under development from the Army's Green Archer land-mobile equipment, was to be put into a twin mounting. The twin 3in/70cal Mk 6 was already well advanced, but the light armament was to be another new mounting, the DACR. Nothing much has come to light about this weapon, apart from the fact that it was to be a 6-barrelled mounting. In all probability it was an updated version of the 40mm Bofors Mk 6. A version of

THE LARGE CRUISER OF 1960

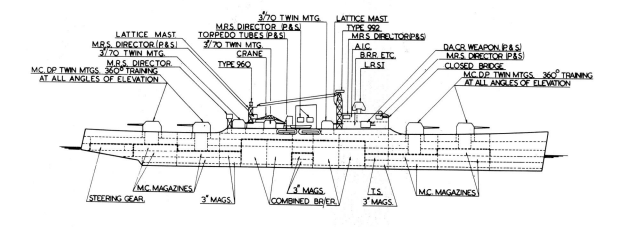

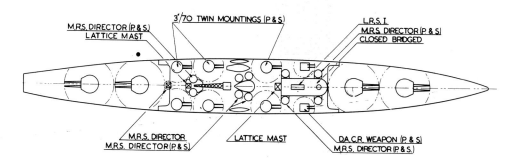

LENGTH. W.L.	645'-0"
BREADTH.	74'-0"
DRAUGHT.	23'-0"
SPEED. (DEEP CLEAN.)	31 KNOTS
S.H.P.	95,000
DISPLACEMENT. (STANDARD.)	14,500 TONS
" (DEEP.)	17,500 "

ARMAMENT
8 – MEDIUM CALIBRE GUNS IN 4 TWIN MOUNTINGS
12 – 3"/70 " 6 " "
2 – D.A. CLOSE RANGE WEAPONS
4 – Q.R. TORPEDO TUBE MOUNTINGS

RADAR TYPE 960
TYPE 992 WITH T.I.U. III

COMPLEMENT 900 – 950

this mounting, known as Mk 12, was planned to have the new L/70 version of the Bofors 40mm gun.

ACCEPTED DESIGN

In the cruiser designs, it proved possible to improve the missile-stowage considerably over the County design. A shorter loading bay was served directly from a 48-round magazine five decks below. The boosters were housed in a separate magazine abaft the main magazine, and assembly took place during the loading sequence, at which point various automatic checks, engine warm-up and other operations were carried out.

The design finally approved was a 14,000-ton ship driven by 4-shaft geared steam turbines developing 95,000shp, for a speed of 31kts at deep load (17,000 tons). The armament was to be two twin 5in gun mount-

ings forward and a twin Seaslug missile launcher aft. A very heavy secondary armament of three twin 3in Mk 6 mountings each side was mounted amidships, and two DACR 6-barrelled light AA guns forward, on either side of the bridge. The adoption of unit machinery, standard since 1945, made it necessary to have two funnels. Not much is known about the sensors, apart from the fact that the ships would have had Type 960 long-range air-warning radar, Type 992 for surface-warning and target-indication, and Type 901 for missile-control. Clearly there would have been additional gunnery sets, and a sonar would have been fitted.

PROJECT CANCELLATION

It had been hoped to order the first of the class under the 1960-61 Naval Estimates (hence the name) but Treas-

THE LARGE CRUISER OF 1960 WITH "SEASLUG"   SKETCH II

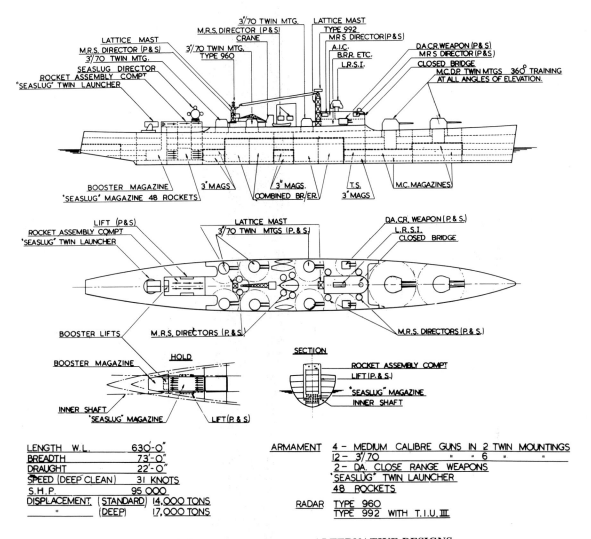

LENGTH W.L.	630'-0"
BREADTH	73'-0"
DRAUGHT	22'-0"
SPEED (DEEP CLEAN)	31 KNOTS
S.H.P.	95 000
DISPLACEMENT. (STANDARD)	14,000 TONS
" (DEEP)	17,000 TONS

ARMAMENT 4 – MEDIUM CALIBRE GUNS IN 2 TWIN MOUNTINGS
12 – 3"/70 " " 6 " "
2 – DA. CLOSE RANGE WEAPONS
'SEASLUG" TWIN LAUNCHER
48 ROCKETS

RADAR   TYPE 960
TYPE 992 WITH T.I.U. III

ury approval was not given, and the request was never put before Parliament. We can work out for ourselves that lack of finance was the most likely reason, but with the advantage of hindsight we can also see that other reasons were probably as influential. The disadvantages of a missile using line-of-sight beam-riding were now becoming apparent, and the designers now had hopes of changing to semi-active radar homing, in a project known as CF 299 but later to emerge as Sea Dart. Another shadow hanging over plans for a new generation of cruisers was the rising cost of the carrier CVA-01. It was becoming obvious to the naval planners that Treasury approval for the class of cruisers as well as two fleet carriers and four DLG escorts was less and less likely. Given such a conflict of priorities it was the cruiser which had to be dropped.

ALTERNATIVE DESIGNS

However this was not the end of the 1960 Cruiser story. The Board had asked for other designs: a purely gun-armed version, a medium-sized 12,250-tonner and a small 10,500-tonner. The large cruiser was simply a revision of the Seaslug cruiser, with two more twin 5in/56 turrets aft and four trainable 21in torpedo tubes amidships. To accommodate the extra turrets and magazines aft, as well as the torpedo tubes, dimensions had to be slightly increased.

The smaller designs owed something to a defunct cruiser-destroyer planned in the 1950s, and had a combined mast and forefunnel, as in the *Daring* and 'Weapon' class destroyers. The medium cruiser had three twin 6in/45cal Mk 26 turrets, two forward on the forecastle, and one aft. The same DACR light AA guns were sited on either side of the bridge, but the forward pair of twin 3in/70cal Mk 6 turrets were dropped. Fire-control was more elaborate than in the previous design: two type 984 3-D surveillance radars, the same LRS 1 director over the bridge and seven MRS light directors, including one on the centreline aft. Torpedo tubes were retained, but this time in fixed quadruple positions with reloads stowed above them.

The small cruiser was even less orthodox, with a twin 3in/70cal Mk 6 turret forward, and a twin 5in/56cal mounting further aft on the same level. DACR close-range AA guns were mounted on either side of the bridge, as before, but another pair was sited port and starboard of the after fire-control position, and there was also a pair of twin 3in/70cal amidships. The trainable quadruple torpedo-tubes reappeared but this time

with two pairs of sets abreast the after funnel. Fire-control was provided by a single LRS 1 director and five MRS directors, but the Type 984 3-D radars were omitted.

CONCLUSION

The 1960 Cruisers were an unusual set of designs, coming after a long break, and so it is hardly surprising that they should bear little resemblance to any other British designs. Whether they would have been a success is hard to guess. Seaslug was not the most successful anti-aircraft missile, but it was accurate within the limits of the technology available at the time. However, as time would show, the impact of the missile system on the hull

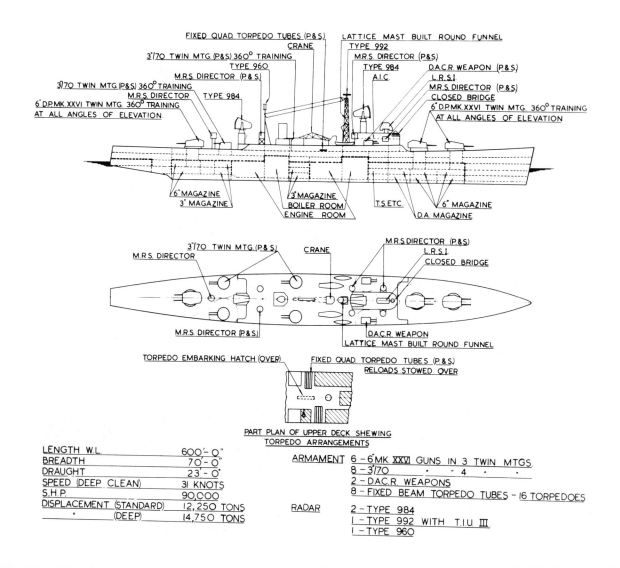

THE MEDIUM CRUISER OF 1960 (4 SHAFTS).   SKETCH IV

LENGTH W.L.	600'-0"
BREADTH	70'-0"
DRAUGHT	23'-0"
SPEED (DEEP CLEAN)	31 KNOTS
S.H.P.	90,000
DISPLACEMENT (STANDARD)	12,250 TONS
" (DEEP)	14,750 TONS

ARMAMENT 6-6"MK. XXVI GUNS IN 3 TWIN MTGS.
8-3"/70   "   4   "   "
2-D.A.C.R. WEAPONS
8-FIXED BEAM TORPEDO TUBES - 16 TORPEDOES

RADAR 2-TYPE 984
1-TYPE 992 WITH T.I.U. III
1-TYPE 960

design was excessive. Had the ships been built there would now be an acrimonious debate about what to do with them. It is significant that none of the customers for the 'Counties' (Egypt for the *Devonshire*, Chile for the *Norfolk* and Pakistan for the *London*) chose to retain the Seaslug missile system.

Without a medium-range missile armament, the all-gun variants did not look very convincing. We now know that the Royal Navy lost faith in the gun prematurely, and within only a decade and a half it realised that the threat from conventional air strikes had been greatly exaggerated, but the evidence for that conclusion was not available in the late 1950s. Even so, it is hard to imagine an independent role for any of these ships, and their replacement by the Type 82 Sea Dart-armed large destroyer was almost certainly the best outcome.

Further information on postwar warship designs will be available in The British section (by Antony Preston) of Conway's All the World's Fighting Ships 1947-1982 *to be published early in 1983.*

THE SMALL CRUISER OF 1960

SKETCH III

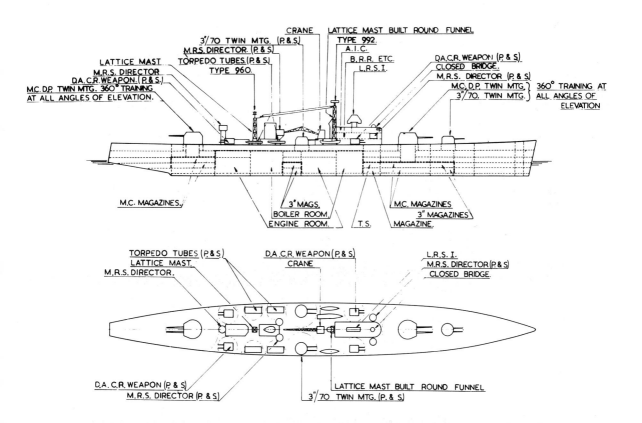

LENGTH. W.L.	585'-0"
BREADTH.	68'-0"
DRAUGHT.	22'-0"
SPEED. (DEEP CLEAN)	31 KNOTS
S.H.P.	90,000
DISPLACEMENT (STANDARD)	10,500 TONS
" (DEEP)	13,000 TONS

ARMAMENT	4 - MEDIUM CALIBRE GUNS IN 2 TWIN MOUNTINGS
	6 - 3"/70. " " 3 " "
	4 - D.A. CLOSE RANGE WEAPONS
	4 - Q.R. TORPEDO TUBES
RADAR	TYPE 960
	TYPE 992 WITH T.I.U. III

DUTCH LEANDERS
The Van Speijk Class
by Thomas A Adams

The *Isaac Sweers* in November 1979.   *C & S Taylor*

The *Leander* (Improved Type 12) class of general purpose frigates has been one of Britain's most successful warship designs with 26 units built for the Royal Navy, 2 for the Chilean Navy, 6 for the Indian Navy, 2 for the Royal New Zealand Navy, 2 units of the Royal Australian Navy's 'River' class and 6 for the Koninklijke Marine – the *Van Speijk* class. However, the *Leander* was a design of the 1950s and they have required midlife refits to up-arm and modernise them. In some cases, as with the Royal Navy, a number have been converted from general purpose frigates to specialised vessels, armed with the Ikara anti-submarine weapon system or with the Exocet surface-to-surface missiles. (see Table 1). Indeed these Royal Navy conversions have been the subject of much discussion and controversy. The other European *Leander*s – the Dutch *Van Speijk*

class have been most interestingly and efficiently modified: modified, not converted, because they still retain their general purpose capability.

ORIGIN

The *Van Speijk* class of the Royal Netherlands Navy emerged in the early 1960s from a need to replace their six *Van Amstel* (ex-US *Cannon*) class frigates. The *Van Speijk*s were ordered in two stages – 4 in October 1962 and 2 in 1964. Building was undertaken by two yards – Nederlandse Dok en Scheepsbouw Mij, Amsterdam and Koninkiuijke Maatschappij De Schelde, Flushing, with all six ships being launched over a period of only two years – March 1965 to March 1967. (See Table 2).

Based on the British *Leander* class, the *Van Speijk*s have an identical hull form and the same steam turbines driving two shafts via double-reduction gearboxes. Internal arrangements were altered to suit metric measurement and Dutch Naval requirements, such as the installation of electronic and electrical equipment of Dutch manufacture.

The basic British armament was retained – twin 4.5in (114mm) Mk 6 dual purpose guns, Limbo Mk 10 triple-barrelled anti-submarine mortar, Seacat surface-to-air missile system and the Westland Wasp anti-submarine helicopter. The British Admiralty Type 965 long-range air surveillance radar with its aerial on the mainmast was replaced by a Hollandse Signaal Aparaten HSA LW-02 system. The type 993 tactical air/sur-face surveillance radar with its aerial on the foremast was replaced by a HSA DA-02 medium range air/surface search set. The British MRS-3 gun director system on the bridge top was replaced by a HSA M45 combined radar and optical fire control system for medium calibre guns.

Two Seacat SAM launchers are on the hangar top, each with its own HSA M44 director sited in a tub on either side of the mainmast. The M44 being an efficient radar/visual director allowing automatic target tracking in bearing and elevation meant that two Seacat launchers could be accommodated as opposed to the one launcher in the original British design.

TABLE 1: PRINCIPAL PARTICULARS AND LEANDER COMPARISONS

	Van Speijk	Modernised Van Speijk	RN Leander	Ikara Conversions	Exocet Conversions	Chilean Navy
Length oa (ft)	372	372	372	372	372	372
Length wl (ft)	360	360	360	360	360	360
Beam (ft)	41	41	43	41	41	43
Draught (ft)	18	18	18	18	18½	18
Standard displacement (tons)	2200	2155	2450	2600	2550	2500
Full load displacement (tons)	2850	2735	2800	2860	3200	2962
Speed (kts)	28	28	30	30	30	29
Crew	254	175	260	257	234	263
Guns	2 × 4.5in	1 × 76mm	2 × 4.5in 2 × 20mm	– 2 × 40mm	– 2 × 40mm	2 × 4.5in 2 × 20mm
SSM	–	8 Harpoon	–	–	4 Exocet MM38	4 Exocet MM38
SAM Launchers	2 × 4 Seacat	2 × 4 Seacat	1 × 4 Seacat	2 × 4 Seacat	3 × 4 Seacat	1 × 4 Seacat
Anti-submarine	1 Limbo mortar	–	1 Limbo	GWS40 Ikara 1 Limbo	–	–
A/S torpedo tubes	–	2 × 3 Mk 32	–	–	2 × 3 Mk32	2 × 3 Mk32
Air Search Radar	LW-02	LW-03	965	–	965	965
Tactical/surface Radar	DA-02	DA-05	993	993	993	992Q
Sonar	VDS/Hull	VDS/Hull	VDS/Hull	VDS/Hull	Hull	Hull
Fire Control	M44/M45	M44/M45	MRS3/ GWS22	GWS22	GWS22	MRS3/GWS22
Helicopter	1 Wasp + hangar	1 Lynx + hangar	1 Wasp + hangar	1 Wasp + hangar	1 Lynx + hangar	1 Wasp + hangar

TABLE 2: VAN SPEIJK CLASS CONSTRUCTION

	Laid down	Launched	Completed	Midlife Mods commenced
Van Speijk (F802)	1 10 1963	5 3 1965	14 2 1967	1 1976
Van Galen (F803)	25 7 1963	19 6 1965	1 3 1967	7 1977
Tjerk Hiddes (F804)	1 6 1964	17 12 1965	16 8 1967	12 1978
Van Nes (F805)	25 7 1963	26 3 1966	9 8 1967	3 1978
Isaac Sweers (F814)	5 5 1965	10 3 1967	15 5 1968	7 1980
Evertsen (F815)	6 7 1965	18 6 1966	21 12 1967	7 1979

194

MIDLIFE MODERNISATION

During the mid-1970s, the Dutch authorities carefully planned the midlife modernisation of these six frigates. Commencing in December 1976, all work was to be undertaken by the same yard, Rykswerke at Den Helder, with one vessel being taken in hand at roughly eight month intervals. This major work was programmed to take about two years, itself an achievement when compared with the 'at least' three years taken on the Royal Navy conversions. However, in practice it has taken the Dutch over two years to complete each vessel.

The finished Dutch products look very different from their British counterparts and, after a detailed examination one cannot but admire this Dutch programme. Utilising the original hull and machinery they have improved their ships to a standard of armament and electronics similar to that in the new *Kortenaer* Standard Frigates. Details of the changes are as follows:

Armament: The midlife modernisation has removed the obsolete twin 4.5in Mk 6 turret and replaced it with a single 76/62mm (3in) Compact Oto-Melara rapid-fire installation.

Anti-submarine weapons: The Mk 10 Limbo anti-submarine mortar has been removed together with its associated sonar, and replaced by two triple Mk 32 anti-submarine torpedo tube mountings, these being fitted on the weather deck, port and starboard of the hangar.

Surface-to-air missiles: The two quadruple Seacat launchers on the hangar top have been retained together with their associated M44 directors.

Surface-to-surface missiles: After some speculation that the Exocet SSM would be fitted, the Dutch have followed the standard applied to the *Tromp* and *Kortenaer* classes and have installed eight (2 × 4) carriers/launchers for the Harpoon missile.

Aircraft facilities: With the removal of the Limbo anti-submarine mortar, the well has been plated over to extend the flight deck. The hangar and helicopter handling facilities have been increased to allow the Wasp helicopter to be replaced by the larger and more versatile Westland Lynx. (see Table 3).

Electronics: The updating of the operations room has been a major step in the use of automation. A SEnsoren, WApens and COmandusysteem (SEWACO) – sensor, weapons and command system – Type V was developed by Hollandse Signaal Aparaten specifically for the *Van Speijk*'s programme of modernisation. This system receives its information from the LW-03 and the DA-05 radars, the navigational radar, the IFF, the optical target designation sights and from the hull-mounted and VDS sonars. Additional input comes from the ship's helicopter IFF system, the ship's electronic support measures and from automatic data links with other ships and aircraft. This SEWACO V is integrated with a Digital Action Information System (DAISY) which processes and evaluates all incoming information and via a number of horizontal tactical displays presents the Operations Officer and the Captain with information in a clear and logical alpha-numeric form.

TABLE 3: COMPARISON OF WASP AND LYNX HELICOPTERS

	Westland Wasp	Westland Lynx
Power Plant	Rolls Royce Nimbus derated to 685shp	2 Rolls Royce Gem each rated at 830shp
Rotor dia (ft-in)	32–3	42
Length of aircraft (ft-in)	30–4	38–3¼
Height of aircraft (ft-in)	8–10	11–3
Maximum take-off Weight (lbs)	5300	8000
Range (nautical miles)	315	489
Weapons load	A/S torpedoes	A/S torpedoes (two) Sea Skua missiles (four)
Notes	–	All weather capability, carry Sonar

Other facilities: The propulsion system received a major overhaul, including the introduction of full automation of the two Babcock and Wilcox boilers. Internal and external communications systems have been improved. Overall the extensive use of automation has resulted in a major decrease in complement from 254 to around 175. This has resulted in a significant decrease in running costs and obviously greatly improved standards of habitability.

During its Eight Year Plan (1975-1983), the Royal Netherlands Navy will have replaced a high percentage of its fleet with new construction. However, the midlife modernisation of the *Van Speijk*s will take these ships into the 1990s.

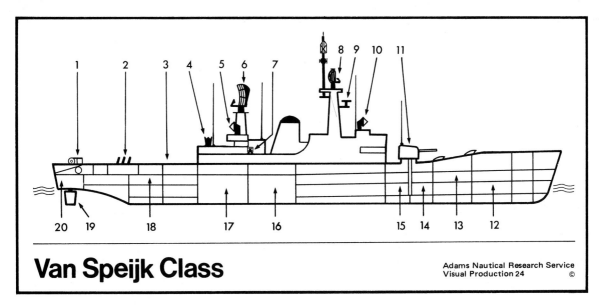

Van Speijk Class

Adams Nautical Research Service
Visual Production 24   ©

KEY TO DRAWING

VAN SPEIJK CLASS As completed: 1 Variable depth sonar; **2** Mk 10 anti-submarine mortar; **3** Flight deck with hangar (fwd); **4** Two quadruple Seacat SAM launchers (one to port and one to starboard); **5** M44 Seacat directors (one to port and one to starboard); **6** HSA LW-02 long-range air surveillance radar; **7** 8-barrelled Corvus launcher (one to port and one to starboard); **8** HSA DA-02 air/surface search radar, incorporating IFF; **9** Type 925 Navigation radar; **10** M45 4.5in gun director; **11** Twin 4.5in Mk 6 gun mounting; **12** Sonar compartments; **13** Accommodation area; **14** Shell room; **15** Magazine; **16** Boiler room; **17** Engine room; **18** Accommodation area; **19** Twin rudders; **20** Steering gear.

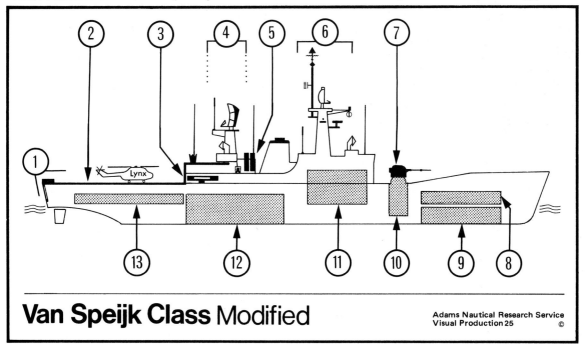

Van Speijk Class Modified

Adams Nautical Research Service
Visual Production 25   ©

KEY TO DRAWING

VAN SPEIJK CLASS Modified: 1 Enclosed VDS area, stern hatch fitted; **2** Flight deck extended and hangar enlarged; **3** Triple anti-submarine torpedo tubes (port and starboard); **4** Modified mainmast, carrying LW-03 'D' Band air surveillance radar and additional ESM aerials; **5** Harpoon SSM installation (port and starboard); **6** Modified foremast, carrying an improved configuration of DA-05 radar, communications and ESM aerials; **7** 76mm Oto-Melara automatic gun; **8** Improved accommodation facilities; **9** Improved sonar installation; **10** Magazine and shell handling installation for the automatic 76mm gun; **11** Operations equipment and external/internal communications outfits improved; **12** Main machinery automated; **13** After accommodation and messing arrangements improved.

Warship Details No.2
The US Mk 37 Director

by John Roberts

The accompanying drawings show the external and internal details of the director of the US Mk 37 DP fire-control system for the control of 5in main and secondary armaments. Developed in the late 1930s the Mk 37 was reliable, accurate and one of the most successful fire-control systems of the Second World War. It was fitted in all US ships of destroyer size and upward constructed after about 1940. It also saw service in the Royal Navy; initially in the cruiser *Delhi*, which was refitted at New York in 1941 with a new armament of five 5in/38 guns, and later (with a British Type 275 radar installation) in the battleship *Vanguard*, the 1943 'Battle' class destroyers and the aircraft carriers *Ark Royal* and *Eagle*.

The full system consisted of the director, containing a 15ft rangefinder stabilised for level and cross level (hence the slotted openings for the rangefinder in the sides of the shield), the director sights and instruments, and a control officer's position, and below decks, a separate fire-control computer and stable element. The early directors carried the antenna for Mk 4 fire-control radar

but this was later replaced by the Mk 12/22 installation. The Mk 12 antenna was similar in appearance to the Mk 4 but the set incorporated several improvements including blind-fire capability while the Mk 22 was a height finding set with a parabolic orange-peel antenna. A few directors had Mk 28/22 instead of Mk 12/22 but postwar the latter sets were superseded by Mk 25 radar which employed a dish antenna.

Another wartime addition was the provision of a slewing sight for the control officer; fitted on the shield in front of the officer's observation hatch in early models but in later models fitted inside a control officer's cockpit (with canvas pram cover) which replaced the original sighting port and observation hatch. In addition the trainer's and pointer's observation hatches were combined into a single hatch. Other variations included the shape of the rear shield – either square or with tapered sides – and several arrangements of the structure supporting the radar antennas. When Mk 12/22 radar was fitted boxes were fitted on the rear of the shield to accommodate some of the radar equipment.

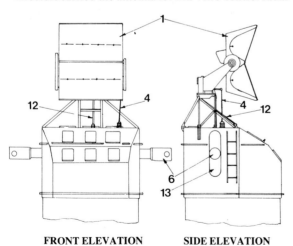

FRONT ELEVATION   **SIDE ELEVATION**

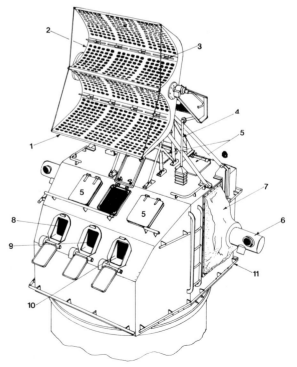

GENERAL VIEW OF Mk 37 DIRECTOR

1 Mk 4 radar antenna; **2** Reflector; **3** Dipoles; **4** Cross-level connecting rod to radar antenna; **5** Observation hatches; **6** 15ft rangefinder; **7** Canvas weather cover over rangefinder slot; **8** Trainer's telescope port; **9** Pointer's telescope port; **10** Control officer's sight port; **11** Handrail; **12** Elevation connecting rod to radar antenna; **13** Rangefinder slot – to allow clearance for cross level movement.

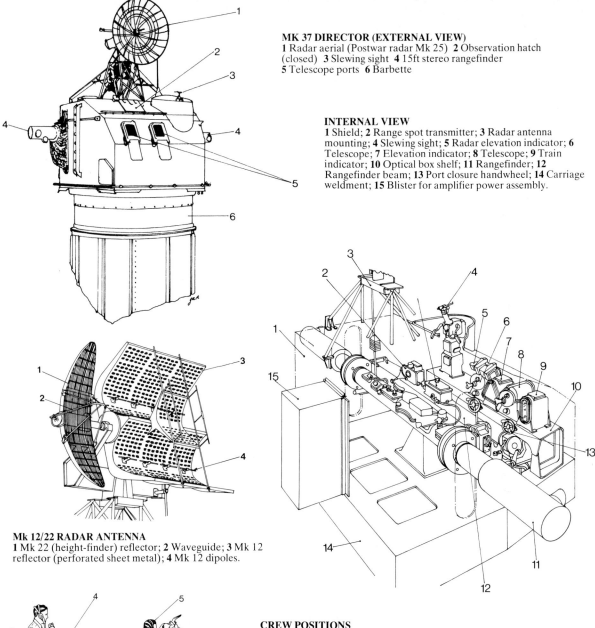

MK 37 DIRECTOR (EXTERNAL VIEW)
1 Radar aerial (Postwar radar Mk 25) **2** Observation hatch (closed) **3** Slewing sight **4** 15ft stereo rangefinder
5 Telescope ports **6** Barbette

INTERNAL VIEW
1 Shield; **2** Range spot transmitter; **3** Radar antenna mounting; **4** Slewing sight; **5** Radar elevation indicator; **6** Telescope; **7** Elevation indicator; **8** Telescope; **9** Train indicator; **10** Optical box shelf; **11** Rangefinder; **12** Rangefinder beam; **13** Port closure handwheel; **14** Carriage weldment; **15** Blister for amplifier power assembly.

Mk 12/22 RADAR ANTENNA
1 Mk 22 (height-finder) reflector; **2** Waveguide; **3** Mk 12 reflector (perforated sheet metal); **4** Mk 12 dipoles.

CREW POSITIONS
1 Range talker; **2** Rangefinder operator; **3** illumination control officer; **4** Talker; **5** Control officer; **6** Pointer; **7** Trainer.

The 'Internal View' and 'Crew Positions' drawings are from *Destroyer Weapons of World War 2* by Norman Friedman and Peter Hodges, and the remaining illustrations are from John Roberts' new 'Anatomy of the Ship' volume, *The Aircraft Carrier Intrepid*. Both are available from Conway Maritime Press (or the Naval Institute Press in North America).

The Bad Weather Flotilla Part 2

by Przemysław Budzbon & Boris Lemachko

The 45mm gun is clearly visible in this shot, which was probably taken on the Black Sea in the late 1930s. If this supposition is correct, the ship would be *Shkval*.

Boris Lemachko Collection

Uragan was launched successfully on 4 September 1928 but the hull was to rust afloat for almost two years pending the completion of the powerplant which was still in the early stages of design and construction. The *Sudotrest* only began experimental work on the first type of boiler for the guard ships programme in the summer of 1928 but because of unsatisfactory results the boiler was dismantled in the spring of the following year. Trials on a second type were begun in August 1929 but were not finished by the end of that year. Ultimately, the planned output and steam parameters were achieved but only at the cost of numerous corrections and alterations. The main fault of this boiler was the impossibility of forcing it above the specified limits, but despite this disadvantage, it was approved for fitting in the *Uragan* class. (An improved type would have delayed by at least

another year a programme that was already considerably over schedule – the planned date of commissioning the prototype was passed on 1 October 1929.) In the meantime four further ships of both series were launched during the summer of 1929 and these were followed by the others of Series I in 1930.

It was not only naval boilers that were new to Soviet shipbuilders at that time. Almost every part of the mechanical equipment had to be tested in order to improve its construction or eliminate faults. The most important items were the turbines, which were the prototypes of a whole generation of Soviet naval turbines. After balancing the rotors, each turbine ran trials before assembly. Lack of suitable space condemned these trials to be carried out in a deckhouse taken from the old battleship *Tsessarevich*. The first set of turbines was assembled at the beginning of 1930 but was not finished until the end of May that year – then, at least, the first Soviet naval turbine could be fitted to the *Uragan* and connected with the port shaft. The starboard turbine ran trials during July – August 1930 and was placed on its mounting soon afterwards.

Fitting-out took a few months and *Uragan* was finally ready for sea at the end of 1930 – 3½ years after the official beginning of work. She was accepted by the government commission on 16 December 1930 and began her sea trials, which gave disappointing results. Because of weight added to the hull, machinery and fittings, the standard displacement had risen by at least 20 tons and fully loaded *Uragan* drew almost 2.6m, leaving only 1m of freeboard. To make things worse the boat was top-heavy, which, in connection with such small freeboard, left her stability and seakeeping much reduced. The main deck was permanently wet in a sea-way – or in anything short of a calm sea. The speed trials proved even worse – *Uragan* could steam at 26.5kts for short periods, but on a longer run she could attain only 23kts at best. Thus, the guard ships proved complete failures – too slow for use as torpedo boats and of no value as ASW vessels because of their lack of depth charge handling equipment and underwater detection devices.

The failure in the speed trials was the result of lack of experience and practice among both the designers and builders. The short period rating of the powerplant did not exceed 7200shp while for extended steaming it fell as low as 6400shp, mainly because of the limited output of the boilers. They were designed to deliver enough steam to feed the turbines, but nothing more. Moreover, to produce this quantity of steam, the boilers had to work at their maximum power, not allowing for any overloading. Thus with the turbines consuming 4-5 per cent more steam than had been specified and with numerous steam driven auxiliaries of vital importance, it was necessary to sacrifice some turbine power to drive those systems properly.

Trials, and necessary alterations and additions delayed the commissioning of *Uragan* but could do little to improve her performance. She was finally commissioned on 12 September 1931 as the first entirely Soviet-built surface warship.[1] She was followed two days later by *Tajfun*, which had undergone exhaustive trials of her powerplant during September. The remaining ships of Series I and Series II entered service during 1932–33.

THE FURTHER SERIES
The 1926 Programme progressed very slowly as Soviet industrial capacity proved to be inadequate for building modern warships in a reasonable time. With the exception of *Uragan*, the guard ships were still on the stocks at the end of 1928 and in the submarine arm the situation was similar. Only MTBs entered into series production, 6 of them being commissioned by November 1928. In the circumstances the Soviet of Work and Defence criti-

[1] The very first, strictly speaking, was the MTB *Pervenec* (see *Warship* 8) but she was classified as a boat rather than a ship.

Shkval at the beginning of the war. At that time she carried 2 single 37mm guns (visible on each side of her forward 4in mounting), 2 single 45mm guns aft (one visible abaft the after 4in gun) and 2 single 0.5in MGs on both sides of the bridge. The searchlight was still carried on the after platform.

Boris Lemachko Collection

Tajfun awaiting repairs during winter in the besieged city of Leningrad.

Przemyslaw Budzbon Collection

cally reviewed the actual progress and potential of the 1926 Programme and decided to change it radically. This opportunity allowed the building times authorised in 1926 to be extended, and at the same time the naval programmes were coordinated with the five-year plans of the whole Soviet economy. On 4 February 1929 the new five-year programme was approved, sanctioning all ships of the 1926 Programme plus 3 flotilla leaders, 10 submarines, additional MTBs and 2 river monitors. Modernisation of 3 battleships, the completion of an old

Smerch during the war. Note the shields on the main guns, built up bridge, camouflage and the mainmast still in place. Guard ships of the Northern Fleet, in contrast to the ships in other areas, had pendant numbers painted on the hull during the war. Those allocated to the *Uragan* class were: SKR 10 – *Groza,* SKR 15 – *Smerch* and SKR 16 – *Uragan*. The SKR stands for 'Storozhevoj Korabl'.

Boris Lemachko Collection

cruiser to a modified design and the rebuilding of the former imperial yacht as a minelayer were also planned. A total of 174.3 million roubles were assigned during the first 3 years for naval shipbuilding. In addition, funds were provided for the very necessary reorganisation and expansion of the shipbuilding industry in the Soviet Union.

As a further extension of the guard ships programme had been decided on, in April 1929 the *Sudotrest* was ordered to prepare an improved design for these ships. Giving this order, the C-in-C of the Naval Forces urged the necessity of increasing the speed by at least 1kt to achieve 30kts as was originally planned. The *Sudotrest,* however, was unable to provide any increase of power, simply because no complete set of turbines existed at that time. Some attempts were made at streamlining and at reducing hull weight (which had been increased due to design alterations) but his was all that could be done.

'Black Monday' did not save the Soviet Union and with serious financial troubles the Soviets had to consider a reduction in the naval programme which had been expanded just a few months before. However, because of the closed character of the Soviet economy, and by great sacrifices in the living standards of its people, it was possible to resume full scale armaments in the Soviet Union within just a year. The first five-year programme was even expanded by adding a total of 53 fighting ships (mainly submarines for the Far East, in response to the Japanese military presence in Manchuria in 1931, by which this power had become a neighbour to the Soviet Union and its satellite, Outer Mongolia).

The above-mentioned events undoubtedly affected the further progress of the guard ships programme. Despite poor results from the sea trials of *Uragan* and *Tajfun*, the Russians decided to continue further construction of the first series because no other design was available at that time. Thus, two pairs were laid down in the Zhdanov Yard (*Metel'* and *V'yuga*) and in the Marti Yard (*Buran* and *Grom*) during 1931–32. Although these ships were destined for the Far East, their construction had to be carried out in the western part of the Soviet Union because of the lack of suitable industrial facilities in the East. Similarly, most of the fittings and armaments for these ships were produced in the Soviet western provinces. The hulls were completed by the end of 1933 and after subsequent dismantling they were transported in sections to Vladivostok by the Trans-Siberian Railway. The ships were reassembled at the Dalzavod (Far Eastern Works) and completed during 1934-35.

These craft were the only ships of the *Uragan* class to be laid down during the first five-year plan. The naval construction programme did not end with unmitigated success during these years, however, since only 77 of a planned total of 98 ships were laid down after 1927. Fourteen of these entered service (8 guard ships and 6 submarines) accompanied by 59 MTBs. The remaining ships had to be rescheduled for the second five-year programme.

The design of the guard ships was revised, but no radical changes were made to the original concept, except the correction of hull lines and hull construction already mentioned. Those efforts, together with some improvements in the turbines gave reason to expect 1.0 or 1.5kts more speed than in the preceding series. Ordnance for the new guard ships was to be modernised as a new 100mm/56 dual-purpose gun was expected to enter service during the second five-year plan. The improved design of the guard ship received the designation *Project No 39* and construction of Series III, comprising 4 ships, was begun in 1933. Three of them were laid down in the Zhdanov Yard (*Burya* and *Purga* for the Baltic and *Molniya* for the Far East) while the fourth one (*Yarnitsa*, intended for the Far East) was to be built by the Marti Yard. They were followed by Series IV, comprising 2 ships (*Sneg* and *Tucha*), which were laid down in the Zhdanov Yard in 1934 and 1935 respectively for employment with the Baltic Fleet. All four of Series III entered service during 1936 while the last pair was completed during 1937–38. The commissioning of *Tucha* on 18 September 1938 finally concluded the guard ships programme, which slightly exceeded 50 million roubles, giving an average cost for each ship of approximately 2.8 million roubles.

MODIFICATIONS

After completion, the guard ships of Series I appeared without their designed AA armament, since the Soviets lacked their own contemporary weapon and did not succeed in obtaining Vickers 2pdr pom-poms. This was the result of the reduction in British credits and imports in May 1927 when the premises of the Soviet trading corporation in London were raided by the police, which severed diplomatic relations between the Soviet Union and Great Britain.

Lack of a suitable AA weapon in any quantity, initially prevented the mounting of any MGs, but these were introduced during the early 1930s. Three 0.5in MGs were mounted when available, one on either side of the bridge, with the third on the quarterdeck.

At first the *Uragan* class was completed with open bridges but these were covered in all ships, probably during their first major refit.

By the mid-1930s the light semi-automatic 45mm/46 Model 1932 AA gun had been introduced on most guard ships already in service. Usually two such guns were mounted – forward and abaft the after 4in gun with two 0.5in MGs added on both sides of the latter. On some ships the second 45mm guns was placed on the forecastle, instead of the aftermost position. The others carried one 45mm gun abaft the after main gun mounting with one or two MGs slightly forward and two MGs on both sides of the front of the bridge.

As a result of experience gained during the Winter War with Finland and news from the Western war theatre, the AA defence of most Russian warships was augmented during 1940–41. This was possibly due to the introudction of the new 37mm/67 auto Model 1939 gun, but because of limited numbers, it was introduced in only a few warships prior to the outbreak of war. In most *Uragan* class ships in European waters, two 37mm guns were mounted in addition to the 45mm pieces, usually on either side of the bridge. In some ships both 45mm guns were removed (on *Uragan* and *Tajfun*, for example).

In the course of the War the armament of most *Uragan* class ships was changed during various refits, repairs and modernisations. The most notable feature was the fitting of large shields to the main guns. This change was introduced from 1942 onwards, together with further additions to the light AA defence. Both *Shtorm* and *Shkval* of the Black Sea Fleet were given two 37mm guns in place of the remaining pair of 45mm pieces aft as well as one 0.5in DShK MG which was fitted on the searchlight platform aft, in place of the projector. This latter innovation was introduced on the majority of remaining ships. By the end of the war, ships from the Northern and Baltic Fleets appeared with two or three 37mm guns and three to four 0.5in DShK MGs. Some of them retained one 45mm piece on the forecastle instead of the 37mm. The most spectacular exception was *Smerch* which at that time carried one 4in/60 and one 3in/55 AA guns on the forecastle, and three 3in/55 AA guns and two 0.5in DShK MGs on the quarterdeck.

The guard ships in service with the Pacific Fleet did not see action until September 1945 and so could be rearmed in a more uniform fashion. During 1943 their 45mm guns were replaced by two or three 37mm. One 0.5in DShK MG was placed on the searchlight platform or two such pieces were mounted on wings added to both sides of this platform.

The A/S armament on most of the *Uragan* class ships was modernised (or was introduced, to be exact) during the war by mounting two DCTs on the stern. Up to 30 DCs were carried on the main deck.

Some of the surviving boats had their mainmast removed at that time, with the wireless antennas spread between the foremast and the booms on the after funnel.

As a result of these modifications and additional fittings, the complement – in the case of *Metel'*, for example – reached 108 men. Because of increased draught the endurance of the *Uragan* class ships was reduced to 1200nm at economical speed.

PRE-WAR SERVICE

The *Uragan* class ships appeared during 1931–32 as the first warships built in Russia after a 14 year 'holiday' in naval construction. No wonder the Russian seamen viewed them with great pride and sentiment, despite their ugly silhouettes and poor characteristics. This sentiment was undoubtedly intensified by their homely sounding names – pleasant to the ear of every Russian, compared to such strange character names as *Marat, Marx* or *Libknekht*. This reversion to tradition was a significant event for the Soviet Navy at the beginning of the 1930s and has been continued to the present day. The new guard ships were named after weather phenomena, previously carried by the Amur Flotilla monitors of 1911, the flatiron gunboats of 1878, coast defence monitors of 1869 and the small gunboats of the Russo-Turkish war. Due to such names as 'storm', 'hurricane' and 'typhoon' the new guard ships earned the nickname 'The Bad Weather Flotilla' among Russian sailors.

In the West the new Soviet guard ships were known at first as those numbered with a pendant letter C. This derived from the building numerals which were painted on the ships sides during their trials periods, the Russian S being erroneously deciphered as latin C. The first 6 craft built by the Zhdanov Yard received numbers reflecting their positions in the series, while ships of the other series carried the yard numbers of their builders.[2]

At the beginning of 1933 Soviet naval expansion was under way – the fleet had 2 battleships (with a third under refit), 4 cruisers, 17 destroyers, 20 submarines, 8 guard ships and 59 MTBs. With the exception of a dozen fast boats transferred to the Pacific in 1932, all ships were distributed between the Baltic and the Black Sea. However the completion of the Baltic-White Sea 'Stalin Canal' gave the opportunity to re-establish naval forces in northern waters. The Northern Flotilla had been formed in April 1933 and a group of six ships from the Baltic Fleet was chosen for the initial transfer via the new canal. On 18 May 1933 the EON 1 (Ekspeditsya Osobovo Naznachenya No 13 – Expedition of Special Purpose No 1), comprising the destroyers *Uritskij* and *Rykov* and submarines *Dekabrist* and *Narodovolets*, as well as the guard ships *Uragan* and *Smerch*, left Kron-

1 Wartime close up of *Groza* in camouflage.

Boris Lemachko Collection

2 Differences in the wartime fittings of individual *Uragan* class ships are evident when comparing this photograph with the other shots accompanying this article. This craft has had her mainmast removed, large rectangular shields placed on the 4in mountings, two 37mm AA guns aft, two 45mm AA guns placed on the widened after platform and MGs in the bow.

Boris Lemachko Collection

shtadt and entered the Neva River estuary. This force under the command of Z Zakupev traversed the fortress of Schlusselbourg and entered Lake Ladoga. On the south-eastern coast of this lake the ships squeezed into the Svir River estuary and proceeded eastwards to reach Lake Onega. North bound the EON 1 flotilla steamed through the Onega to enter the 'Stalin Canal' south of Medvezhegorsk. The most difficult part of the journey involved negotiating 19 locks spread along 227km of the canal. To reduce draught as much as possible the armament and most of the moveable deck fittings were dismantled and followed the ships in barges. Sometimes pontoons had to be used to pass the numerous shallows. On 20 July 1933 the flotilla passed the last lock gate and concluded the first navigation of the 'Stalin Canal'. In Beomorsk the force was reviewed by Stalin, Voroshilov and Kirov and on the next day *Uritskij* and *Dekabrist*, as well as both the guard ships, were visited by them personally. The EON 1 finally arrived at Murmansk on 5 August 1933 while 20 days later the EON 2 force steamed off Kronshtadt. This second expedition, consisting of the destroyer *Karl Libknekht*[3], the submarine *Krasnogvardeets* and the guard ship *Groza*, arrived at Murmansk within four weeks thanks to the experience gained during the first transfer.

Three ships of the *Uragan* class remained in the Baltic and one of them – *Tajfun* – took part in the first Soviet experiments with use of thermodetection at sea during the autumn of 1934. The prototype thermodetector of the TU 1 type was installed at Fort K in Kronshtadt and could keep a contact with *Tajfun* at a range of 15,000nm. Further experiments were conducted on the destroyer *Volodarskij* and the battleship *Marat*, the latter having the apparatus installed on board. The thermodetection devices were used on some ships and coastal batteries during the war.

With the completion of the last Series IV ship in 1938 the total number of the *Uragan* class reached the planned level of 18 ships; their distribution is given in table 5.

1

2

THE URAGANS AT WAR

1938-1940 *Metal'* was the first of the *Uragan* class to engage in combat. During the Soviet-Japanese battle off Chasan Lake, during 22 July – 11 August 1938, she transported wounded Russians to Vladivostok and screened three convoys delivering troops and material to Poset Bay.

After the partition of Poland, Stalin began to pressurise the Baltic states. In the case of Estonia this was excused by the attacks made on Soviet ships in Estonian waters. The steamer *Pioner* was unsuccessfully attacked by an unknown submarine at that time, while the steamer *Metalist* was sunk on 26 September 1939 in

Narva Bay by – the Russians claimed – a Polish submarine. However, *Orzel*, the only operational Polish submarine left in the Baltic, was on her way to Britain at the time. According to Finnish information (based on statements made by a Soviet POW) the *Metalist* was actually sunk (with loss of life) by the guard ship *Tucha* after being missed by the submarine *Shch 303*, in order to give the Soviets an excuse to claim rights to defend Estonian waters. By the end of September the Estonian government had signed an agreement allowing the Soviet Union to establish bases in Estonia.

On 30 November 1939 Russia invaded Finland and surface units of the Baltic Fleet participated in landing operations on the small Finnish held islands in the inner Gulf of Finland. The guard ships *Burya, Vikhr', Sneg* and *Purga* took part in these operations, providing fire support during the first week of the war. Of the Northern Fleet *Groza* was mentioned for her participation in landing the 104th Rifle Division on the barely defended Liinahamaraii, and at Petsamo during 30 November – 2 December 1939 when, together with the old destroyer *Karl Libknekht* she supported the assault forces.

[2] S Breyer gives different numbers to those cited in this work from recent Russian sources. According to the 'Geleitfahrzeuge der Sowjetischen Marine', *Marine Rundschau* 1968, Heft 3, the *Uragan* class ships were numbered as following: *Shtorm* – S1, *Tajfun* – S2, *Vikhr'* – S3, *Tsiklon* – S4, *Shkval* – S5, *Groza* – S6, *Metel'* – S7, *Smerch* – S8, *Uragan* – S9, *V'yuga* – S10, *Purga* – S11, *Burya* – S12, *Grom* – S13.

[3] Official Russian orthography of this name.

To be continued

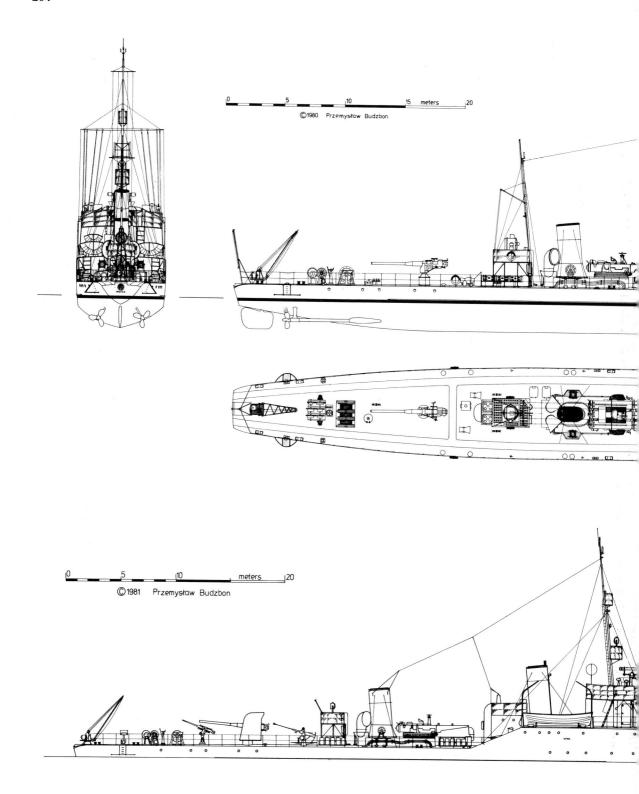

0   5   10   15   meters   20

©1980   Przemysław Budzbon

0   5   10   meters   20

©1981   Przemysław Budzbon

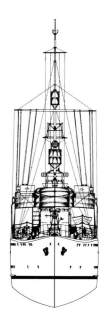

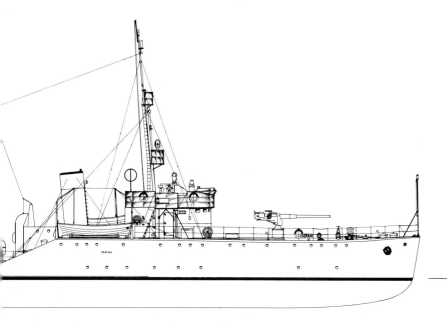

URAGAN in the early 1930s

	BS	ISO
БУРАН	Buran	Buran
БУРЯ	Burya	Burja
ГРОМ	Grom	Grom
ГРОЗА	Groza	Groza
МЕТЕЛЬ	Metel'	Metel'
МОЛНИЯ	Molniya	Molnija
ПУРГА	Purga	Purga
ШКВАЛ	Shkval	Škval
ШТОРМ	Shtorm	Štorm
СМЕРЧ	Smerch	Smerč
СНЕГ	Sneg	Sneg
ТАЙФУН	Tajfun	Tajfun
ЦИКЛОН	Tsiklon	Ciklon
ТУЧА	Tucha	Tuča
УРАГАН	Uragan	Uragan
ВИХРЬ	Vikhr'	Vihr'
ВЬЮГА	V'yuga	V'juga
ЗАРНИЦА	Zarnitsa	Zarnica

Russian and Latin ortography of names
of the URAGAN class.

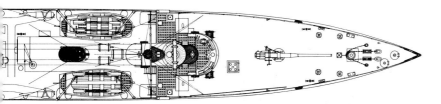

TUCHA at the end of war

A^s&A^s

HMS CAVALIER TO OPEN THIS YEAR from Antony Preston, London

After ten years in limbo the Royal Navy's last 'conventional' destroyer HMS *Cavalier* is to open to the public on 16 June this year. The destroyer paid off at Chatham in 1972 and was later bought outright from the Ministry of Defence by the HMS *Cavalier* Trust. Since then matters have progressed slowly for lack of funds, and the ship has been in care and maintenance at Husbands' repair yard at Southampton until recently. Now, however, thanks to the help of the late Admiral of the Fleet Earl Mountbatten it is possible to proceed with Phase 1 of the conversion, and this must be complete by mid-June.

The trustees intend to open the ship in phases, using the proceeds of the first year's visitor-flow to fund further improvement. The ship will be docked on 23 March for about nine days and then return to her buoys until near the end of the month. She will then be moved to 45 Berth in Southampton Docks, at the head of the Ocean Dock. There she will be only 300 yards from the gate, and easily accessible to the public.

M CLASS SUBMARINES

Two printing errors occured in the article on the War service of the Soviet 'M' class submarines in *Warship* 21. On page 15 under the entry for 24 August 1942 'M179' should read '. . . *M173* was sunk by *Uj1112* . . .' and on page 17 the entry under 25/26 October 1943 should read '*M172* and *M174* reported in for the last time, it seems they were probably lost on the mine barrages . . .'. In addition the photograph on page 16 of the Series XV 'M' class transferred to Poland cannot be one of the *M100–M105* ships. These belonged to the Series XIIbis and furthermore *M100* and *M101* were renumbered *M45* and *M46* respectively. Does any reader know the correct numbers of the six vessels transferred to Poland? Note that this caption was not the author's.

COLONIAL BATTLESHIP

In an excess of zeal the editor provided two photographs of the armoured cruiser *Nelson* for Ross Gillett's article the 'Colonial Cruiser' in *Warship* 21 and corrected the author's classification of *Nelson* from 'battleship' to 'armoured cruiser'. In fact this referred to the old 1st Rate line-of-battleship *Nelson* launched at Woolwich in 1814 and subsequently converted to a screw ship. She was given to the colony of Victoria in 1867 and served as

a training ship until 1893; she was hulked in 1898 and broken up in 1928-29. The armoured cruiser *Nelson* was launched by Elders in 1876 and was commissioned as commodore's ship for the Australia station in July 1881, hence the confusion. My apologies to the author and to our readers.

PHOTO IDENTIFICATION from the Editor

Many years ago I purchased the accompanying photograph in a secondhand bookshop. It was completely unmarked with either caption or source. The row of vessels in the foreground are First World War motor launches, obviously newly completed and as yet not fitted with roofs to their wheelhouses. On the left is an icebreaker which I have not been able to identify, in the centre background an armoured cruiser of the *Devonshire* class, probably *Carnarvon*, and on the right two floating docks (one only just in view). It seems virtually certain, given the icebreaker and the new motor launches, that this view was taken in Canada, possibly at Montreal, as that is where the motor launches were assembled prior to shipping to the UK. The Canada location is reinforced by the fact that the *Devonshire* class ships served on the NA and WI station during 1916 (*Carnarvon* 1915) to 1918. The cruiser still has her main deck 6in guns (moved to the upper deck in the *Devonshire* class, 1915-16) and the first motor launches completed in 1915 so the photograph was taken during 1915 or 1916. Can any reader confirm the location, provide a more accurate date, and identify the icebreaker.

Newly completed motor launches, at a Canadian port in 1915 or 1916.

*W*arship *P*ictorial

USS NORTH CAROLINA

by Kenneth L Eagle

North Carolina was the first of the US Navy's final generation of battleships, her keel being laid down at the New York Navy Yard on 27 October 1937. She was launched on 13 June 1940 and commissioned on 9 April 1941 but her active service life was to last only six years. Decommissioned and later stricken from the navy list she was purchased with donations from a group of citizens in North Carolina for $250,000 and on 2 October 1961 moved to her present berth at Wilmington, North Carolina as a state memorial. The photographs were taken by Kenneth L Eagle on a recent visit to the ship.

The forward 16in turrets and the ship's side showing the fore-end of the belt armour.

1

2

1 A view taken from abreast the after superstructure, on the port side looking forward. In the foreground is a quadruple 40mm Bofors Mk 2 mounting and beyond some of the ship's ten 5in/38 twin mountings of her secondary DP gun battery.

2 The bridge tower viewed from the port side; the horn on the side of the tower is the port steam whistle and the large antenna on the masthead platform is for the air-search SC2 radar. An SG surface-search radar antenna has replaced the Mk 13 antenna originally fitted on the main Mk 38 director.

3 The after section of the superstructure showing the mainmast, funnels and part of the port 5in battery. The after Mk 37 director carries the antennas of Mk 12/22 radar and the main battery director, forward of it, the antenna of Mk 13 surface fire-control radar.

4 A Mk 51 director for one of the quadruple 40mm Bofors mountings. The box at the top is a Mk 15 gyro gunsight.

4

3

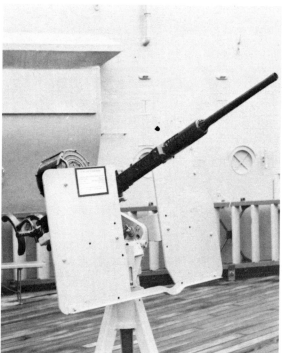

1 A close-up of the Mk 37 director on the bridge, one of four fitted to control the 5in guns. The Mk 4 radar antenna on its roof has been added since the ship was preserved the original having been replaced by the similar Mk 12/22 in 1944 – when first preserved she carried a small antenna in this position.

2 One of the ship's single 20mm Oerlikon Mk 10 mountings. In the background, stowed against the superstructure, is one of the ship's side ladders.

3 The after triple 16in gun turret, looking forward. In the right foreground is one of the ship's spare anchors. Note the ship's bell under the overhang of the platform on the after superstructure.

4 Close-up of the midships structure and funnels from the port side.

5 The forward 16in gun turrets and bridge structure viewed from the forecastle. Note that the starboard steam whistle on the bridge tower is smaller than the port whistle, and.the tops of the Mk 57 directors (with the small dish antenna of Mk 34 radar) visible abreast the Mk 37 director. The Mk 57 replaced the Mk 51 director for control of several of the ships 40mm guns.

6 The ship's quarterdeck viewed from the starboard side.

3

4

5

6

1

2

3

4

5

1 The 5in loading machine, which was used to train guns' crews for the twin 5in/38 mountings.

2 One of the ship's quadruple 40mm Bofors Mk 2 mountings viewed from above. The splinter shield originally fitted across the front and sides of the mounting has been removed.

3 The ship's reconnaissance aircraft, the OS2U Vought Kingfisher. Although the ship still carries the crane (visible in the background) fitted for handling aircraft, the two catapults originally fitted on the sides of the quarterdeck have been removed.

4 One of the ship's spare propellers displayed on the main deck.

5 A close-up of the gunhouse of a 5in/38 mounting with various types of ammunition displayed on its side – from left to right, 5in cases, 5in shells, 40mm ammunition, 20mm ammunition and a 5in case with shell above it.

British Naval Guns 1880~1945 No.6
by NJM Campbell

9.2in Mk I This gun, designed by Woolwich in 1881, was originally a 26 calibre trunnioned gun with no chase hooping, but when the dangers of an unsupported chase became evident they were chase hooped to the muzzle with a reduction in bore length to 25.6cals. It had originally been intended to mount 8 guns each in the ironclads *Sultan* and *Hercules* but this was cancelled in 1885, while a project to rearm the turret ship *Rupert* and to arm the cruisers *Imperieuse* and *Warspite* with these guns had also been abandoned in 1884 with the hoped-for advent of later marks. It must be remembered that for most of the 1880s Woolwich was quite incapable of meeting the navy's demands. The next project was to rearm the armoured ram *Belleisle* with 4 guns in 1886 but two years later the guns still required chase hooping and repair so that this was cancelled. Finally, an attempt to overcome the delays in completing the cruisers *Galatea* and *Aurora*, due to late delivery of their 9.2in Mk Vs, was given up as their VCPII mountings only allowed 12° elevation and the performance of the Mk I gun was quite inadequate for this. In the event the only ship with Mk I was the gunnery school gunboat *Cuckoo*, the mounting being a VBI and later a VCPIII with elevations of 10° and 15° respectively.

The gun was to be found in coast defence batteries at Slough Fort (Thames), Inchkeith, Lough Swilly and

The small monitor *M21* during her trials in 1915. On the forecastle she carries a Mk VI 9.2in gun on a VCPIII mounting, formerly fitted in an *Edgar* class cruiser. Her remaining armament consists of a 6pdr QF gun on a HA Mk IC mounting (a conversion from a low-angle weapon) at the after end of the superstructure and a 12pdr, 18cwt gun on a PIV mounting on the quarterdeck.

MoD

Jamaica. Altogether 17 were made of which 11 were naval but 4 of these were later transferred to the army.

After chase hooping the structure of the Mk I was – 'A' tube taking breech screw, with 141in liner secured by screwed ring/breech piece (coiled wrought iron) '1B' and '2B' coils, 4 hoops to muzzle/'D' coil (wrought iron) with trunnions, 'C' coil (wrought iron). All parts were steel unless noted. A bronze balance sheath and steel elevating band were shrunk over the breech end.

The 'D' and 'C' coils were replaced in the naval guns by steel hoops, the Mark becoming IA. The breech block, of interrupted screw cylindrical type, had a hand worked 3-motion mechanism, but in some army guns there was no hinged carrier, the block being withdrawn by handles, and these had the prefix 'UC' while those with 3-motion mechanism had the prefix 'C' and also had the '2B' and part of the 'C' coil replaced by steel hoops.

9.2in Mk II This was originally a 28.4 calibre gun with no chase hooping, and was intended for rearming the *Rupert* but this project was cancelled in 1886, and on chase hooping the bore was reduced to 25.6cals. It only differed from Mk I in having the trunnions 2.65in nearer the muzzle, and as in naval Mk Is the 'D' and 'C' coils were replaced by steel hoops, the guns becoming Mk IIA.

Only 2 were made, one being in the gunnery school gunboat *Snake*, on an experimental hydraulic mounting, and the other being kept as a spare.

9.2in Mks III,IV,V,VI,VII These trunnioned 31.5 calibre guns only differed in construction and in some external dimensions. Originally Mks III and IV were not chase hooped but this was rectified. Their allocation was:

Mk III: VCPI (15° elevation) – 4 guns in *Imperieuse*.

Mk IV: Coast defence – 19 guns distributed between Lough Swilly, Malta, Singapore, Hong Kong, Colombo, Table Bay and Sierra Leone.

Mk V: VCPII (12° elevation) – 2 guns each in *Australia*, *Orlando* and *Undaunted*.

MKs V and/or VI: VCPI (15° elevation) – 4 guns in *Warspite*; VCPII (12° elevation) – 2 guns each in *Aurora*, *Galatea*, *Immortalite* and *Narcissus*; VCPIII (15° elevation) – 1 gun in *Pincher*.

Mk V1: Turret (13° elevation) – 2 guns in rearmed *Rupert*; VBI (10° elevation) – 4 guns in rearmed *Alexandra*; VCPIII (15° elevation) – 2 guns each in *Blake*, *Blenheim*, *Edgar*, *Endymion*, *Gibraltar*, *Grafton*, *Hawke*, *St George* and *Theseus*; 1 gun each in *Crescent* and *Royal Arthur*; Coast defence – 14 guns distributed between Sheerness, Malta, Gibraltar, Colombo, Mauritius and Simons Bay.

Mk VII: P and E – I naval gun at Shoeburyness.

The total number of guns made were 4 Mk III, 28 Mk IV, 18 Mk V, 61 Mk VI (of which 47 were naval) and 1 Mk VII. As ships were scrapped some transfers to the army occurred: 4 Mk VI in 1904, 8 Mk V and 11 Mk VI in 1906, and 4 Mk VI in 1907, but the only result of this was that 4 Mk VI on high-angle 45° mountings were installed at Gibraltar and moved to Plymouth in 1906. By the First World War, when these obsolescent guns became important again, the army were very short of them as most had been scrapped.

In the navy the *M19* to *M28* class of small monitors built in 1915, were each to have a Mk VI gun, taken from the *Edgar* class, on a VCPIII mounting altered to give 30° elevation, but the demand for Mk VI guns in the naval batteries in Flanders was such that *M25, 26* and *27* never had 9.2in, and the guns in *M21, 23* and *24* were replaced by 7.5in weapons in 1916-17. Originally there was only one mounting on a railway truck but later there were 4 in fixed positions and a total of 9 Mk VI and 1 Mk V were supplied. 2 Mk III and 2 Mk VI guns were sent to Antwerp in 1914 where they were destroyed, and 2 Mk III and 2 MK VI were transferred to the army for use on railway trucks. A list of October 1917 shows that in addition to the above, 7 Mk IV, 6 army Mk VI and 2 Australian Mk IVE had been supplied for railway mountings. The principal features of construction were:

Mk III: On first issue, no liner. 'A' tube/breech piece taking breech screw, 'B' tube, 5 'B' hoops to muzzle/jacket, '1C' hoop, trunnion ring, '2C' hoop. Bronze sheath over jacket for balancing.

Mk IV: Differed in having half 'A' tube lined, no '1C' hoop and no bronze sheath.

Mk IVA: As Mk IV but separate bore and chamber liners.

Mk V: Liner and alpha tube/'A' tube/breech piece taking breech screw, 'B' tube, 'B' hoop not to muzzle/jacket, trunnion ring, 'C' hoop.

Mk V:* No 44 only, after reconstructing as a partly wire wound gun. It had burst in 1897 in *Galatea*.

Mk VI: 'A' tube/breech piece taking breech screw, '1B', '2B' tubes to muzzle with '1C' and '2C' tubes for part length/jacket, trunnion ring, 'D' hoop.

Mk VIA: Thicker 'A' tube and shorter '1B'.

Mk VIB: '1B' tube replaced by '1B' and '2B' hoops. '2C' tube replaced by 'C' hoop.

Mk VIC: '1B' tube replaced by '1B' and '2B' hoops. Breech screw in bush screwed into jacket.

Mk VII: 'A' tube/breech piece, 'B' hoop, 'B' tube to muzzle/'1C', '2C', '3C'/jacket, trunnion ring, 'D' hoop. The breech screw was in a bush screwed into the breech piece and '1C'.

All these had an interrupted screw, cylindrical type breech block normally with hand worked 3-motion mechanism.

The addition of a star to the Mark, and an extra star to Mk V*, indicated that the front slope of the chamber had been altered to prevent slip back at high elevation. The prefix 'B', indicating continuous motion BM, only applied to guns in the 45° coast defence mountings. A few early army Mks IV, IVA, VI and VIB had the prefixes 'UC' or 'C' indicating the absence or presence of a hinged carrier.

The Australian guns were 4 25cal Elswick Pattern 'B' at Port Phillip, 2 Pattern 'C' for Adelaide but never mounted, and 4 Pattern 'G¹' of which 3 were mounted at Sydney. The last was virtually identical to the Mk VIC and the spare gun, when sent to England, became Mk VIE. The two Pattern 'C' guns were sent earlier and were known as Mk IVE. The main difference was the large chamber.

Mk VIII This was a part wire wound 40 calibre trunnioned gun mounted in the cruisers *Powerful* and *Terrible*, each ship having 2 guns on CPIV mountings, allowing 15° elevation. A total of 6 guns were made. The 2 guns from *Powerful* and one of the spares were mounted in coast defence batteries at Cromarty in 1913–14, while one of the *Terrible's* guns was briefly mounted in *Marshal Ney* in 1916, and it and the other *Terrible* gun were added to the naval batteries in Flanders in 1917, the last of the 6 following as a spare in 1918.

The construction was – inner 'A' tube/'A' tube/wire over rear half of 'A'/jacket and 'B' tube to 150in from muzzle/trunnion hoop over join jacket and 'B'. The breech bush screwed into the 'A' tube and a collar between the 'A' tube and jacket screwed into the latter. The breech block was of interrupted screw cylindrical type with hand worked continuous mechanism.

Mk VIII* indicated alterations to the front slope of the chamber to prevent slip back but no guns were so altered.

The armoured ram *Belleisle* in the late 1880s; her intended re-arming with four 9.2in Mk I guns was cancelled in 1888.

Photomatic

PARTICULARS OF 9.2in GUNS

	Mk I, II	Mk III-VII	Mk VIII
Weight (tons)	Mk I 21.9, Mk II 20.9	Mk III 24.2, Mk IV 22.8, Mk V 22.2, Mk VI and VII 22.3	25
Length oa (in)	255.8	310	384
Length bore (cal)	25.57	31.5	40.08
Chamber (cu in)	4300	4950	4600
Chamber length (in)	44	43	53.4
Projectile (lb)	380	380	380
Charge (lb-type)	140-Pr Br, 42-Cord 30	163-Pr Br, 53.5-Cord 30, 59.25-MD 19	66-Cord 40+3¾, 77.25-MD 37
Muzzle Velocity (fs)	1781	2065 (Pr Br), 2119 (Cord), 2095 (MD)	2329 (Cord)
Range (yds)	7500/10°, 9800/15°5′	11,423/15° (2100 fs), 16,664/30° (2100 fs)	12,846/15°

Notes: These ranges are for 2crh shells as fired by the above guns. They are taken from old tables and are all optimistic, particularly the 30° figure. The two Mk IVE guns were 31.4 and 31.9cals with chambers of 5881 and 6000cu in, both had a charge of 66lb MD19 and MV of 2100fs. The Mk VI guns in 45° coast defence mountings had a 44.75lb MD16 charge and fired a 290lb shell at 2065fs.

The Iron Screw Frigate Greenock Part 1

by John M Maber

It is believed by many that the Royal Navy spurned the use of iron for warship hulls until the order was placed in June 1859 for the construction of the iron-hulled armoured battleship *Warrior* (initially classed as a frigate since she had but one gundeck, but soon reclassified as a third class battleship). Although this move followed developments in France, where Depuy de Lôme had been responsible for the construction of the armoured, but wooden-hulled, ship of the line *Gloire*, the British Admiralty had in fact been to the forefront in its appreciation of the advantages, such as comparative cost, ready availability and relative strength/lightness of structure, of iron over wood for ship construction.

There remained, however, the apparently intractable problem of the disturbing effect of an iron hull upon the magnetic compass which rendered accurate ocean navigation all but impossible. It was not until 1838 that some means of correction was evolved as a result of trials conducted by George Airy, the Astronomer Royal, aboard the 580-ton iron steamship *Rainbow* belonging to the General Steam Navigation Co of London.

FIRST IRON SHIPS FOR THE RN
In the meantime, in 1837, the Admiralty had taken over from the Post Office responsibility for the mail packet service and it was as one of a number of replacement vessels for the Dover/Calais route that John Laird of Birkenhead launched the 228-ton iron paddle steamer *Dover* in May 1840. This small craft, the first iron vessel built for the Royal Navy, was later sent out to west Africa where she spent many years in and around the Gambia until she was finally sold in 1866! Two years later John Laird put afloat the 878-ton iron hulled paddle frigate *Guadaloupe*, a private venture which having failed to excite the attention of the Admiralty had been acquired on behalf of the Mexican government (see *Warship* 11). In 1843, however, the compass problem having been finally resolved, the Admiralty placed an order with Messrs Ditchburn & Mare of Blackwall for an iron-hulled paddle sloop of 858 tons. Launched as *Trident* on the 16 December 1845 this vessel was built up on an iron keel with frames of iron angle 4ins by 3½ins by ½in thick and plated with hand-wrought iron plates of ¾in abreast the keel and ¼in at upper deck level. These details apart, the *Trident* was typical of her day with twin-cylinder oscillating machinery of 350nhp, built by Messrs Seaward & Capel of Poplar, and a three-masted (probably barque) rig.

The *Trident* was followed by the 1400-ton iron paddle frigate *Birkenhead* (ex-*Vulcan*) built by John Laird (Yard No 51) which entered the water on the 30 December 1845. By this time, however, the days of the paddle warship were numbered and the last such craft, the 1257-ton wooden-hulled frigate *Valorous*, joined the fleet in 1852. The paddles themselves were vulnerable but this weakness apart they interfered with the conventional broadside arrangement of the armament. Thus the paddle frigates carried many fewer guns than contemporary sailing frigates although the limited broadside battery was supplemented by a number of larger shell guns, either swivel mounted or on traversing carriages.

THE SCREW PROPELLER
In February 1837 Francis Pettit Smith first demonstrated his screw propeller and in the following year the Ship Propeller Co was formed to exploit his patents. This development led to the construction by Henry Wimshurst at Poplar of the 237-ton screw steamship *Archimedes* which, following preliminary trials early in 1839, was sent round the coast visiting Dover, Portsmouth, Plymouth, Bristol and other ports to demonstrate the versatility of the screw propeller. While at Dover in April 1840 the *Archimedes* took part in a series of trials with the Admiralty cross channel packet steamers, including amongst others the 225-ton paddler *Widgeon*, the fastest vessel on the station. In their report to the Board of Admiralty, Captain E Chappell, RN and Thomas Lloyd stated that in their opinion '. . . the propelling power of the screw is equal if not superior to that of the ordinary paddle wheel. In this respect, therefore, Mr Smith's invention may be considered to be completely successful.'[1] On the other hand they pointed out that the step-up spur gearing was very noisy, not that this would have been of great consequence in a warship where the screw '. . . would probably be used only in cases of emergency, . . .'

Despite reservations expressed by the Surveyor of the Navy, Sir William Symonds, the Admiralty Board was impressed and within a month the decision had been made to build a screw steamship for the Royal Navy. Such a vessel was seen as the answer to the shortcomings associated with the paddle steamer; a full broadside could be mounted whilst, with a feathering or lifting

[1]. *Reports Relative to Smith's Patent Screw Propeller as used On Board the Archimedes* by Captain Edward Chappell, RN (London, 1840).

The launch of the *Greenock* screw frigate at Greenock 30 April 1849.

National Maritime Museum

screw, the sailing qualities might be expected to be little impaired. In the first place, however, there were numerous technical problems to be resolved and after some discussion an order was placed with Sheerness Dockyard in December 1840 for the construction of a wooden screw sloop. The vessel entered the water as *Rattler* on the 12 April 1843 and began her trials in October of that same year. Between February 1844 and January 1845 no fewer than 32 propellers of varying form were tried although in the event it was a two-bladed screw of Francis Pettit Smith's design which proved the most successful. These activities culminated in the much publicised 'tug-of-war' between the 1078-ton screw sloop *Rattler* and the paddle sloop *Alecto*, a vessel of similar dimensions, which took place off the Nore on the 3 April 1845.

SCREW SHIP CONSTRUCTION

By this time, however, the Admiralty mind had been made up and already orders had been placed for seven screw frigates, including the iron hulled *Pegasus, Megaera, Simoon* and *Vulcan*, together with sundry smaller vessels, whilst a number of other ships then under construction were to be converted for screw propulsion. In the event, orders for the wood screw frigates *Arrogant, Dauntless* and *Termagant* were followed early in 1845 by that for the 1413-ton (bm) *Pegasus*, the first of the iron vessels, which was placed with John Scott & Sons of Greenock. Orders, placed in March 1845, for the *Megaera, Simoon* and *Vulcan* went in turn to William Fairburn (Millwall), Robert Napier (Govan) and Ditchburn & Mare (Blackwall) respectively.

Machinery layout of the screw frigate *Greenock*.

Courtesy Scott Lithgow Ltd

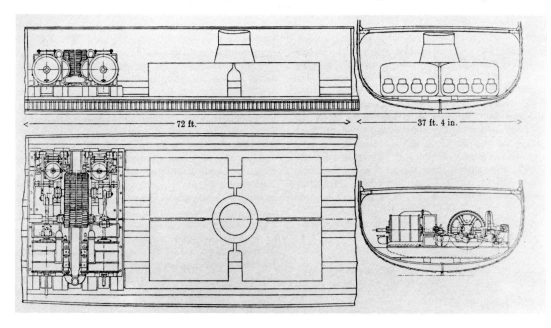

The keel of the *Pegasus* was laid at Greenock in 1845 but a year later her intended name was changed, appropriately, to *Greenock* and it was as such that she entered the water, following a lengthy period of gestation, on 30 April 1849. Without doubt she was massively built, the keel, itself $9\frac{3}{4}$ins deep by $4\frac{3}{4}$in across, the stem and the sternpost being fabricated of solid malleable iron and the transverse frames of iron angle 6ins by $3\frac{1}{2}$ins by $\frac{7}{16}$in thick. In addition each alternate frame was strengthened by a reverse frame of 4in by 3in by $\frac{1}{2}$in angle while, over the length of the machinery compartment, a frame spacing of as little as 1ft ensured a sound foundation for the engine and boilers. Four keelsons of malleable iron, 16ins wide by $\frac{3}{4}$in thick, added to the longitudinal strength of the hull structure. The wrought iron shell plating tapered from $\frac{3}{4}$in thick over the ship's bottom to $\frac{1}{2}$in for the upper strakes under the wales. The *Greenock* was 210ft long between perpendiculars and of $37\frac{1}{2}$ft beam.

Like her wooden hulled contemporaries the *Greenock* carried a figurehead, the unusual choice in her case being a bust of John Scott (1752-1837), late head of the Clyde shipbuilding business by whom she was built. At the time of her launch her hull was painted black, with a black and white chequered strake in the way of the gunports in keeping with the practice of the day.

GREENOCK'S MACHINERY

As a general rule, early commercial screw steamships were engined with geared vertical machinery, the gearing being made necessary by the fact that contemporary technology did not permit engine speeds sufficiently high for the efficient performance of the screw propeller. In the design of a warship, however, the question of affording maximum protection was an important factor and this led to the development of horizontal machinery, likewise geared, which could be sited below the waterline. Thus the *Greenock* received simple twin-cylinder horizontal geared engines of 565nhp designed to meet this requirement and built by Scott, Sinclair & Co of Greenock, a firm closely associated with the shipbuilder.

The engine and gearing occupied some 21ft of the total length of 72ft taken up by the machinery space, the former being so arranged that the two cylinders, each of 71ins diameter[2] with a stroke of 4ft, were positioned to starboard of the crankshaft which carried two cranks displaced by 90°. To port were the two vertical air pumps, each driven off the corresponding crank via a connecting rod and bell crank linkage. Four sets of spur gearing with a step-up ratio of 1 to 2.35 connected at the crankshaft, driven at 42 rpm, to the propeller shaft to give 98.7 rpm at the designed full power. The 14ft diameter two-bladed screw, of the type patented by Francis Pettit Smith, weighed some 7 tons and could be disconnected enabling it to be lifted clear of the water when the ship was under sail.

2. A drawing of 1845 gives the cylinder dimensions as $67\frac{1}{2}$ins diameter by 4ft stroke, the nominal horse power being 510 against the 565nhp of the machinery shown on a drawing of 1848 and eventually fitted.

Steam was supplied by four box through-tube boilers, each with four wet-bottomed furnaces, sited in pairs at the forward end of the machinery space. In keeping with the practice of the day the boilers were fed with sea water necessitating frequent debrining or partial 'blowing down' when the boilers were steamed. Likewise the condensers were of the 'jet' type into which cold salt water was injected or sprayed in order to induce a vacuum once the cylinder, condenser and air pump had been flooded with steam on starting. The salt-laden condensate and ingested air were then passed, via the air pump, to the hot well and thence overboard or into the boiler feed system carrying with it liberal quantities of tallow, the all-purpose lubricant employed for steam plant at the time and in fact the only suitable lubricating agent then readily available.

As in the majority of contemporary steam vessels the air pumps were in fact the only engine driven auxiliaries on board and provision was made for a suction to be taken either from overboard or from the bilge as required. In the latter case ash and cinders were invariably carried over into the feed system, but with the low

The iron screw frigate *Greenock*.
Author's collection

pressures employed a few more impurities were of little consequence. In all probability the bulk of this dross was discharged overboard when debrining the boilers!

Like the majority of her contemporaries the *Greenock* was designed to carry a full ship rig, the intention being that she should cruise under sail, steam being raised only for manoeuvring when winds were adverse or absent. As stated above the screw could be disconnected and hoisted clear of the water, the funnel being lowered at the same time in order to avoid interference with the working of the sails. In appearance of course there was little to distinguish her from the wooden-hulled screw frigates then coming into service.

ARMAMENT

It seems probable that the *Greenock* was first intended to mount ten long 32pdr smooth-bore muzzle-loaders, this being the standard fleet weapon of the day which had replaced the mixed calibre armament fit of the old sailing navy. These truck-mounted guns were to have been carried on the spar deck firing through broadside ports, but early in 1845 the then Secretary of the Admir-

alty, the Right Hon Henry S Corry, proposed the strengthening of the ship's armament by the addition of guns on the main deck firing directly forward and aft. The provision of the two gun ports at the forward end posed no problem but some redesign was necessary aft where the original arrangement for the screw well and rudder interfered with the fitting of the additional guns. The proposed changes are detailed on a drawing dated 22 April 1845.

The eventual armament fit, proposed on 27 June 1845 and detailed on a general arrangement drawing dated 14 January 1848, comprised four 68pr (8in) and two 56pr (8in) shell guns, and four 32pr ML guns on the spar deck and four 32pr ML guns on the main deck.

It was still envisaged, of course, that engagements would be fought out at ranges little greater than those of Nelson's day and it was with this factor in mind that, early in 1845, doubts began to be expressed as to the wisdom of building warships with iron hulls.

To be continued

Amphibious Command Ships:
Past Present & Future Part 1

by Norman Polmar & John J Patrick

Air controllers aboard a US Navy command ship during combat in the Pacific.

USN

HMS *Bulolo* shown as the flagship of Rear Admiral
Troubridge, headquarters ship for the British XIII Corps
landings in Italy during July 1943.

IWM

The amphibious force flagships or, as they were more
recently known, amphibious command ships, have
essentially passed from the naval scene. The only two
ships of the type remaining in service with any navy have
quietly assumed the role of flagships for US Navy numbered fleets.

THE ORIGINS OF AMPHIBIOUS COMMAND SHIPS
It was the frequency and complexity of Second World
War amphibious assaults that led to the development of
the amphibious command ship. The difficulty of coordinating such assaults was first demonstrated in this
century by the notorious disaster of the Gallipoli landing
of 1915, at the southern end of the Turkish Straits. The
Gallipoli landing was called 'one of the greatest disasters
in British history' by military historian J F C Fuller.

Despite this debacle, which hastened the fall of Wins-
ton Churchill from his position as First Lord of the
Admiralty, neither Great Britain nor the United States
drew the correct conclusions concerning the need for
extensive communications and staffs to support
amphibious operations. In fact, the same problems that
had plagued the Gallipoli expedition came close to causing another disaster two decades later, when the Allies
mounted Operation Torch, the joint British-American
landings in French North Africa. French forces nominally loyal to the government of occupied France put up
only sporadic resistance, but poor coordination and lack
of command support confused and even endangered the
landings.

Rear Admiral H K Hewitt, commander of the American Western Task Force, which landed troops on

Morocco's Atlantic coast, flew his flag in the heavy
cruiser *Augusta*. This ship had been fitted with additional radios and extra bunks for the amphibious command staff, but there were still far too few radio circuits
for so large an operation, and the *Augusta* was so
crowded that the staff could hardly carry out its tasks. To
make matters worse, the *Augusta*'s command and communications facilities were often needed at one place
just as her 8in guns were needed for fire support elsewhere. As Admiral Hewitt stated in his report:

'No ship of the Western Naval Task Force was suited
to be a headquarters ship due to the small space alloted
to communications equipment and personnel. The
Torch Operation clearly demonstrates that a headquarters ship with adequate communications facilities is
essential to amphibious operations.'

THE FIRST AMPHIBIOUS COMMAND SHIP
The Royal Navy, after more than three years of war, was
already moving to meet Admiral Hewitt's requirement.
In March 1942, eight months before Operation Torch,
the Admiralty had ordered the conversion of a 9110-ton
armed merchant cruiser, HMS *Bulolo*, into the first ship
specially configured for amphibious command. The British designated this new type a headquarters landing ship
(LSH).

The *Bulolo*'s new communications installation had
separate radio networks for ground, naval and air units,
while joint channels were provided for overall coordination of an amphibious operation. To minimize interference, the ship's many transmitters were located aft and
her even more numerous receivers well forward. The
Bulolo had separate operations rooms for the different
service staffs, plus an inter-service room for coordination. This ship also carried several landing craft to take
the ground force commander and his staff ashore.

1

2

1 The first of the modern command ships: HMS *Bulolo*,
photographed with HM the King embarked.
IWM

2 The wireless room of a British Second World War command
ship with operators from the Army, Royal Navy, and Royal Air
Force working side-by-side.
IWM

3 The USS *Ancon* (AGC-4) in San Francisco Bay, 1945-46.
USN

As an LSH, the *Bulolo* had a complement of approximately 300, plus about 200 officers and men of the embarked amphibious staffs. For self-defence, she had four 4in anti-aircraft guns in twin mounts, plus numerous single 40mm and 20mm anti-aircraft guns. The Royal Navy was so impressed with the *Bulolo*'s high-volume information handling and communications that it assigned her to support Prime Minister Churchill during the January 1943 Casablanca Conference with President Roosevelt.

In addition to the *Bulolo*, the Royal Navy converted three other merchant ships to large LSHs during the war, the *Hilary, Largs,* and *Lothian* (several destroyers, frigates, and gunboats were also temporarily employed in the LSH role between 1943 and 1945).

US NAVY DEVELOPMENTS

Spurred by Admiral Hewitt's report on Operation Torch, the US Navy's Bureau of Ships (BuShips) belatedly began a programme to produce amphibious command ships. BuShips had completed plans for the first American counterparts of the *Bulolo* by the end of 1942 and these were approved on 3 February 1943, not quite three months after Operation Torch. The new ships were to bear the designation amphibious force flagship (AGC).

The US Navy acquired the necessary ships by taking over several of the ubiquitous, single-screw C-2 cargo ships then building under contract from the US

3

Maritime Commission, forerunner of today's Maritime Administration. The first ships (MC Hulls 200-203) were acquired on 15 March 1943 and would become AGC-1, -2 and -3, respectively. Twelve additional C-2 hulls would later be diverted to the AGC programme to meet the growing demand for command ships.

To help meet the need for AGCs while C-2 hulls were still undergoing conversion, the Navy also took in hand the SS *Ancon*, a passenger-freight liner completed in 1938. Following Pearl Harbor, this 14,150-ton ship had become a troop transport under US Army control but was subsequently transferred to the Navy. She carried troops from the United States to North Africa for the Torch landings, where she was barely missed by U-boat torpedoes that sank a nearby ship. This was the beginning of her reputation as a 'lucky' ship, a reputation that endured through extensive wartime operations in which she was never hit by enemy weapons.

Although the *Ancon* was designated AGC-4, she was actually the first amphibious force flagship commissioned into the US Navy, and the first to see combat. In addition, the *Ancon* was by far the largest of the AGCs: 453ft overall, with a 64ft beam and a 26ft draught.

Shortly after Operation Torch, the *Ancon* reported to Norfolk for conversion, which was completed on 20 April 1943. Like the C-2 conversions, she received the standard US Navy armament for large amphibious and auxiliary ships: two single, open-mount 5in/38 guns and several 40mm anti-aircraft guns (unlike the C-2s, however, she did not have 20mm guns). Her combat debut came during the July 1943 invasion of Sicily, where she was flagship of Task Force 85, commanded by Rear Admiral A G Kirk. She was also the afloat headquarters of II Corps, commanded by Major General Omar Bradley (Bradley's Corp was the lead unit of Lieutenant General George S Patton's Seventh Army).

When Allied troops subsequently landed on the Italian mainland at Salerno in September 1943, the *Ancon* served as the flagship of newly promoted Vice Admiral H K Hewitt, the officer whose report had helped spark the US AGC programme. Also on board was Lieutenant General Mark Clark, commanding the US Fifth Army. It was this landing that brought the amphibious flagship concept to the attention of historian Samuel Eliot Morison, who mistakenly reported that the new ship type had been 'improvised for Admiral Hewitt in the Salerno operation'. Despite this misunderstanding of the *Ancon*'s origins, Morison was correct in his conclusion that the new ship type had come about because:

'the network of communications in modern amphibious warfare had become so vast and complicated, and the officers and men necessary to staff amphibious force headquarters so numerous, that no ordinary combatant or auxiliary ship could hold them.'

After Salerno, the *Ancon* changed her base of operations from the Mediterranean to the British Isles, joining the huge amphibious armada being organised for the Normandy invasion. On 6 June 1944, she was the flagship of the US amphibious task force that assaulted Omaha Beach.

Returning to the United States for a six-month refit, the *Ancon* then departed for action in the Pacific where other AGCs had been active since the invasion of the Marshall Islands early in 1944. Although the US Navy withheld information on these ships throughout the war, the Japanese may have become aware of their importance. In any event, the commanders of the Easter 1945 assault on Okinawa reportedly ordered the *Ancon* to operate on the eastern side of the island to draw Japanese attention away from the main landings on the Western shore. The *Ancon*'s luck held, and she survived this decoy duty without damage.

The *Ancon* remained a lucky ship right up to the surrender ceremony in Tokyo Bay, during which she provided workspace and long-range radio communications for the American and Allied press. At anchor alongside the battleship *Missouri*, the *Ancon* gave her crew a front-row seat at that historic event of 2 September 1945.

THE C-2 COMMAND SHIPS

The 15 AGCs converted from C-2 merchant hulls were by far the most numerous and significant of the Second World War amphibious force flagships. The first four ships, which had the C2-S-B1 hull, formed the *Appalachian* class (AGC-1, -2, -3 and -5); the remainder, which had the C2-S-AJ1 hull, became the *Mount McKinley* class (AGC-7 to -17).

All 15 AGCs were basically similar. They had an overall length of 459ft, a beam of 63ft, and a 24ft draught. Their full load displacement was about 12,800 tons. Twin boilers and a single steam turbine produced 6,000shp for a trial speed of slightly over 16kts (sustained speed being somewhat less). All C-2 AGCs had a single open-mount 5in/38 on the forecastle and a second on the fantail, four to eight 40mm guns in dual or quadruple mounts, and up to twenty 20mm guns.

The exact number of officers and men on board varied from one operation to the next. Most C-2 AGCs had accommodation for approximately 55 officers and 580 enlisted men, but they could embark a larger number of men when necessary. Each ship carried a few landing craft with which to carry ashore the commander of the landing force and his staff.

---

1 The USCGC *Duane*, early 1945, as an amphibious command ship. Note the 40mm main gun batteries forward and aft. Six of the 327ft 'Treasury' class ships, which earlier carried up to three 5in guns, were extensively modified for the AGC role. After the war they reverted to the patrol gunboat configuration.

US Coast Guard

2 The USCGC *Spencer* as an amphibious flagship in September 1944. An open 5in gun mount was retained forward and aft. Note the camouflage paint scheme.

US Coast Guard

1

2

The bridge of HMS *Bulolo*, showing the damage from a bomb hit received on 7 June 1944 while she was operating as Commadore Douglas-Pennant's HQ ship off the Normandy beachhead.

IWM

The USCGC *Bibb* on 29 January 1945. Note the open 5in mount on the quarterdeck and the twin 10mm mountings on the after superstructure.
USN

The command ship *Adirondack* standing out from the Philadelphia Naval Shipyard. She was typical of the highly capable C-2 command ships that served the US navy into the 1970s.

The principal feature of the AGCs was, of course, the great amount of internal space devoted to command and communications. As a result, the conversion plan for the C-2 AGCs called for an added enclosed deck amidships, between the forward and aft kingposts. The exact internal arrangements varied both from ship to ship and from operation to operation. However, the following table, which describes the arrangement of the *Mount McKinley* in 1944, gives some idea of the layout of her principal command and communications spaces:

MOUNT McKINLEY (AGC-7)
Arrangement of Key Command
Support/Communications Spaces, 1944:

Level	Command Support/Communications Spaces
Flag Bridge	Radar Room, Flag Plotting Room
Navigation Bridge	Aerological (Meteorological Office)
Superstructure Deck	War (Army/Marine) Command Office, Intelligence Office
Main Deck	CIC, Joint Operations Room, Navy Operations Room, Voice Circuits Filter Room, Staff Gunnery and Air Office, Radio II (main transmitting room)
Second Deck	Coding Room, Communications Room, Flag and Staff Officers' Offices, Radio III (secondary transmitting room)
First Platform	Radio I (central receiving room)
Second Platform	Photographic and Photo Interpretation Facilities, Print Shop

The first of the C-2 AGCs to join the fleet was the *Rocky Mount* (AGC-3), commissioned on 2 October 1943. Together with her sister ship, *Appalachian*, the *Rocky Mount* went into action for the first time in the January 1944 assault on Kwajalein Atoll in the Marshall Islands, where she served as flagship of the amphibious force commanded by Rear Admiral Richmond Kelly Turner. Six months later, the *Rocky Mount* again carried Turner's flag, this time as a vice admiral commanding all US amphibious forces in the Pacific theatre during the massive June 1944 landings on Saipan.

As more and more AGCs joined the fleet, it became commonplace for several of these ships to participate on the same operation, and for individual ships to take on special duties while still performing their main function as amphibious command ships. In the February 1945 assault on Iwo Jima, for example, the *Estes* (AGC-12) was assigned to control underwater demolition work and pre-assault shore bombardment in addition to other duties. Her sister ship *Eldorado* (AGC-11) served as

Vice Admiral Turner's flagship for the assault and headquarters for US war correspondents covering the landings, providing the long-range communications needed to broadcast dispatches directly to the home front (Secretary of the Navy James Forrestal visited on board the *Eldorado* during the operation). Still another command ship, the converted seaplane tender *Biscayne* (AGC-16), was tasked with coordinating the destroyer screen protecting the entire invasion force.

During the subsequent invasion of Okinawa in April 1945, the *Eldorado* carried both the Commander, Air Support Control Unit, and the Amphibious Force Fighter Director Officer. She thus served as the main control centre for around-the-clock air defence of the entire assault force, coordinating air traffic over the beaches and directing fighter intercepts of kamikaze and conventional air attacks. The *Eldorado*'s primary mission was to carry Vice Admiral Turner, again in command of the amphibious operation, and his staff. A total of five AGCs took part in the Okinawa assault.·

On numerous occasions the AGCs were in combat. This usually took the form of fighting off enemy aircraft, particularly the kamikaze planes that menaced US amphibious forces as the US landings drew closer to Japan. However, at least one AGC took on enemy forces ashore. Off Leyte in October 1944, the *Rocky Mount* used her 5in guns to silence Japanese mortars that had damaged several LSTs on the beach.

Not all of an AGC's wartime duties were this arduous. In January 1945, the *Catoctin* (AGC-5) sailed from the Mediterranean to Sevastopol on the Black Sea, where she became the advanced American headquarters for the Yalta Conference. During that conference, the *Catoctin* provided communications support for President Roosevelt, and her crew operated transportation, canteen, hospital, and dental services for the American delegation ashore.

There was one more Navy-developed AGC, the *Biscayne*. She was one of 35 *Barnegat* class small seaplane tenders (AVP) built during the war. These were 1695-ton, 310ft 8in ships, with several being completed as PT-boat tenders. The *Biscayne* was completed in 1941 and serviced seaplanes as the AVP-11 in the Atlantic and North Africa areas. In May 1943, while at Mers-el-Kebir, Algeria, she was converted to a command ship (although not redesignated, as AGC-18, until October 1944).

The *Biscayne* served in the AGC role for the invasions of Sicily, Salerno, Anzio, Southern France, Iwo Jima and Okinawa, and also operated immediately after the war in Korean and Chinese waters. She was later transferred to the Coast Guard for duty as a patrol vessel.

THE COAST GUARD COMMAND SHIPS
Besides the *Ancon*, the converted seaplane tender *Biscayne*, and the numerous C-2 AGCs – all of which served as commissioned ships in the US Navy – there were six Coast Guard amphibious command ships. These were large cutters of the 327ft 'Secretary' class, built between 1935 and 1937, used as anti-submarine escorts in the early stages of the war and later converted to meet the

The USS *Estes*, flagship of the Commander, US Seventh Fleet, underway in the Whangpoo River while the United States was providing support for Nationalist Chinese forces in 1946.

USN

The USS *Mount Olympus* in Antarctic ice while serving as flagship for Rear Admiral Richard E Byrd's expedition to the South Pole in 1946–47.

USN

A formal portrait of the presidential yacht *Williamsburg*. From 1941 to 1945 she served as a gunboat (designated PG-56). In the role of presidential yacht she did not wear her hull designation AGC-369.

White House

growing demand for AGCs. One of them, the *Duane* (WPG-33), received a Navy designation (AGC-6) in anticipation of being taken over by the Navy, but neither she nor her five sisters, which retained their wartime Coast Guard designations (WPG-31, 32, 35–37) were ever transferred from Coast Guard control. The six converted cutters had Coast Guard captains and crews throughout the war who jealously guarded the separate status of their ships. However, the premature redesignation of the *Duane* as a Navy AGC appears to have caused some misunderstanding in the Navy. This eventually led to the following memorandum, issued shortly after the end of the war, from the Chief of Naval Operations to the Commander, Amphibious Force Training Command, US Atlantic Fleet:

'1. In reference (a), the *Duane* is referred to as the USS *Duane* (AGC-6).

2. Attention is invited to the status of the *Duane*. It is a Coast Guard vessel, owned and manned by the Coast Guard. However it operates under the Navy. In order to avoid any misunderstanding, it should be called the CGC *Duane*'.

Since the 'Secretary' class cutters were the largest ships in Coast Guard service, a distinction they retained until the completion of the *Hamilton* in 1975, they had adequate size and stability for the amphibious flagship role. However, the flagship conversion did require that their after superstructure be built up to hold offices, berthing spaces, and communications facilities. Even then, command and communications facilities were inferior to those in the *Ancon* and the C-2 hulls. During conversion, the cutters also beached most of their 5in/52 single-purpose guns.

To be continued

X1-Cruiser Submarine

by D K Brown RCNC

During the early years of the First World War both British and German submarines achieved considerable success with small guns against merchant ships. In both countries the Naval Staffs began to dream of heavily-armed submarine cruisers and from 1916 such vessels were built in Germany. As Preston says 'The importance of the gun-calibre was grossly over-estimated in the minds of both the British and the Germans'. In practice a U-Cruiser could do nothing that a smaller U-boat could not do . . .' (Ref 1).

The British Submarine Committee had considered similar ships in 1915 but had decided not to go ahead with the design, presumably because of a lack of suitable targets. After the war, the victorious Allies had the chance to inspect surrendered German U-Cruisers and many countries decided to build their own monsters (Ref 2). Even Italy, with the *Balila* class, developed from *UE11*, approached the submarine cruiser category. None of these ships was successful and only the Japanese craft even formed the basis for future development.

DESIGN OF X1

Towards the end of 1920 the Royal Navy decided to build an experimental submarine to study the submerged handling of large vessels and also the practicability of mounting and using a heavy gun armament. The new submarine was expected to remain at sea for long periods and to be sufficiently well-armed to engage a destroyer (Ref 3). Provision was made for this submarine, *X1*, in the 1921/22 estimates and she was laid down on 2 November 1921. The design particulars are given in Table 2.

The *X1* was an unusual design for the Royal Navy and for A W Johns, RCNC who was still in charge of submarine design. Her pressure hull, which was one inch thick, was almost completely surrounded by an external hull which contained both the main ballast tanks and most of the fuel. She had 9 water-tight bulkheads, and frames about 1ft 6in apart. The internal diameter of the pressure hull amidships was 19ft 7½in. The service displacement on the surface was about 3050 tons giving a reserve of buoyancy of 18 per cent (Ref 4).

GUN ARMAMENT

There were two twin mountings for 5.2in/42cal QF Mk I guns sited one ahead of the bridge and the other about 50ft aft of the bridge. These guns had a range of 16,000yds. A circular trunk 4½ft in diameter ran from the mounting to the magazine in the pressure hull which contained 100 rounds per gun. There was a working chamber 10ft in diameter round the trunk between the pressure hull and the gun mounting. Special ballast tanks were fitted to compensate for the loss of weight as ammunition was fired.

Elaborate gunnery control arrangments were fitted in compartments which had to be bolted water-tight and resist full diving pressure. The director tower was arranged at the level of the bridge canopy and had a top which could be raised 2ft when in use. The upper control room was between the director and the pressure hull. Just abaft the control room was the rangefinding room with a 9ft rangefinder on the bridge. The conning tower was abaft the gunnery control rooms to which it provided access.

MACHINERY

Unfortunately *X1* had novel machinery which consisted of:

a Two 8-cylinder diesels, Admiralty design and built at Chatham, each giving 3000bhp at 390rpm.

b Two auxiliary diesels, removed from the German submarine *U126* (not the *Deutschland* as is often stated) with a nominal rating of 1200bhp each. These engines drove the generators which charged the batteries and

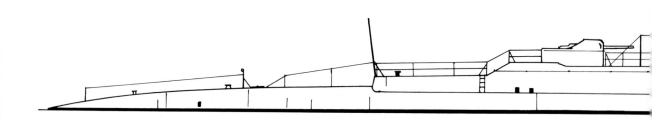

could also drive the main motors direct.

c Two main electric motors of 1000hp driven directly by the auxiliary engines through the generators.

Each of the twin shafts could be driven using either the main diesels or the motors or both together. This should have given a total of 8000hp but the German diesels failed to give anything like their full power (the best they could do was 940bhp) and the recorded power on trial was 7135hp giving 19.5kts. By 1930 speed had dropped to 18.6kts at 3048 tons (probably on main engines only). At the same date her endurance was recorded as 5300nm at 18kts or 16,200 at 10kts using 95 per cent of her 452 tons of fuel. The battery was in three groups of 110 cells each and weighed 221 tons in all.

SERVICE CAREER

X1 was commissioned in December 1925 and ran successful full power trials in March 1926 before acceptance in April of that year. After a voyage to Gibraltar and back it was found that the main engine drive wheels were damaged and had to be replaced. After refit she returned to the Mediterranean under Captain P E Phillips, DSO,RN with a very experienced 1st Lieutenant – D Friedberger (Ref 5). *X1* carried out a long series of exercises in the Mediterranean, with the fleet, against the fleet, on observation patrol and in simulated attacks. Her gunnery officer (Ref 5) recalls her as a beautiful ship with clean lines and good in a sea; a pig to dive though, taking 3 or 4 minutes to get under.

In January 1928 her starboard shaft broke during a full power run and a new set of gears was needed but after repairs at Malta, in April 1928 the port shaft broke in the same place. By 1930 the CO reported 'internal arrangements not very satisfactory because of overcrowding with auxiliary machinery, accommodation is cramped, ventilation poor and the ship suffers from humidity, diving arrangements good.' Both the main and auxiliary engines continued to give trouble and *X1* spent most of her time in dockyard hands. The rules of life on ships in the London Naval Treaty meant that she could not be replaced with new building until 1938 so it was decided to lay her up. Her main Kingston valves were blanked and she lay in Fareham Creek until she was scrapped in 1937.

Inevitably there were many rumours about this large and experimental craft and some are still quoted. It was often stated that she was a great success and scrapped either because the Admiralty disliked submarines or because they were afraid that our enemies would copy her. Apart from her unreliable machinery *X1* seems to have achieved her creator's intentions but there was no role for such a submarine in the RN. It is interesting that the German Navy, who had experience of cruiser submarines in the First World War did not repeat their mistake in the Second.

REFERENCES

1 *The First Submarines*. A Preston, Purnell.
2 *All the World's Fighting Ships 1922-1946*. (Conway Maritime Press 1980)
3 *DNC Department History of World War II*. Naval Library
4 *The Development of HM Submarines*. A N Harrison, RCNC
5 *Captain Gilbert Harrison RN*. Mark Williams (Cassell 1979)

TABLE 1: CRUISER SUBMARINE DESIGNS

Country	Submarine	Launched	Guns	Submerged Displacement
United Kingdom	X1	1923	4–5.2in	3600 tons
Japan	I1	1924	2–5.5in	2790 tons
USA	V4, V5, V6	1927	2–6in	c4000 tons
France	Surcouf	1929	2–8in	4300 tons

TABLE 2: PARTICULARS OF X1

Length (oa):	363ft 6in
Breadth (extreme):	29ft 10in
Displacement (surface):	2780 tons
Displacement (submerged):	3600 tons
Speed (surface):	19.5 – 20kts
Speed (submerged):	9kts
Endurance (surface):	14,500nm
Endurance (submerged):	50nm at 4kts
Torpedo tubes:	6-21in with 12 MkIV SX torpedoes
Guns:	2-twin 5.2in mountings
Diving Depth:	500ft (later reduced to 350ft)
Test depth:	200ft
Complement:	11 officers, 100 men

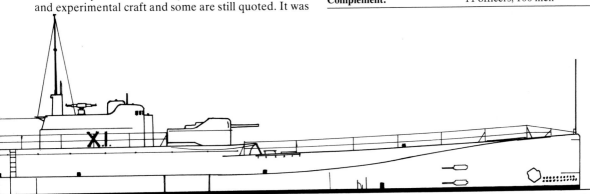

Lesser Known Warships of the Kriegsmarine No1:
The Light Cruiser Nürnberg

by MJ Whitley

Nürnberg at a fleet review pre-war. She carries a vice admiral's flag at the fore truck as flagship (Scouting Forces). Note the old He60 floatplane still carried.

Drüppel

The light cruiser *Nürnberg* was the sixth and final cruiser planned by the Reichsmarine in the build-up of the new German fleet and the replacement of out-dated ships retained under the Treaty of Versailles. In fact she was never to sail under the Reichsmarine ensign for in May 1935, with the advent of the National Socialist government, the fleet became known as the Kriegsmarine – a prophetic change of title.

The new cruiser, named after the Bavarian town in South Germany, was the third to carry the name. It had first been borne by the 3550-ton 'Kleiner Kreuzer' completed in 1908, armed with ten 10.5cm guns; this ship was part of Von Spee's East Asiatic Squadron and was sunk off the Falkland Islands in December 1914 by the British cruiser *Kent*. She was replaced by a new vessel of 5300 tons, completed in 1917 by Howald at Kiel, which was ceded to Britain after the war, being finally sunk as a target off the Isle of Wight in July 1922.

DESIGN AND CONSTRUCTION

The design of the third *Nürnberg* was a modification of the previous Reichsmarine cruiser, *Leipzig*; the new ship displaced 6980 tons standard, 9114 tons full load, on a longer and slightly broader hull than her predecessor. The propulsion unit consisted of a mixed steam and diesel system, with six marine boilers (16atm) grouped in pairs in three boiler rooms providing steam for two sets of Krupp-Germania geared turbines driving the two outer shafts from separate compartments. To extend her cruising range, she, like all previous designs (except *Emden*) was equipped with diesel power on the centre shaft. Four MAN 7-cylinder two-stroke double action motors were geared through a Vulcan gearbox to give 12,400bhp on this shaft. The steam turbine installation provided 66,000hp giving a designed top speed of 32kts, with 18kts maintainable on the diesels alone. When running on diesel power the outer shafts were rotated by electric motors to reduce drag.

As with all German warships of the period, her electrical installation was extensive by contemporary British standards. Four separate generating units were provided, comprising two turbo-generators of 350kW each (one in each turbine room) and two diesel compartments forward, each containing a pair of 150kW diesel

The *Nürnberg* in superb condition, pre-war. No 3.7cm guns appear to be shipped at this time.

Drüppel

generators making a total capacity of 1300kW. Power distribution was on the 'tree' and not the ring main system. During the war, when protection against magnetic mines became necessary, a degaussing alternator was fitted. Her DG arrangements consisted of three main and five subsidiary coils to afford the requisite protection. Two Anschutz master gyros were fitted but the only other navigational aids were two D/F sets.

The hull, longitudinally framed and incorporating a high degree of welding to conserve weight, was fitted with a bulbous bow and side bulges, and was divided into fourteen water-tight compartments. A double bottom extended some 83 per cent of her length. The main armour belt, 50mm thick at its maximum, was extended to the stem, whilst the protective deck carried between 20mm and 25mm plating and the turrets up to 80mm thickness of armour. In technical details, she differed little from *Leipzig* but was aesthetically more pleasing in appearance. Her main armament, consisting of the well proven 15cm SK C/25 pattern gun, was shipped in three triple turrets disposed in typical continental fashion with one forward and two aft. The after pair were, like those of *Leipzig*, disposed on the centreline. The massive block bridge carried the conning tower and the navigation, signal and flag bridges. This structure also carried the two main 6.5m base rangefinders, one atop the navigating bridge and the second on the foremast tower.

Between the bridge structure and the single funnel, the ship's boats were clustered, being handled by a pair of derricks stepped against the after end of the superstructure. Abaft the funnel, the aircraft installation consisted of a catapult, crane and accommodation for two reconnaisance aircraft – initially obsolete, 170kt, He60 biplanes, but these had been replaced by the more modern and faster Arado Ar196 by the outbreak of war.

The after superstructure carried the secondary control position, flak director, a third 6.5m rangefinder and two twin 3.7cm flak mountings. Between the after end of this superstructure and 'B' turret, the exhausts for the diesel installation were taken up. Her secondary armament of eight 8.8cm guns in twin mountings was carried at forecastle deck level and disposed on the beam, forward and aft of the after triple 53.3cm torpedo tube banks.

All boiler uptakes were trunked into a large single funnel, like her near sister *Leipzig*, but of slightly different design. In contrast to the *Leipzig*, *Nürnberg* carried a large platform around the funnel on which were mounted four searchlights. Later, during the war, the after pair were replaced by light flak guns. Finally, an unusual feature of her appearance was the stepping of three masts, one on the bridge, one on the after side of the funnel and a mizzen just forward of the flak director aft.

As designed, her ship's company numbered 25 officers and 648 men, with a further 17 officers and 66 men when serving as a flagship. Later her complement rose to 870 men. By British standards, her galleys were small and both officers and men were fed from the same galley, a legacy of the 1918 mutinies. Particular attention had been paid to office accommodation, which was typical of all German warships. In addition, there was a canteen, barber's shop and laundry. Accommodation was also provided for the transport of troops when required. One thousand men could be carried for a day or 600 for longer periods. Alternatively, 200 tons of supercargo could be carried.

The contract for her construction as cruiser 'F', (the name remained secret until her launch in accordance with German practice) went to the Deutschewerke at Kiel, where she was laid down in 1934 under the 1933 programme. Launched on 8 December 1934 she was finally commissioned on 2 November 1935 under the command of Kpt z S Schmundt.

ARMAMENT

Like previous light cruisers, the main armament of *Nürnberg* was carried in three triple turrets. (Drehturm LC/25), which differed slightly from earlier mountings. The guns themselves were 149.1mm calibre SK C/25, firing a 45.5kg shell with a maximum range of 25,700m. The turret fronts carried 80mm of Krupp 'Wotan h' armour, with 20mm on the sides and 35mm on the rear. Each complete turret weighed 147,150kg. Power was part electric, part hydraulic with hand loading and ramming. For the main armament, 150rpg were provided (30 AP, 50 HE base-fuzed and 70 HE nose-fuzed). Of these, 16 (12 time-fuzed and 4 CRBF) were stowed in ready-use clips in the gunhouse. A further 10 shells and charges were stowed in each handing room. For illumination, 250 star shell were carried and at night 'A' turret carried star shell in its ready-use racks. The magazines were directly under the armoured deck, shells and charges being stowed in the same space. both shells and charges were man-handled from their bins and cases to the revolving structure through double hand-troughs, one each for shells and charges. Chain hoists delivered the ammunition to the guns but separate auxiliary bucket hoists were also provided at the rear of the main hoists. All magazines, shell rooms and handing spaces were fitted with a spray drenching system although it was not possible to drench the revolving structure. Brine magazine cooling arrangements were fitted. The ammunition arrangements were claimed to achieve a rate of fire of 10 to 12 rounds per minute. Each gun was fitted with its own individual gyro firing and TIC gear, thus eliminating laying errors at the gun.

The heavy anti-aircraft weapons consisted of twin 8.8cm guns from the outset and were of the SK C/32 pattern in twin LC/32 mountings. Light flak weapons comprised four twin 3.7cm SK C/30 in twin LC/30 mountings and several 2cm/30 guns in single L/30 mountings. Her torpedo armament consisted of 12 tubes for 53.3cm G7a torpedoes in four triple mountings. Five torpedo control sights, each with its own binoculars, were fitted. Two were on the bridge, one in the control tower forward and two in the after control position.

Her design also made provision for carrying 182 EMC mines but this prevented her using 'C' turret or her torpedo armament.

Fire control was exercised by means of optical stereoscopic rangefinders and a fire control room incorporating range and bearing plots as well as a vertical panel (giving elevation data). The 8.8cm guns were controlled by a combined 3m base rangefinder/height finder/director, on the centreline aft.

WARTIME MODIFICATIONS

Until 1942, *Nürnberg* was not greatly altered except for the addition of a few 2cm guns and the installation of a radar set whose aerial mattress was mounted atop the navigating bridge. The German equivalent of Asdic (but working on magnetostriction principles), *S Gerate*, was installed to supplement the pre-war fitted passive hydrophone system GHG (*Gruppenhochgerate*) with its 32 hydrophones and the navigational hydrophone (HNG). The latter was a single rotatable microphone, more accurate in bearing than the GHG.

In 1942, she underwent a major refit during which the catapult and aircraft installations were removed as well as the after banks of tubes. Newer radar was installed with the aerial mounted on the foremast tower.

By late 1944, she was equipped with FuMO21 and FuMO25 radar sets and then, in December 1944, the FuMO21 set was replaced by the new 50cm FuMO63 *Hohentwiel* equipment. The FuMO25 set, carried at the war's end had a wavelength of 81cm and was fitted with a range and bearing panel for low-angle gunnery. Its performance was given as detecting a battleship at 25km, destroyer at 17km and low flying aircraft at 40km. The *Hohentwiel* outfit on the other hand was a shorter range equipment. Other electrical equipment included an IFF device (*Wespe*) mounted on the foremast truck and four METOX radar search receivers. One, type *Palau* was mounted above the forward FuMO25 mattress and was rotatable, whilst two more similar but fixed aerials were mounted abaft the fore top at bearings of red and green 125° respectively. The fourth, type *Cuba* and operating on 1m to 2m wavelengths, was mounted on the forward *Palau* array. By 1945, this radar outfit was hopelessly out of date, there being no aircraft warning on the gunnery set aft. Neither were there any radar jamming devices.

In common with warships of all combatant navies during the Second World War, it was found necessary to greatly augment the light flak outfit. However, due to the almost peacetime situation in Baltic waters, where the cruiser spent much of her time until the autumn of 1942, there was no pressing need for additions. Some additions were made before her transfer to northern waters later that same year, when she received two army pattern 2cm *vierling* (quadruple) mountings shipped atop the navigating bridge (the foremost rangefinder having been landed) and aft on a bandstand on the roof of 'B' turret. Five single 2cm guns were also carried at this time. After her return from Norwegian waters to the Baltic in 1943, no further additions were made until 1944, when, in May, it was proposed to allocate her some of the 4cm flak 28 (Bofors) which were then being fitted to many of the Kriegsmarine's ships to counter the vastly increased dangers of air attack as the Luftwaffe lost command of the skies. These 4cm guns were part of

Nürnberg about 1937.

CPL

a large reserve which had fallen into German hands in the course of their conquest of Europe, principally originating from Polish stocks. Fitted in single, shielded mountings, they added a much needed extra 'punch' to the ship's flak outfit. *Nürnberg* was originally scheduled

TABLE 1: TECHNICAL DATA

Displacement:	6980 tons standard, 9114 tons full load
Length:	170m (pp), 181m (oa)
Beam:	16.4m
Draught:	5.0/6.4m
Machinery:	Six Marine boilers, (16atm = 235psi), two sets Krupp-Germania geared turbines developing 66,000hp on the outer shafts. Four double-acting two-stroke 7-cylinder MAN diesels developing 12,400hp on the centre shaft. Max speed 32kts
Auxiliary machinery:	Two 350kW turbo-generators and four 150kW diesel generators = 1300kW
Fuel capacity:	1055cu m furnace oil fuel, 255 cu m diesel fuel
Radius of action:	740nm at full speed, 2400nm at 13kts
Armour:	Main deck: 20mm (flat), 25mm (slope); Conning tower 50mm (front), 100mm (side), 30mm (rear); Conning tower tube: 60mm; Forward rangefinder: 15mm; flak director: 14mm; foretop: 20mm; side: bows 0 to 35mm, main belt 50mm, stern 18–20mm; barbettes: 60mm
Armament (as designed):	9–15cm SK C/25 in Dreh T LC/25 (150 rpg); 8–8.8cm SK C/32 in Dop LC/32 (400 rpg); 8–3.7cm SK C/30 in Dop L C/30 (1200 rpg); 4–2cm C/30 in single C/30 mountings; 12–53.3cm G7a torpedoes in four triple mountings (no reserve torpedoes).

TABLE 2: PARTICULARS OF GUNS

	15cm SKC/25 in LC/25	8.8cm SKC/32 in LC/32
Calibre (mm):	149.1	88
Muzzle velocity (m/s):	960	950
Shell weight (kg):	45.5	9
Shell length (mm):	655	397
Burster (kg):	19.3	3.1
Cartridge weight (kg):	33.4	15*
Cartridge length (mm):	1192	932*
Maximum range (m):	25,700	17,200
Barrel length (cal/mm):	60/9080	76/6690
Liner length (cal/mm):	57.7/8570	72/6340
Constructional gas pressure (kg/cm²):	3000	3150
Barrel life (rounds):	500	3200
MOUNTING:		
Elevation/Depression:	+40°/−10°	+80°/−10°
Training arc:	±360° (720°)	±360° (720°)
Armour, Whn/A (mm):		
front	80	12
side	20	10
deck	20–35	10
rear	35	–
Weight of barrel & breech (kg):	11,970	3640
Weight of cradle & brakes (kg):	2457	1120
Weight of mounting (kg):	55,450	6275
Weight of shielding (kg):	31,500	5830
Weight of complete turret (kg):	147,150	23,650

* Fixed ammunition

TABLE 3: COMMANDING OFFICERS OF NÜRNBERG

Kpt z See	Hubert Schmundt	2.11.35	to Autumn 1936
Kpt z See	Theodore Riedel		to Autumn 1937
Kpt z See	Walter Krastel		to Autumn 1938
Kpt z See	Otto Klüber		to 7.8.40
Kpt z See	Leo Kreisch	8.8.40	to 19.3.41
Kpt z See	Ernst von Stüdnitz	20.3.41	to 6.43
Kpt z See	Gerhardt Böhmig	6.43	to 7.10.44
Kpt z See	Helmuth Geissler	8.10.44	to end of war

Taken late in 1944, this view shows the two forecastle LM44
2cm twins and the 4cm Flak 28 mounted on the bridge top.
Only one bridge wing is swung out.

Drüppel

to receive four 4cm guns, which were to displace the two
Vierlings from the bridge and 'B' turret, while two of the
twin 3.7cm SK/C30 mountings were to be landed to
accommodate a third and fourth 4cm gun. The single
2cm guns were to be replaced by eight twin 2cm LM44
mountings. Each 4cm and 3.7cm gun was allowed 1000
rounds whilst each 2cm gun shipped 1500 rounds.

For some unknown reason, *Nürnberg* was allocated a
very low priority in the refit programme and seems to
have been regarded less favourably than her older sister,
Köln. The programme schedule called for refits to be
carried out in the order *Hipper, Prinz Eugen, Köln,
Scheer, Lützow* and *Nürnberg*. Probably as a result of the
delay in reaching *Nürnberg* and of diversions of guns to
the very active light surface forces, the cruiser did not in
fact receive this planned outfit. In the final event, only
two 4cm guns were shipped, one on the bridge and a
second on the former catapult tower, which had been
removed by this time along with the rest of the aircraft
equipment. Two naval pattern *vierlings* were mounted,
one on 'B' turret, the second forward of the flak director,
while the two former army pattern mountings were
retained as 'of the ration' extras now mounted to port

and starboard between the 8.8cm mountings. Ten 2cm
twin LM44 mountings and one single 2cm mounting
completed the light flak outfit. These were carried: two
on the forecastle, two on the bridge wings, two at the
after end of the funnel platform, two in the waist of the
main deck and two on the quarterdeck. The single gun
was carried on the bridge front above 'A' turret.

By December 1944, a further plan was finalised to
increase flak outfits yet again with the availability of the
new 3.7cm flak 43M gun. Under these arrangements,
Nürnberg's armament was to consist of eight 3.7cm
43M, two *vierlings* and ten 2cm twins, (all 3.7 SKC/30s
being landed). However, the critical war situation prevented these plans from being realised and she finished
the war with the following outfit: 2 – 4cm(2×1), 8 –
3.7cm(4×2), 37 – 2cm(4×4, 10×2, 1×1). Finally, the
after torpedo tubes were also landed to reduce top
weight and, although she was not nominally allocated
re-loads, by the war's end, four re-loads were in fact
held.

To be continued

Naval History Classics

Conway Maritime are pleased to offer WARSHIP readers a series of newly reprinted classic works of naval interest, encompassing both technical and operational history. These highly-regarded but scarce works will be made available in good quality editions at moderate prices, but readers should note that numbers will be strictly limited. The first title is:

THE WARSHIPS AND NAVIES OF THE WORLD, 1880
by Chief Engineer
J W King, USN

This book is based on two highly detailed official reports written in the late 1870s by Chief Engineer J W King following several tours of Europe to study the latest developments in warship construction as preparation for the vast modernisation programme that brought the United States' 'New Navy' into existence.

The 1870s were a period of rapid technical advance and most of the European navies were undergoing radical change. Furthermore, new navies were in the process of formation in recently independent countries or politically reconstructed states in South America and the Far East; all in all, public interest in naval developments had never been so high. King realised that the

information at his command was unique, and therefore he rewrote his works for publication, *The Warships of Europe* being followed by the up-dated and expanded *War-ships and Navies of the World*. In this volume King included British, French and US developments as well as those of smaller navies, and added special chapters on armament, armour-plate and engineering advances. The result was a thorough and highly valuable survey of the state of warship design in 1880 together with an appraisal of the material strengths of the navies of the world.

9½″ × 6″, 768 pages, 66 plates. ISBN 0 85177 269 2. £18.00

Available July 1982. Further volumes in the series will be published in the autumn, beginning with *Naval Gunnery* by Howard Douglas in October.

Copies may be obtained from your WARSHIP supplier or direct (post free) from Conway Maritime Press Ltd.

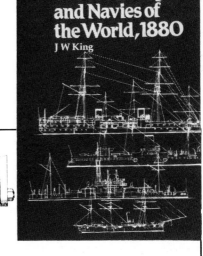

The War-Ships and Navies of the World, 1880
J W King

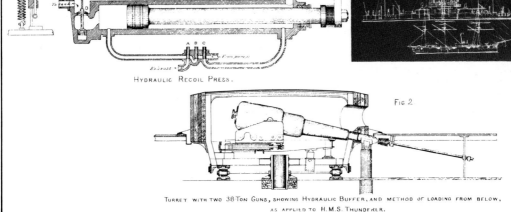

Fig. 1.

HYDRAULIC RECOIL PRESS.

Fig 2

TURRET WITH TWO 38 TON GUNS, SHOWING HYDRAULIC BUFFER, AND METHOD OF LOADING FROM BELOW, AS APPLIED TO H.M.S. THUNDERER.

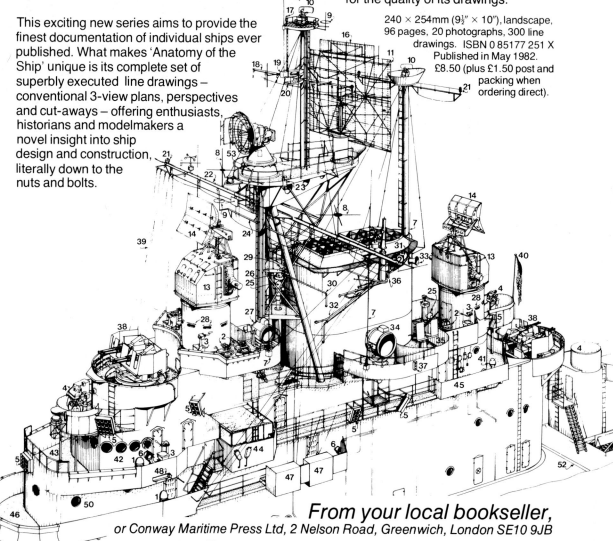

Editorial

John Roberts

The *Glasgow* nearing Portsmouth on her return from the Falklands. Aft of the vertical recognition stripe, near the waterline, is the patched hole from the bomb which passed through the ship without detonating on 19 June.

MG Photographic

The editorial in this issue has been greatly extended to provide some comment on the naval aspects of the Falklands War. Some consideration was given to a separate article on the subject but there has been such a mixture of information and misinformation eminating from the media, particularly on the technical side, in the last six months that any detailed appraisal must contain a good deal of supposition. When more official information is released, *Warship* will be able to provide a more accurate study of events. Oddly enough the most relevant article in this issue – Exocet by Antony Preston – was scheduled to appear in *Warship 24* well before the Falklands War began, while the choice of the Skyhawk for our Warship Wings feature was only partially influenced by recent events.

STRATEGY

The basis upon which the Royal Navy is organised has in recent years become more and more tied up with NATO and the possibilities of World War Three. In the past, planning has always been related to the next possible major enemy, which, in the event of a minor conflict, was almost guaranteed to provide the vessels required to cope with a lesser situation. However, this involved well

balanced fleets capable of a variety of functions whereas the NATO organisation is increasingly moving towards specialisation from its member countries. Hence, the US Navy provides the main strike force and vital air cover with its carriers, the Royal Navy provides the main anti-submarine force, the Belgium Navy the mine clearance facilities, and so on – theoretically an ideal system, unless as in Britain's case, one finds oneself in a war to which NATO has no commitment.

Warships are versatile and can be employed in many situations for which they were not designed, but two fundamental problems come immediately to mind. Firstly, isolation from the other naval forces of NATO also means isolation from the primary source of naval air power (the US carriers), and secondly, the somewhat limited area of operations for NATO forces (the North Atlantic and Arctic) produces ships designed to operate comparatively close to their main bases. This latter has a major effect on endurance requirements (in relation to stores, spare parts, etc, as well as fuel) and the provision of a fleet train (much of which might again come from other members of NATO). In the Falklands context Britain was very lucky indeed that *Hermes* and *Invincible* had not yet been sold; without the barely adequate air cover they provided the recovery of the Falklands would have been impossible.

Britain still depends to a large extent on seaborne trade and, although the RN's world-wide commitment has been abandoned, there is still scope for considerable interference with the country's interests in many parts of the world. The real question is avoided by those in power, for to say, outside the NATO context, that Britain alone can no longer adequately defend herself is politically unacceptable, but in the circumstances it has to be accepted that our interests in distant parts of the world must rely on treaties and diplomacy. The alternative is a reconsideration of the role of the Royal Navy with a view to providing a balanced fleet capable of operating far from home, such as the Falklands Islands Task Force did, should the need arise. At the moment this would seem financially impractical unless Britain's nuclear deterrent is abandoned and the money intended for Trident diverted to strengthening the surface fleet and rebuilding the Fleet Air Arm.

TACTICS

The early stages of the conflict seem to have largely revolved around a mixture of propaganda and threats (in the shape of the exclusion zones) designed to keep the Argentinians guessing as to exactly how many vessels (particularly submarines) the Royal Navy had in the area of the Falklands. Once the Task Force arrived it made the obvious move of taking South Georgia first, thereby providing a shore base, which has most probably been used as a storage and repair facility, and as a safe anchorage. This was followed by softening-up operations in preparation for the landings which, judging by the loss of *Sheffield*, do not seem to have been possible at a distance sufficient to keep beyond the range of Argentinian aircraft. At the same time the cruiser *Belgrano* was torpedoed and sunk by HMS *Conqueror* outside the exclusion zone – the official reason was the threat it and its two escorts posed to the task force but one suspects that it was also intended as a demonstration of what might happen to ships of the Argentinian Navy should they venture into waters patrolled by submarines. It seems to have been very effective in that once the 12 mile coastal limit was imposed little more was heard of the Argentinian Navy.

The choice of landing area seems to have been governed by two main naval considerations (there were obviously other military considerations). San Carlos Bay and Falkland Sound provided sheltered water for the assault ships and their escort and the surrounding hills prevented low flying aircraft from having more than a few seconds to line up on their targets. The first line of defence was the Sea Harriers which proved very effective against enemy aircraft but were, unfortunately too few to prevent large groups of Argentinian planes breaking through to the bridgehead. A second line of defence was provided by the warships in, and off the entrance of, Falkland Sound. These ships, although they should not have been the prime target, were very vulnerable being in restricted water with little room for manoeuvre or early warning of air attack (in the Second World War such an operation would have been suicide for warships without adequate air cover). This latter seems to have been worsened by the reported lack of MTI (moving target indication) in the RN's main air search radar which made it difficult to locate low flying aircraft

among the reflections produced by the surrounding land mass. Once fired the navy's missile systems worked well as is obvious from the number of aircraft shot down in circumstances where reaction time was short. However, they could not cope with the number and frequency of attacks and seem to have been swamped regularly. With Sea Dart for example, once the two missiles on the launcher have been fired there is a substantial delay (for arming, warm up and loading) before the next pair are ready – hence if four aircraft attack, one has serious problems. In fact it seems likely that the success of the Type 22 frigates with their Sea Wolf missiles had a good deal to do with the fact that their two launchers carry six rounds each.

I have seen no evidence of how effective the 4.5in guns of the fleet were as AA weapons but it has been reported that at least one aircraft was brought down by a 20mm Oerlikon – not bad for a weapon over 40 years old. This situation (and the need for an anti Exocet weapon) produced a reaction reminiscent of the proliferation of CRAA in the Second World War. One Type 42 sailed for the South Atlantic with several 20mm Oerlikons bolted to her deck and the RN has shown interest in the Vulcan Phalanx point defence gun, two of which are being installed aboard *Invincible*'s sister *Illustrious*.

EXOCET

It seems, but is by no means certain, that the Task Force did not expect attack from the air with anything other than bombs and that the Exocet attack on *Sheffield* on 4 May came as a surprise. Although it was known that the Argentinians had these missiles, it was also believed that they were not operationally ready and could not be made so without technical assistance from France (which had been withdrawn). Judging from the film of the incident taken from *Hermes*, the *Sheffield* and other ships of the Task Force were operating very close to each other when one would have expected the ships to be widely separated to provide early warning and area defence against an air launched missile attack. Given that *Hermes* and *Invincible* were the prime targets (in fact the only ones which would have prevented the British continuing their mission), AA escorts like the Type 42s should have been at a distance from them which ensured that the attacking aircraft could be brought down by their Sea Darts before it came close enough to launch its missile. According to the *New Scientist* (29 July) the Argentinian aircraft was located by AEW helicopters (this is by no means certain as other reports suggest the conversion of helicopters for this role was not considered until later) and by the 'area command ship' (presumably *Hermes*) giving 17 minutes warning of an attack, but the radar emissions were mistaken for those of a Sea Harrier – presumably the IFF returns were similar, a very odd coincidence if true; it would seem unlikely that reliance would be placed on other radar emissions for recognition purposes.

As there was no warning of an attack *Sheffield* was not fully alert, but to what degree is uncertain. She was using a satellite communication link at the time, which appar-

The *Glamorgan* passing Southsea as she approaches Portsmouth on her return from the Falklands. She was hit by an Exocet missile, fired from the shore, while carring out a bombardment of East Falkland.

MG Photographic

On board view of *Glamorgan* taken from the portside, abreast the hangar looking forward. A canvas sheet covers the hole in the wrecked hangar and steel plates cover the holes in the upper deck caused by the Exocet missile which struck the ship.

MG Photographic

ently produces interference on radar – it has been denied that her radar was off but at the same time no indication was given as to whether this meant that *all* her radar sets were operational. Some may have been off or even out of action for maintenance – it is impossible to keep a full set of radars fully operational 100% of the time. Why *Sheffield*, and not the command ship, was using the satellite link has yet to be answered.

It now seems that the attacking aircraft launched the Exocets at close and not extreme range as originally suggested, which would indicate that the real target, as might be expected, was *Hermes* and that *Sheffield* was unlucky in being the largest target to hand when the missile switched on its homing radar. The Exocet's emissions were apparently picked up by *Sheffield*'s passive defence system but too late for reaction, as witnessed by the ship's armament still stowed fore-and-aft in the photographs taken after the attack. The missile struck just below the mainmast at about the level of No 2 deck and passed through the machinery spaces. The warhead did not detonate (or only partially detonated) but the remaining rocket fuel started a fire in a diesel fuel service tank through which the missile had passed. This rapidly filled the central part of the ship with dense smoke, rendering the area untenable and preventing the crew from getting at the fire. Consequently the fire rapidly spread, assisted by the ship's furnishings, electric cables and (according to the *New Scientist*, 22 July) hydraulic fluid from broken pipes. It seems the fire fighting was also hampered by:

a A considerable reduction in electricity generating capacity due to damage and equipment faults.
b Faults in several of the fire pumps.
c Fire fighting equipment (extinguishers and breathing apparatus) insufficient in quantity and quality.
d Spread of smoke through ventilators and non fume tight doors and hatches.
e Difficulty in shutting-off damaged sections of the fire main.

Sheffield had to be abandoned and subsequently foundered, or was scuttled – neither story has been confirmed – while under tow by *Yarmouth* (it seems

The survey ship *Herald* moored at South Railway Jetty Portsmouth on 21 July 1982. Like other vessels in the hydrographic service she was converted into a hospital ship for the Falklands War.

MG Photographic

Antrim anchored in Spithead on 17 July 1982.

MG Photographic

probable she was scuttled when heavy weather caused flooding which made the tow too difficult). The ship was obviously lost because of the impossibility of preventing the fire from spreading, the hull itself standing up well and showing no signs of flooding or serious structural damage from the missile itself.

DAMAGE TO GLAMORGAN

An Exocet hit the destroyer *Glamorgan* at the end of a bombardment operation off the Falklands. Launched from the shore it was detected in time for the ship to turn away (presenting a smaller target) and fire a Seacat missile (which missed). The missile just reached the ship at the end of its run and hit the upper deck abreast the hangar, gouged a lump out of the deck and bounced against or into the hangar where it failed to detonate, (visible signs of damage are slight; compare photo of *Undaunted* in *Warship 22*, page 119). It caused a fire

which burnt out the hangar and the Wessex helicopter inside it and caused damage in the galley below.

Two Exocets were also fired at *Hermes* but by this time, according to the *New Scientist* (29 July) helicopters had been equipped with jamming gear to decoy the missiles' homing radar (also attributed to chaff from a Type 21) and the attack was unsuccessful. These missiles subsequently locked themselves onto *Atlantic Conveyor* which was, of course, sunk. This does not line up with the earlier story that *Atlantic Conveyor* was the actual target as she, having a similar radar profile, had been mistaken for one of the carriers.

BOMB ATTACKS

Four ships were lost to bomb attacks – the *Ardent* (11 May), *Antelope* (24 May), *Coventry* (25 May) and the *Sir Galahad* (8 June). The loss of *Coventry* was straight forward, if tragic – three bombs hit her, blowing away a large part of her port side, and causing her to capsize. *Antelope* was lost when an unexploded bomb detonated while being defused in her after machinery room, causing a fuel fire which ultimately got out of control and detonated her after missile and/or torpedo magazine situated directly over the machinery room in question. The other vessels were also lost due to the spread of fire, and much the same circumstances apply to these as to *Sheffield*, except for the Type 21's in which much has been made of the fact that they had aluminium superstructures. It is something of a red herring because, like the other items of concern, it contributed to the difficulties of fighting fires but was not in itself the cause of loss – it is simply a case of whether or not the increased vulnerability of aluminium to fire is acceptable to gain the design advantages.

LESSONS

Assuming the above to be a correct analysis which, as I have already said, is by no means certain, the following conclusions can be made. If modern warships follow previous sub-division practice, the area below No 2 deck would have vertical access only while that above would give a high level of fore-and-aft movement. If the considerable inconvenience of losing fore-and-aft communication could be accepted, extension of vertical access as much as is practical to the full depth of the ship would assist in preventing the spread of smoke and fire, provided inflammable gear is kept away from the dividing bulkheads. Provision could also be made for eliminating non-essential inflammable items, providing fume tight doors and hatches, and avoidance of long runs in the ventilation trunks and communication passages. The provision of fire proof cable is more difficult, as this costs about ten times as much as PVC and is more difficult to bend. A possible alternative is to provide fire proof junction boxes where cables pass through decks and primary bulkheads.

There are obvious advantages in providing splinter protection to cable runs, hydraulic systems, etc and the provision of armoured trunks for these has been under consideration since before the Falklands conflict. It has a weight penalty of course but this is not a prime problem in modern ships. Splinter proof bulkheads would also assist in reducing the effects of damage but here the weight problems might well be too much to accept, particularly as it would be a non-visible asset to tax payers who like to see lots of weapons for their money.

The flagship of the Falklands Task Force, HMS *Hermes*, following her return, 21 July.

W Sartori

Money, one suspects has been the prime cause of some of the problems encountered with fire fighting equipment where the supply has been both inadequate in numbers and quality. Steps have in fact already been taken to provide the ships of the RN with more and

F3, one of the *Fearless*'s landing craft, in drydock at Portsmouth on 21 July.

W Sartori

The assault ship *Intrepid*, with her sister *Fearless* beyond, moored at Portsmouth on 14 July.

MG Photographic

improved fire extinguishers and breathing sets. Similar problems may apply to equipment where maintenance is difficult due to a limited supply of spare parts. However, this is pure supposition; keeping machinery running constantly is not and never will be an easy task and it is certainly a major achievement to keep a task force at sea for so long and so far from a dockyard. By way of example the *Invincible* is reported to have had one of her main gas turbines replaced at sea (she carries two spares).

The *Canberra* nears Southampton after her highly successful service as a troopship for the Falklands War.

MG Photographic

CONCLUSIONS

Several other technical points could be made but space precludes a lengthy debate; besides it must be remembered that this is but a small aspect of a much wider subject. There has been too much concentration in the media on the technical details of ships and their faults and not enough on the adequacy of the overall lessons of operating a fleet at sea. The most obvious conclusion is that a fleet cannot operate in areas dominated by enemy aircraft without adequate air cover; and 20 Harriers, however superb the aircraft, is not adequate. The only alternative is a substantial improvement in the AA capability of ships, which means more AA missile launchers, and more control systems to go with them and consequently bigger ships – another one of those financially/politically unacceptable statements!

Considering that Argentina is far from being a first class military power her aircraft managed to do considerable damage and one wonders what would happen in a conflict with a more efficient enemy. At least five warships were damaged by bombs (*Plymouth, Broadsword, Antrim, Glasgow* and *Argonaut*), some badly, but none of these bombs appear to have exploded. Add to this the apparent 50% effectiveness, or lack of it, of Exocet in detonating and one wonders what the losses would have been if the Argentinians had had some decent ammunition.

John Roberts

CHANGE OF ADDRESS

Please note as from 6 September 1982 the address of the publishers of *Warship* will be:
Conway Maritime Press, 24 Bride Lane, Fleet Street, London EC4Y 8DR. Tel: 01-583 2412

The Iron Screw Frigate Greenock Part 2

by John M Maber

Back in 1842 the Admiralty had been informed of claims made in the United States to have developed a form of iron armour, resistant to ball shot, which comprised a 6in thick sandwich of ⅜in wrought iron plates rivetted together. Upon receipt of this intelligence the Admiralty had arranged with the captain of the gunnery school, HMS *Excellent*, for a series of trials to confirm or disprove these reports. In the event it was shown that a 32lb shot could penetrate 'compound armour' of this description at 400yds and that likewise little protection was offered against shellfire. Although this demonstration had shown iron laminate to be of little use by way of protection, other factors such as the escalating shortage and cost of suitable timber, together with the satisfactory mercantile experience, had had an influence on Admiralty thinking, and it was within this context that a decision in favour of wrought iron for warship hulls had been made. Now, with the wisdom of this choice in question, it was only too apparent that little consideration had been given to the effects of gunfire against an iron structure.

Faced with mounting criticism of its policy favouring iron, the Admiralty arranged for a series of trials to be carried out in great secrecy at Woolwich Arsenal in order to assess the possible effects of gunfire on the iron hull structure of a warship.

PROTECTION TRIALS

A 32pdr gun firing solid shot was employed in these trials which were conducted at a fixed range, the weight of the charge being varied to simulate change of range and thus impact velocity against targets mocked up from iron plate of different thicknesses and quality to represent a ship's side structure, in some cases backed by timber or a composite material known as 'kamptulicon'[3]. It was hoped that the latter, after passage of the shot, would expand to form a watertight seal in the way of the shot hole but although the idea showed some promise it was, to all intents and purposes, not really a practical proposition.

The trials demonstrated that at short ranges against an unbacked target, the shot easily penetrated the iron plate making a relatively clean hole but that in almost all cases the shot broke up into a mass of splinters which within the interior of a ship could result in heavy casualties. On the other hand it was shown that a 14in thick timber backing effectively contained the splinter hazard and in fact the 1980-ton (bm) iron frigate *Simoon* was built with a 10in backing of timber along the ship's sides. However, no such provision was made in the case of the *Greenock* whose ship's sides were lined only with 1in thick tongued and grooved deal.

By this time the matter of whether or not to build warships of iron had become a political issue and eventually in December 1846 the Admiralty, having lost faith in its own enterprise, sought to cancel the contracts. In the event, this proved too expensive and in 1847 it was decided that the *Simoon, Megaera* and *Vulcan* should be completed as troopships with, for reasons of economy, lower powered machinery than that originally planned. Likewise the iron paddle frigate *Birkenhead* was to be relegated to the trooping service being assured thus of a place in history by the circumstances accompanying her

[3] A mixture of india rubber, gutta percha and cork on canvas (Oxford English Dictionary).

tragic loss in February 1852 on an uncharted rock in False Bay, Cape Colony.

GREENOCK'S CONSTRUCTION

For a time in 1847 work stopped on the *Greenock* but eventually her construction was resumed on the lines of the general arrangement drawing dated the 14 January 1848; that is, as a screw frigate. A surviving sail plan dated March 1848 shows the proposed arrangement for her ship rig. Chief Engineer Thomas Bullions took up his appointment to oversee the installation of the ship's machinery in January 1849 and on 30 April following the *Greenock* entered the water to be towed away to an alongside berth for the final stages of fitting out. Thereafter, the Admiralty appears to have lost interest in the vessel. However, trials were run on completion of fitting-out (excluding armament) and under steam alone the *Greenock* achieved a mean speed of 9.6kts at 719ihp.

At last, in June 1850, the *Greenock* manned by a scratch steaming crew left the Clyde for Devonport where she lay for some fourteen months, without armament or stores, awaiting a decision as to her future. Presumably consideration was given to her possible transfer to the trooping service but, in the event, in August 1851 she moved round to Woolwich Dockyard on the Thames. A month later Chief Engineer Samuel B Meredith relieved Thomas Bullions but, this event apart, she remained laid up until August 1852 when the Admiralty gave approval for her sale to the London-based Australian Royal Mail Steam Navigation Co. Although never commissioned for Royal Navy service, the *Greenock* retained her designation in the Navy List as an 'Iron Screw Frigate' from 1849 when her name first appeared until it was finally deleted following her sale in 1852.

The Australian Royal Mail S N Co had been awarded in 1852 a contract valued at £26,000 per annum for the carriage of the mails to Australia via the Cape. In the wake of this agreement, which actually became effective on 3 June 1852, the first departure from London had been taken on 29 May by the 1392-ton screw steamship *Australian* but it is the subsequent purchase of the *Greenock* in August of that year which is of greater relevance in the present context.

MELBOURNE, ex-GREENOCK

Renamed *Melbourne*, the former *Greenock* was fitted out to meet her new owners' requirements in little more than six weeks, which would appear to indicate that some preliminary work might have been carried out already towards her conversion for trooping duty. There is some support for this belief in the details accompanying her entry in Lloyd's Register which was posted in August 1852. The nominal horse power is given as 260 against the 565nhp of the machinery installed by her builders. Certainly the former frigates *Simoon*, *Megaera* and *Vulcan* had been completed as troopships with machinery of lower power than originally planned, so it is possible that the *Greenock* may have been re-engined in the course of her twelve-month lay-up at Woolwich.

In the event, the *Melbourne* was handed over to the Australian Royal Mail Co towards the end of September 1852 and on the 29th of that month left London bound for the Cape and thence, via King George's Sound, to Melbourne and Sydney. All was not smooth sailing, however, and having put into Plymouth, where the mails were to be embarked, the *Melbourne* was delayed for the repair of weather damage sustained during the passage down Channel. She was under way again on 13 October but fouled two hulks resulting in further delay whilst repairs were effected. Finally on 15 October the vessel made a successful departure with 35 first class, 58 second class and 57 steerage passengers, only to sustain more storm damage necessitating a call at Lisbon where she was detained until 21 November. Fortunately the remainder of her outward passage appears to have been uneventful and she arrived in Sydney on 4 February 1853.

Homeward bound it was not long before the *Melbourne* was once again in trouble, for soon after leaving Sydney she dropped a propeller blade. The spare was fitted at Port Phillip but part of this too was lost on 12 April after which the ship's engineers made good the worst of the damage utilising spare iron plate held on board. Presumably this jury propeller proved reasonably successful since the vessel made good time until 23 June when, off Fayal in the Azores, one of the engine cranks fractured. The voyage was completed under sail.

CHARTER SERVICE

Thereafter the *Melbourne* was laid up for a time awaiting repair, having completed but one voyage in the Australian trade. In any event, largely as the result of mismanagement, the fortunes of the Australian Steam Navigation Co[4] were at a low ebb and it was only the outbreak of war in the Crimea in March 1854 which brought some relief through the charter of the fleet for transport work. Both the *Melbourne* and her consort *Victoria* were taken up on 22 April in that year although, in fact, it seems unlikely that the former ever sailed for the Crimea under Australian S N Co management. A few weeks later she passed into the hands of J Scott Russell, the Millwall shipbuilder, presumably in part settlement of outstanding debts[5].

Under Scott Russell's ownership the *Melbourne* continued on charter for the transport service but the end of the war saw her laid up and offered for sale. Thus in 1857 she was purchased by Martin & Co of London without change of name and returned to the Australian trade. Three years later she changed hands again becoming the property of 'W F'rlnge' (W Furlonge?) of London by whom she was first employed in the China trade and subsequently to the Mediterranean.

The frequent changes of ownership continued in 1863 when the *Melbourne* was acquired by Gellatly & Co of London, primarily for the Indian trade although in 1864 she was listed by Lloyd's as working between Liverpool and New York.

[4] The mail contract had been withdrawn in April 1853.
[5] The company's iron steamships *Adelaide* and *Victoria* had been built on the Thames by J Scott Russell.

The screw steamship *Melbourne* (ex-*Greenock*) probably leaving London with migrants for Australia.

Author's collection

In 1861 the *Melbourne* had been remeasured in accordance with the formula for the calculation of tonnage set out in the Merchant Shipping Act of 1854 and from this time was listed by Lloyd's as being of 1636 tons gross and 899 tons net. She was first registered (Official Number 26,402) in 1863 and in June 1866 appeared in the 'Return . . . of the Steam Vessels Registered in the United Kingdom' under the ownership of 'E Gellatly and others' (Gellatly, Hankey, Sewell & Co). By this time, however, some seventeen years since she had first been put afloat, the *Melbourne* with her outmoded machinery must have been decidedly uneconomic in operation although in fact she was to continue in the Indian trade under Gellatly's houseflag, working out from Liverpool, until 1867 when she was sold, again without change of name, to E Bates & Sons of that port.

IRON FRIGATE FATES

The career of the *Melbourne* as a screw steamship was now over since her new owners removed the machinery and fitted her out as a sailing vessel, still however with her full ship rig. In the course of her survey some repairs were carried out and her bilges 'cemented' to make good the wastage of her hull plating. For the next seven years she plied between Liverpool or Dundee and India, apparently without untoward incident, until early 1875 when she was posted missing thus putting a period to a career which had spanned a quarter of a century.

Of her consorts, the paddler *Birkenhead* had been wrecked in 1852 as mentioned above; the *Megaera*, much neglected whilst laid-up in reserve, survived until June 1871 when, en route for Australia with naval reliefs, she had to be beached in an unseaworthy condition on St Paul's Island in the southern Indian Ocean; the *Simoon*, was commissioned as a troopship in 1852, achieved no notoriety, however, and was broken up at Dartmouth in 1887; and lastly the *Vulcan*, first commissioned as a troopship in 1851, served until 1867 when she was sold commercially and converted as the barque *Jorawur*. The group had been conceived in haste without taking fully into account the current state of the art of naval warfare but, on the other hand, abandonment of the iron screw frigate was possibly an over-reaction to public criticsm. Certainly no one should accuse the Admiralty of the day of being dilatory in the acceptance of new ideas; the matter of delays in their implementation was, on the other hand, all too frequently a direct result of the lack of adequate funds and one can only conclude that circumstances in the mid-nineteenth century appear to have had much in common with those prevailing at the present time!

Lesser Known Warships of the Kriegsmarine No2
The Light Cruiser Nürnberg

by MJ Whitley

SERVICE CAREER

Following the usual pattern of trials and working up, *Nürnberg* joined the reconnaissance forces as flagship. In August 1936, she sailed for Spanish waters wearing the flag of Konter Admiral Boehm, for service as part of the International non-intervention patrols during the civil war in that country. Her first tour lasted until December, when she returned once more to Germany. The following year saw her carrying out two further deployments, between April and May, then later from June to August 1937. There were few incidents worthy of note, except that on 16 July 1937 she claimed to have been attacked by an unidentified submarine south of the Balearic Islands.

Back in Germany once more, in August 1938, *Nürnberg* joined the large fleet review in Kiel Bay, when Adolf Hitler and the Hungarian regent, Admiral Horthy, inspected the Kriegsmarine. In March 1939 she formed part of the overwhelming force which was sent to occupy Memel; with her were the *Deutschland, Scheer, Admiral Graf Spee, Leipzig, Köln*, seven destroyers and numerous torpedo-boats, minesweepers and smaller craft. The Lithuanian navy consisted only of the ancient ex-German minesweeper *Prezidente Smetona* mounting two 7.5cm guns! On completion of this task, *Nürnberg*, with *Admiral Graf Spee*, the two other light cruisers and escorted by destroyers of the 1st, 3rd and 5th divisions, as well as U-boats, embarked upon a major exercise out in the Atlantic and down to the Mediterranean. After visiting a number of Spanish ports, the fleet did not finally return to Germany until May. Then, as the world slid towards war once again, the fleet continued its training in the Baltic. Here in the course of one exercise off Bornholm on 27 August when *Nürnberg* was working with the 1st destroyer division, and torpedo-boats, *Max Schultz* rammed and sank the torpedo-boat *Tiger*.

The German attack on Poland opened on 1 September 1939 and at sea, the cruisers under the command of Vice Admiral Densch (Flag Officer Reconnaisance Forces) with *Nürnberg* (flag), *Leipzig* and *Köln* took part on the first day but were withdrawn westwards two days later without having seen action. In the west *Nürnberg*, with other cruisers (all except *Karlsruhe* – under reconstruction at Wilhelmshaven) and light forces, began to lay the 'West Wall' mine barrages to protect the German North Sea coasts. By October, she had returned to the Baltic where she remained until early November when she sailed back to the North Sea.

MINELAYING OPERATIONS

In the North Sea, Naval Group Command West was using destroyers with great success to lay minefields off Britain's east coast during the dark winter nights. Admiral Boehm, C-in-C (fleet), wanted to use cruisers to cover the destroyers on their return and employed *Nürnberg, Leipzig,* and *Köln* under the command of Vice Admiral Densch to do so. This was an extremely risky process bearing in mind the presence of several British submarines in the North Sea but at first all went well. However, on the 13th, an ominous day, the three cruisers were in the German Bight awaiting the destroyer's return. Late in the forenoon, *Leipzig* had stopped to search a Danish steamer, whilst the other two cruisers carried out anti-submarine patrols. Finding no contraband, the steamer was released and the three cruisers steamed off on a southerly course. Suddenly, at 11.24, a torpedo explosion rocked *Leipzig* on her port side amidships, destroying her forward boiler room and causing very severe damage. *Nürnberg* immediately went up to full speed and turned hard to starboard to comb the torpedoes' tracks. Two minutes later, lookouts reported two torpedoes on the starboard quarter on a

The half-sister upon which the design of *Nürnberg* was based, the light cruiser *Leipzig*, seen here in the early 1930s

CPL

course which, if the cruiser's starboard turn continued, would cause them to hit the cruiser amidships. Desperately port full rudder was applied, but with the ship still in a starboard turn, her head could not come round fast enough. One torpedo passed only 20 metres ahead of her forefoot but the second hit the cruiser on the starboard bow, throwing a column of water high into the air. Reducing speed to 12kts and steadying on a course of 250° the crew began to take stock of the damage. Hardly had the engine room reported 'no damage' when three further torpedo tracks were sighted on the port quarter. Increasing speed once more to 'full ahead' and turning hard-a-starboard, Kpt z See Kluber managed to avoid the torpedoes which exploded some distance astern. The heavy flak guns opened fire on a submarine

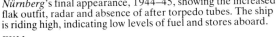

Nürnberg's final appearance, 1944–45, showing the increased flak outfit, radar and absence of after torpedo tubes. The ship is riding high, indicating low levels of fuel and stores aboard.

IWM

sighting but this was thought in retrospect to be the torpedoes exploding. Unlike *Leipzig*, *Nürnberg* had escaped relatively lightly from the torpedo hit. The torpedo had struck right forward in compartment AV causing flooding in some adjacent compartments and fuel bunkers in the hold and 'tween decks. She was only slightly down by the bows, however. Only some 14 minutes had passed since the torpedo hit when the submarine (HMS/M *Salmon*) was sighted briefly in the wake. 'C' turret fired a few rounds but without effect – probably the only time this ship ever fired her main armament at a low-angle target. Aircraft now found the damaged cruiser and near-missed her with their bombs. With 90 tonnes of water aboard, *Nürnberg* got under way again at 18kts with her lower bows hanging off to starboard. The heavily damaged *Leipzig* was only able to use her diesels. For over an hour, the damaged pair, covered only by *Köln* remained in danger until, at 13.55, the destroyers returned. *Künne* stood by *Nürnberg* whilst the rest joined *Leipzig* and *Köln*.

The lame ducks were slowly escorted back to the Jade river, but the danger was not yet passed. Early on the 14th, almost within sight of safety, the British submarine *Ursula* managed to make a last minute attack on *Nürn-*

berg, now escorted by *Künne* and *F9*. Her torpedo salvo struck the escort vessel *F9*, which sank quickly with heavy loss of life. Despite counter attacks by the German destroyers, *Ursula* escaped. By 09.50 that morning, *Nürnberg* had entered the locks at Brunsbuttel from whence she proceeded to the Deutschewerke yard in Kiel for repairs; these took until the end of April 1940, when she re-ammunitioned in the Scheerhafen prior to running trials. The unlucky *Leipzig* was never fully repaired, so great was her damage, and was mainly used for training for the remainder of the war until late 1944.

NORWAY

Lying in Kiel, with *Scharnhorst, Gneisenau* and *Hipper* early in June 1940, Kpt z See Kluber was disappointed to be told that *Nürnberg* was to be excluded from Operation 'Juno' on the grounds of her lack of range. This was ironic in view of the specific inclusion of diesels for long range cruising, a design feature common to all the light cruisers (except *Emden*), which was never utilised by any of them for their intended purpose. Having missed participation in the occupation of Norway, and the 'Juno' sortie, *Nürnberg* did not move to Northern waters until 10 June, when, on a fine, calm evening, under blue skies, she slipped from her buoy, escorted by the torpedo-boats *Jaguar* and *Falke*, bound for Trondheim. Stowed aboard were Luftwaffe stores and mining equipment for the defence of Trondheim. Joined briefly by the fleet escort vessel *F3*, the small squadron steamed northwards, encountering thick fog in the western Skaggerak. By late afternoon on 12 June, both torpedo-boats

A close-up of *Nürnberg*'s bridge structure taken during the mid-war period, probably in Norway. Note the dark stripe which formed part of her painted camouflage scheme, and the less permanent camouflage netting designed to blend the ships angular shape into the shoreline.

Drüppel

had to be detached to Stavanger for fuel, leaving the cruiser unprotected. *Nürnberg* continued north zig-zagging at 27kts until met by an escort of the 2nd mine-sweeper flotilla off Trondheim on the 13th. Four days later, she was riding at anchor in Herjangsfjord, Narvik. She remained in northern waters until late in July, during which time her aircraft attacked a submarine off Trondheim but without success.

On 25 July, the damaged *Gneisenau* sailed, homeward bound from Trondheim, escorted by *Nürnberg* and the destroyers *Lody, Jacobi, Ihn* and *Galster*. The passage was uneventful until the afternoon of the 27th, when, off the SW coast of Norway, the torpedo-boat *Luchs* was sunk, probably by a torpedo from the submarine *Thames* (aimed at the battlecruiser) or by a drifting mine. The unfortunate torpedo-boat, which had only joined the escort some 3 hours previously, broke in two and sank. The squadron continued its passage, arriving safely in Kiel by the forenoon of the 28th.

THE BALTIC

Kpt z See Kreisch relieved Kluber as commanding officer on 8 August and the ship spent the remainder of 1940 in the Baltic. In September whilst in Gotenhafen, she was visited by Admiral Mavagini of the Royal Italian Navy and in October and November she had a short machinery overhaul at the Deutschewerke yard in Kiel.

In 1941, whilst in Baltic waters, *Nürnberg* became a training ship – on 15 February by orders of the OKM. Together with all the surviving light cruisers she formed part of the Fleet Training Squadron, the main object of which was to train the large numbers of men required to man the rapidly expanding U-boat fleet, as well as mine-sweepers and smaller craft, in the basic arts of seamanship and engineering. In February numbers of her existing trained crew were drafted to U-boats and her operational efficiency fell drastically. Kpt z See Kreisch (who had assumed command after his previous

Nürnberg surrendered in Copenhagen, May 1945.
IWM

ship *Lützow* had been torpedoed in June 1940), left the cruiser shortly after she was detailed for training duties. Kreisch had a distinguished career in the Kriegsmarine and later reached flag rank as Flag Officer (Destroyers) towards the end of the war.

The invasion of Russia in the middle of 1941 resulted in the formation of the 'Baltenflotte' with *Tirpitz, Scheer, Nürnberg, Köln* and seven destroyers and torpedoboats. After standing by in the Aaland See for a few days, it became obvious that the Red Fleet was not going to intervene in strength so the fleet was soon dispersed. For the remainder of the year, *Nürnberg* took part in various fleet exercises until she began a major refit in January 1942. The refit was carried out by the same yard as repaired her in 1939, Deutschwerke at Kiel, where she docked on 11 January 1942. During the course of this refit, as well as having the machinery overhauled, the catapult and aircraft installations were landed as well as the after torpedo tubes. Modifications and additions were also made to her light flak outfit. Some delay was caused by air-raid damage, so that it was not until 23 August that she left the yard for Gotenhafen and post refit work-up which lasted until October. Operational once more, the ship, by now under the command of Kpt z See von Studnitz, was ordered to northern waters to join the considerable force already deployed in Norway.

RETURN TO NORWAY

Late in the afternoon of 11 November the cruiser, escorted by *Z25* and *T23*, sailed from Gotenhafen bound for the Skaggerak. On passage through the Sound, *T23* was detached to Kiel, but *Z29* and *Z25*

joined from Copenhagen. Despite air attacks off Stadtlandet, the force had reached Trondheim by the 18th and, after a stay in that port, arrived in Bogen Bay, Narvik, on 2 December. Here, apart from very occasional exercises with the other heavy units in Norway, *Nürnberg* remained virtually inactive in the Narvik area throughout her stay in northern waters. Finally, on 27 April 1943, the cruiser sailed south once more to Trondheim on the first leg of her journey back to Germany. Under orders issued in February 1943 following the Barents Sea debacle in December 1942, major units of the fleet were to be paid-off or reduced to training status. *Nürnberg* was scheduled to form part of the Baltic training squadron but remain temporarily operational in the Norwegian theatre until 1 August 1943. It would appear, however, that the plans were expedited and the ship was to be brought home early. Escorted by *Griff, Jaguar* and *Blitzen*, the cruiser reached Trondheim without incident and then, reinforced by the addition of *T24* continued south for Kiel, where she arrived on 3 May 1943.

TRAINING DUTIES

Nürnberg transitted the Kiel canal to the Naval dockyard at Wilhelmshaven where she underwent a machinery overhaul until the end of May, after which she returned to the Baltic once more and joined the Fleet Training Squadron under the command of Vice Admiral Thiele. Here, in the still peaceful waters of the Eastern Baltic, together with several other heavy units remaining to the Kriegsmarine, she was once more grossly misemployed in training cadets, a task which could equally well have been done by smaller craft and auxiliary vessels. Morale declined and none of the ships in the squadron could be considered battle-worthy in view of the

Admiral Makarov in the Neva River about 1955. The ship is in a well kept state and differs only in detail from her pre-war appearance. All light AA has been landed and new radars fitted at the fore-top as well as on the new tripod mizzen.

Drüppel

constant crew changes. She remained on this duty throughout 1943 and 1944, during which time the ship saw no action at all, although some of the heavy units of Admiral Thiele's squadron were, by October 1944, engaged on shore bombardment duties in support of the retreating German armies. For some reason, *Nürnberg* took little or no part in these operations. Instead, she remained on battle training until the turn of the year and in the new year was ordered to the Skaggerak for mine-laying duties. By the first week of January 1945, *Nürnberg*, now wearing the flag of Flag Officer (Destroyers), Vice Adm Kreisch, was based in Oslo Fjord with destroyers, torpedo-boats, minelayers and S-boats. After exercises in company, the cruiser sailed on her first and only minelaying sortie, Operation 'Titus', on the afternoon of the 13 January. Accompanying her were the destroyers *Ihn* and *Riedel*, the torpedo-boats *T19* and *T20* and the minelaying *Linz*. Seven R-boats of the 8th flotilla were to join later. All except the R-boats were laden with mines, *Nürnberg* carrying 130 EMC mines. The squadron steamed parallel to the coast, beating off air attacks off Arandal, until shortly before midnight, when south of Lillesand the R-boat escort joined. With sweeps streamed, the R-boats took up an arrowhead formation ahead of the cruiser, which had *Linz* and *T20* in starboard echelon and *Riedel*, *Ihn* and *T19* in echelon to port as the squadron turned to port to lay the mines in a line across the entrance to the Skaggerak. The lay was completed without incident and by mid-morning, the ships were safely back in Oslo Fjord.

SURRENDER

Probably because of the critical fuel situation, *Nürnberg* took no further part in minelaying operations and on 24 January both she and *Linz*, escorted by *Galster*, *T19* and *T20*, sailed for Copenhagen. The Naval Command had scheduled her to take part in operations in the Eastern Baltic (when she was to relieve *Emden*) after gunnery training off Bornholm in March, but the ship was far from operational. Her ship's company was in a very low state of training, many being mere cadets who had served only a short time abroad, and the fuel position was desperate – only 270 tons of synthetic pitch-oil was aboard. In consequence, *Nürnberg* lay idle in Copenhagen until, at 0200 on 5 May 1945, a signal was received ordering a cease-fire as from 0800hrs. On 22nd, the ship was taken over on behalf of the Royal Navy by the cruisers *Devonshire* and *Dido* in Copenhagen and both she and *Prinz Eugen* prepared for their move to Wilhemlshaven. The two ex-Kriegsmarine cruisers sailed for Germany on 24 May, escorted by HM ships *Devonshire*, *Dido*, *Iroquois* and *Savage*, arriving in Wilhelmshaven on 28 May 1945. *Nürnberg* was taken to Wilhelmshaven under British escort where she lay while the Allies discussed the division of the surrendered tonnage at the Tripartite Commission. By the end of the year, it had been decided that the *Nürnberg* would become part of the Soviet spoils of war. Then rumours of discontent and sabotage aboard the cruiser reached the ears of the British, who, mindful of the events of 1919, laid plans to sieze the ex-German ships. For security reasons, *Nürnberg* was left in dry dock whilst all the remaining ships were seized on 16 December, when the Russian crews were put on board. On 2 January, 1946, wearing the flag of Vice Admiral Rall of the Soviet Navy, the cruiser sailed for Libau accompanied by *Hessen, Blitz, Z15, T33* and *T107*.

POST-WAR SERVICE

After examination in detail by the technical experts of the Soviet Navy and following the instruction of a suitable ship's company, *Admiral Makarov*, as she was now named, joined the Baltic naval forces as part of the 8th Fleet, based at Tallin (formerly Reval). The officer after whom the ship was now named lost his life when, as commander in chief of the Imperial Russian Far East fleet, his flagship, *Petropavlosk*, was mined and sunk outside Port Arthur on 10 April 1904. By late 1948, the cruiser had become the flagship of the 8th Fleet (Vice Admiral F V Zozulya).

In the early 1950s, with the appearance of the three new *Chapaev* class cruisers in the Baltic, which probably incorporated some aspects of the ex-German cruiser, *Admiral Makarov* was withdrawn from active service and became a training vessel, based at Kronstadt and attached to the training detachment there. During the summer of 1954, this detachment also included the old battleship *Oktyabrskaya Revolyutsia*, the destroyers *Leningrad, Odarennyi* and *Provornyi* as well as the escort *Berkut* and minesweepers *Vladimir Polukhin* and *Vladimir Trefolev*. The old gunboat *Krasnoye Znamya*, submarines *Shch 303* and *Lembrit* also servied with this squadron. During her time in this employment, *Makarov* carried various pennant numbers: 1954/55 – 46; 1955/56 – 36; 1956/57 – 98; 1957/58 – 47; 1958/59 – 96.

Pennant numbers were allocated on a twelve-monthly basis and changed on 30 April each year. Operating with the training squadron, the ship was kept in a very smart condition, but had landed most, if not all, of her light flak

De-ammunitioning in Copenhagen.

IWM

outfit. New radars had been fitted, but otherwise the cruisers' appearance remained little different from that of her Kriegsmarine days. It was reported from German sources (ex-Kriegsmarine POWs?) that at this time too, her main turbines were removed to provide space for cadets' classrooms and the ship had to rely on her diesels. This is, however, considered rather improbable and it is more likely that two boilers were removed to provide a boiler room space for conversion.

On 1 May 1959 the cruiser was not allocated a new pennant number and was seen on that date partially stripped. She was also believed to have been seen as a bare hull at Kronstadt in August 1959 while in the summer of 1960 it was reported that she was being finally broken-up in the coaling harbour at Leningrad.

Nürnberg thus out-lived all her sister cruisers of the Kriegsmarine, but in truth she had very little to show for her 24 years in service. She took part in no major actions at all and it is doubtful if in fact her main armament was ever fired in anger. Uneventful as were the lives of her sister light cruisers, they at least took part in the Norway operation, the capture of the Baltic Islands in 1941 and contributed supporting gunfire to cover the army's retreat in 1944–45. *Nürnberg*, the most modern of them all, was always in the wrong place at the wrong time and her main contribution to the Kriegsmarine probably lies in the large numbers of men trained in her pre-war cruises who subsequently manned U-boats and minor surface craft during the Second World War.

ACKNOWLEDGEMENTS

I am indebted to Mr R Erikson for data on *Nürnberg*'s Soviet service.

Amphibious Command Ships:
Past Present & Future
Part 2

by Norman Polmar & John J Patrick

THE FACILITIES OF THE AGC

The Second World War AGCs owed their usefulness and flexibility first and foremost to what has been called their true 'main battery', their extensive communications installations. A wartime Navy document prepared to familiarise prospective users with AGCs as a generic type highlights the unique capability of these ships:

> To meet with the communications requirements of all services during the Assault Phase of an amphibious operation, the AGC is equipped with the most extensive communications installation afloat. In fact, there are few, if any, shore stations in the world that are equipped to handle a comparable number of diversified radio circuits as the AGC.

The central clearing-house for all written radio messages was the communications room, also called the joint communications office. It served the commanders of the various amphibious components and their staffs by supervising all routing and delivery of written messages and all encrypting and decrypting, which took place in separate but adjoining spaces. Another space, known as the filter room, 'filtered' and evaluated most voice messages. The numerous remote control radio units and internal communications terminals in the voice filter room enabled its operators to connect external voice circuits throughout the ship.

RADIO ROOMS

The main receiving room was located forward. Designated Radio I, this space was also known as radio central since, besides controlling receivers, it exercised direct control over the numerous transmitters in the main and secondary transmitting rooms (designated Radio II and Radio III, respectively). Thus, all written radio messages were actually received or sent out by personnel in the main receiving room, and most of the ship's external voice circuits also passed through this space.

The radio rooms described in the 1944 orientation document typically contained the following equipment:

Radio I 66 general purpose receivers (HF to LF), grouped in pairs; 4 VHF receiver-transmitter pairs; 44 radio-telegraph operating positions.

Radio II & III 30 general purpose transmitters (HF to LF), ranging from long-range, 2kW LF sets to 25 watt HF sets for local communication; 2 HF receivers (one per room); 2 LF receivers (one per room).

The receivers located in Radio II and Radio III were for emergency use in case of battle damage to Radio I. Both transmitter rooms were aft to avoid interference with the receivers in Radio I, located forward.

While the number of transmitters in a typical AGC appears to have remained more or less the same from 1944 to the end of the war, the number of receivers seems to have grown dramatically. The *Mount McKinley*, a C-2 AGC, is reported to have had 112 receivers by 1946, not counting the portable units sent ashore with the landing force commander. Nevertheless, she retained the same 34 transmitters as noted above.

A Second World War AGC required elaborate switchboards to handle the large number of circuits. The ship's switching system was designed to accommodate frequent variations in the communications plan. The switchboards controlled and connected not only radio nets, but also internal teletype, telephone, and public address systems. Perhaps their most important function, given the need for fast response against enemy aircraft and shore batteries, was to provide remote stations throughout the ship with direct access to voice radio circuits.

THE FUNCTIONS OF THE AGC

The Navy familiarisation document stated that an AGC's primary mission was 'to meet the communications requirements of the naval, landing force and air support commanders during assault operations.' However, it was becoming apparent that an AGC was more than just a communication ship. Although the term 'command and control' had not yet been coined, the

Flag plot aboard the amphibious command ship *Estes* during an exercise.

USN

AGC was, in fact, a remarkably sophisticated command and control centre. Groping to express this fledgling concept, the document credits the AGC with a secondary mission: 'to provide certain special facilities such as aerological, meterological, photographic, map reproduction, printing and operations displays.'

The last phrase, 'operational displays', is the key that distinguishes the AGC from earlier flagships. The AGC's communications installation, however complex, differed from that of earlier flagships only in scope and performance. The AGC's truly revolutionary feature was the numerous displays of all sizes that enabled the men on board to handle the large body of data generated by modern amphibious operations.

Most of the displays of the Second World War period were manual, but they did include the new radar Plan Position Indicators (PPI), which had been developed by the US Naval Research Laboratory at the beginning of the war. A typical AGC had a PPI on the flag bridge of the force commander as well as others in the adjacent flag plot and 'staff watch officer's shelter'. The PPI monitored the surface and air search radars, enabling the naval commander to keep track of the many units under his control and giving him timely warning of approaching threats. Additional PPI's were located in the Combat Information Centre (CIC), a below-decks space that was even then becoming the focal point of many command activities. The CIC concentrated particularly on functions, such as air traffic control and fighter direction, which required specialised personnel, constant monitoring of radars and radio circuits, and very rapid response to changing situations.

The flag plot was the normal situation for the force navigator and other staff officers charged with keeping a dead reckoning for the entire force and controlling its movement. The staff watch officer's shelter provided chart tables for the naval force commander, or, in his absence, the officer of the watch. Both of these spaces had radio remote control stations and internal telephones, supplemented, when necessary, by the nearby

The USS *Adirondack* in a 'Mediterranean moor' at Naples, Italy, in 1953 during the change of command ceremonies for the U.S. C-in-C Naval Forces Eastern Atlantic and Mediterranean.

USN

signal bridge, with its traditional 'flag bag' and its pneumatic tubes for sending written messages throughout the command spaces.

OPERATIONAL COMMAND

Below decks was the war command room, a conference space where a senior officer from any service could station himself and some of his staff during key phases of the operation. If the naval commander remained on the flag bridge, this space served principally as the afloat command post of the landing force commander.

To aid the decision-making of senior commanders, the joint operations room, also known as the support control room, provided large plotting tables, radio remote controls and internal communications for the operations officers responsible for each aspect of the

amphibious assault. The joint operations room was not large enough to accommodate all members of the operational staffs. The remainder could station themselves in a separate auxiliary joint operations room, which occupied a corner of the ship's wardroom. This auxiliary space also provided redundancy in the event of battle damage to the main joint operations room.

The various operations officers – Navy, Army/ Marine, naval air, gunnery and intelligence – also had separate offices in which to work; as did the force aerologist, since accurate weather reports were essential for any amphibious operation. The naval air officer and the gunnery officer shared a single office. Finally, as mentioned earlier, the communications room was also designated as the joint communications office, since it provided written message services for all shipboard staff activities.

The *Estes* underway off San Diego, California, in 1969. After the war the US Navy's AGCs gave up their after armament for a helicopter platform. Note the large AN/SPS-30 radar antenna atop the lattice mast over the bridge and a large TACAN pod on the after kingpost.

USN

A close-up view of the bridge structure of USS *Blue Ridge* in 1977.

Giorgio Arra

THE CIC

As mentioned above, the CIC was one of the most noteworthy AGC features. CIC's of one sort or another became commonplace in many types of ships during the Second World War, including small escorts. The basic feature of the CIC was one or more PPI scopes connected to the ship's air search radar. The AGC, of course, had a very extensive installation rivaling those of the largest warships. In addition to detecting and tracking all friendly ships and aircraft in or near the force, the AGC's CIC directed the fighter aircraft defending both the force and the beachhead from enemy bombers, torpedo planes and, in the last stages of the war, kamikazes. To carry out these complicated tasks, the command ship's CIC had numerous PPI's, plus ancillary radar display equipment such as height-finders. It also had large plotting boards for tracking contacts and numerous voice radio terminals for relaying orders.

The AGC's radar suit, the source of most of the data analysed in the CIC, was equally impressive. In the C-2 ships, a lattice mast above the superstructure carried the large antenna of the SK air-search radar and the smaller antenna of the SG surface-search set. One of the ship's forward kingposts carried a second SG antenna while a YG homing beacon was mounted on a kingpost or mast aft to assist in aircraft control. By the end of the war, the C-2 AGCs had yet another antenna mounted aft for the SP fighter-direction radar. Radio intercept and jamming equipment was also installed.

POST-WAR CUT BACKS

The flexible capabilities of the US Navy's AGC's did not save most of them from being disposed of or layed-up in reserved during the post-war fleet reductions. Not only was the US averse to maintaining a large Navy in the late 1940s, but the attitude of many US military leaders towards the type of operation for which the AGCs were designed is summed up in the late-1940s testimony of General Omar Bradley before a Senate committee: 'I am wondering whether we shall ever have another large-scale amphibious operation. Frankly, the atomic bomb, properly delivered, almost precludes such a possibility.'

Accordingly, the number of active AGCs dropped sharply. The *Ancon* was returned to her civilian owners in February 1946, and the ex-seaplane tender *Biscayne* was transferred to the Coast Guard in July. The six converted Coast Guard cutters reverted to their pre-war function, and all but five of the 15 C-2 AGCs (AGC-7, -8, -11, -15 and -17) were laid up in mothballs.

The few AGCs in commission during the late 1940s performed varied and useful tasks in addition to carrying the flags of the remaining amphibious force com-

Detail of the aft radar tower on USS *Blue Ridge*.

Giorgio Arra

mands. The *Mount McKinley* served as flagship for Operation Crossroads, the first of the postwar atomic bomb tests, which took place at Bikini atoll in July 1946, Two years later the same ship was the floating headquarters for a second series of tests at Eniwetok. Other AGCs carried observers and members of the press to witness these and subsequent nuclear blasts in the Pacific.

During the same period, the *Adirondack* (AGC-15) was flagship of the Navy's new Operational Development Force (OPDEVFOR, predecessor of today's OPTEVFOR, the Operational Test and Evaluation Force). Before being laid up for a short period in 1949, the *Estes* carried the flag of three successive commanders of the US Seventh Fleet and the flag of one Commander, US Naval Forces, Western Pacific. Another ship, the *Mount Olympus* (AGC-8), became the flagship of Rear Admiral Richard E Byrd's 1946-47 expedition to Antarctica – Operation Highjump.

KOREAN OPERATIONS

Partly because of their usefulness in activities such as these, a few AGCs remained active and ready for combat when the Korean War broke out in 1950. The *Mount McKinley* was underway to the Western Pacific for amphibious exercises when North Korean troops crossed the 38th parallel on 25 June and, proceeding immediately to Japan, she helped carry elements of the US occupation force to South Korea to reinforce the badly outnumbered defenders being formed into a United Nations command. In September 1950, after the UN forces had managed to defend a precarious toehold at Pusan, the *Mount McKinley*, carrying General of the Army Douglas MacArthur, directed the brilliant amphibious assault on the Communist-held port of Inchon, far behind the North Korean lines. The Inchon operation, which was instrumental in destroying the North Korean Army, occurred less than one year after General Bradley had predicted the end of large-scale amphibious operations.

The *Mount McKinley* went on to direct the time-consuming assault on the heavily mined North Korean port of Wonson, and then to assist in evacuating US forces and civilian refugees from the North when Chinese intervention suddenly turned the tide against the UN forces.

One other AGC, the *Eldorado*, participated in Korean War amphibious operations, serving as standby ship for the *Mount McKinley* at Inchon, then going on to direct the evacuation of that same port in January 1951, following the Chinese intervention. Returning later in the spring with the advancing UN forces, the *Eldorado* was on hand to transmit the first pictures of the Korean truce talks that began in July 1951.

As a result of the Korean war, two additional AGCs the *Estes* and the *Pocono* (AGC-16), were brought out of mothballs. This, however, was soon balanced by the decommissioning of the *Adirondack* in 1955 and the *Mount Olympus* in 1956, the latter having suffered ice damage while supporting the Distant Early Warning (DEW) radar network in the Arctic. The five AGCs that remained active received helicopter decks during the early 1950s and underwent continued updates of their radar and communications equipment in subsequent years.

SUEZ TO VIETNAM

There were few major crises of the 1950s and 1960s in which these AGCs did not play some part. During the Suez Canal crisis in the fall of 1956, the *Pocono* embarked the C-in-C, US Naval Forces, Eastern Atlantic and Mediterranean, for a period of three months. Both the *Pocono* and the *Mount McKinley* were on hand during the landing of US Marines in Lebanon in 1958. The *Pocono* remained in Beirut for three months after the initial landings to provide air traffic control and to support high-level diplomatic communications. The *Pocono* and *Mount McKinley* were involved in the Cuban missile crisis of 1962, the former as flagship of the Atlantic Fleet Amphibious Force and the latter as flagship of the Fourth Amphibious Group. The *Pocono*

3

1 USS *Blue Ridge* in 1979.

Giorgio Arra

2 An underwater explosion tests the shock resistance of the USS *Blue Ridge* off San Clemente island, California, July 1976.

USN

3 USS *Blue Ridge*. Note the after radio antennas are folded down to permit operation of a UH-1 Huey helicopter from the ship's flight deck.

USN

later served as headquarters for US naval forces supporting the 1965 intervention in the Dominican Republic.

In response to the Tonkin Gulf incident of August 1964, the *Mount McKinley* was ordered to South-east Asia, where she relieved the *Eldorado* as flagship of the Seventh Fleet Amphibious Strike Force. The *Mount McKinley* remained in South-east Asian waters until 1965, directing the Marine landings at Da Nang and Hue, South Vietnam. She then alternated with some other AGCs in tours off the Vietnamese coast, providing communications support for land operations against Vietcong and North Vietnamese forces.

The designation AGC was also assigned after the Second World War to the presidential yacht *Williamsburgh*. Built in 1930 as the private yacht *Aras*, she was used by the Navy from 1941 as a gunboat (PG-56). She

was redesignated AGC-369 on 10 November 1945, to serve as President Truman's yacht, replacing the long-serving *Potomac* (AG-25) in that role. The *Williamsburgh* was laid-up during the Eisenhower Administration and was outfitted as a research ship in 1962 by the National Science Foundation and renamed *Anton Brun*. The *Williamsburgh* was a 1870-ton, 244ft ship, with graceful lines. In White House service she was painted white.

NEW DESIGNATIONS AND NEW SHIPS

The five AGCs active during the Vietnam War were the last of the Second World War amphibious force flagships, the remainder having been stricken between 1959 and 1961. On 1 January 1969, these five ships were redesignated amphibious command ships, and their letter designation was changed from AGC to LCC. However, they retained their original hull numbers.

The Second World War veterans shared the new designation with two new amphibious command ships laid down in the late 1960s. These ships, the *Blue Ridge* (LCC-19) and the *Mount Whitney* (LCC-20), together with a third LCC, had been proposed by the Kennedy Administration as part of the build-up of US amphibious forces in the early 1960s. Intended to increase limited warfare options, the ambitious Kennedy programme originally called not only for three new command ships, but for nine giant LHA helicopter carriers, as well as numerous LSDs, LPDs, and LSTs.

Even as some new ships were being built, however, the amphibious programme was being cut back, in part to help meet operating costs from the Vietnam War. The *Blue Ridge* was commissioned on 14 November 1970 and the *Mount Whitney* on 16 February 1971. Construction of the third ship was first delayed while consideration was given to completing her as a combination amphibious/fleet command ship, and then cancelled altogether.

Meanwhile, the last of the war-built LCCs were retired, the *Estes*, *Mount McKinley*, *Pocono* and *Taconic* (AGC-17) being decommissioned by 1971. The *Eldorado*, veteran of Iwo Jima, Okinawa, and Inchon, was the last of the AGCs to retire, leaving the fleet in 1973, some 30 years after the first amphibious command ship was commissioned.

The principal reason for retiring these ships, apart from their advancing age, was their relatively small size, which precluded the installation of voluminous modern C³ (Command, Control, and Communications) systems. The two new LCCs, based on the earlier LPH helicopter carrier hull design, displaced 19,290 tons, nearly 7000 tons more than their war-built predecessors. The *Blue Ridge* and the *Mount McKinley* were 620ft long, with 83ft beam and a 27ft draught. The large 'flight deck' area, derived from the LPH design, provided ample space for radio antenna farms. Both ships were built with two twin 3in AA gun mountings. These were supplemented in 1974 by two Sea Sparrow point-defence missile systems.

The new command ships had accommodations for a crew of 700 officers and men, plus an additional 200 officers and 500 enlisted men for amphibious command activities. These included the command of the amphibious task force and the landing force, as well as the control of tactical air support by an embarked tactical air control group. A modular amphibious control centre gave the task force commander control of all phases of the landing operation and assisted the ground force commander monitoring his units ashore. An elaborate tactical intelligence centre supported the main control centre, as did the ship's communications unit, which was twice the size of that in any other ship afloat in the early 1970s. The *Blue Ridge* and the *Mount Whitney* also had a complete installation of the Naval Tactical Data System (NTDS), a computerised system for exercising command and control of fast-moving tactical operations.

DECLINE AND FALL?

In service, the two ships' careers were uneventful, with the *Blue Ridge* serving in the Pacific and the *Mount Whitney* in the Atlantic. By 1979, however, it had become obvious that replacements were needed for the older missile cruisers that had served as fleet flagships since the early 1950s. Newer missile cruisers (originally DLG/DLGN 'frigates') lacked the working space, accommodation and communications equipment needed by a numbered fleet commander. At the same time, the post-Vietnam decline of US amphibious lift

Radarmen operate consoles in the air detection and tracking section of the amphibious control centre of the *Mount Whitney*.
USN

capacity to just over one Marine Amphibious Force (Division/Air Wing) spread over two (and, after 1980, three) oceans made a really large-scale amphibious operation increasingly unlikely. The relatively small-scale amphibious operations that might take place could, in any case, be handled by the LHA amphibious assault ships, which had elaborate command and control facilities.

Thus, in October 1979, the flag of Commander, Seventh Fleet in the Western Pacific shifted from the 35-year old cruiser *Oklahoma City* to the *Blue Ridge*, and in January 1981, the flag of Commander, Second Fleet in the Atlantic shifted from the *Albany* to the *Mount Whitney*. Without a bang or a whimper, an important and interesting ship type therefore disappeared from the US fleet and the navies of the world – the amphibious command ship. While the two modern LCCs remain on the Register of US Naval Vessels, their designation is now a misnomer, and their genesis as floating command centres for large-scale amphibious operations merely an interesting chapter in naval history.

1 The *Blue Ridge*. Note open deck spaces, landing craft stowage, and helicopter area aft. No hangar is provided, but an elevator connects the helicopter deck with a vehicle parking area below.
USN

2 The surface/sub-surface plotting section of the amphibious control centre of the *Mount Whitney*.
USN

1

2

The First Submarines for the Royal Navy by Michael Wilson

Holland No 1 at Vickers yard in Burrow-in-Furness, 1901.
MoD (HMS Dolphin)

Since early times man's desire to extend his own habitat and travel underwater has only been exceeded by a similar wish to emulate the birds and take to the air. That he should ultimately have been successful in achieving both these ambitions at roughly the same time must be attributed to the great technological advances that began in the dying years of the last century and which continued at a faster pace in the early years of the present one. But this story is concerned with only the development of underwater travel, with the adoption of the submarine as a weapon of war by the Royal Navy, and with the first years of the Royal Navy's submarine service.

ROBERT FULTON

Over the years inventors in England experimented with various submersibles, as indeed they did elsewhere in Europe and America, but it was on 4 October 1805, only days before Admiral Nelson's famous victory at Trafalgar, that the American inventor Robert Fulton at last gave a convincing demonstration of the potential of a submarine boat by exploding a charge beneath the hull of the 200-ton brig *Dorothea* at anchor in Walmer Roads off the Kent coast. The motive power for this craft was necessarily by means of a hand-cranked screw propeller, while the explosive charge had to be fixed to the target. Despite the patronage of the Prime Minister, Mr William Pitt, Fulton did not receive any encouragement for his achievement since the First Sea Lord, the redoubtable Admiral the Earl of St Vincent, was resolutely against the development of such a weapon, and it was on this occasion that he made the remark that was to colour the British Admiralty's view of submarine warfare for almost a hundred years: 'Pitt was the greatest fool that ever existed to encourage a mode of warfare which those who command the seas [ie the Royal Navy] did not want, and which, if successful, would deprive them of it.'

This view, as much as the victory at Trafalgar which

followed Fulton's success less than three weeks later, became the keel on which the Admirals built their opposition to the submarine. To be fair, the correctness of St Vincent's statement was shown by the events of 1916 and 1917, and again in 1940–42 when Britain's lifeline was very nearly cut by the activities of Germany's U-boats. So it was that the development of the submarine was left to other nations, and many different designs were built and tested before the end of the century. In both Russia and France experimentation was carried out with the official backing of the naval authorities. On the other hand, across the Atlantic in the USA it was left to two men, John P Holland and Simon Lake, who individually and with no assistance from the US Navy, designed and produced several successful submersibles.

THE PRACTICAL SUBMARINE

The true development of the submarine needed the impetus of two other technological advances: a satisfactory engine to propel the boat underwater; and a weapon that would not only justify the use of the submarine against an enemy but which would give the crew of the submarine a chance to survive their attack. Both these advances came before the end of the nineteenth century. During the American Civil War a hand-propelled submarine built for the Confederate Navy was fitted with a spar torpedo which, on 17 February 1864, was exploded against the side of the Northern 200-ton screw-sloop *Housatonic*. The resulting explosion sank both vessels – not a very satisfactory way of using a submarine! Not until Whitehead's self-propelled torpedo was developed in 1868 could this difficulty be overcome. In 1886 a Spanish Naval Officer, Lieutenant Peral, developed a submarine in which the propulsion was at last independent of man-power and relied instead on an electric motor driven from the newly developed accumulator storage batteries. Lack of official support led to Peral's design going no further than an unsatisfactory prototype, and it was left to the French to seize the opportunity and become the dominant submarine power in the first years of the current theory.

Relying on one electric motor with the necessary electric batteries, however good an improvement this was on a hand-powered system, had the drawback of leaving the submarine with a short and finite range, limited by the need to return to harbour to recharge the batteries before they became exhausted. Yet a number of French and Russian submarines were built with this limitation, and were considered operational, but because they were intended primarily for harbour defence duties, it was felt that this need not be inhibiting.

The French *Narval* was the first submarine to be completed with dual propulsion systems, whereby one was used for surface running and the other when dived, and with the added advantage of being able to recharge the electric batteries while still at sea. That the *Narval*'s primary motive power was from steam engines was an obvious disadvantage for a submarine, but to criticise the design for this reason is to ignore the great step forward that had been taken. Following the great success

Holland No 3 at Portsmouth *c*1903–05, with HMS *Victory* in the background. The tall mast abaft the conning tower is the periscope, the remaining three vertical pipes being ventilators.
Courtesy J A Roberts

of the *Narval* on trials in 1899 the French were not slow to recognise the potential of this design and further orders immediately followed making France the first naval power to have an appreciable submarine force. The fact that this force was just across the Channel from Britain's premier naval base at Portsmouth was not lost on the Admiralty for, despite the improving political relations that were to lead within a few years to the *Entente Cordiale*, there remained a traditional suspicion of the French surviving from centuries of warfare between the two countries. It was this suspicion that led the Admiralty to look seriously at the necessity for submarine development. But first, it remains to look briefly at how the Americans had responded to this new mode of warfare.

DEVELOPMENT IN THE USA

As already mentioned, during the American Civil War the *Housatonic* made history not only in being the first ship sunk in war by a submarine but also by causing – unwittingly perhaps – the first submarine war casualty. When John Philip Holland left his native Limerick in 1873 at the age of 32 to settle in the USA, he took with him in his few belongings a sketch of a submarine design. Support for his ideas came from fellow exiles who believed that this was just the weapon to wage war against the English. So with $6000 raised from Irish Americans his first submarine was built and launched on 22 May 1878. The boat was a mere 14½ft long and weighed 2¼ tons. Larger boats followed. One, hijacked after a dispute with Holland's backers, foundered in choppy seas while under tow. Another, which thieves found they could not operate safely, was left in a lumber shed for many years before being put on display in New York. Later, another attempt had a disastrous beginning when the submarine hit a log pile on launching, was holed and went straight to the bottom! Penniless but undeterred, Holland was saved when strained relations with both Great Britain and France in 1893 decided the US Congress to pass an appropriation of $200,000 for a submarine. Not ordered until 1895 this submarine, to have been called the *Plunger*, would have been 85ft in length, displaced 149 tons and have been armed with

TABLE 1: PARTICULARS OF SUBMARINES

	French *Narval*	USS *Holland*	HMS/M *No 1*	HMS/M *A1*	HMS/M *XE 3*	HMS/M *Valiant*
Completed	1899	1900	1903*	1903	1944	1966
Length	111ft 6in	53ft 10in	63ft 10in	103ft 3in	53ft 1½in	266ft
Beam	12ft	10ft 3in	11ft 9in	11ft 10in	5ft 9½in	32ft
Draught	9ft	8ft 6in	9ft 11in	10ft 1in	7ft 0in	27ft
Length: Beam	9.2:1	5.25:1	5.4:1	8.7:1	9.1:1	8.3:1
Surface Displacement	104 tons	64 tons	105 tons	190 tons	30.3 tons	3485 tons
Dived Displacement	146 tons	74 tons	120 tons	207 tons	33.6 tons	3940 tons
Torpedo Tubes	4 × 18in (external	1 × 18in	1 × 18in	1 × 18in	None**	6 × 21in
Crew	13	1 + 6	2 + 6	2 + 9	3 + 1	11 + 78
Main Engines	Steam, triple expansion Electric motor	4-cyl petrol engine Electric motor	4-cyl petrol engine Electric motor	16-cyl petrol engine Electric motor	42hp diesel Electric motor	Pressurised water reactor, steam turbine Aux electric motor

Notes: *Because of first of class trials *No 1* was not completed until early 1903, but *No 2* was completed first in Aug 1902. ** Armed with side charges

two torpedo tubes. Although never completed it shows the strides Holland had made in less than twenty years since his first boat in 1878. To replace this submarine Congress allocated some money and another Holland submarine began to take shape in the winter of 1896, and appropriately carried out its first dive on St Patrick's Day 1898. Two years later, after numerous alterations and trials, the boat was purchased by the US Government on 11 April 1900, and on 12 October that year Lieutenant Harry H Caldwell became the commanding officer of the USS *Holland*, the first submarine captain in the US Navy.

FIRST BRITISH STEPS

Back in England the Admiralty was concerned to note the additional provision for submarine boats in the French Naval Programme following the *Narval*'s trials. In the summer of 1900 Mr Isaac L Rice, of the Electric Boat Company, which had built Holland's latest submarine for the US Navy, visited England hoping to obtain further orders for his company to build submarines. He was introduced to the Admiralty by Lord Rothschild and after a number of negotiations it was agreed that Messrs Vickers Sons and Maxim Ltd at Barrow would build five submarines for the Royal Navy on behalf of the American Company. Negotiations had been conducted so swiftly that in November the Admiralty were forced to approach the Treasury asking that money be allocated to pay for the submarines. Once again the speed with which the matter was dealt with is surprising, for a favourable reply was received only three days later! It was a radical change of policy for the Admiralty who had been so firmly set against submarine development for so long, but it may be partly excused for it was stated in the following 1901/1902 Naval Esti-

mates that the submarines were being built so as to allow our destroyer commanding officers the opportunity of working against them.

A firm order was placed with Vickers in December of that year and Captain R H S Bacon, a torpedo specialist, was sent to Barrow with HMS *Hazard* to oversee the work of construction. Lieutenant F D Arnold-Forster, another torpedo specialist, followed, destined to become the first commanding officer of the Royal Navy's first submarine. At Barrow the work of building the submarine was carried on with much secrecy; Arnold-Forster recalls that on arrival in the shipyard he was anxious to sight his first command but soon found that no-one seemed to have heard of any submarine. Eventually the boat was found in a large shed prominently marked 'Yacht Shed', while parts were made and delivered marked 'Pontoon No One'.

THE HOLLAND CLASS

Holland No 1 was launched on 2 October 1901 and began her sea trials on 15 January the following year. These were completed in April, though not without the excitement that could be expected with any new type of ship, especially one as revolutionary as this. Early in February she ran into a dockyard wall damaging the bow. Two days later the blank flange over the opening for the torpedo tube failed – in the haste to complete this boat she was initially built without a torpedo tube – and the ingress of water caused 'the boat to stand on her hind legs, alarming the men working inside'. Although accepted on completion of these trials the boat was not finally completed until nearly a year later. Meanwhile *Holland No 2* had been launched on 21 February 1902 and was able to leave for Portsmouth in the middle of the year, being towed by HMS *Hazard*. *No 4* left at the same time being towed by *Torpedo Boat 42*. These dates are of interest since the contract between the Admiralty and the Electric Boat Company was for Vickers to build repeats in all particulars of the boats then building for the US Navy, yet the first of these, the USS *Adder*, did not start trials until November 1902 some months after *Holland No 4* had been completed at Barrow.

Another interesting aspect is the degree of autonomy afforded Captain Bacon; it was as if the Admiralty, having once taken a distasteful step in ordering submarines, would then rather have as little to do with the project as possible. Even the American liaison engineer was removed as soon as *Holland No 1* was accepted, and Bacon and his team of officers together with the design staff of Vickers were left to their own devices. Bacon quickly realised that these first five submarines could never be anything more than experimental boats, despite their initial encouraging performance. With the co-operation of the Vickers design staff the plans for a new class of submarine were produced, and the Admiralty was persuaded to include an order for four of these in the 1902/1903 Programme and a further nine in the 1903/1904 Programme. It was the beginning of a regular and progressive annual programme for submarines which continued until the outbreak of war in 1914.

FEATURES OF THE HOLLAND BOATS
Before concluding it is necessary to look more closely at the design of these two classes of submarine, the early

Early RN submarines alongside the old 'Admiral' class battleship *Camperdown*, which served as a mooring ship for submarines at Harwich from 1908 until 1911. In the foreground are the *C7* (37), *C8* (38) and *C9* (39).

Courtesy J A Roberts

ancestors of the present day nuclear-powered boats of the modern Royal Navy of which HMS *Valiant* was the first to be wholly British designed and built (HMS *Dreadnought*, it will be recalled, included many American features in her design, not the least being the power-plant).

The *Holland* class boats were single-hulled vessels of spindle form, ie the main ballast tanks were internal to the pressure hull and the hull itself was circular in shape with the centre of all sections on a straight line. At the forward end there was a single 18in torpedo tube. There were no internal watertight bulkheads, or any provision for crew comfort and the cluttered interior was devoted to the working of the submarine. A 60-cell battery powered a single electric motor giving a nominal range of 25 miles at a maximum underwater speed of 7kts. On the surface a 4cyl Wolseley petrol engine was expected to give a range of some 250 miles at the maximum speed of 8kts. A single rudder was fitted and there was a single set of diving rudders to control the depth of the submarine. When on the surface there was little freeboard and even a small sea could cause a serious likelihood of foundering if the hatches were not shut. The problem of surface navigation was not helped by the small amount of deck casing and an almost complete absence of what was later to be called a conning tower. The diving time was a matter of a few minutes depending on the actual reserve of buoyancy in the submarine when running on the surface, something which could vary from time to time depending on the conditions. On the other hand the *Narval*, because of her steam propulsion unit, could take up to twenty minutes for diving. However, the periscope was perhaps the most novel arrangement in these submarines. Previously such instruments were not available

and the commanding officer would have to break surface and take what bearings he could through the ports fitted in the sides of the conning tower. Even when the *Holland*s began to be built no provision was made for an 'optical tube', and that it was finally added to the design was due to the work of Captain Bacon. It was called a 'Unifocal Ball Joint Type' and was stowed horizontally along the hull, being raised about a ball joint by hand. Once it was raised, it was also trained by hand by means of a geared handwheel. Primitive though this sounds it was a great advance and compares with the periscope in the USS *Adder* which carried out her trials shortly after *Holland No 1* and which had a fixed periscope rigged through the forward ventilator with a field of view limited to only 15° on either bow.

THE 'A' CLASS

The following 'A' class kept to the same spindle hull form but had an increase in length of some 40ft with a corresponding increase in displacement by two-thirds. The power of the engine and the main motor was increased as was the battery capacity and the amount of fuel carried. This gave a better performance on the surface, but when dived 'A' class boats were comparable with the earlier *Holland*s, though they showed a greater stability. They were fitted with a larger conning tower and the periscope was now made to slide up and down. By 1905 the advantages of a larger conning tower were fully acknowledged and they were then fitted to the earlier *Holland*s. One other major change was made: from the *A2* onwards the bow was made blunter so as to accommodate two torpedo tubes.

The dangers of using a petrol engine in a confined space were obvious, yet there was no reliable alternative – not that the early petrol engines were all that reliable! However the *A13* was selected to test the adoption of a heavy oil engine for submarines, and though these trials took some time they did lead to the adoption of the diesel engine for the 'D' and later classes.

The *Holland*s, despite being a completely new concept of warship for the Royal Navy, were lucky in that they suffered no serious accidents during their period of service. The 'A's were not so fortunate. The *A1* (Lieut-

H M Submarine *C29* prior to the First World War.
Cribb

enant L Mansergh) was rammed and sunk by the SS *Berwick Castle* in the Solent on 18 March 1904; there were no survivors and though the submarine was subsequently salvaged she was never recommissioned. The *A8* foundered while running on the surface and sank in Plymouth Sound, though she was both salvaged and repaired. The *A3* was rammed and sunk by *HMS Hazard* off the Isle of Wight in February 1912, while just months before the outbreak of war in 1914 the *A7* failed to surface after exercises in Whitesand Bay. On the other hand Royal confidence in this new type of warship was shown when the *A3* was visited while in harbour at Portsmouth in March 1905 by Her Majesty Queen Alexandra and one of her daughters.

These 'A' class submarines never actually met the enemy at sea but were still operational when the war started in August 1914. Three were nominated as the 9th Submarine Flotilla in 1914 for defence of the Clyde area while the remainder were made available for training duties. A proposal by Vice Admiral Sir Reginald Bacon, at that time commanding the Dover Patrol, would have used some of them as navigational beacons to aid the monitors in bombarding the Belgian coast. (In June 1944 two X-craft were used as markers off the D-day beaches). The proposal was not pursued. All the boats of the class were taken out of service during the war and scrapped soon after. But it is *Holland No 1* that has once again been in the news. She had been sold to Thomas Ward for scrap in 1913 but was lost while under tow from Plymouth to the breaker's yard. Early in 1981 the wreck was located by HMS *Bossington* using the latest minehunting equipment. Now it is to be hoped that money can be found to raise her, carry out the essential restoration and preservation work and then place her as a permanent memorial alongside HMS *Alliance* at the Submarine Museum in Gosport.

Thus the submarine entered the Royal Navy, though because of the Admiralty's early firm line against their adoption and use little had been done in Britain in their development. Germany, under the direction of Admiral Tirpitz, also had a 'wait and see' policy. Neither nation lost much by this stand-off attitude, as was shown in the years following 1914; meanwhile other nations had been left to bear much of the cost and frustration of development.

This view of *D4* demonstrates how quickly the submarine developed. Completed in 1911 only 8 years after *Holland No 1*, she was over four times the displacement of the earlier vessel and has already the general appearance associated with the submarine type for the next forty years, except for the lack of a deck gun.

Courtesy J A Roberts

Warship Pictorial

Richelieu & Jean Bart

The French battleships *Richelieu* and *Jean Bart* were provided under the 1935 Programme, and launched in 1939 and 1940 respectively. On the verge of completion *Richelieu* had to leave Brest in June 1940, to avoid capture by the Germans, and sailed for Dakar. There she was damaged by aircraft from HMS *Hermes* and temporarily immobilised. In September 1940 she provided gunfire defence during the abortive Anglo-Free French attack on Dakar but following the successful Allied landings in North Africa she sailed to the USA where she was refitted prior to joining the British Home, and later Eastern, Fleets. She returned to France in August 1945 and then went for refit to Casablanca before rejoining the Eastern Fleet for the remainder of her war service.

The *Jean Bart* escaped from St Nazaire in a partially complete condition in June 1940 and sailed for Casablanca. Construction was resumed at the end of the war at Brest and she finally entered service in 1949. The accompanying photographs originate from the US Naval Historical Centre.

The *Richelieu* at Dakar on 25 July 1940.

1 The *Richelieu*'s main armament of two quadruple 15in turrets viewed from the forecastle during the ship's passage to the Far East, 24 March 1944.

2 Floats supporting anti-torpedo nets surround the *Richelieu* at Dakar, 25 July 1940.

3 *Richelieu* at Trincomalee in mid-1944. In the background is the British battleship *Queen Elizabeth*.

4 *Richelieu* at Trincomalee 1944.

5 The *Jean Bart* in partially fitted-out condition at Casablanca on 23 June 1940 shortly after her escape from France. Note the incomplete superstructure and the lack of AA weapons, secondary armament, 15in guns in B turret and fire control gear.

6 *Richelieu* in August 1943 after completion of her US refit and modernisation.

Jean Bart on 23 June 1940, the day after her arrival at
Casablanca. Two 37mm AA mountings, fitted hastily on 18
June at St Nazaire, can be seen abaft the funnel.

The *Jean Bart* at Casablanca in 1943 with the French cruiser
Duguay-Trouin in the foreground. She was damaged during
the North African landings and this view shows her after
repairs – note that the 15in guns have been removed from A
turret.

EXOCET ~ the Worlds first Sea Skimmer
by Antony Preston

The two MM-40 fibreglass canisters on the port side of the *d'Estienne d'Orves*. Note that the two canisters are simply bolted onto the existing MM-38 ramp.

Aérospatiale

The sinking of the Israeli destroyer *Eilat* off Port Said on 21 October 1967 marked the beginning of a 'missile panic' which swept Western navies in a manner unknown since Sinope, just 114 years earlier. Although the surface-to-surface guided weapon was by no means new, the Russian SS-N-2 *Styx* was suddenly promoted to the status of No 1 ship-killer, and every front-line navy began to study countermeasures to it.

By great good fortune the French company Aéro-spatiale (Societé Nationale Industrielle Aérospatiale Systemes) had already begun research into an anti-ship system. The company (actually still called Nord Avia-tion at that time) had developed its CT20 target drone into the Rb08A for the Royal Swedish Navy in 1964 and so the designers were already familiar with many of the problems. There is an apocryphal story to the effect that the President of the Tactical Missile Division of SNIAS gave authority for the development of the new project in the same week as the sinking of the *Eilat*. Whether true or not, the project was very soon dubbed MM-38, an abbreviation for *Mer-Mer 38 kilometres* (referring to the

designed range) and given the name Exocet (Flying Fish). It was under way in 1968 and by the end of 1973 (phase 1, the development stage) 18 firings had taken place. These test-firings showed that it was necessary to modify the warhead and to improve the interface bet-ween the homing head and the firing installation. Then phase 2, the operational and evaluation firings, began early in 1974 and a further 96 rounds were fired.

In 1971 the Royal Navy joined the French Navy in choosing the MM-38 Exocet as its new (and first) surface-to-surface missile system. A total of 300 rounds were ordered, with up to 17 per cent of the equipment being manufactured in Great Britain. This purchase by a major navy was just the sort of endorsement needed and by mid-1977 no fewer than 17 navies had ordered 1000 Exocets and it is still in quantity production at Bourges five years later.

The first firings at sea were made in 1971-72 by the trials ship *Ile d'Oleron* followed by the experimental patrol boat *la Combattante*, which had a single ramp fitted on the quarterdeck. In April-May 1974 the British guided missile destroyer *Norfolk* carried out firing trials in the Mediterranean, following the French destroyer *Duperré*. The French ship had four MM-38 ramps fitted amidships, angled out to allow the efflux to clear the after funnel, whereas the British chose to site the four ramps in the position formerly occupied by 'B' 4.5in Mk

The first operational deployment of MM-38 was in the French destroyer *Duperré*, with four ramps angled out to port and starboard between the funnels.

Aérospatiale

The French sloop *d'Estienne d'Orves* firing an Exocet MM-40 missile during the 1981 development trials in the Mediterranean.

CEM via Aérospatiale

An MM-38 round photographed one-thousandth of a second
before impact against the target.

Aérospatiale

6 gun mounting. Blast proved comparatively easy to deal with, the normal means being a curved steel ramp behind the launcher, to deflect the blast and flame upward.

THE METHOD OF GUIDANCE

Exocet was the first of the 'fire-and-forget' missiles, using the *Installation de Tir Standard* (ITS or Standard Firing Installation) to set the missile's gyroscope axes to predetermined angles. The ITS also gathers pre-launch information such as target coordinates, trajectory commands, launch-speed, true vertical reference (basically what the aviator knows as his artificial horizon) and platform movements, from the ship's radar, optical sights, vertical reference-unit and the ship's log. The data is processed by a coordinate-calculator based on an analogue computer and transmitted to the missile, the ITS initiates the firing sequence and the missile takes off from its cannister. At a distance of about 24km (the outer limit of a circle within which the target has been predicted to be) the radar seeker switches itself on and begins to search for the target. Lock-on is normally achieved within two seconds, permitting the missile to correct its bearings. Although the missile is intended to fly into the hull of the ship at the same height, should radar contact with the target be lost (if it disappears in a heavy swell, for example) a proximity fuze will trigger off the warhead as it passes over the target.

THE MISSILE

The MM-38 is 5.2m long and 384mm in diameter, with four cruciform wings about two-thirds of the length from the nose and four more aerodynamic control-surfaces at the rear. The nose cone contains the ADAC active radar homing head, while the remainder of the body contains, first, the front equipment bay and wings, then the warhead, sustainer motor, the booster motor and finally the rear equipment bay and control surfaces.

The ADAC head houses a radar antenna which scans over a limited bearing and azimuth, housed inside a laminated fibreglass radome. The front equipment bay houses the computer which gives commands to the control surfaces, the radio-altimeter, the gyros and accelerometers, and the thermal batteries which provide electrical power for the homing head.

The 165kg (364lb) warhead is of the semi armour piercing (SAP) type, calculated to do the maximum damage to a medium-sized warship by penetrating through the hull-plating before detonating. Against small targets the high rate of fragmentation and the blast ensures maximum damage to superstructure and electronics.

The body of the sustainer and booster motors is made of light alloy with an internal coat of heat-resistant material. The solid-fuel booster motor burns for about 2.5 seconds, ejecting the missile from its container and raising its velocity to near Mach 1. After a short delay the Epervier sustainer rocket-motor ignites, and it burns on average for about 110 seconds, behaving much like a cigarette.

The flame tube passes through the rear equipment bay, which also contains the actuators of the control surfaces, the main 1350W thermal battery for powering the systems in the missile, the AC/DC converter and the gyro which controls a self-destruction device.

The missile is supplied complete with its container-launcher, a rectangular box of 3mm light alloy which is closed at both ends by hinged doors. Inflatable seals are needed to keep the interior of the box filled with an inert gas at slight pressure, thus ensuring a stable and dry environment for the missile. The missile is suspended and locked on a ramp, along which its attaching points slide during launching. A series of twelve plastic dampers provide an elastic support to protect the missile from shock and vibration during transport and loading.

At the end of the firing-sequence the sequence-box inside the container fires explosive bolts on the doors to allow them to be pushed open by spring actuators. This movement automatically triggers pistons which lock the missile to the ramp, so that there is no movement which can effect the firing coordinates. A locking device to prevent the missile from launching itself is disengaged the moment the booster-motor ignites.

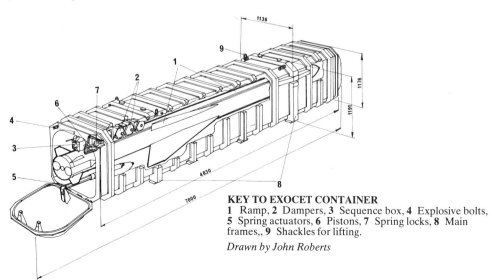

KEY TO EXOCET CONTAINER
1 Ramp, **2** Dampers, **3** Sequence box, **4** Explosive bolts, **5** Spring actuators, **6** Pistons, **7** Spring locks, **8** Main frames,, **9** Shackles for lifting.

Drawn by John Roberts

OPERATION OF THE SYSTEM

The Exocet missiles are fired by one man from the operations room or CIC. When the ship enters its operational zone the magnetron in the homing head is warmed up, a process which takes about 60 seconds. As soon as a target is detected (it must be within an angle of ±30° to the axis of the missile) the gyros of the missiles are run up, taking a further 30 seconds, and as soon as the decision to engage has been taken the axial gyro is aligned, taking a further 6 seconds. At this point, a minimum of 96 seconds after the first warning of a threat (assuming that the gyros were not run up) the ITS takes over automatically and the sequence is irreversible, and in 2-5 seconds after the 'fire' button is pressed the missile is launched.

In $2\frac{1}{2}$ seconds the boost motor lifts the missile clear of the launcher and takes it up to an average height of 30m (98ft); it then pitches over into level flight before coming down to its cruise-height of 15m (49-50ft) within 4km ($2\frac{1}{2}$ miles) of the ship, travelling now on the sustainer motor at a speed of about 300m/sec (nearly 1000ft/sec). At about 24km a radio-altimeter in the missile brings it down to the sea-skimming height of about 7m (23ft), which is preset according to the sea state, and if the target is at 40km range the missile will have been in flight for about 2 minutes 20 seconds.

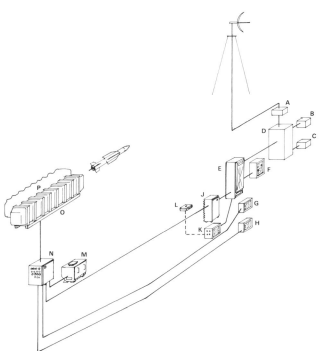

LAYOUT OF A TYPICAL EXOCET SYSTEM:
A Radar, **B** Vertical reference centre, **C** Log, **D** Coordinate changer, **E** Inter-connection panel, **F** Command panel, **G** Doors command unit, **H** Anti-icing command unit, **J** Technical unit, **K** Switch unit, **L** Test unit, **M** Power-supply unit, **N** Junction boxes, **O** Pallet, **P** Missile container.

Drawn by John Roberts

DEPLOYMENT

The successful trials in 1972-74 led the French and Royal navies to instal Exocet in a number of warships:

FRENCH NAVY	ROYAL NAVY
1 *Duperré* (4)	4 County class (4 each)
3 *Tourville* class (6 each)	4 *Amazon* class (4 each)
2 *Suffren* class (4 each)	8 *Broadsword* class (4 each)[1]
1 *Colbert* (4)	18 *Leander* class (4 each)[2]
1 *Jeanne d'Arc* (6)	
3 *Georges Leygues* class (4 each)[1]	
1 *Aconit* (4)	
9 *Commandant Riviere* class (2 each)	
14 *d'Estienne d'Orves* class (2 each)[2]	

Notes
1 More of class to be built
2 Not all completed or refitted

There is no space to list all the other ships in overseas navies which have been fitted with Exocet, but the following summary shows just how rapidly the weapon system became accepted:

ARGENTINA– 4 destroyers, 3 frigates
BELGIUM – 4 frigates
BRAZIL – 2 frigates
BRUNEI – 3 fast patrol boats
CHILE – 2 destroyers, 2 frigates
ECUADOR – 3 fast patrol boats
GERMANY – 4 destroyers, 30 fast patrol boats
GREECE – 14 fast patrol boats
INDONESIA – 3 frigates, 4 fast patrol boats
MALAYSIA – 8 fast patrol boats
PERU – 2 destroyers, 6 fast patrol boats
THAILAND – 3 fast patrol boats

THE NEXT STEP

The only valid criticism of the MM-38 Exocet were its comparatively modest range of 40km and the weight of the missile. Although it was as good as any other missile of its generation in practical terms, there was a demand from customers for more range, and so in 1976 development of the MM-40 started. There was also a demand for more firepower, and as problems had been encountered in trying to transfer the containers at sea the designers were told to simplify and lighten the whole installation as well.

Advantage could be taken of experience with the air-launched AM-39 variant, in which the weight of the round had been reduced substantially. Eventually, in spite of increasing range from 42km to 70km, it proved possible to reduce the total weight of missile and canister from 1750kg to 1150kg. It was also possible to reduce the volume significantly by fitting the missile with folding wings and adopting a fibreglass canister in place of the alloy box-launcher. Using a later generation of electronics the designers were able to reduce the weight and volume of the below-decks equipment and at the same time the method of installing the missile was simplified.

The missile itself is basically similar to the MM-38 round but has a longer sustainer-motor to provide a longer burn-time. This accounts for the extra length of 590mm. A digital computer replaces the analogue type used before but in other respects the missiles use virtually the same components. The ITS has been replaced by a much lighter *Installation de Tir Légère* (ITL) which can handle both MM-40 and MM-38 missiles.

The new canister is simply a cylinder of wound fibreglass and as the missiles wings are folded the total diameter is 350mm as against 1000mm for the box-launcher. The weight of the missile went up from 735kg to 850kg but the all-up weight of the missile and canister is 600kg less. The twin canister-tubes are fitted with two reinforced sections to allow them to be secured to the launching ramp, and two can fit into the space occupied by one MM-38. In fact the modular design of the canisters allows them to be mounted in threes, fours or even sixes, and makes for more rapid installation than before. Eight MM-40s with ITL weigh about the same as four MM-38s with ITS.

An important improvement over MM-38 is the ability to angle the gyros through 60° which permits the ship to engage on a wider bearing. The altitude-control system has also been improved, so that in a flat calm the missile can be brought to as little as 2.5m above the sea, making it even harder to detect.

OVER-THE-HORIZON GUIDANCE

The principal of guidance for the MM-40 is little different from the older MM-38. The missile is programmed with the coordinates of the target before the launch, as usual, but if the target is over the horizon these coordinates must be provided by an external sensor such as a radar in a helicopter. The missile is designed to accept data from any type of airborne radar currently in service, and the minimum requirement is a single-track radar (preferably with a track-while-scan facility), a gyro-compass and a radio set for transmitting data.

The helicopter locates the target and then provides the firing ship with the distance between itself and the target and the azimuth. The ITL can then calculate the triangulation needed to plot the range and bearing of the target, and once this information is in the missile's digital computer the firing sequence can be initiated. If it is necessary for the firing ship to maintain radar silence the helicopter can transmit the range and bearing for both the firing ship and the target, and from these figures the ITL could produce the same information.

DEPLOYMENT

Following trials on the *Ile d'Oleron* in 1979-80 the sloop *d'Estienne d'Orves* was fitted with two MM-40 canisters early in 1980 for trials over the French Navy's *Centre d'Essais de la Mediterranée* firing range. Using a Lynx helicopter as a relay it proved possible to hit a target 65km away. What was also proved was the ability of the ITL to handle both MM-38 and MM-40 missiles, for although the *d'Estienne d'Orves* was given two MM-40 canisters on the port side, the starboard single MM-38 launcher was retained and used in the trials programme.

The Mediterranean trials in 1980 brought the development phase to an end and the MM-40 is now in production at Bourges. Details of orders have not been made public but it is known that apart from the French Navy the customers include Argentina, Ecuador, Israel,

Nigeria and Oman as well as at least three other navies. South Africa would have been the first to have it in service in the sloops *Good Hope* and *Transvaal* but when the two ships were bought by Argentina they were given MM-38 instead. The first ship in service is likely to be the Ecuadorean corvette *Esmeraldas*, currently running trials in Italy.

AM39

The importance of the ship-to-ship version of Exocet has been overshadowed by the frighteningly successful use of AM-39 by Argentinian Super Etendard aircraft against British ships in the Falklands conflict. At the beginning of May the DDG HMS *Sheffield* was hit by one Exocet launched at a distance of about 20 miles, and after the San Carlos landings the Ro-Ro ship *Atlantic Conveyor* was hit by another. The most disturbing feature of the *Sheffield* sinking was not the damage done by the warhead (the superstructure of the ship remained intact) but the rapidity of which a fire took hold. There is also the question of how the ship's passive defences appear to have been overwhelmed. The *Atlantic Conveyor* stayed afloat for several days, despite having been hit by two Exocets, a reflection of the ability of a big hull to asborb damage.

Clearly the South Atlantic baptism of fire for Exocet has stimulated sales, and the manufacturers reported a massive increase in orders. However it must also stimulate the search for effective countermeasures. Undoubtedly a countermeasure does exist, whether in the form of jamming or in the form of a counter-attack by guns or missiles, but until such time as live missiles are flown in a full-scale test of point-defence systems, the missile will continue to dominate surface warfare.

EXOCET DATA

	MM-38	MM-40
Length (round)	5.21m	5.80m
Length oa	5.44m	6.20m
Span	1.0m	1.0m
Weight (round)	735kg	850kg
Total weight	1750kg	1150kg
Speed	Mach 0.93	Mach 0.93
Range	42km	70km
Warhead	165kg	165kg

Comparison of the sizes of MM-38, AM-39 and MM-40
Key to MM-38: **1** Rear equipment bay, **2** Booster motor, **3** Sustainer motor, **4** Warhead, **5** Logic frame, **6** Vertical gyro, **7** Radio altimeter, **8** Guidance computer, **9** Homing head, **10** Radio altimeter, **11** Axial gyro, **12** Radio altimeter antenna.

Drawn by John Roberts

12 — ITL 6 MM40 ON PATROL BOAT

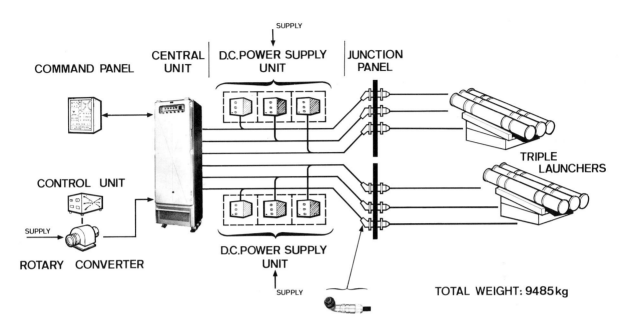

A typical MM-40 outfit for a patrol boat

Aérospatiale

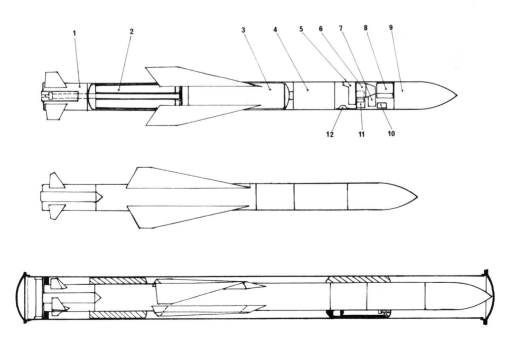

British Naval Guns 1880~1945 No7
by NJM Campbell

9.2in Mk IX Only 14 of this 46.7 calibre gun were made and, except for one modified and known as Mk X/IX in the gunnery school gunboat *Drudge* on a Mk VS mounting, they were only used for coast defence. They were mounted at the Needles, Malta and Gibraltar, and one gun was for a time mounted at Bere Island. The Gibraltar guns were on the crest in special mountings allowing 20° depression. Mk IX was of wire-wound construction, with the wire extending for about 60 per cent of the barrel's length, and was trunnioned. The breech mechanism was of the 3-motion type and the interrupted screw block was cylindrical. Most guns were later converted to 'C' IX with single-motion breech mechanism, and alterations to suit modified coast defence mountings for the Mk X gun.

Mk X/IX was more extensively modified, being altered to take a Welin breech block, while the trunnion ring was replaced by a seating for the naval mounting and two additional short tubes were screwed and shrunk on.

9.2in Mk X This was another 46.7 calibre gun extensively used by both the Navy and Army. It was carried in Mk V mountings by the armoured cruisers *Aboukir, Cressy, Drake* and *Levianthan*; in Mk VS by the battleships of the *King Edward VII* class and the armoured cruisers of the *Black Prince* and *Achilles* classes, as well as for a time by the gunnery school gunboats *Drudge* and *Excellent* (ex-*Handy*); and in Mk VI by the cruisers *Bacchante, Euryalus, Hogue, Sutlej* and *King Alfred*. All these single mountings allowed 15° elevation though in two of the *King Edward*s – *Commonwealth* and *Zealandia* – this was increased to 30° in the latter part of the first World War. Spare Mk V mountings converted to 30° were also fitted in the small monitors *M15, 16, 17* and *18*.

Early in 1917 3 Mk VS mountings altered to give 45° elevation were installed in the RN siege gun batteries on the Belgian coast, and it is interesting to note that the Mk X guns could run out at maximum elevation.

Army guns were primarily for coast defence in single mountings allowing 15°, 30° or 35° elevation though a number were used on railway mountings. Altogether 112 guns were made for the Navy of which 12 were later transferred to land service, and excluding these, about 170 for the Army.

The Mk X gun was of standard wire-wound construction with forward shoulders on the inner 'A' tube, no trunnions and single-motion breech mechanism with Welin block. It suffered from steel choke and from the use of too large a propellant grain, and these defects remained in naval guns which were obsolete after the First World War, 3 guns with tapered inner 'A' tubes being cancelled. In Army guns a smaller grain propellant was eventually adopted, and tapered inner 'A' tubes gradually introduced, so that the Mk X remained the standard coast defence gun until the end of the fixed coastal batteries.

The prefix 'A' is sometimes found and indicates 'pure couple' breech mechanism.

The designation Mk X^V was used for 2 army guns wire-wound over part of their length only, and with no 'B' tube, while Mk XT was used for the 2 guns made by Vickers for the reconstructed Turkish ship *Messudieh* but never delivered. The latter were designed for a lower working pressure, with about 200fs less MV, but would take the standard MD37 charge. They were to have had Elswick 3-motion short arm BMs and were kept as special reserve railway guns.

The Mk X^X designation covered guns with tapered inner 'A' tubes, while the suffix RT following Mk X, X^V or X^X indicated modifications to fit the Second World War Mk V railway mounting. It is not thought that any were so modified.

9.2 Mk XI A 50.15 calibre gun for the Navy mounted in twin Mk VII and single Mk VIII mountings in the battleships of the *Lord Nelson* class and in twin Mk VII mountings in the armoured cruisers of the *Minotaur* class. Both allowed 15° elevation. Altogether 45 guns

The battleship *Commonwealth* in 1920. She carried a secondary armament of four 9.2in Mk X in single Mk VS mountings, seen here abreast the fore and main masts on the upper deck. The remainder of her original scecondary battery of 6in guns on the main deck were removed during the First World War and replaced by four shielded 6in guns mounted on the upper deck between the 9.2in turrets.

IWM

were made of which 12 were still in existence during the Second World War, though the last cradles and slides, which came under a different department, had been scrapped in September 1938. The guns were declined by the Army, apparently due to problems in adapting the mountings of Mk X guns.

The Mk XI was of standard wire-wound construction with an inner 'A' tube with forward shoulders, most guns having cannelured rings, and single motion BM with Welin block. The prefix 'A' indicated 'pure-couple' breech mechanism, while 'Mk XI' covered 2 guns with a thinner 'A' tube and smaller diameter chase, made to an earlier Elswick design, Mk XI being a Vickers design. Another Elswick design, their pattern J, was intended for a higher working pressure and had no forward shoulders on the inner 'A' tube. It was numbered E572, but on relining to the standard Mk XI design became No 433 in the service series. None of these were segregated in use.

9.2in Mk XII This 51.35 calibre gun was originally the 50cal 9.45in Elswick pattern 'E' intended for the Norwegian coast defence ships *Nidaros* and *Björgvin* which

were taken over by the RN as the *Gorgon* and *Glatton* in the First World War. The single Mk IX mountings allowed 40° elevation. In all, 6 guns were made of which 2 were lost in the *Glatton*, and the remaining 4 offered to the Army after the First World War but unwisely declined. The guns were of normal wire-wound type with tapered inner 'A' tubes and Elswick 3-motion short-arm breech mechanism. The first 3 were relined to 9.2in and the others completed to this size. The last 2 differed in having a thicker 'A' tube and thinner inner 'A' along the chase.

9.2in Mk XIII This was an Army gun on a railway mounting and was only 35 calibres long – a curious figure for a new railway gun, but presumably justified by the special circumstances of the Western Front in the First World War. About 23 guns were made. It was trunnioned and of normal wire-wound construction with Welin block and 'pure-couple' BM. It was in service in the Second World War, and two new versions were designed, Mk XIII[x] without wire and otherwise with inner 'A', 'A', jacket, breech ring, breech bush, shrunk collar and trunnion ring, and Mk XIIIA differing in having a loose liner, full length jacket and no shrunk collar. It is not thought that any of these two were completed.

9.2in Mk XIV A 45 calibre gun from Vickers intended for a cancelled armoured cruiser to be built in Italy and similar to the Elswick pattern 'H' in the Greek cruiser

Averov, except that the wire-winding extended for half the barrel's length and not the whole. Of the 4 guns, 3 were used on railway mountings in the First World War and the other on the Vickers range.

9.2in Mk XV A 46.7 calibre gun and in effect an updated Mk X. It was intended for the twin Mk VIII coast defence mounting which allowed 44° elevation, but this was never completed. A total of 36 guns were ordered and some at least passed proof, but it is doubtful if any

The *Cressy* class armoured cruiser *Bacchante* and three of her sisters carried two 9.2in Mk X guns in single Mk VI mountings fore and aft while the remaining two, *Cressy* and *Hogue*, were fitted with Mk V mountings.

Tom Molland

were actually used in the existing single coast defence mountings. The construction comprised inner 'A' and 'A' tubes, jacket, breech ring, breech bush and shrunk collar with Welin block and Asbury BM.

PARTICULARS OF 9.2IN GUNS, Mks IX – XV

	9.2in Mk IX	9.2in Mk X, XV	9.2in Mk XI	9.2in Mk XII	9.2in Mk XIII	9.2in Mk XIV
Weight (tons)	26.8 (Mk X/IX 28.4)	28.3 (Mk XT 27.8, Mk XV 27.9)	28.4 (Mk XIx 28.2, No 433 28.8)	31.2	24.2	26.6
Length oa (in)	445.3 (Mk X/IX 442.6)	442.4	474.4	485.4	335	427
Length bore (cal)	46.74 (Mk X/IX 46.68)	46.66	50.15	51.35	35	45
Chamber (cu in)	8123	8123 (Mk XV 8158)	9000	8600	5800	8123
Chamber length (in)	71	71 (Mk XV 71.48)	65.28	65.28	45.23	71
Projectile (lb)	380	380	380	380/391	380	380
Charge (lb)/type	120/MD 37, 107/MD 26, 109/SC 150	120/MD 37, 107/MD 26, 109/SC 150, 123.6/SC 205*	128.5/MD 37	128.5/MD 37 152/MD 45*	82/ MD 26 81.1/SC 150	120/MD 37 107/MD 26
Muzzle Velocity (fs)	2778 (MD 37), 2748 (others)	2778 (MD 37), 2872 (SC 205), 2748 (others)	2890	2940 (MD 37) 3060 (MD 45)	c2480	2748 (MD 37), c2720 (MD 26)
Range (yds)	15,500/15° (2crh/2778fs)	15,500/15° (2crh/2778fs), 25,700/30° (4crh/2778fs)	16,200/15° (2crh)	c31,000/40° (4crh/2940fs), c39,000/40° (8crh/3060fs)		

*Supercharge

Attack and Defence Part 3 by D K Brown RCNC

One of the most difficult tasks for the twentieth century naval constructor has been the protection of ships against underwater explosions from mines or torpedoes. The first recorded test of underwater protection was initiated by Sir William White in 1886 and carried out against the old battleship *Resistance* in conditions of secrecy unusual in that era of open government. The aim was to find out whether empty or coal filled compartments provided the better protection against torpedo explosion. The test charge was 120lb of wet gun-cotton, much larger than most of the then current torpedo warheads. The conclusion reached was that coal filled compartments provided some degree of protection.

It seems that there were no further trials until 1903 by which time typical torpedoes had a warhead of about 230lbs of wet gun-cotton. The old coast defence ship *Belleisle* was fitted with an experimental protection system which consisted of a series of longitudinal watertight bulkheads arranged to form five rows of compartments and containing, in order from the outside, Water, Cork, Coal, Air, Coal with an overall width of 12ft (Fig 1). A charge of 230lbs of gun-cotton was exploded against the skin and caused very extensive damage – all six bulkheads were ruptured and a boiler was shifted by 2ft. (Gunnery trials against *Resistance* and *Belleisle* will be described in a later article.)

The test was followed up in 1905-6 by a further series of trials against an old merchant ship, the *Ridsdale*. It had been learnt that the Russian battleship *Tsarevitch* had been torpedoed several times in the Russo-Japanese war and had remained afloat. This ship had a thick bulkhead abreast of the engine rooms, boiler rooms and magazines formed by turning down the protective deck over these spaces and continuing it to the bottom of the ship. *Ridsdale* was given a strong, inner bulkhead which was able to resist a 230lb charge, though details of the trial remain obscure.

This scheme, with a thick bulkhead well inboard, was incorporated into the design of the *Dreadnought* though, due to weight limitations, such protection was confined to short lengths abreast the magazines. Later ships had a more complete protection until 1910 when it proved impossible in *Hercules* and *Colossus* in way of their wing turrets. In 1912 complete protection was once again provided in the design of the *Queen Elizabeth*.

The battleship *Majestic* sinking off Cape Helles on 27 May 1915, after being torpedoed by the submarine *U21*. Such incidents in the early part of the war emphasised the need for some form of additional underwater protection in older ships and led to the general adoption of the bulge.

Courtesy J A Roberts

HOOD TRIALS

Such protection involved a considerable amount of both weight and cost and in 1913 it was decided by the Board of Admiralty that large scale tests should be carried out against the old battleship *Hood*. She was taken in hand in Portsmouth for extensive alterations which involved building-in two longitudinal bulkheads over a length of 120ft alongside the engine and boiler rooms. Abreast the engine room a heavy (80lbs/ft) bulkhead was built 7ft outboard of the 17lb engine room bulkhead (Fig 2). For the second test, at a boiler room, the 80lb bulkhead was inboard and the lighter one closer to the explosion. In both cases the existing double bottom structure was retained (Fig 3).

The first test was carried out in the Beaulieu River on 9 February 1914 (Ref 1). A charge of 280lbs of wet gun-cotton was exploded 12ft below the surface abreast the middle of the engine room. The two watertight compartments forward of the point of the explosion were empty and those aft were full of water. The double bottom spaces were all empty. The explosion made a hole 18ft high and 30ft long, its effects being directed mainly against the empty compartments. The thin wing bulkhead was blown right in until brought to rest by the 80lb bulkhead which was itself seriously dished. In the empty compartments the thick bulkhead was pierced by a fairly large number of fragments of the shell plating, shattered by the explosion. The innermost (17lb) bulkhead was slightly distorted and leaked at the rivets but the flow of water was well within the normal capacity of the ship's pumps. It was noted that the horizontal struts connecting the bulkheads had transmitted the blow to the innermost bulkhead and it was decided that for the second experiment these should be cut and joined in such a way that they could carry tension loads only. The projectile effect of broken shell plating also indicated that the outer space should be water filled.

The second experiment was held at Spithead on 7 May 1914 with the double bottom and outer space full and the inner compartment next to the boiler room bulkhead (80lb) empty. The 280lb charge made a slightly smaller hole than the previous shot but the tamping effect of the adjacent water filled compartments caused more extensive structural damage. The heavy bulkhead was only slightly dished and the slow leakage was again within the capacity of the pumps. The conclusion drawn from these two tests were: a) There should be a thin bulkhead inboard of the thick protective bulkhead to retain the water which would inevitably break through the main bulkhead. b) The bulkheads should be joined by ties only (not struts). c) A thick bulkhead could be made strong enough to prevent serious flooding of main compartments.

A conference was held at Portsmouth in September 1914 to consider the results of the *Hood* trials together with the earlier ones, described above and those on *Terpsichore* (1913).

The conference noted that it was still unclear which spaces should be full and which empty, though that next to the charge should certainly be empty to avoid a tamping effect. They also considered that the space outboard of the thick bulkhead should be liquid filled in order to slow down pieces of flying plate. proposals were made for further work to determine the optimum arrangement of compartments, the design of the thick bulkhead and the value of venting arrangements, but due to the war this work was not carried out. The conference endorsed the design of the protection in *Queen Elizabeth. Hood*, herself, was sunk on 4 November 1914 to block the southern entrance to Portland harbour where her hull may yet be seen on still days.

The charge used against *Hood* was reasonably typical of 1914 torpedoes (British 21in Mk II had a charge of 225lbs) but both sides were to introduce torpedoes with charges of over 500lbs during the war, eg: the 23.6in German torpedo of 1916 with a 550lb charge, and the 21in Mk IV British torpedo of 1917 with a 515lb charge. The radius of damage is roughly proportional to the cube root of the charge weight.

THE BULGE

The outbreak of war and the numerous casualties from mine and torpedo showed that a form of protection was needed which could be applied to existing ships. The Director of Naval Construction himself, Sir Eustace Tennyson d'Eyncourt, devised a form of protection known as the bulge (Fig 4), and without any preliminary trials, this system was fitted to four old cruisers of the *Edgar* class. The bulge stuck out some 15ft from the original ship's sides serving both to detonate the torpedo at a distance and absorbing part of the energy of the explosion. The outer part of the bulge was air filled and the inner compartment was freeflooding. Transverse bulkheads were fitted about 20ft apart to limit flooding. This large addition to the hull reduced speed by about 4kts which mattered little in their new role as coastal bombardment ships. Both *Edgar* and *Grafton* were torpedoed in 1917, the bulge proving very effective in minimising damage. A somewhat similar bulge was incorporated in all the monitors designed by C S Lillicrap and a modified – reduced – bulge was fitted to many ships designed in the First World War, including *Renown, Hood, Courageous, Hermes, Raleigh*, etc. Later, the battleships of the *Royal Sovereign* and *Queen Elizabeth* class were bulged, the loss of speed being kept down to about one knot. This simple protection further proved its value in December 1939 when the *Barham* was hit in the region of A & B turret shell rooms. Though the hole in the bulge was 17ft × 32ft the damage was localised and the ship was able to make her own way to the repair yard at 16kts. D'Eyncourt was very proud of his work on bulge protection and was even to write to the Prime Minister complaining that lack of technical understanding had unduly restricted its use (Ref 2).

1 The ironclad *Resistance*, seen here as built, was employed in the first recorded tests of underwater protection in 1886.
P A Vicary

2 The destroyer leader *Bruce* at the moment of being destroyed by an 18in aerial torpedo, in a test carried out off the Isle of Wight on 22 November 1939. Torpedo employed a magnetic pistol and detonated under the ship.
IWM

1

2

288

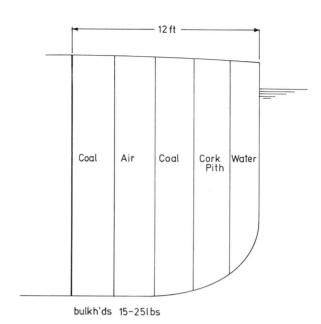

bulkh'ds 15–25 lbs

FIG 1 : BELLEISLE

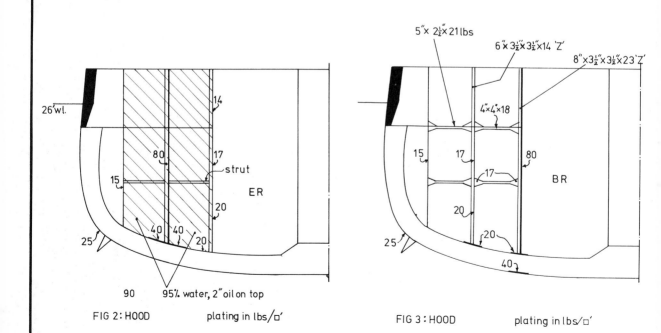

FIG 2 : HOOD   plating in lbs/□′

FIG 3 : HOOD   plating in lbs/□′

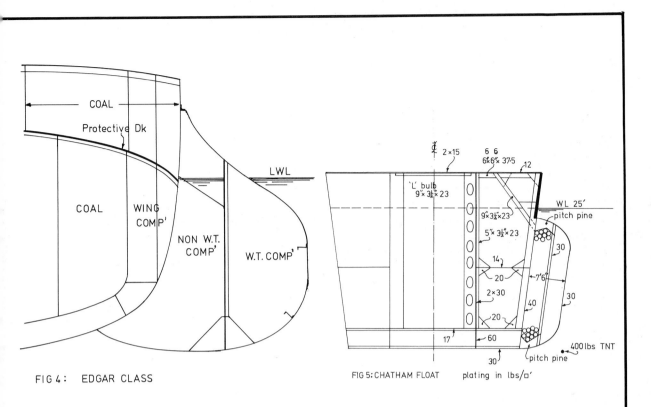

FIG 4: EDGAR CLASS

FIG 5: CHATHAM FLOAT   plating in lbs/□′

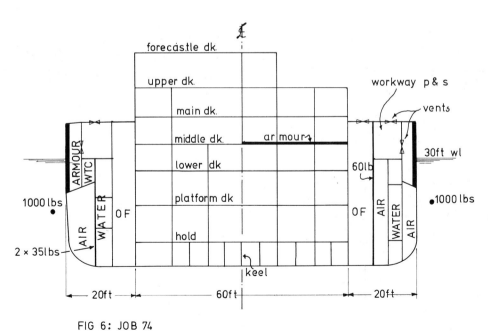

FIG 6: JOB 74

In the meantime, Professor Hopkinson of Cambridge, working on behalf of the DNC, had developed a scaling law which enabled model tests to be representative of full scale explosions. After proving his work on very small models, a $\frac{1}{4}$ scale model was made and tested of a detachable bulge used on the merchant ship *City of Oxford* and later, in modified form on the old battleship *Revenge*.

This is probably the appropriate moment at which to outline the phenomena associated with an underwater explosion. The almost instantaneous conversion of several hundred pounds of explosive into gas leads to both a shock wave, which travels at the speed of sound in water, and a bubble of gas, which expands very rapidly at first, then contracts or expands again with further oscillations which die away. When the explosion takes place against the hull plating it will be shattered and pieces of plate flung with great velocity into the ship. For this reason side armour does not extend far below the water line where it can be broken by a torpedo hit – even the thickest armour will fracture. It is usual to have an air space next to the hull into which the gas can expand, followed by a water filled space to slow down pieces of plating.

Small scale tests in 1915 at Portsmouth showed that the damage caused by an explosion could be reduced by filling the inner compartments of a bulge with steel tubes, sealed at each end. Later that year a large pontoon was built at Chatham representing, at full scale, half the section of a large warship with a bulge. The 'Chatham Float', as it was known, was 80ft long, 31ft 6in wide and 31ft 6in deep (Fig 5). The outside compartment of the bulge was air filled and the inner space was packed with steel tubes, 9in in diameter, $\frac{1}{4}$in thick, sealed at both ends. A 400lb charge of TNT made a hole about 15ft diameter in the bulge crushing the tubes in way of the explosion. Damage to the main structure was very slight with only limited leakage through riveted seams, which would have been well within the capacity of ship's pumps.

In 1920 a replica of the bulge system, with tubes, used in the battlecruiser *Hood* was built onto the float, together with an alternative scheme using a water filled compartment instead of tubes. A 500lb charge of Trotyl was exploded against the protective systems and both successfully resisted the explosion with only the usual slight leakage at rivets. It will be noted that the charge used was smaller that that of torpedoes already in service and much smaller than new designs in hand (about 750lbs).

POST WAR TRIALS

By 1921, there was interest in the American protection system which relied on a number of longitudinal bulkheads of more or less uniform thickness rather than the British concentration on a thick bulkhead furthest from the hull. Scale models of both schemes were made and attached to the Chatham Float for test. The charge was 20lbs of TNT which represented a 1000lb charge at full scale. From these tests it was concluded that, weight for weight, the British system was superior though it was noted that similar experiments in the USA led to exactly

the opposite conclusion. The British also concluded that venting the explosion outside the armour was effective.

The lessons of all these tests were incorporated in the design of the protection for the *Nelson* and *Rodney*. Water filled spaces were used instead of tubes and the British negotiators at the Washington Treaty were briefed to ensure that water was excluded from 'standard' displacement. A full scale replica of the *Nelson* scheme was built into the Chatham float and a 1000lb charge exploded against it. The thick bulkhead received a permanent set of $3\frac{1}{2}$in and would probably have withstood a considerably larger charge.

Further trials in the early 1920s included some on the effect of depth charges against surrendered U-boats, the effect of near miss bombs exploding underwater against the *Gorgon* and some more elaborate trials with *Monarch*. She was fitted with a modified bulge and in 1923 was tested against large near miss bombs. From these trials much was learnt concerning the effect of shock and the dangers of fractures in the main circulating water system.

By 1925 money was very scarce and for many years only small scale, model tests were possible. After some initial, basic experiments at Portsmouth a strong box was built, some 10ft × 12ft, which could accommodate different arrangements of bulkheads. The device, known as the 'bulge model' remained in use until the mid-1940s by which time over 130 trials had been carried out together with another 240 against a simpler box target.

With considerable difficulty, permission was obtained to defer the scrapping of *Roberts* and between 1929 and 1935 some 11 trials were carried out against larger scale models ($\frac{1}{3}$ or $\frac{3}{4}$ scale) attached to her bulge. Charges of various sizes up to $16\frac{1}{2}$lbs (representing 1000lbs full scale) were used. These tests enabled the Constructors in charge to get a real understanding of the way in which protection systems worked and led up to the design of the sandwich protection used in later ships. The importance of the overall depth of the side protection was clearly shown; a 12ft system withstood a 1000lb charge while a 9ft depth failed against 500lbs (scale figures). Several vent plates failed to function and it was concluded that, after all, venting was unnecessary. Welded construction overcame the old problems of leaking and tearing along riveted seams.

All these model tests showed the importance of getting all the details right. It was found that an air-water-air sandwich was the best arrangement with the three layers of equal thickness, though quite considerable changes in proportion could be made with little loss. The liquid space had to be less than completely full to prevent the deck cover from rupture by the hydraulic pulse developed. Various arrangements of stiffeners and transverse bulkheads were tried. During this period the diving (or B) bomb was seen as a greater menace than the torpedo.

JOB 74

By 1934 the design of *Ark Royal* was in hand and advance thinking on the new battleships had started; the DNC, Sir Arthur Johns, persuaded the Board to build a new full size target. Job 74, as it was known, was designed by D E J Offord RCNC and his assistant D W Smithers RCNC (Ref 3). Job 74 was 72ft long, 60ft wide and 50ft deep from deck to keel (Fig 6). Full scale targets were attached at the ends. The interior was fitted out to represent compartments typical of both battleship and cruiser practice. Since Job 74 was also to be used for bombing trials, she was given a heavy armoured deck.

For the first underwater trial Job 74 was given a sandwich system on one side and a modified d'Eyncourt bulge on the other leading to an overall width of 100ft. A 1000lb charge was exploded against each side in turn causing a hole about 25ft × 16ft in the outer plating. Both the intermediate longitudinal bulkheads in the sandwich were destroyed over a length of about 36ft and the main protective bulkhead deflected 18in but not ruptured. The rapid distortion of this bulkhead set up a pressure pulse in the oil tank behind it which caused some damage to the main hull. The other system failed, the main bulkhead being ruptured over an area 14ft long by 28ft deep.

Once again, many specific lessons were learnt emphasising the need for great care in the design of every structural detail. While the value of welding was demonstrated in general, it was shown that available techniques were not satisfactory for welding thick (over 1in) high tensile (D1) plates.

Job 74 continued to lead an exciting life. Offord was much concerned over the risk of explosion of the warheads in *Hood*'s above water torpedo tubes. To study this hazard, three 750lb warheads were exploded on the main deck of Job 74. Some years later, Offord was to give evidence to the inquiry into the loss of the *Hood*

The *Rodney* (shown her in 1939) and *Nelson* were the first RN warships to incorporate a built-in underwater protection system utilising water filled spaces.

IWM

maintaining that the cause was explosion of the torpedo warheads. He still (1980) holds this view. She was also used for bombing trials which demonstrated very clearly the difficulty of hitting even a stationary target; 34 hits were scored with bombs where weights totalled 10,000lbs. Turret flash trials were also held and the contents of 6in and 8in magazines were deliberately ignited to imitate an explosion. An aircraft hangar (of cruiser type) was fitted to study hangar fires and fire fighting. During the war Job 74 was used as an air raid shelter and Offord has said 'the shelterers had a certain amount of confidence in her'.

Other trials from the late 1930s included some rather unsuccessful shots against the old submarine *L19*. A special submarine section, Job 81, was built and tried in 1938. After she had been tested to destruction, another section, Job 9, was built and remained in use for shock trials, particularly against batteries, throughout the war. Other trials were aimed at testing weapons, rather than ships, and of these the most notable was the sinking of *Bruce* by a torpedo with a magnetic pistol on 22 November 1939 off the Isle of Wight (Ref 4).

A later article will show that these trials enabled British warships to withstand very severe attack during the Second World War. Ships which get home are not regarded as 'news' – we hear too much of those which were lost.

REFERENCES

1 *Records of Warship Construction 1914-18*, DNC.
2 d'Eyncourt papers. National Maritime Museum.
3 *A Century of Naval Construction. A History of the RCNC*. D K Brown (To be published by Conway Maritime Press in 1983).
4 *V & W Class Destroyers 1917-1945*. A Preston, Macdonald 1971.

The Bad Weather Flotilla Part 3

by Przemysław Budzbon & Boris Lemachko

On 22 June 1941 the Russians found themselves facing the full weight of a German onslaught which shattered their defences. The main bases of the Soviet Navy were threatened by the German advance and in the early stages of the war it became necessary for the Red Navy to participate in the defence of its own bases.

The Russian defence was most successful in the north, where heavy mountain terrain and embittered defence prevented German troops from overrunning the main base of the Northern Fleet – Polyarnoe. Northern Fleet ships participated in the defence of the Rybachyj Peninsula and along the Litsa River. At the beginning of July *Groza* and *Smerch* repeatedly supported Soviet troops resisting the German bridgehead on the right bank of the Litsa. The Germans began the second phase of their attack, from a widened Litsa bridgehead, on 13 July and *Smerch* shelled their positions from the Bay of Litsa. On the following day Soviet ships, supported by the destroyer *Kujbyshev*, 4 subchasers and *Groza*, landed a large party of troops on the western bank of the river. The German advance was halted, and on 16 July, a second landing was made in the Bay of Litsa with the support of *Kujbyshev*, guard ships *Groza*, *Smerch* and *Priliv*, and the subchasers.

A group of 4 German submarines operating off the Kola coast during August – September achieved some successes, of which the most significant was the damaging of the Soviet transport *Mariya Ulyanovna* (3879 BRT) by *U 571* off Cape Teriberski on 26 August. The damaged ship was helped by *Groza* during her attempts to reach port but she had to be beached two days later.

The third guard ship of the Northern Fleet – *Uragan* – was waiting at the Polyarnoe yard's pier for replacement parts for her damaged turbines. The parts were to come from Leningrad, but after German forces encircled that city, it was impossible to supply them until the blockade was broken in 1944. The *Uragan* was not therefore recommissioned until late 1944.

DEFENCE OF THE BALTIC

The Soviet defenders were not so successful on the Baltic coast. The Germans occupied the naval base at Libau on 27 June and three days later the Soviets had to evacuate Riga and the Dvina Estuary. In futile

One of the Northern Fleet 'troika' – possible *Groza* at the end of war. Note the difference as compared with the earlier appearance of the ship – absence of a mainmast, 37mm gun carried in place of the searchlight and new camouflage painting. In 1945 the pendant numbers of the *Uragan* class ships with the Northern Fleet were changed: *01* in the case of *Smerch*, *02* – *Groza* and *03* – *Uragan*. The submarines in the foreground are *K 21* and *L 15* respectively.

Boris Lemachko Collection

Vikhr' dressed overall after the war. The new 100mm gun is particularly noticeable, while other modifications include the built up bridge, antennae booms on the after funnel, canvassed 37mm single mounting and the MGs in the bow.

Boris Lemachko Collection

attempts to halt the German advance 7 Soviet destroyers, accompanied by *Sneg* and *Tucha* under Rear Admiral Drozd, tried on 13 July to intercept off the Dvina River estuary a German convoy, protected only by minesweepers and on its way from Libau to Riga. Both guard ships had only just completed a major overhaul when the war broke out.

A desperate defence did not slow the German troops who, on 19 August, reached Tallin – the main base of the Baltic Fleet at that time. After a week of furious fighting the Soviet supreme command – Stavka – had to order the evacuation of Tallin, for which three convoys and their covering forces assembled during 28 August off Tallin. The rearguard under Rear Admiral Rall consisted of 3 old destroyers, the guard ships *Burya, Sneg* and *Tsiklon*, the minelayer *Vaindlo* and a number of small boats. After the departure of the convoy, *Vaindlo* and the guard ships laid a mine barrage in the harbour and the approaches to Tallin. En route to Kronshtadt, the withdrawing forces were heavily attacked by German aircraft, but the heaviest losses were sustained in breaking through the 'Juminda' mine barrage during the night of 29 August. Among the numerous ships lost on mines that night were all 3 destroyers of the rearguard as well as *Sneg* and *Tsiklon*. During the day the main forces, still under continuous attack by German

bombers, entered Kronshtadt, thus ending the largest and most expensive operation the Soviet Navy had yet undertaken. Of the total of 195 units involved, 53 with over 4000 men on board were lost.

Those ships of the Baltic Fleet which survived the first two months of the war soon found themselves under attack by the Luftwaffe. In September, during three days of intensive bombardment, Stuka dive bombers severely damaged or sunk in Kronshtadt 10 major surface units. Among the lesser warships lost was *Vikhr'*, sunk on 21 September, while *Tajfun* was severely damaged two days later. Thus only *Burya* and *Tucha* of the original seven remained in service with the Baltic Fleet in the beseiged city of Leningrad, while *Purga* was at that time temporarily attached to the Lake Ladoga Flotilla, formed at the beginning of July to face the advances of German and Finnish forces. *Purga*, together with the old torpedo boat *Konstrucktor*, convoyed ships to Leningrad and during September – November about 45,000 tons of food, petrol and ammunition was shipped into Leningrad for the loss of 6 steamers and 24 barges. On 4 November *Konstrucktor* was sunk by German bombers while *Purga* remained in service until the beginning of December, when navigation on the Ladoga was halted by heavy ice.

THE BLACK SEA

When the war began, one of the two guard ships of the Black Sea Fleet – *Shtorm* – had been under refit in the fleet's main base of Sevastopol since March 1939. At that time her power plant was stripped-down but,

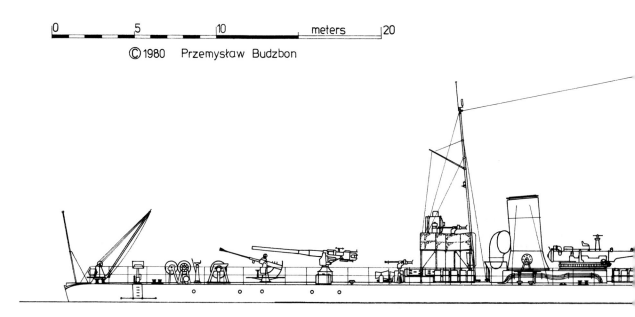

despite urgent orders, work proceeded slowly and was not entirely complete before the initial German attacks on Sevastopol began on 30 November. Because the other immobilised ships were menaced by the Luftwaffe, it was decided to evacuate all ships undergoing repairs either to Poti or other Caucasian ports. So *Shtorm,* with her turbines only just completed, in company with *Shkval* convoyed the incomplete ships to the Caucasian ports and escorted convoys with troops and material to the beseiged base. It was planned to complete the remaining work on the *Shtorm* at Poti but, because of a shortage of ships, she was appointed to a large assault operation on the Kerch Peninsula intended to break the blockade of Sevastopol. *Shtorm,* assisted by 3 gunboats, formed the support force during the landing of Group B near Kamysh-Burun on 29 December. The refitting of *Shtorm* was finally completed in June 1942.

THE GERMAN OFFENSIVE OF 1942
Before the Germans resumed their offensive in the summer, the Soviet command made the most of the time available to strengthen their forces and harrass the German regrouping. In the Arctic, guard ships took part in numerous patrol and escort duties protecting convoys from Britain and between the Russian har-

bours. *Smerch* was mentioned for her A/S patrol duty off the Kola inlet with the guard ship *Rubin* and some subchasers during the PQ13 convoy of March 1942. The same pair, assisted by the destroyer *Gromkij,* reverted to shore support during the assault of the 12th Brigade of the Morskaya Piekhota (Naval Troops, as the Russians call their Marines) on the southern coast of Motovska Bay. This landing, on 28 April, was intended to upset German preparations for their summer offensive in the north.

The defenders of Sevastopol found themselves in a critical condition in the spring, despite the continuous efforts of the Black Sea Fleet to supply the city. In one such operation the destroyers *Bditelnyj* and *Bezuprechnyj* and the guard ship *Shkval* brought 800 men and 360 tons of material into the southern bay of Sevastopol on 20 June. In spite of these efforts the Soviets had to evacuate Sevastopol on 4 July allowing the strong German offensive on the southern flank of the Eastern Front to push the Russians to the foot of the Caucasus mountains. During the above operations *Shtorm* participated in the evacuation of isolated elements of the Soviet 47th Army from the Taman Peninsula during 2 – 5 September.

On the opposite flank of the Eastern Front both sides paid particular attention to Leningrad – the last base of

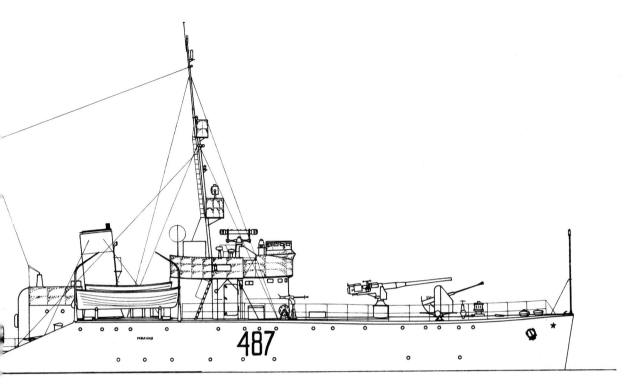

487

MOLNIYA in 1953

the Baltic Fleet remaining in Russian hands. The most important factor upon which the defence of this beseiged city depended was communication. Navigation on Lake Ladoga was resumed on 24 May and was utilised with more vigour than during the 1941 season. To break the lifeline of the beseiged city, the Germans began intensive air attacks on ships and bases on Ladoga. This resulted in heavy losses to Soviet craft, one of the victims being *Purga*, which was sunk near Marja on 1 September. The armament and fittings of *Purga* were removed from the wreck in the same year. The hull was raised in 1943 and some parts of the power plant were removed to refit *Vikhr'* which had been salved and taken in hand during the meantime: she was recommissioned in 1944. Of the remaining guard ships of the Baltic Fleet, *Burya* and *Tucha* were overhauled and refitted during 1942 and were followed by *Tajfun* which was repaired after damage sustained in 1941. On 24 August during attempts to shell enemy installations *Burya* was lost on mines off Suursaari Island.

As a result of the German occupation of Sevastopol, ships of the Black Sea Fleet had to be evacuated to the small Caucasian ports, but the German offensive in the summer – autumn of 1942 menaced the Caucasian coast and threatened to deprive the Soviet warships of their last bases in the Black Sea. The fall of Novorssisk on 7 September left Tuapse as the next objective of the German advance, so Soviet warships were employed in reinforcing Tuapse with troops and material. *Shtorm* participated in two such operations, undertaken during the course of September. The Russian defence off Tuapse subsequently became critical and in one attempt to soften the German pressure, the destroyer *Nezamozhnik* and the guard ship *Shkval* shelled land targets near Sarygol and Kiik-Atlama during the night on 14 October. The supplying of Tuapse was resumed six days later and in one of these operations, carried out during 24 – 28 October, the destroyers *Nezamozhnik*, *Bojkij* and *Besposhchadnyj* and the guard ships *Shtorm* and *Shkval*, as well as some transports bringing more troops and supplies from Sochi took part. As a result of these enterprises the German advance had been stopped by the end of the month. As a result the situation on the Caucasian coast stabilised itself and the Russians were able to undertake harassment operations against the German held shore. During the night of 20 December the leader *Kharkov* and destroyer *Bojkij* shelled Yalta, while *Nezamozhnik* and *Shkval* bombarded Feodasia. On the way back the Soviet force encountered the German 1st E-boat Flotilla but no success was achieved by either side.

TABLE 1: BUILDING DATES

Name	Laid down*	Launched	Commissioned	Fate
SERIES 1				
Uragan	13.8.1927	4.9.1928	12.9.1931	Scrapped 1959
Tajfun	13.8.1927	1.6.1929	14.9.1931	Deleted c1959
Smerch	13.8.1927	1929	Sept 1932	DOSAAF training ship 1950
Tsiklon	24.10.1927	1930	8.7.1932	Lost 28.8.1941
Vikhr'	24.10.1927	1930	12.9.1932	Deleted c1959
Groza	24.10.1927	1930	22.7.1932	Scrapped 1959
Metel'	18.12.1931	1934	18.9.1934	Training ship 1950
V'yuga	1932	June 1934	18.11.1934	Scrapped 1959
SERIES II				
Shkval	24.9.1927	1.7.1929	13.10.1932	Deleted c1959
Shtorm	24.9.1927	1.9.1929	5.3.1933	Deleted c1959
Buran	22.4.1932	1934	1935	Deleted c1959
Grom	22.4.1932	1934	1935	Deleted c1959
SERIES III				
Burya	1933	1935	6.11.1936	Lost 24.8.1942
Molniya	1933	1935	1936	Deleted c1959
Purga	1933	1935	4.9.1936	Lost 1.9.1942
Zarnitsa	1933	1935	1936	Deleted c1959
SERIES IV				
Sneg	1934	1936	Oct 1937	Lost 28.8.1941
Tucha	27.4.1935	20.10.1936	18.9.1938	Deleted c1959

Builders: Zhdanov Yd, Leningrad (*Uragan*, *Tajfun*, *Smerch*, *Tsiklon*, *Vikhr'*, *Groza*, *Metel'***, *V'yuga*,**, *Burya*, *Molniya***,
Purga, *Sneg*, *Tucha*).
Marti Yd, Nikolaiev (*Shkval*, *Shtorm*, *Buran***, *Grom***, *Zarnitsa***)
*Official dates.
**Assembled by the Dalzavod, Valdivostok

After her service in Arctic waters in 1941–42, *Smerch* was taken in hand in a small northern yard for necessary overhaul and repairs. The work was complete by the end of 1942 but during the acceptance trials on 8 December she was caught by enemy bombers and subsequently sank. She was raised however in 1943 and found suitable for repair. Thus she remained in the yard until late 1944.

Only *Groza* of the original 'troika' remained in service with the Northern Fleet at the beginning of 1943. Apart from participation in convoy operations she undertook, with other ships, the close screening of the main base at Polyarnoe. However, her intensive use caused considerable deterioration and she had to be detached to the yard for a refit in 1943, from which she did not emerge until the beginning of 1945.

COUNTER OFFENSIVE

The 1943 campaign was the crisis point for the Eastern Front and was marked by a growing initiative by Russian forces, encouraged by the victory at Stalingrad. On 4 February a large landing was made by the Russians off Novorossisk but did not ultimately succeed, while a simultaneous feint assault by guard boats at Cape Myshanko withheld German attacks and, after reinforcement, was consolidated. To help the defenders of this bridgehead the destroyer *Zheleznyakov*, accompanied by *Shkval* and *Shtorm*, shelled Anapa on the night of 1 May.

During the above operations both sides ran supply convoys and attacked those of their opponents. Both *Shtorm* and *Shkval* participated in escort duties and following an air attack off Geledzhik in one such operation they had to take in tow the damaged troopship *Internatsional*. To prevent further attacks by the Luftwaffe on the supply convoys, the Russians undertook numerous bombardments of the airfield in Anapa. In these actions both *Shtorm* and *Shkval* participated in the shelling in June and August.

Such intensive use of surface units during the 1941–43 campaigns, without proper maintenance and only provisional repairs, resulted in fighting efficiency being considerably decreased. At the end of 1943 *Shkval* was taken in hand for a refit and overhaul originally planned for the end of 1941! She was completed by the end of the war. Repairs, and lack of them, in the remaining vessels of all three fleets, together with the unsuccessful bombardment of Yalta (resulting in the loss of 3 destroyers on 6 October), prevented the Soviet command from employing the larger surface ships. Thus during the offensive operations of the Red Army in the summer of 1944, when the main naval bases in European waters were recaptured, the landing operations and close support of the land forces was largely carried out by small vessels and naval aircraft.

The last time during the European War that the ships of the *Uragan* class are mentioned is in a mid-October 1944 convoy consisting of *Uragan* and *Smerch* and the survey ship *Masshtab* escorted by minesweepers which entered the freshly taken port of Liinahamarii. This took place during a complex operation which resulted in the Germans evacuating Kirkenes (Norway).

THE FAR EAST

The situation in the Far East was quite different: here according to the Yalta agreement, the Soviet Union declared war on Japan three months after the capitulation of Germany.

Initially landings were made on the east coast of Korea in support of an advance by the Soviet 25th

Army. The largest operation was a landing in Chongjin where the first wave landed on 12 August, while the main landing flotilla, under Admiral Yumashev, arrived three days later. This second force consisted of the old destroyer *Vohkov*, 5 Lend-Lease frigates, the guard ships *Meter'* and *V'yuga*, 6 minesweepers and 11 Lend-Lease landing craft, as well as minor units embarking a total of 5000 men. Both guard ships, accompanied by *Vojkov* and the minelayer *Argun*, shelled enemy positions during two days of fighting which ended in the evening of 16 August. In support of the subsequent Soviet offensive in Korea, small landings were made in the harbours of Odaejin and Wonsan during 19 and 21 August respectively with *Metel'* participating in the former assault.

Operations against Sakhalin begun on 11 August with attacks by elements of the 16th Army on the southern part of the island. To suppress the strong Japanese defence, assault operations were carried out by the Soviet North Pacific Flotilla. The landing force,

Molniya in 1953, practically unchanged since the war. Note the low freeboard at the stern with only a few mines onboard.

Przemyslaw Budzbon Collection

consisting of *Zarnitsa*, the minelayer *Okean*, 14 MTBs and other craft, landed over 1500 men behind the Japanese positions in Toro on 16 August. On 20 August the Soviet 133th Rifle Brigade was landed in Maoka opposite to the Soviet advance with both *Zarnitsa* and *Okean* participating in the action.

TABLE 2: TRANSLATION OF SHIP NAMES

Buran	– Snowstorm	*Smerch*	– Whirlwind
Burya	– Storm	*Sneg*	– Snow
Grom	– Thunderbolt	*Tajfun*	– Typhoon
Groza	– Thunderstorm	*Tsiklon*	– Cyclone
Metel'	– Blizzard	*Tucha*	– Cloud
Molniya	– Lightning	*Uragan*	– Hurricane
Purga	– Snowsquall	*Vikhr'*	– Strong wind
Shkval	– Squall	*V'yuga*	– Windstorm
Shtorm	– Gale	*Zarnitsa*	– Summer lightning

CONCLUSION

Fourteen of the original eighteen *Uragan* class remained in service after the war, but these ships, already of dubious value at the time of their completion, were completely obsolete in the atomic age. In 1950 *Smerch* was handed to the paramilitary organisation DOSAAF for training duties and once again covered great distances on the Russian inland waterways, being transferred from the Arctic to the Caspian Sea in 1951.

Virtually unchanged, ships of the *Uragan* class remaining in service until the great clearing of old ships (comparable to Fisher's selling of obsolete RN ships in 1905) was carried out at the end of the 1950s by Gorshkov. With the exception of *Smerch*, all the remaining ships of this class were disposed of or relegated to other duties at that time.

Thus, for practical purposes, the story of the first Soviet surface warships ended but it seems worth looking at the subsequent development of the Soviet guard ships of which the *Uragan* class were the immediate ancestors. It was not until 1938 when the last ship of the *Uragan* class was completed that work on a new class of guard ships began. Eight vessels, known as the *Yastreb* class, were begun as Project No 29 during 1939–40 in the Zhdanov Yard. Displacement was doubled compared with the undersized *Uragan* class, while 23,000shp 2-shaft geared steam turbines, fed by four

A *Kola* class frigate before modernisation of the fire control gear.

Boris Lemachko Collection

TABLE 3: DISTRIBUTION OF THE URAGAN CLASS AT THE END OF THE 1930s

Northern Fleet	Baltic Fleet	Black Sea Fleet	Pacific Fleet
Groza	Burya	Shkval	Buran
Smerch	Purga	Shtorm	Grom
Uragan	Sneg		Metel'
	Tajfun		Molniya
	Tsiklon		V'yuga
	Tucha		Zarnitsa
	Vikhr'		

watertube boilers arranged en echelon, provided for a respectable speed of 31kts – far better than the 23kts of the preceding class. The planned armament was three single 85mm/55 AA and four single 37mm/67 AA guns, three 0.5in DShK MGs and one triple 18in torpedo tube mounting. The *Yastreb* class craft with a short forecastle, raked stem and two distinctive raked funnels had a more warlike silhouette than the *Uragan* class and were comparable to the escorts developed by the Western Allies during the war and could therefore be classified as frigates. Only three of the *Yastreb* class were completed by the end of hostilities, albeit with the armament altered to use what was available at that time. The 85mm guns were replaced with heavier 100mm pieces, causing some stability problems, so in order to lower the centre of gravity, 'X' mounting was placed on the main deck instead of in a superfiring position over 'Y' mounting. The remaining ships were completed with a reduced armament post war. However, the exact number finally commissioned is not known – 7 were reported which were in service until 1962, at the latest. Eight of the *Yastreb* class were planned for the Baltic Fleet while at least a dozen ships of modified design were ordered before the war for the Pacific Fleet (*Albatross* class) and the Black Sea Fleet (*Kaguar* class), but only 7 were laid down prior to the outbreak of hostilities. Two of the former were commissioned by the end of 1945 while the incomplete hulls of the latter were captured by the Germans in Nikolaiev and subsequently scrapped.

POST WAR GUARD SHIPS

The first post war design of Soviet guard ship appeared in service in 1954. Code named the *Kola* class by NATO, ten such boats were allegedly built in the Baltic and Black Sea yards during 1950 – 55. War experience and studies of ex-German torpedo-boats resulted in the adoption of a flush-deck and a deeper freeboard compared with the *Yastreb* class, both innovations being representative of a new post war design philosophy in Soviet naval construction. The *Kola* class ships displaced 1500 tons and carried four single 100mm/56 AA guns as well as two twin 37mm/67 AA guns, one triple 21in torpedo tube mounting and four DCTs. A two-shaft power plant arranged en echelon provided a speed of 30kts with 30,000shp. They seemed to have disappeared from active service by the end of the 1970s.

The succeeding group was the *Riga* class, which first appeared in 1955, apparently as a reduced version of the *Kola* class. In comparison, the *Riga* class vessels displaced 25 per cent less, carried a reduced main armament and had a speed which did not exceed 28kts. This simplified design produced a cheap and compact ship allowing for mass production. Much effort had been put into designing a hull which would enable the weapons to be used in a heavy sea. The flush-deck and high sheer, commencing with a sharply raked stem, provided a distinctive, new Russian style. The significant novelty which appeared on these new frigates was modern electronic and fire control equipment. Approximately 65 of this class were built during 1952–59 in the Baltic and the Black Sea yards and 16 of these were sold abroad.

The *Riga* class ended the development line which had been initiated by the *Uragan* class in 1927. Development since the 1960s produced ships which could be more accurately described as corvettes rather than frigates to which both the *Kola* and *Riga* classes corresponded. The latter constituted the bulk of the frigate force of the Soviet navy during the 1960s and 1970s. They are now being replaced by the *Koni* class – frigates of a new generation.

The first guard ships of Soviet construction were not a brilliant achievement: they were slow, weakly built, bad sea boats, and were overgunned for their size. Nevertheless the design and construction of these ships enabled Soviet naval engineers to begin a basis of experience which has been amassing ever since and has resulted in the present sophisticated Soviet naval construction.

1 *Yastreb* in 1945. Note the Type 291 antennae on the foremast. The cramped ships of the *Uragan* class had no space for such luxury.
Boris Lemachko Collection

2 A *Riga* class frigate. This is *Karl Libknecht* of the East German Navy.
Przemyslaw Budzbon Collection

3 The *Koni* class guided missile frigate *Rostock* of the East German Navy in July 1980.
Marek Twardowski Collection

1

3

2

Warship Wings No.3
McDonnell Douglas A~4 Skyhawk
by Roger Chesneau

It is fair to say that one of the fundamental problems facing designers of both naval aircraft and aircraft carriers themselves has been the trend, especially marked since the Second World War and the advent of jet aircraft, towards even greater airframe dimensions. This is of course but one element in the intricate pattern of strategic and tactical requirements confronting designers, but it is one that seems impossible to stop – given the need for the maximum number of aircraft to carry more and more weapons over greater and greater distances at higher and higher speeds.

As a solitary successful example of a completely deliberate attempt to put the brake on this trend, the A-4 Skyhawk is a fascinating aircraft and one that has not been without impact on naval aircraft thinking. In simple terms, it was born out of an idea to produce a single-capability machine with absolutely minimum all-up weight and dimensions. The original concept was for an ultra-light fighter, but the design team was quickly persuaded to reconfigure its project to meet the demand for a US Navy replacement for the propeller-driven attack/close-support AD Skyraider.

The most obvious limitations that could be set were the length and width of contemporary US carrier lifts, thereby negating the need to provide a wing folding facility, and almost incidentally, saving weight. Carrier take-off and landing, however, dictated that maximum wing area be available in the quest for optimum near-deck handling: the full delta would have provided a wing of sufficient size but in the absence of stabilizers would have resulted in unacceptable approach speeds and poor airborne agility; the compromise was achieved via a foreshortened delta platform. Even so, manoeuvrability was reduced, even though the balance was partially restored by introducing leading-edge slats.

Further savings could be accomplished through simplification. For example, the Skyhawk has only two internal fuel tanks, one behind the pilot and a second running the complete span of the wing: this was possible because the wing is a single integral structure, with the minimum number of spars and ribs; strength is maintained by mounting the main undercarriage gear in fairings outside the structure – albeit with an aerodynamic drag penalty.

The lower the weight of an aircraft, the less powerful the plant required to drive it through the air at a given speed, assuming a constant aerodynamic factor. The A-4 uses a minimum engine – J52 at (currently) 11,200lb thrust, although earlier models were fitted with licence-built Sapphires (J65) at some 7000lb thrust – and hence keeps weights down in this department too; even so, the airframe can lift five tons (about its own weight) of ordnance by means of five external stations.

The success of the Skyhawk concept can be measured by the fact that it remained in production from 1953 until 1979 – a US record. Upgraded continuously from A4D-1 (A-4A) through to A-4M in US service, the installation of more powerful engines, improved avionics and other modern requirements finally meant that the contents would not fit the box, and the type is now no longer in US Navy front-line combat service; however, it is still widely used by the USN in its two-seat trainer variants, and a large number are held in reserve. At the time of writing, reactivation of *Oriskany* and *Bon Homme Richard* is still being mooted, which may see the reintroduction of the type in USN colours on board carriers. The Royal Australian Navy still operates shipboard Skyhawks (A-4G *Melbourne*), as does the Argentine Navy (A-4B, *25 de Mayo*), whilst the US Marine Corps still has A-4s very much in strength, preferring new-build aircraft to A-7 Corsairs when it came to re-equipment some twelve years ago. Land-based A-4s are operated by a number of air forces too, notably those of Israel, New Zealand and Indonesia.

POSTSCRIPT

Of recent interest have been the Skyhawks operated by the Argentine Navy. Orders totalling 91 A-4s have been placed since 1965, comprising 50 A-4Bs (ex-US machines, 25 A-4Cs and 16 A-4Qs (rebuilt A-4Bs), although normal attrition and combat losses in the Falklands War have reduced these numbers to a figure that is now probably below 40. The A-4Qs have been operated on a detachment basis aboard *25 de Mayo*, these variants being equipped with the simple APG-53A radar enabling them to work in less than perfect weather.

McDONNELL DOUGLAS A-4M SKYHAWK – SPECIFICATION

Overall length:	40ft 4in
Span:	27ft 6in
Max height:	15ft
Wing area:	260ft²
Engine:	1 × J-52-P-408A turbojet, 11,200lb thrust
Max speed:	675mph (M0.89) at sea level; climb from sea level 500ft/sec (clean)
Combat radius:	400nm
Weight:	11,000lb empty; 25,000lb fully loaded
Weapons:	2 × 20mm Mk 12 cannon; five external stations totalling 10,000lb

All A-4 missions during the Falklands War were conducted from land bases, and, clearly, the fact that all but a handful of Argentine Skyhawks were unable to operate in conditions of poor visibility goes some way to explain their less than fulsome reaction to the British landings. However, as British commanders commented at the time, given that the aircraft were a quarter of a century old, were operating beyond their theoretical maximum radius and were often flown in weather environments for which they were never designed, the wonder is that they were able to mount any kind of effective offensive; that they were able to says a good deal for the pilots.

1 Factory-fresh A-4M for the US Marine Corps. Note prominent in-flight refuelling probe, undercarriage fairings, wing leading-edge slats and dorsal avionics 'hump'. The aircraft carries two wing-root 20mm cannon, one of which is clearly evident.

McDonnell Douglas

2 An A-4G Skyhawk of the Royal Australian Navy lands aboard the carrier *Melbourne*, showing to good effect the long-stroke oleos of the undercarriage legs and the trailing hook.

RAN

Notes & Comments on the 4.5in, 8cwt GUN

by Geoffrey Hudson

The after 4.5in gun of a Fairmile 'D' fast patrol boat.

This article was originally sent by Geoffrey Hudson as a letter providing additional information and comment to Anthony Preston's article 'The Sad Story of the 4.5in 8cwt gun' which appeared in Warship 20. *However, it was much too long for inclusion in A's and A's, and as shortening it would have reduced its information value considerably, it has been reproduced here as a supplement to the original article.*

By the Spring of 1943, it had been found possible to fit the Army's 6pdr tank gun into the existing naval 2pdr Mk XVI power operated mounting. This weapon entered service with Coastal Forces towards the end of 1943 and was known as the 6pdr Mk VII. However, even before this, it was realised that the 6pdr would not sink armed trawlers and that something in the nature of

the US Navy 4.5in rocket would be necessary for increased destructive power.

Consideration was given to two alternative large calibre gun projects, namely the light 4.5in and the 95mm tank howitzer (modified). By May 1944, 18 equipments of each type had been ordered, both types being designed for a power operated mounting then in service in Coastal Forces, for the 6pdr Mk IIA 7cwt gun. One type was to be abandoned subsequent to the results of firing trials (see table).

COASTAL FORCES TRIAL WEAPONS

	4.5in	95mm
Muzzle Velocity (fs)	1500	1050
Weight of complete round (lbs)	22	28
Weight of projectile (lbs)	15 (5½ HE)	25 (3 HE)
Breech	semi-automatic	semi-auto may be fitted
Rate of fire (rpm)	10 – 15	10–15

The 4.5in Mk I of *FPB 1033* (ex-*MTB 533*) in 1953.

After land trials in June-July 1944 the 4.5in was selected and at the time it was expected that sea trials in MTBs would be possible in August 1944. Also at that time, it was still intended to fit the gun in the Mk XVI power mounting while a hand operated mount was also contemplated. The 4.5in shell was filled with RDX/TNT and fitted with a modified base fuze. (The day following receipt of *Warship 20* in October 1981, with the article on the 4.5in gun, I was in Leamington Spa on an overnight stay. My host had two 4.5in shell cases, both cut-down 3.7in AA cases, dated 1942 and 1943.)

The intention, in August 1944, to develop a hand operated mounting was to enable the six flotillas of Fairmile 'B' type gunboats, at that time earmarked for the Far East, to replace their 6pdrs with what was to be known as the 4.5in 8cwt Mk II; the power operated version had been designated Mk I. In the event, the time scale was lengthened for both mountings.

By January 1945, it was stated that production of the 4.5in 8cwt Mk I and Mk II was unlikely to start before April 1945. At the same time, it was announced that *MGB 538* (the last of the Vosper 1944 class, which by this time had been earmarked as a development vessel) would have the 4.5in Mk I.

In April 1945, it was stated that the 4.5in was delayed further and that the design of a development mounting was in hand. This new mounting was to incorporate either the new 4.5in Mk I, or the existing 6pdr Mk IIA gun, and was to have electro-hydraulic drive and redesigned hydraulic components. This development mounting was then destined for *MGB 538*.

THE 4.5in IN SERVICE

The first 4.5in/8cwt Mk I, power mounts were seen by April 1946 on *MTB 528* and *509* ('short' boats, Vosper 1944 class and BPB 1944 class respectively). These replaced the 6pdr Mk VII which these boats received on completion. By the summer of 1946 Fairmile 'D' type boats *MTB 5007* and *5008* had the new mount fitted fore and aft respectively, again in place of their original 6pdr and around that time 3 Camper & Nicholson 1943 class boats, *MTB 2016* to *2018* had their forward 6pdr replaced by a 4.5in.

Coastal Forces craft were renumbered in mid-1949, after which MTBs and MGBs were known as FPBs. Prior to that date, the following boats are known to have mounted the 4.5in Mk I: 71ft 6in BPB 1944 class – *MTB 509* and *520*; 73ft Vosper 1944 class – *MTB 528* and *530*; the Vosper experimental 'short' boat *538* (originally intended to carry the first mounting, completed in August 1948 as *MTB 538*, but with a twin oerlikon and four 18in torpedo tubes. She landed this armament and at the beginning of 1949 and, as *MGB 538*, was fitted with a 4.5in forward and the twin oerlikon aft); 'long' boats include the three Campers already mentioned and the Fairmile 'D' type *MTB 790, 5007, 5008* and *5009*. Until 1949, the 4.5in in these latter boats merely replaced the forward 6pdr (apart from *5008*, where originally the after 6pdr was replaced; later, she too had her 4.5in forward).

After mid-1949, the combined torpedo and gun armament was dropped and boats were generally fitted as either gunboats or torpedo boats. 'Short' boats with the 4.5in forward and a twin oerlikon aft included *FPB 1027, 1030, 1032* and *1033*. 'Long' boats after mid-1949, when fitted as gunboats, generally carried

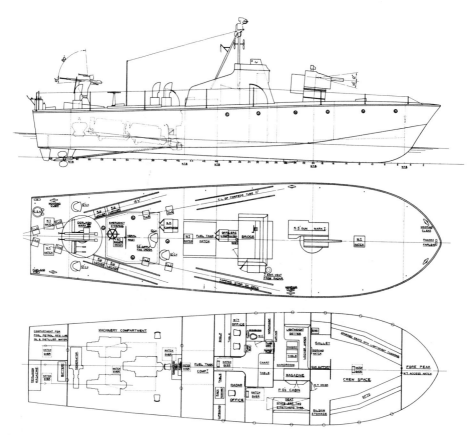

Official general arrangement drawing for *MGB 538* showing the 4.5in Mk I mounting on the forecastle; aft she carries a twin hand-operated Mk XII Oerlikon mounting.

NMM

two 4.5in, and a twin oerlikon amidships. The following Fairmile 'D' type were so fitted: *FPB 5001 (ex-MTB 780), 5002, 5003 (ex-MTB 790), 5007, 5008, 5009, 5015, 5020, 5031 (ex-MTB 758), 5032 (ex-MTB 779), 5033 (ex-MTB 785), 5035 (ex-MTB 793), 5036 (ex-MTB 794)*.

By 1949, the ·4.5in Mk I had become the main gun armament in coastal forces and after that time no 6pdrs appear to have been mounted. Its use continued with the *Gay* class of 1953-54 and the *Dark* class of 1955-57, when fitted as gunboats, but came to an end with the two operational squadrons of *Dark*s paid-off in 1957.

THE Mk II MOUNTING

As far as the hand operated Mk II mounting was concerned, the need for this arose from a requirement for the Far East, where base facilities were less readily available, but the large calibre gun was needed for the 1945 Burma and Malaya campaign, in order to sink Japanese sampans and barges.

The first vessel fitted with the 4.5in Mk II was *ML 570*, which in early 1946 carried this gun on her foredeck while operating from HMS *Hornet* at Gosport. The only

other craft known to have been fitted with the Mk II, were *Bold Pathfinder* and *Bold Pioneer*. These two experimental 'long' boats carried two such mounts when fitted as gunboats in 1953 to 1955. In addition they carried a single 40mm Bofors amidships. The last 4.5in Mk II appears to have been the single gun fitted on the fore deck of *Bold Pathfinder* in 1961 when she was Senior Officer of the Trials Squadron (see photo in *Warship 20*).

Regarding the boats listed in the Warship article and in Janes, as carrying 4.5in, I have never seen other evidence that *FPB 5514, 5517* or *1601* had this mounting. *MTB 2017* (later *FPB 5517*) had one, as did MGB 538 (later *FPB 1601*), but not as *FPB 5517* or *1601* as far as I can see. I wrote to Francis McMurtrie in about 1947-49 with comments about the 4.5in and believe I told him that *MTB 2014* had one. I made a mistake in reading a photo! Perhaps this is the original source of this error, unless someone actually has a photo showing a 4.5in on this vessel.

An idea, albeit somewhat dramatised, of the limited accuracy and muzzle velocity of the 4.5in/8cwt can possibly be gained from the following (humourous) comments made by former COs in conversation with the author. 'The instructions said — place yourself (ie the gun) alongside the enemy and pull the trigger/fire' and 'you could watch the shell all the way from it coming out of the barrel to hitting the target!'

Akagi & Kaga Part 3

by Hans Lengerer

A close-up of *Kaga*'s starboard quarter prior to her modernisation, showing her after starboard 8in casemate battery and funnel outlet.

Just four days after returning to Staring Bay, following the attack on Darwin, at 08.30 on 25 February, Vice Admiral Nagumo's group sailed once more. The group now comprised the air attack group with the carriers *Akagi, Kaga, Hiryu* and *Soryu*, the support group with the battleships *Hiei, Kirishima, Haruna* and *Kongo* and the cruisers *Tone* and *Chikuma*, the first destroyer squadron as escort with the light cruiser *Abukuma*, the second group of the 4th destroyer division (*Maikaze, Hagikaze*), the 17th destroyer division (*Tanikaze, Urakaze, Isokaze, Hamakaze*), the first group of the 18th destroyer division (*Shiranui, Kasumi*), the second group of the 27th destroyer division (*Ariake*) and the destroyer *Akigumo*. From the 6 to 11 March the first group of the 15th destroyer division (*Kuroshio, Oyashio*) was also under his command. Supply was the task of the first supply group (*Kyokuto Maru, Kenyo, Maru, Nippon Maru, Toei Maru* and *Teijo Maru*).

Vice Admiral Nagumo's task was two-fold: he was to obstruct the supply of reinforcements for Java from Australia, Ceylon and India, and sink enemy ships attempting to escape. His operational orders alloted the task of attacking enemy fleet units and commercial shipping to his air attack group, while the support group was to assist and also attack enemy ships. The security group's task was to carry out reconnaissance, to protect, and, where necessary, to attack commercial ships.

At 08.30 on 26 February the ships had passed through Ombai Straits, and were heading for their operational area to the south of the island of Java. The next day they received information that an enemy aircraft carrier had been discovered in the vicinity of Bali (US aircraft tender *Langley*). Vice Admiral Nagumo reacted immediately, and hoped to be able to attack on the following day, 28 February, but aircraft of the *Takao* flight group damaged *Langley* so severely on 27 February that she was scuttled the same day. On 28 February a reconnaissance aircraft from a cruiser sighted an unarmed merchant ship and dropped a 60kg bomb, which missed. The ship was not sighted again.

On 1 March the group was 140nm distant, bearing 190°, from Christmas Island, when a Kate returning

TABLE 14: RESULTS OF ATTACKS BY THE SHIP ATTACK UNIT

Aircraft (Vals)	Carrier	No of Bombs Released	Hits	%	Target
17	*Akagi*	16	15	94	*Dorsetshire* and *Cornwall*
18	*Soryu*	18	17	78	*Dorsetshire* and *Cornwall*
18	*Hiryu*	18	17	94	*Dorsetshire* and *Cornwall*
2	*Akagi*	2	2	100	*Hermes*
11	*Hiryu*	11	9	82	*Hermes*
14	*Zuikaku*	14	13	93	*Hermes*
18	*Shokaku*	18	13	72	*Hermes*
12	*Akagi*	12	12	100	*Vampire*
4	*Hiryu*	4	1	25	*Vampire*
3	*Akagi*	3	3	100	*British Sergeant*,
3	*Soryu*	6	6	83	*Athelstone*
3	*Hiryu*	3	3	100	

Note: Bombs employed were 250kg Type 98 for ground attack and 250kg Type 99 general purpose. It is possible that some near misses were judged as hits.

from reconnaissance sighted the US tanker *Pecos*. About 90 minutes later the first Val from *Soryu* attacked, followed by further machines which had taken off about an hour later. Nine Vals from *Akagi* also attacked and the tanker was finally sunk after sustaining 5 hits and 6 near misses by 250kg bombs. A total of 18 Vals took part in the attack.

THE SINKING OF EDSALL

A little later the US destroyer *Edsall* was sighted by one of the three aircraft operating as aerial security for the *Soryu*, and was reported as being a light cruiser. At 17.22 Vice Admiral Nagumo ordered Gunichi Mikawa to sink the vessel. *Kongo, Haruna, Tone* and *Chikuma* turned towards the destroyer, and, eleven minutes after the order to attack, *Chikuma* opened fire at 21,000m. At the same time three aircraft took off from *Kongo* and *Haruna* in order to direct the fire. At 17.47 the battleships began to fire their 35.6cm guns at 20,700m. The *Tone* joined the battle at 18.14 from 20,300m. The *Edsall* zigzagged violently and, although she often disappeared behind the columns of water thrown up by shells striking the water nearby, she received no direct hits.

At 18.00 8 Vals took off from *Akagi*, followed at 18.05 by 9 Vals from *Soryu*. Between 18.27 and 18.57 they bombed the *Edsall* with eight 250kg and nine 500kg bombs and, after suffering hits and near misses, the destroyer sank at 19.01. The *Tone* did not stop firing until 18.42, while the battleships fired their last salvo at 18.59. In the battle, which lasted about an hour, they fired 297 35.6cm shells, and 132 15cm shells. *Tone* and *Chikuma* used 844 20,3cm and 63 12.7cm shells. If you add to this total the 17 bombs, it is hardly likely that more ammunition could have been expended on a destroyer. Shortly after *Edsall* was sunk, the Dutch merchantman *Madjokerto* ran into the group, and was sunk by *Chikuma* and destroyers.

TJILATJAP

On 2 and 3 March the group crossed into its operational area without further incident. At this time Vice Admiral Nagumo's orders for the attack on Tjilatjap assumed it would commence on the following day, but bad weather, which was to affect the whole operation, necessitated a two-day postponement until 5 March.

On 4 March a reconnaissance aircraft located a destroyer and a merchantman and bombed the former without success. Ten Vals, which had taken-off immediately on receipt of the sighting report, failed to find the ships due to the poor weather. Later, an aircraft from the *Hiryu* found a burning freighter, the Dutch *Enggano*, in position 12°04′S/108°1.5′E. *Chikuma* and *Urakaze* sank the ship with torpedoes at 12.43, after discovering that *Chikuma*'s AP shells passed through *Enggano*'s hull without detonating.

At 11.00 on 5 March, 180 aircraft took-off from the carriers, 230nm south west of Tjilatjap.[1] This was the same distance as from Pearl Harbor, but in the opposite direction. The Kates flew at the lowest level, led by the aircraft from the *Soryu*, with the Vals behind and above them, and the Zeros higher still. Eighteen Kates and nine Zeros from the *Akagi* took part. As for *Kaga* and the other carriers, no information is available on numbers or pilots. It is known that none of the *Akagi*'s aircraft were shot down, but again there is no information about the other aircraft. However, it can hardly be assumed that the 32 P-40s, which the *Langley* had transported to Tjilatjap, had not yet been assembled, and in addition, Japanese reports indicate that AA fire was strong. In the air attack on 5 March which lasted about one hour, 8 ships were sunk and in the following days 12 more were scuttled; the town was taken by Japanese troops on 8 March. Railway installations, harbour equipment, the auxiliary minesweeper *Ram* (at that time under construction) and about 200 buildings in the town were destroyed.

At 10.30 on 6 March the group divided: *Hiryu, Soryu, Haruna, Kongo* and the 17 Destroyer Division (*Tanikaze, Urakaze, Isokaze* and *Hamakaze*) steamed in the direction of Christmas Island, while the main group

[1] Remarkably Japanese sources record virtually nothing of Nagumo's operations South of Java; even the offical work by the War History Institute of the Japanese Defence Ministry *Rannin, Bengaru wan Homen Kaigun Shinko Sakusen* (Japanese Navy offensives in Dutch Indies waters and the Bengali Gulf) by Masao Sasaki accords only 6 lines to this attack.

Akagi c1940, note the port side island superstructure.
Bfz

headed further east, but met no enemy. On the morning of 7 March the *Kongo* and *Haruna* shelled buildings, oil tanks, radio installations and a bridge on Christmas Island for about 20 minutes, and then steamed off to the east. Aircraft from the *Soryu* located two armed merchant ships which were sunk about 90nm bearing 300° from Christmas Island. The two groups rejoined on 10 March and entered Staring Bay on the following day; Java surrendered on 9 March. The *Kaga* sailed on 15 March, reached Sasebo on the 22nd and entered dock there on the 27th for attention to the damage she had received when she struck a reef on 9 February.

OPERATIONS IN THE INDIAN OCEAN
On 24 March the 5th carrier division (*Shokaku, Zuikaku*), which had left Yokosuka on 17 March again joined Nagumo's group in Staring Bay, where prepara-

Akagi c1941.
Bfz

tions were underway for operations in the Indian Ocean. This followed a decision by Imperial headquarters not to occupy Ceylon, which prompted the Combined Fleet to plan several raids in the Indian Ocean, including one against Ceylon itself. The purpose was to secure the newly conquered territories and to provide for supplying the troops fighting in Burma direct from the sea by defeating the British Eastern Fleet and destroying British air power in the area.

On 26 March, at 08.00, the battle group sailed from Staring Bay. Vice Admiral Nagumo had at his disposal 5 carriers (*Akagi, Hiryu, Soryu, Shokaku, Zuikaku*) 4 battleships (*Hiei, Kirishima, Kongo, Haruna*), 2 heavy cruisers (*Tone, Chikuma*) the light cruiser *Abukuma*, 8 destroyers (*Tanikaze, Urakaze, Isokaze, Hamakaze, Shiranui, Kasumi, Kagero* and *Arare*) plus a train of 6 supply vessels (*Shinkoku Maru, Kyokuto Maru, Kenyo Maru, Nippon Maru, Toei Maru, Kokuyo Maru*) escorted by the destroyers *Hagikaze, Maikaze* and *Akigumo*.

The ships steamed into the Indian Ocean via the Ombai Straits, took on supplies for the last time before the attack on 3 April and increased speed to 20kts,

The carrier *Shokaku* which operated with the *Akagi* and *Kaga* in the Indian Ocean in March-April 1942.
IWM

(formerly 9 – 14kts) at 13.30, in order to attack Colombo on Easter Sunday (5th). The intention was to attack in the early hours of a Sunday, as at Pearl Harbor, but this proved impossible. On the one hand British Intelligence had fairly accurate information, and on the other a Catalina sighted the group on 4 April, and was able to send a sighting report before being shot down (*Akagi, Soryu, Shokaku* and *Zuikaku* launched 3 Zeros each and *Hiryu* 6 at 19.20; by 19.45 all aircraft had returned). However, the message reached Admiral Sir James Somerville at an awkward time, and caused him to make a series of errors, with the result that, fortunately for the British, the opposing fleets did not meet. From 6 April the 'A' and 'B' groups had rejoined after embarking provisions at Addu Atoll.

Vice Admiral Nagumo should have left Staring Bay on 21 March and attacked Ceylon on 1 April, but he was forced to postpone the action because of the delayed arrival of the 5th carrier division, which had been operating in defence of the motherland until 16 March. Admiral Somerville had learned of this and had positioned his fleet to the south and north-east of the island from 31 March to 2 April; after this he assumed that his intelligence officers had obtained the wrong data, and the fleet left the area to resupply.

The message from the Catalina gave Admiral Layton, in Colombo, time to arrange a heightened state of alert, and all ships that were able to leave port were sent to sea.

COLOMBO

At 06.00 on 5 April the air strike took off. Of the total of 360 aircraft (315 operational aircraft, 45 reserve machines), Vice Admiral Nagumo sent 128 into action. Under the command of Commander Mitsuo Fuchida, 54 Kates, 38 Vals and 36 Zeros (Table 12) flew to attack

the ships, harbour installations and airfields of Colombo. On the approach flight, 6 Swordfish of 788 Squadron were intercepted and fell easy prey to the Zeros.

Fuchida flew in a great arc around Colombo, in order to approach the target from the north, and at 10.45 he gave the order to attack. The dive bombers (Vals) began to bombard harbour installations and ships, but were surprised by 14 Hurricanes, which had taken off from an improvised runway on the racecourse. They shot down 5 Vals from the *Zuikaku* and one from the *Shokaku* before being intercepted by the Zeros, which brought down six machines without loss.

Some of the Vals attacked Ratmalana airfield, from where 22 Hurricanes and 6 Fulmars had taken-off. They were immediately engaged in aerial combat by Zeros, which succeeded in shooting down 4 Fulmars and 7 Hurricanes for the loss of 1 Zero from the *Soryu*.

The Kates hindered by the bad weather, dropped their bombs on barracks, a bridge, rail and harbour installations and ships between 10.56 and 11.13. In total the Japanese shot down 15 Hurricanes, 4 Fulmars, 6 Swordfish and 2 Catalinas and lost 7 machines in return. They sank the old destroyer *Tenedos* and the armed merchant cruiser *Hector*, severely damaged the submarine depot ship *Lucia*, and slightly damaged the merchantman *Benledi*. Quays, workshops, repair facilities, railway installations, hangars, administrative buildings, etc, were also damaged or destroyed.

TABLE 15: ORGANISATION OF THE AIR ATTACK UNITS OF AKAGI (TRINCOMALEE)

Commander	Aircraft	Targets
Cdr Mitsuo Fuchida	18 Kates	Vicinity of naval arsenal
Lt Cdr Shigeru Haya	6 Zeros	Direct cover for *Akagi*'s Kates

Note: Fuchida was overall commander. No aircraft were lost.

At 11.28 Fuchida radioed to Vice Admiral Nagumo that he should prepare the second air attack, and seven minutes later he gave the order to return: 121 machines landed on their carriers between 12.48 and 13.25.

At 13.00 a reconnaissance aircraft from the *Tone* sighted two British cruisers and at 14.27, after a second message from the *Abukuma*'s reconnaissance machine Vice Admiral Nagumo gave orders for a strike against

TABLE 16: ORGANISATION OF THE SHIP ATTACK UNIT ON 9 APRIL 1942

Commander	Aircraft	Carrier
Lt Zenji Abe	17 Vals	*Akagi*
Lt Cdr Takashige Egura	18 Vals	*Soryu*
Lt Michio Kobayashi	18 Vals	*Hiryu*
Lt Akira Sakamoto	14 Vals	*Zuikaku*
Lt Cdr Kakuichi Tokahashi	18 Vals	*Shokaku*
Warrant Officer		
Tsugio Matsuyana	3 Zeros	*Hiryu*
Flight Sergeant		
Hayime Sugiyama	3 Zeros	*Soryu*

Note: Tokahashi was overall commander. Four Vals and one Zero from *Soryu* were lost.

these vessels by the ship attack unit. Seventeen Vals took-off from the *Akagi* at 14.49, 18 more from *Hiryu* at 14.59 and 18 from *Soryu* at 15.03. Lieutenant Commander Takashige Egusa, of the *Soryu*, gave the order to attack at 16.29 and between 16.38 and 16.55 the dive bombers of *Akagi* and *Soryu* attacked the cruiser *Dorsetshire*, while those from the *Hiryu* attacked the cruiser *Cornwall*. Both were sunk in textbook dive bombing attacks, in which the hit rate reached the phenomenal average of 88 per cent.

TRINCOMALEE

At 09.00 on 9 April, 100nm east of Trincomalee, the air attack unit began to take off for the strike against that base. Vice Admiral Nagumo's group had been sighted by Catalinas on the 6 and 8 April and, as at Colombo, the ships at Trincomalee were ordered to put to sea, and steam on a southerly course close to the coast. Amongst these ships were the aircraft carrier *Hermes*, the destroyer *Vampire*, the corvette *Hollyhock*, the tanker *British Sergeant* and the auxiliary ship *Athelstone*. When the 91 Kates and 41 Zeros reached their target under the leadership of Commander Mitsuo Fuchida, there were no ships in the harbour, and the British already had 17 Hurricanes and 6 Fulmars in the air, having been forewarned by radar. For the loss of 3 Zeros (2 from the *Zuikaku*, 1 from the *Shokaku*), they shot down 8 Hurricanes and 1 Fulmar.

Between 10.30 and 10.45 the bombers attacked the Naval arsenal, barracks, oil tanks, AA positions, administrative buildings and the airfield at China Bay, where they caused some severe damage. One Kate from the *Hiryu* was lost, and there were 2 dead and 1 severely injured in the aircraft. The aircraft began to land back on the carriers at 12.30.

At 10.55 one of the *Haruna*'s reconnaissance aircraft twice radioed the position of the British ships steaming southwards, in particular that of the *Hermes* (bearing 250°, 155nm distant). At 11.00 Vice Admiral Nagumo gave the order to the ship attack unit to prepare for attack (Tables 16 and 17). Eighty-five Vals and 6 Zeros took off from the *Shokaku* at 11.43 under the leadership of Commander Kakuichi Takahashi. The carrier was sighted at 13.30, was bombed from 13.35 to 13.50, and sank at 13.55; 10 minutes later the escorting destroyer *Vampire* was also sunk. The corvette *Hollyhock*, the tanker *British Sergeant* and the auxiliary ship *Athelstone* suffered the same fate.

On the return flight the Vals were attacked by 8 Fulmars between 15.15 and 15.40, which had been sent in from Ratmalana as fighter protection for the *Hermes*. They shot down four of the *Soryu*'s Vals, and 1 Zero, while the Japanese claimed to have shot down 7 machines (Spitfires), although 2 of these were not confirmed: official British records state that 2 Fulmars were shot down.

Around 15.45 the aircraft began landing on the carriers but, in the meantime, a group of 9 Bristol Blenheim bombers had taken off to attack Vice Admiral Nagumo's group. Its position could be calculated with some certainty from the incomplete radio message received from the Catalina which had sighted the Japanese on the morning of 9 April and had subsequently been shot down by the Zeros of the *Shokaku* and the *Zuikaku* at 10.10. The Blenheims did indeed find the group, surprised the fighter protection, and dropped their bombs onto *Akagi* and *Tone* at 13.25. Although they caused no damage, this was the first time that an enemy aircraft

A view looking forward along *Akagi*'s port side showing the rear of the bridge and two of the ship's AA mountings.

The carrier *Soryu* operated with *Akagi* and *Kaga* throughout their war service and was present at the Battle of Midway when the two big carriers were sunk.
IWM

group had been able to penetrate the defence system, and carry out an organised attack. The Zeros shot down 5 Blenheims and damaged another seriously, for the loss of 1 aircraft.

After the ship attack unit had landed, the group altered course to the East, took on supplies on 10 April, steamed through the Malacca Straits on the morning of 13th and entered the South China Sea on the following day, where the *Shokaku* and the *Zuikaku* separated from the main group to follow a NNE course towards Japan. As a result of the attack by Colonel Doolittle's bombers on 18 April, the group was ordered to take part in the search for the American carrier battle group, which had been sighted by a picket boat. Vice Admiral Nagumo altered course from north-east, but on 20 April the search was given up, and from 22.00 the ships steamed on a NW course. At 10.30 on 22 April *Akagi* dropped anchor in Yokosuka harbour.

THE SINKING OF AKAGI AND KAGA

Akagi and *Kaga* were sunk, together with the *Hiryu* and the *Soryu*, at the battle of Midway. There have been many analyses of this battle so it will not be discussed again here. On 5 June 1942 *Akagi* was hit by two bombs at 07.24 and 07.25 dropped by Dauntless aircraft from the *Enterprise* from an altitude of 500m. One bomb struck the corner of the centre lift, passed through the shaft and detonated the torpedoes and bombs stored – against regulations – on the hangar deck. The second bomb hit aft on the port side, and exploded amidst the aircraft which were standing ready to take off to attack the American group. In spite of all the emergency measures taken (flooding of the torpedo and bomb storage rooms, use of CO_2 to combat the fire) the carrier became a sea of flames and after 10.50 was steaming around out of control. Around 13.00 the destroyers *Arashi* and *Nowaki* had taken on board the majority of the crew. After Captain Taijiro Aoki had given the order to abandon ship, the same destroyers rescued the remaining survivors from 17.00. A radioed order from Captain Aoki to sink the *Akagi* with torpedoes, was cancelled at 19.25 by Admiral Yamomoto who ordered a delay, but at 01.30 on 6 June 1942 he ordered the ship to be sunk by the 4th destroyer division (*Hagikaze, Maikaze Nowaki* and *Arashi*). At 01.50 the destroyers launched their

torpedoes and at 02.00 the *Akagi* sank in position 30°30'N/179°40'W. 220 members of the crew were lost.

Between 07.27 and 07.30 on 5 June 1942 the *Kaga* received four hits by bombs dropped by the dive bombers of the *Enterprise*. The first bomb struck aft on the starboard side, and exploded amongst the aircraft waiting for take off. The second and third also hit on the starboard side, one close to the bridge, and the other further forward. The fourth exploded on the hangar deck, after it had penetrated the flight deck on the port side, slightly aft of the bridge. As with the *Akagi*, the carrier turned into a mass of flames after bombs and torpedoes, stored on the flight and hangar decks exploded and petrol fires began amongst the fuelling vehicles and aircraft ready for take off. Here too attempts were made to extinguish the fire with CO_2, but the fires were too violent. In addition, the fire extinguisher pumps went out of action.

At 14.00 the order to abandon ship was given, and the destroyers *Hagikaze* and *Maikaze* had taken survivors on board by 14.50. By 15.25 the fire had found its way to the forward petrol tanks and after two gigantic explosions which literally tore the carrier apart, the *Kaga* sank at 16.26 in position 30°20.3'N/79°17.2'W, with the loss of 800 lives.

The *Kaga* was stricken from the list of Imperial Japanese warships on 10 August 1942, and the *Akagi* on 25 September 1942. With their loss began the beginning of the end of the once proud Imperial Japanese Navy.

TABLE 12: ORGANISATION OF AIR ATTACK UNITS OF AKAGI (COLOMBO)

Commander	Aircraft	Targets
Cdr Mitsuo Fuchida	18 Kates	Buildings and ships
Lt Cdr Shigeru Haya	9 Zeros	Escort, and attacks on enemy aircraft in the air and on the ground

Note: Cdr Fuchida was overall commander. No aircraft were lost.

TABLE 13: ORGANISATION OF SHIP ATTACK UNIT ON 5 APRIL 1942

Commander	Aircraft	Carrier	Target
Lt Zenji Abe	17 Vals	*Akagi*	Enemy
Lt Cdr Takashige Egusa	18 Vals	*Soryu*	ships
Lt Michio Kobayashi	18 Vals	*Hiryu*	

Note: The ship Attack Unit was not designated as part of the order of battle on 19 March 1942, but VA Nagumo altered his orders at 23.40 on 4 April. Ltd Cdr Egusa was overall commander. No aircraft were lost.

BATTLESHIPS
of the Grand Fleet

A pictorial review of the British Battleships and Battlecruisers of the First World War
R. A. Burt and W. P. Trotter, MC

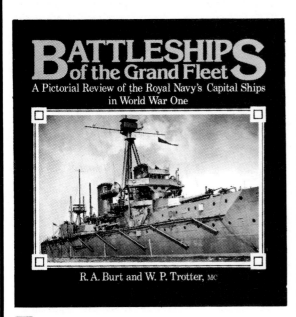

BATTLESHIPS of the Grand Fleet
A Pictorial Review of the Royal Navy's Capital Ships in World War One

R. A. Burt and W. P. Trotter, MC

Here is a unique selection from the collection of Pym Trotter, who has been collecting warship photographs for over 70 years. These superb pictures give a panoramic view of British battleships from the completion of the *Dreadnought* to the signing of the Washington Treaty of 1921. The photographs have been chosen both for their rarity and for their value in showing the constructional changes most of the ships underwent. Even the dedicated naval historian can expect to find new views of old favourites in this volume. All classes of dreadnought type battleships are included, and the accompanying text has been researched from official Admiralty sources. Reference tables are included.
10″ × 7″ (24.6 × 18.4cm); 96pp; over 170 photographs and 21 tables. £10.95 hardback; £7.50 paperback.

Other naval books from Arms and Armour Press include:
American Battleships 1886-1923 by John C. Reilly and Robert L. Sheina
Atlas of Naval Warfare by Helmut Pemsel
British Battleships of World War Two by Alan Raven and John Roberts
British Cruisers of World War Two by Alan Raven and John Roberts

The Mary Rose

The Excavation and Raising of Henry VIII's Flagship
by Margaret Rule
Foreword by HRH The Prince of Wales

The raising of the *Mary Rose* in September will be the climax of over ten years' work on this unique Tudor 'time capsule', preserved since 1545 by the seabed silt of the Solent. This definitive account by the director of the excavation covers the history of the *Mary Rose* from her launching at Portsmouth Dockyard in 1509 to her raising and return to the Dockyard in 1982. In addition, there is a detailed review of the findings of the archaeological team based on a study of the construction of the ship, and on the objects found preserved inside her: guns, rigging, and navigational instruments, as well as clothes and other personal items. As Mrs Rule explains, these findings will radically alter our view of Tudor life at sea and increase dramatically our knowledge of the history of ship construction.

263 ×194mm (10⅜" × 7⅝"), 256 pages, 200 illustrations in colour and in black and white.
ISBN 0 85177 255 2.
£12.50 (plus £1.90 post and packing when ordering direct). Published September 1982.

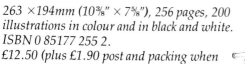

From your local bookseller
or Conway Maritime Press Ltd
2 Nelson Road, Greenwich, London SE10 9JB

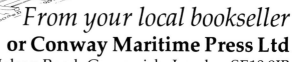